# Advancements in Instrumentation and Control in Applied System Applications

Srijan Bhattacharya
*RCC Institute of Information Technology, India*

A volume in the Advances in
Systems Analysis, Software
Engineering, and High Performance
Computing (ASASEHPC) Book Series

Published in the United States of America by
    IGI Global
    Engineering Science Reference (an imprint of IGI Global)
    701 E. Chocolate Avenue
    Hershey PA, USA 17033
    Tel: 717-533-8845
    Fax:  717-533-8661
    E-mail: cust@igi-global.com
    Web site: http://www.igi-global.com

Library of Congress Cataloging-in-Publication Data

Names: Bhattacharya, Srijan, 1980- editor.
Title: Advancements in instrumentation and control in applied system
  applications / Srijan Bhattacharya, editor.
Description: Hershey PA : Engineering Science Reference, [2020] | Includes
  bibliographical references and index. | Summary: "This book explores the
  advancement of instrumentation in various applications"-- Provided by
  publisher.
Identifiers: LCCN 2019042050 (print) | LCCN 2019042051 (ebook) | ISBN
  9781799825845 (hardcover) | ISBN 9781799825876 (paperback) | ISBN
  9781799825852 (ebook)
Subjects: LCSH: Engineering instruments. | Control theory. | Expert systems
  (Computer science)
Classification: LCC TA165 .A5588 2020  (print) | LCC TA165  (ebook) | DDC
  620.0028/4--dc23
LC record available at https://lccn.loc.gov/2019042050
LC ebook record available at https://lccn.loc.gov/2019042051

This book is published in the IGI Global book series Advances in Systems Analysis, Software Engineering, and High Performance Computing (ASASEHPC) (ISSN: 2327-3453; eISSN: 2327-3461)

British Cataloguing in Publication Data
A Cataloguing in Publication record for this book is available from the British Library.

All work contributed to this book is new, previously-unpublished material.
The views expressed in this book are those of the authors, but not necessarily of the publisher.

For electronic access to this publication, please contact: eresources@igi-global.com.

# Advances in Systems Analysis, Software Engineering, and High Performance Computing (ASASEHPC) Book Series

ISSN:2327-3453
EISSN:2327-3461

Editor-in-Chief: Vijayan Sugumaran, Oakland University, USA

## MISSION

The theory and practice of computing applications and distributed systems has emerged as one of the key areas of research driving innovations in business, engineering, and science. The fields of software engineering, systems analysis, and high performance computing offer a wide range of applications and solutions in solving computational problems for any modern organization.

The **Advances in Systems Analysis, Software Engineering, and High Performance Computing (ASASEHPC) Book Series** brings together research in the areas of distributed computing, systems and software engineering, high performance computing, and service science. This collection of publications is useful for academics, researchers, and practitioners seeking the latest practices and knowledge in this field.

## COVERAGE

- Distributed Cloud Computing
- Software Engineering
- Computer Graphics
- Metadata and Semantic Web
- Network Management
- Storage Systems
- Computer Networking
- Computer System Analysis
- Enterprise Information Systems
- Parallel Architectures

IGI Global is currently accepting manuscripts for publication within this series. To submit a proposal for a volume in this series, please contact our Acquisition Editors at Acquisitions@igi-global.com or visit: http://www.igi-global.com/publish/.

# Titles in this Series

*For a list of additional titles in this series, please visit:*
*https://www.igi-global.com/book-series/advances-systems-analysis-software-engineering/73689*

701 East Chocolate Avenue, Hershey, PA 17033, USA
Tel: 717-533-8845 x100 • Fax: 717-533-8661
E-Mail: cust@igi-global.com • www.igi-global.com

# Editorial Advisory Board

# Table of Contents

# Detailed Table of Contents

**Chapter 1**
Similarity Analysis of IPMC and EMG Signal With Comparative Study of
Statistical Features .......................................................................................... 1

Ankita Paul, Tata Consultancy Services Ltd, India
Naiwrita Dey, RCC Institute of Information Technology, India
Srijan Bhattacharya, RCC Institute of Information Technology, India

Ionic Polymer Metal Composite is a popular sensor and actuator due to its Electroactive property to show bending abilities under low applied voltage while Electromyography is a widely used technique in Biomechanical field to analyze human bio signals to compare different motions and predict muscular anomalies and diseases. IPMC having electroactive resistive and capacitive properties as a smart sensor shows a possibility of offering equivalent precision and accuracy in determining human muscular movement predictions and analyses. This chapter correlates the EMG data method with IPMC data method for feature extraction. The process includes use of the EMG electrodes and IPMC strips to retrieve signals from the muscle movement, amplify them, clean and scale the data, and conduct the similarity analysis.

**Chapter 2**
Vision and Sensor-Based Human Activity Recognition: Challenges Ahead....... 17

Md Atiqur Rahman Ahad, University of Dhaka, Bangladesh

Human action or activity or behavior analysis, recognition, and understanding are very important research areas in the field of computer vison, internet of things (IoT) sensor-based analysis, human-computer interaction (HCI), affective computing, intelligent system, healthcare facilities, and so on. There is much importance in human action recognition. This chapter introduces the core aspects of human action or activity recognition (HAR). These are split into two different domains: computer vision-based action/activity recognition, action localization, etc.; and wearable IoT sensor-based HAR. Though cameras are also sensors that provide vision-based information, the author puts camera-based or vision-based methods in another category. The chapter introduces core challenges and strategies to move forward.

# Chapter 3

Nowadays, the most common neurological disorder is Epilepsy. An epileptic seizure is a sudden synchronous and repetitive discharge from brain cells. The seizure is very dangerous and life-threatening for people affected by Epilepsy, as this may occur anywhere and anytime. The analysis of Electroencephalogram data (EEG) is a difficult task for a neurologist to go through the entire EEG records visually, in consideration with an increasing number of channels and more extended EEG recording. Authors are working to develop a system that gives a warning message so a safety measure can be taken before the seizure occurs. To do that, authors analyze epileptic EEG data in depth to get unique characteristics from EEG data, namely, disrupts background; sharply define components, Electrocerebral negativity, and electrical field. With the consideration of all of the above attributes of Epilepsy, an algorithm is developed, which is able to segment out the susceptible seizure waveform occurrence from EEG recording (onset) in different channels.

The actuator is an integrated part of every robotic system which can actuate the joint for the necessary movement of the device. Depending on the energy conversion mechanism, the actuators are subdivided into three classes, namely electric, pneumatic, and hydraulic. The electric actuators are very popular in the field of engineering and technology due to their ease of use and low maintenance. In this chapter, an electric linear actuator (Manufactured by TiMOTION, Model: TA1) has been modeled by considering its each and every associated physical parameter and also simulated in MATLAB Simscape to observe its performance. Also, different control actions like PID, LQR, and Sliding mode methods have been studied to select the best control action for the actuator. Finally, as an application of the developed actuator model, a one DOF robotic assistive device called human knee exoskeleton has been designed in the MATLAB Simscape. It has been tested that the knee joint trajectory has been followed by the actuator with suitable control action.

**Chapter 5**

    *Soumyajit Goswami, IBM India Pvt. Ltd., India*
    *Arghya Sarkar, MCKV Institute of Engineering, India*
    *Samarjit Sengupta, University of Calcutta, India*

In this chapter, the design and implementation of the self-synchronized adaptive linear neural (S-ADALINE) network approach for harmonic detection and the measurement of electrical power components (active power, reactive power, apparent power, power factor, etc.) at non-sinusoidal state have been discussed. A brief of the importance of electrical power measurement has been specified in Section 2. Section 3 is to discuss on the modern techniques of power measurement. The use of ADALINE style for harmonic estimation has been reflected in Section 4. In Section 5, harmonic tracking using S-ADALINE has been presented. Section 6 has been utilized to compare between ADALINE and S-ADALINE. In Section 7, S-ADALINE based power components measurement has been enlightened. A set of simulation tests in terms of accuracy, speed, and convergence of the S-ADALINE has been performed in MATLAB and deliberated in Section 8. The developed prototype is presented in Section 9 with experimental results.

**Chapter 6**

    *Srijan Bhattacharya, RCC Institute of Information Technology, India*
    *Satwik Halder, RCC Institute of Information Technology, India*
    *Ankana Sadhu, RCC Institute of Information Technology, India*
    *Saurav Banerjee, RCC Institute of Information Technology, India*
    *Suvojit Sinha, RCC Institute of Information Technology, India*
    *Saheli Banerjee, RCC Institute of Information Technology, India*
    *Sankita Kundu, RCC Institute of Information Technology, India*
    *Bikash Bepari, Haldia Institute of Technology, India*
    *Subhasis Bhaumik, Indian Institute of Engineering Science and
        Technology, India*

The following chapter is a comparative study of signals obtained using Electromyogram sensors and Ionic Polymer Metal Composite (IPMC) sensors. This chapter studies in detail the behavior of the electromechanical sensor, i.e., IPMC as an EMG sensor. The former being an electromechanical sensor picks up the electrochemical gradient due to flow of ions through the axon ends released within the muscle which ultimately causes the muscle contraction, and also detects the mechanical tension created because of muscle contraction. EMG sensors are an electrical sensor that is able to detect voltage changes due to electrochemical changes under our skin due to voluntary muscle movements. During the relaxed phase, both the sensors stay stagnant at different reference voltage levels, and shows variation in voltages only during the instants of contraction. The characteristic obtained by plotting the experimental readings are compared in the chapter.

**Chapter 7**

Pradip Saha, Heritage Institute of Technology, India
Santanu Ghorai, Heritage Institute of Technology, India
Bipan Tudu, Jadavpur University, India
Rajib Bandyopadhyay, Jadavpur University, India
Nabarun Bhattacharyya, Centre for the Development of Advanced
        Computing, Kolkata, India

Biochemical means of tea quality evaluation is quite accurate, but it requires very costly instruments and takes a long time to conduct the experiment. Researches show that thearubigin (TR) and theaflavin (TF) are the two most important biochemical compounds present in tea liquor on which liquor characteristics of black CTC tea depends. Consequently, this fact may be the basis of determining tea quality by assessment of TR and TF via electronic tongue (ET) response. This technique is free from subjective factors. In literature, there are only two research works using this technique so more research work is required to address the problem. This chapter proposes a modeling technique of ET response using sparse decomposition technique to estimate TR and TF content in a given tea sample. For each tea sample, sparse model coefficients obtained from the ET response is considered as a characteristic attribute of it. Experimental results using dissimilar regression models show high prediction accuracies which justify the efficacy of the proposed method.

**Chapter 8**

Arpan Deyasi, RCC Institute of Information Technology, India
Pampa Debnath, RCC Institute of Information Technology, India

This chapter shows the measurement procedure of junction depth using SIMS method with detailed experimental procedure, and the result is verified by theoretical computation. SIMS profile is analytically characterized by Pearson's distribution function, and all the results together established the fact that the device can be utilized for operating as a diode in RF range; where ion dose is considered as a variable parameter with ion energy. Implanted impurity distribution profile is obtained as a function of depletion width from which junction depth can be evaluated. Straggle parameters and projected range profile near the ion energy range is computed for which depth is evaluated, and skewness & kurtosis are estimated to get a theoretical knowledge of all the moments assuming the Pearson IV distribution. Results suggest that distribution of atoms may be considered as Gaussian in nature.

**Chapter 9**

Mandakinee Bandopadhyay, Asansol Engineering College, India
Subrata Chattopadhyay, National Institute of Technical Teachers'
Training and Research, Kolkata, India

With the development of mobile communication technologies and the popularity of relating devices, GSM network-based intelligent systems have been used more and more widely. Most existing intelligent systems have built on mobile platforms, but those systems don't provide any facility that could save time and energy. But people suffer from lack of time and energy to buy essential needs like medicine, etc. and they like to communicate to the supplier to get confirmation instantly before leaving home or office to collect the same. So, in society, it needs to give alignment without going on field. This chapter copes this problem using wireless database searching scheme using GSM technology, which is very useful in smart cities, where cell phone is an essential part of living. The system receives information from outsiders and customers through GSM modem database searches of all the suppliers connected in a common server and sends the result through short messages independently to the customer showing the availability.

**Chapter 10**

Shreem Ghosh, Johnson Controls Inc, India
Arijit Ghosh, RCC Institute of Information Technology, India

In any electrical or electronic systems, unwanted signals known as noise signals are encountered which interact with the true signal and thus affecting signal quality. Noise may enter into a device or system in many forms and have a different order of impacts. Prevention and elimination of noise had attained paramount importance to ensure signal fidelity. This chapter presents a comprehensive analysis on elimination of noise by electronic grounding of instrumentation and automation systems as well as various engineering considerations for the same.

Thin film is used for sensing and electronic devices applications. Various techniques are used for thin film deposition. This chapter presents the Spray pyrolysis deposition technique used for the growth of thin films sensing and device material. Spray pyrolysis is an inexpensive method to grow good crystalline thin film compared to other thin film deposition techniques. The chapter gives an overview of the spray process used for thin film deposition. Basic setup for this process is explained. Parameters affecting the deposition process is explained, as are the various spray methods. Finally, some examples of spray pyrolysis in different applications like a gas sensor, UV photodetector, solar cell, photocatalysis, and supercapacitor are discussed.

# Chapter 12

The tremendous area of application of microprocessors and microcontrollers has exhausted the demand for polymers as sensors among the fastest growing technologies of the $18 billion sensor market worldwide. This chapter presents the study of characteristic behavior of a compliance structure made of PVDF (Poly Vinylidene Fluoride) material which is acting as an actuator and sensor, too. The inverse piezoelectric nature of PVDF has been used to produce the required amount of force by applying the voltage at a specific point at the base of the structure which is generating the opening and closing of the end effector. The displacement of the tip of the end effector can be sensed by generated voltage of piezoelectric effect of PVDF.

Nowadays, it is very often that some portion of the Indian traction system is still suffering from a single line railway transportation. This in turn creates a havoc disturbance in maintaining the proper sequence of traction control system. Also, passengers are taking risk to catch the train which is already in motion but no such action has been taken to eliminate these consequences. It has been found that more or less various works have been done on Automation in Railway Crossing Gate using Microcontroller and IR Sensor. Thus, it is often decided to develop an idea for the Indian traction system to ensure better controlling action by introducing Limit Switches as Tactile Sensors and by introducing HMI using PLC. The purpose here to take control over various controlling domains, including Railway crossing gate are as follows: Track signal, crossing level signal, alarm notification, and platform edge fence. The proper sequencing needs to be operated via a 128 I/O module with 2 KB memory size small PLC kit.

Many automated health monitoring devices detect health abnormalities based on gleaned data. One of the effective approaches of monitoring a senior cardiac patient is the analysis of an Electrocardiogram (ECG) signal, as proven by various studies and applications. However, diagnosis results must be communicated to an expert. An intelligent and effective technology gaining wide popularity known as 'internet of things' or 'IoT' allows remote monitoring of the patient.

# Foreword

Among the PhD colleagues, some have forgotten new techniques in their tools in their work. Srijan Bhattacharya does not fall into this category. Bio-medical instrumentation and use in robotics system design makes visible their mastery of the subject matter, their insightfulness, and their expository skill.

This book engrossed on the advanced technology applied in Instrumentation and Control, for any discipline sensors are continually plays an important role. Design of sensor for various biological field is contributed by the authors. Detection of diseases by advance computational techniques also contributed by authors of this book.

Sensors application in robotics for disable persons and design of unique device to assist them enhances the potential of this book. From Nano scale to macro scale sensor application and measurement system will be found by the researcher and readers. Compliant structure in sensor design can contribute new research domain for the readers.

For the industry personnel also this book will be interesting as industry standards, programmable logic controller (PLC) application in practical online system also contributed in this book.

Readers/Researchers interested in biological signal processing as electrocardiogram (ECG or EKG), electroencephalogram (EEG), electromyogram (EMG) with smart Electro active polymer (EAP) are a few chapters in this book. A unique technique of extracting EMG signal with Ionic Polymer Metal Composite (IPMC) with computational analysis is surges the impact of the book.

The most interesting part of electrical measurement system and control strategy will attract the upcoming researcher at the same time application of IoT in medicine and biological application will give new research domain for all.

Moreover, a chapter is contributed by an author in the field of vision sensor and its recent trends in global research domain.

Overall, this book is essential reading for the upcoming researcher and will be a future asset for the new field of instrumentation, control, and sensor design.

*Habib Masum*
*Ghani Khan Choudhury Institute of Engineering and Technology, India*

# Preface

## OVERVIEW

Present scientific community is in a high dimension to enrich the technology where we cannot say "sky is the limit". Presently developed algorithm with Artificial Intelligence (AI) with Machine Learning (ML) and Deep Learning (DL) changed the world that all we are experiencing. Conventional engineering is the backbone of every developed system where sensors plays an important role, better to say that sensors are the key element for this development. Measurement systems are the support of those sensors and control engineering gives the ultimate stability of the products. Instrumentation is a field of engineering which deals with sensors, process control, signal conditioning, Measurement system and many more. The book *Advancements in Instrumentation and Control in Applied System Applications* is focused on highlighting the above mentioned application and research area for present researcher and interested readers.

Another important application of Instrumentation is Internet of Things (IoT). If we think in this area the major authority of this field is dominating with the sensor application in different aspect to make the mankind much more comfortable. Signal conditioning for the different sensors and calibration of the same is challenging task for the present researcher. This book focused on this topic with some chapters contributed by the young researcher in biomedical application and medicine delivery system.

Mechatronics system design a multidisciplinary research domain where measurement, control and sensor calibration are so essential to develop the system for mankind. The present research gap is highlighted through this book for the upcoming researcher. At the same time bio-signal capturing and processing with proper signal conditioning is most challenging part for all new researcher. Few chapters will fulfill the demand of the said bio-medical instrumentation application research gap to find a new research domain for the readers.

Nano sensor development changes this new era of research that we all can experience this in our daily life. This interesting topic also covered by a contributor for this book, not only that smart sensors example electro active polymer (EAP) application in biomedical sensor calibration and computational process also part of few book chapters here. One chapter is contributed to enlighten the sensor application through image processing for bioengineering for the present state of art.

From the above discussion the importance of this book can be realize by the readers and new researchers where a wide range of application in the instrumentation field is highlighted. The main focus is to grow interest to the upcoming students, researchers, readers in system design for the mankind.

## TOPIC IN THE WORLD TODAY

As discussed earlier the topic includes for this book are relevant towards the upcoming researcher in Instrumentation and allied field. Sensor is always an important topic for the researcher and for the today's world. This book containing sensor application in various field of engineering as well as recent topic of AI, IoT, also recent trends on image processing and sensor application in biomedical application.

## TARGET AUDIENCE

The target audience is the future researcher, to found upcoming research topic in the field of Instrumentation, control, sensor design and measurement, Image Processing, micro and smart sensor design.

## ORGANIZATION OF THE BOOK

The book is organized into 14 chapters. A brief description of each of the chapters follows:

Chapter 1 focused on smart sensor application in biomedical signal capturing. Electro active polymer (EAP) sensor Ionic polymer metal composite (IPMC) is take as challenge to replace conventional clinical EMG sensor.

Chapter 2 shows a vision-based sensor application for human activity in biomedical application. This chapter is a review of research gap and challenges in recent trends in bio-engineering and image processing.

Chapter 3 is focused on epileptic seizure detection from the EEG signal using algorithms, soft computing of clinical data is taken and processed for disease detection.

Chapter 4 focused on biomedical application in robotics and control of lower body exoskeleton where system modeling and control is highlighted. This system is helpful for the disabled persons unable to walk and perform exercise in clinical aspect.

Chapter 5 is on electrical measurement process and control of smart grid, an overview of several classical methods applicable for electrical power measurement in the presence of harmonics and/or inter-harmonics have been discussed. Different modern technologies with their pros and cons are presented for power components measurement.

Chapter 6 focused on Electro Active Polymer sensor for biomedical application. Process of signal conditioning from the IPMC is shown in this chapter. It's also an open problem for development of alternative clinical sensor for EMG, EEG, ECG.

Chapter 7 is on design and development of taste sensor, tea quality is the main aim of it. Technique of determining the concentration of bio-chemical compounds in black tea samples by using electronic tongue signals are enriched in this chapter.

Chapter 8 is focused on measurement of electronic circuit. Junction depth measurement and corresponding process analysis is hereby presented where the total design is based in RF range.

Chapter 9 synchronize the medical and IoT. Smart city with useful information about the availability of medicine in any medicine store through wireless database.

Chapter 10 related to industry standards. Hence under all practical conditions design and implementation of a reliable, maintainable and stable earth pit considering the local soil characteristics are focused in this chapter.

Chapter 11 related to micro sensors development, challenges on spray pyrolysis method, technique in single-step deposition/synthesis method to deposit or synthesize binary, ternary or more complex compounds. This technique gives different nanostructured based thin film. Due to the presence of nanostructures in the film, it increases the efficiency of the sensors.

Chapter 12 related to robotics, smart sensors and there control. Moreover on miniaturized polymer micro-gripper applied for manipulating micro particles and micro components in micro assembly.

Chapter 13 related to PLC application in Indian railways, automation in the Indian traction system by introducing PLC is hereby reported.

Chapter 14 is of health monitoring using IoT. This chapter provided an insight into the current state and curved a path for future improvements in order to integrate remote health monitoring technologies into the clinical practice of medicine.

## CONCLUSION

To conclude this book will enlighten the new research area of different aspect of Instrumentation researcher as well as it may give some solutions to other engineering discipline like Mechatronics, Robotics, Computer science etc., after going through the chapter details it may be clear to the readers a wide range of research aspect and recent trends are focused around the globe. All the recent upcoming topics AI, IoT, application in smart to conventional sensors are focused also vision sensors its recent application in medical application also focused.

*Srijan Bhattacharya*
*RCC Institute of Information Technology, India*

# Acknowledgment

First of all, I would like to thank all the authors, reviewers, advisory committee members for their support and help for this edited book "Advancements in Instrumentation and Control in Applied System Applications". This is my proud privilege to share that more than 45 authors contributed for this book with 20 submitted chapters from this more than 40 reviewers offered their valuable time to evaluate the chapters with their expert comments and finally 14 chapters are published from five nations (India, Australia, Bangladesh, Japan, Norway) and 23 Institute/University/Industry/Health Organization.

I would like to thank management of RCC Institute of Information Technology, Kolkata, India for providing me all the necessary stuff to complete this project.

Finally, I am blessed by my parents Dr. Sanat Kumar Bhattacharya and Dr. Tapasi Bhattacharya for their endless support and help.

*Srijan Bhattacharya*
*RCC Institute of Information Technology, India*

# Chapter 1
# Similarity Analysis of IPMC and EMG Signal With Comparative Study of Statistical Features

**Ankita Paul**
*Tata Consultancy Services Ltd, India*

**Naiwrita Dey**
*RCC Institute of Information Technology, India*

**Srijan Bhattacharya**
ⓘD https://orcid.org/0000-0002-5405-2231
*RCC Institute of Information Technology, India*

## ABSTRACT

*Ionic Polymer Metal Composite is a popular sensor and actuator due to its Electroactive property to show bending abilities under low applied voltage while Electromyography is a widely used technique in Biomechanical field to analyze human bio signals to compare different motions and predict muscular anomalies and diseases. IPMC having electroactive resistive and capacitive properties as a smart sensor shows a possibility of offering equivalent precision and accuracy in determining human muscular movement predictions and analyses. This chapter correlates the EMG data method with IPMC data method for feature extraction. The process includes use of the EMG electrodes and IPMC strips to retrieve signals from the muscle movement, amplify them, clean and scale the data, and conduct the similarity analysis.*

DOI: 10.4018/978-1-7998-2584-5.ch001

## INTRODUCTION

For years, Electromyography (EMG) techniques have been used in the bio sensing methods to retrieve bio signals for muscle movement. EMG data has been processed and analytical research on the retrieved data has been proven to help in muscular disease prediction, analysis and preventive measures with the help of Machine Learning. Ionic Polymer Metal Composites are electroactive polymers that operate as actuators as well as sensors to detect bio signals. This research proposes IPMC as a potential alternative and a possible successor to the present EMG techniques to collect bio signal data and offer better data in that case to apply Machine Learning for regression model predictions.

Electromyography (EMG) techniques help in analytic methods to record and evaluate a series of electrical signals emanating from body muscles; these EMG signals are formed by physiological variations in the state of muscle fiber membranes, based upon action potentials resulting from depolarization and repolarization. According to Raez et al., the combination of muscle fiber action potentials from all the muscle fibers of a single motor unit is called as Motor Unit Action Potential (MUAP) (Farina, 2002; Reax, 2003). A non-invasive technique is used wherein by placing electrodes or sensors directly on the skin, EMG signals are detected and recorded (Hummel, 2005; Andersen, 2008; Burnett, 2007). But usual collective EMG data retrieved from human muscles can be prone to ambient noise, electrode intrinsic errors or crosstalk that may contaminate the EMG signal data generated from the muscles leading to anomalous interpretation of data.

## IPMC SENSOR

Ionic Polymer Metal Composites (IPMC) are a type of Electro Active Polymer (EAP) sensor, with perfluorinated polymer membrane of Nafion or Flemion(Fig 2), normally electroplated with noble metal like Platinum (Pt) or Gold (Au) or with Silver (Ag) (Chung, 2005) and on application of low voltages, IPMC shows ion exchange capabilities with a high capacitance showcased at low voltages. Upon application of external force (muscle contraction or relaxation in this case), there is a small (in few millivolts) amplitude electrical signal generated between the electrodes of IPMC. This activity is believed to be a mechanically-induced ionic motion and thus, at a steady deformation state, the electrical signal is dissipated (Koser B et al, 2013). In IPMC, the resistance depends on its curvature so that the resistance of convex electrode increases while that of a concave decreases, the change in resistance is asymmetric with higher variation in electrode expansion (convex side) than that of electrode compression (concave side). Even though active input is needed for

*Figure 1. The phenomenon of ion exchange in IPMC Strip*
Source: Bhattacharya et al, 2014

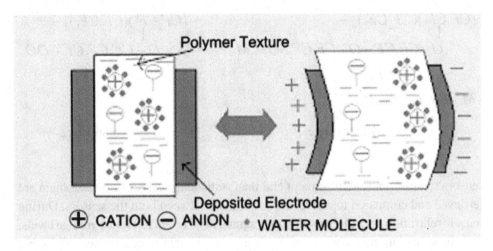

measuring the resistance of the electrode, the sensing signal is easily detectable and can be used to estimate actuator position for stable states(Punning A,et al, 2007). The high energy density, efficiency and very low power consumption makes it advantageous. In general, IPMC is a bending actuator aimed at applications that . The usual force generated at the tip of the IPMC is 10 gf for a 45 ×15 ×0.35 mm IPMC strip approximately.

The IPMC strips are made in two steps – a) Compositing Process and (ii) Surface Electroding process. The polymers go through ionic salt solution of Platinum ammine treatment (Pt(NH3)4 HCl, with free ions – H+, Li+, or Na+) and then chemically reduced to yield IPMC. The metal Pt penetrates within the membrane to a thickness of 1 – 20 _m. and then the polymer is soaked in salt solution which results in platinum (containing cations) to diffuse through the ion exchange process (Figure 1). LiBH4 (Lithium Borohydride) or NaBH4 (Sodium Borohydride or Sodium Tetrahydridoborate) are the reducing agents used to metalize the polymer. The primary reaction of platinum composite is noted below (Bhattacharya et al, 2014):-

LiBH4 + 4_Pt_NH3_4_2+ + 8OH− Þ 4Pt0 + 16NH3 + LiBO2 + 6H2O

When the IPMC strips are placed on a human arm, the electromagnetic radiation varies based on muscle contraction and relaxation, making the strip act as a sensor to detect the changes of muscle movement. This electroactive property lets it pick up the electrochemical gradient due to flow of ions through the axon ends released within the muscle which ultimately causes the muscle contraction and detect the mechanical tension. In this experiment we use both IPMC and EMG as electroactive

*Figure 2. IPMC Nafion and Flemion Structure*
Source: Bhattacharya et al, 2014

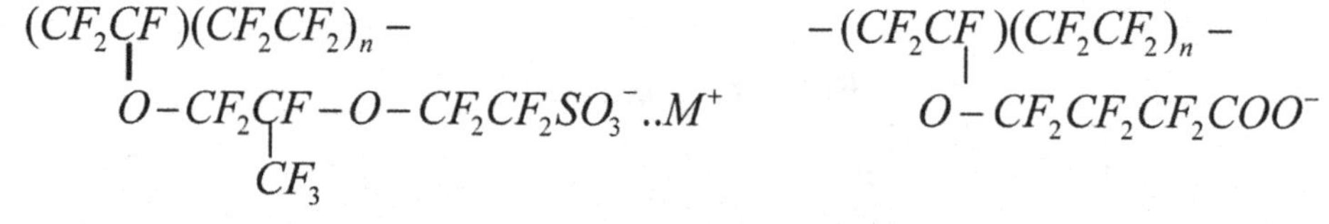

$$(CF_2CF)(CF_2CF_2)_n - \atop O-CF_2CF-O-CF_2CF_2SO_3^- ..M^+ \atop CF_3$$

$$-(CF_2CF)(CF_2CF_2)_n - \atop O-CF_2CF_2CF_2COO^-$$

$M^+$ : Counter ion ($H^+$, $Li^+$ or $Na^+$)

Nafion Structure          Flemion Structure

sensors to sense muscle movement and then statistical features of time domain are retrieved and compared to arrive at a correlation between both the sensors. During muscle relaxation both the sensors stay stagnant at different reference voltage levels, and shows variation in voltages only during the instants of contraction. We apply the same technique for data retrieval when the human arm is put under pressure and the muscles come under the effect of a strain. Time domain features are calculated and visually represented for analytical purpose with the help of Machine Learning using Python to reaffirm the similarities obtained between IPMC and EMG. With the help of Statistical Analysis and mathematical tests we correlate the data obtained from both IPMC and EMG sensors to obtain a similarity between the nature of their data and it is indicative of the fact that IPMC can be a good fit as a bio sensor to obtain and train models for disease prediction of muscles and movements for human beings, using Machine Learning.

## WORKING PRINCIPLE

EMG sensor detects the action potential generated by motor neuron of muscles with the help of electrodes placed over muscles in low fat region of body. Two electrodes were placed over the skin of upper arm (mainly over biceps muscles) to get the two voltage values and a third electrode was attached to the elbow joint to provide the reference potential (Fig1). The low amplitude voltage signals were fed as input to the AD620 amplifier for amplification. IPMC has been employed as a pressure sensor and thus works on the principle that it will give different output voltage on different extent of curvature. This curvature of IPMC in turn depends on the extent of pressure exerted on it by the muscles over which it is placed. Varying extent of curvature gives peaks of different amplitude in the characteristics thus indicating an idea of the force exerted on the IPMC. This in turn indicates the extent of action potential generated during the application of force. It has been verified experimentally that

*Figure 3. Block diagram for the data acquisition unit*

application of pressure causes ionic movement in between the metal plates resulting in generation of voltage signal (Gudarzi, 2017). The behavior including the electrical sensing ability of IPMC, which is caused due to the electrochemical changes due to muscle activity causes the IPMC to respond in electric field surrounding the generated action potential (i.e. Flow of charge), is also to be noted.

## DATA COLLECTION PROCESS AND CONTRIBUTION TO THE CHAPTER

Three electrodes of the Electromyogram sensor were used, two of them placed on the bicep muscles for differential input voltage into the instrumentational amplifier, and one on the elbow as the reference potential. The IPMC was placed on the bicep muscle, the same actuation area where the EMG electrodes were placed, and the voltage generated due to the pressure and the electrochemical change created due to voluntary muscle activity was fed into the current to voltage converter circuit. The given circuit also assists to amplify the voltage which is provided as input into the PCI-1711 data acquisition card and the data was logged into the excel sheet using the 'Write to Measurement file' of LabVIEW.(Fig 4) Similarly, the output from the instrumentational amplifier was fed into the data acquisition card as an input and the data was logged into another excel sheet with respect to the system time. Data acquisition tool is used to retrieve the data from the respective sensors. The 'Write to Measurement File' tool has been implemented to log the data into an excel files sheet. The waveform chart was employed to observe the signal being generated from the sensors. Two circuits were drawn for both the sensors (EMG and IPMC) and inserted within an infinite while loop.

### Proposed Method

In this present study EMG Electrodes and IPMC strips have been used as sensors of muscle motion. A trans-impedance amplifier using TL082 as Current to Voltage Amplifier, an instrumentation amplifier (AD 620) is used to amplify the signals of EMG. For data acquisition PCI 1711 is used, it contains 16 single-ended channels

*Figure 4. Experimental setup for data acquisition from IPMC sensor and EMG electrodes placed on the human arm*

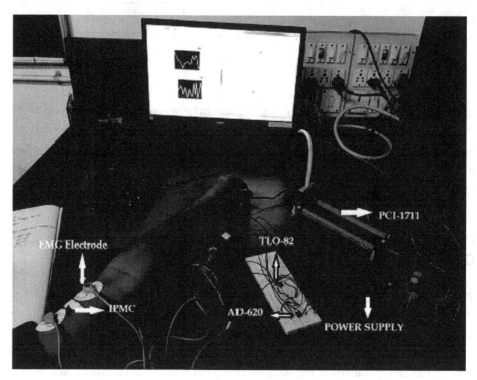

with 12-bit resolution for each and maximum sampling rate 100 KS/s, having software trigger mode. It provides two D/A output channels. In PCI 1711 the maximum reference input voltage is $\pm 10$ V and maximum output scaling is $\pm 10$ V. It is used to log the data using LabVIEW. LabVIEW 2015 is used to observe and store the characteristics of the output signals instantaneously while conducting the experiment. Digital Multimeter (DMM) is used to measure the signals in the range of milli-volts and micro ampere of IPMC and EMG electrodes. The IPMC strip used in this investigation is composed of a per fluorinated ion exchange membrane (IEM), which is chemically composited with a noble metal such as Gold or Platinum. For software simulation, Spyder 3 has been utilized for Python programming.

## Statistical Analysis

In the attempt to correlate the nature of data obtained from both IPMC and EMG sensors, the extraction of data, cleansing of data were followed by the computation of the statistical features for both the datasets.

Statistical features - These are attributes that throw an insight upon the statistical properties of a dataset. In order to achieve our similarity analysis we obtained features that designate the nature of the dataset, their relativity and correlation, going forward which can help us with designing a machine learning model based on the features collected. The features can be either Time domain, Frequency domain or Time-Frequency domain. In this experiment Time Domain features have been analysed because it has been found to give higher accuracy with respect to Frequency domain features and is also easy to be accumulated from raw signal data making it easier to implement (Altin, 2016).

**Time Domain Statistical Features**: The variability of the amplitude of a signal with respect to time depends upon the condition of the muscles (relaxed or under pressure) when the data was extracted using EMG and IPMC. The TD Features used in this experiment to draw the comparative study are (Zhou, 2012; Chai, 2014; Altman, 2005; Gurland, 1971) - Mean, Median, Standard Deviation, Entropy, Root Mean Square, Variance, Skewness, Kurtosis, Mean Absolute Variance.

The Mean and Standard Deviation of both the IPMC generated data and the EMG signal data is computed. The results of the Standard Deviation indicate, that the IPMC data is more constricted near the mean while the EMG data is more spread out away from the mean, implying that the dataset of EMG signal has high variability and less closer to the expected value (Fig 3). A more spread out data around the mean, as in the case of EMG can make it difficult to demarcate statistical features or make robust predictive analysis from the dataset using Machine Learning models. The IPMC Data on the other hand shows a comparatively low variability around the mean, making the dataset more suitable for predictability analysis. The more spread out a data, the less the reliability and vice versa.

## Application of Kolmogorov– Smirnov Test

The Kolmogorov–Smirnov test (K–S test) is a non-parametric test of one-dimensional probability distributions used in Statistics to compare a sample with a reference probability distribution (one-sample K–S test), or to compare two samples (two-sample K–S test) (Stephens, 1974). The Kolmogorov–Smirnov statistic can quantify a distance between the empirical distribution functions of two samples of IPMC and EMG data. The null distribution of the K-S statistic is calculated under the null hypothesis that the sample is drawn from the reference distribution (in a one-sample case scenario) or that the samples are drawn from the same distribution (in a two-sample case). In the two-sample case, the distribution considered under the null

*Figure 5. Notched Box plot of EMG and IPMC data showing a correlated mean*

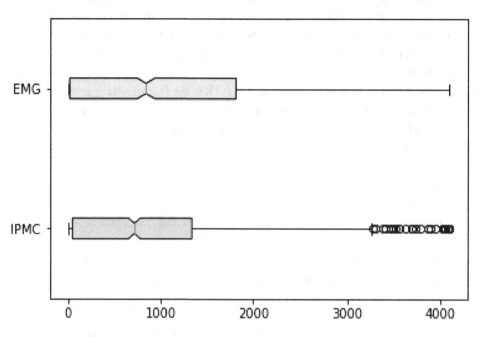

hypothesis is a continuous distribution but is otherwise unrestricted. In this case, the K-S Test is applied to test whether the two underlying probability distributions of IPMC and EMG are similar. The statistic is mathematically expressed as –

$$D_{n,m} = \sup[[F_{(1,n)}(x) - F_{(2,m)}(x)]]$$

Where F1,n(x) and F2,m(x) are the empirical distribution functions of the first and the second sample respectively, and sup is the supremum of the functions .The Scipy module of Python has been applied to predict the similarity of the nature of data values retrieved from IPMC and EMG .The Ks_2samp function used from the Scipy module along with matplotlib and numpy modules and we obtained the following result:

The K-S test returns a D statistic and a p-value corresponding to the D statistic. The D statistic is the absolute max distance (supremum: sup) between the Cumulative Distributive Function (CDF) of the two samples. The closer this number is to 0 the more likely it is that the two samples will tend to have higher similarity. The p-value returned by the K-S test is an accurate mode of interpretation of the statistic in practical applications. The tests assume that the sample was drawn from a Gaussian distribution or in this case, are showing close resemblance to each other. Technically

*Table 1. P value and D-statistic values obtained from correlating IPMC and EMG datasets during normal muscle contraction and gripping a ball*

|  | **Muscle Contraction Normal** | **Muscle Contraction during Ball Grip** |
|---|---|---|
| P Value | 2.000041630 | 0.972715155 |
| D Statistic | 0.113765642 | 0.050847457 |

this is called the null hypothesis, or H0. The significance level mentioned earlier called alpha, is chosen typically 5% (or 0.05), that is used to interpret the p-value.

In this case, we interpret the p value as follows.

$P <= (0.05)$: reject H0, lack of resemblance

$P > (0.05)$: fail to reject H0, close resemblance.

The P Value and D-Statistic obtained in two conditions, during normal contraction of arm and while gripping a ball, using both EMG electrode and IPMC strip.

This test result returns a p-value of 2.000041630 in case of normal muscle contraction and 0.972715155 in case of muscle contraction during ball grip, which is above the significance level of 5%, that gives a hint about the similarity of data distribution between the EMG signal data and the IPMC signal data for both the cases of muscle contraction – normal as well as ball grip. We cannot reject the null hypotheses (H0) and it can be a favourable inclination towards the resemblance in the nature of data collected from both IPMC and EMG data. The empirical distribution functions are plotted together for both the data samples (fig below) using the ecdf module from the mlxtend library of Python.

The ECDF is made by sorting the data and plotting it along the horizontal axis. It is a non-decreasing stair-step function that rises by 1/n at each of the n sorted data points. The cumulative distribution function (CDF) of the probability distribution from which the data was randomly sampled is approximated by the ECDF. The resemblance between the nature of distribution of both EMG and IPMC makes it a possibility to use IPMC data for prediction models that can interpret muscle movement of human arms.

## Histogram Analysis of the IPMC and EMG Data Distribution

A histogram is a representation of the distribution of numerical data. It is an estimate of the probability distribution of a continuous variable and was first introduced by Karl Pearson. We "bin" (or "bucket") the range of values—that is, divide the entire

*Figure 6. ECDF plot of IPMC and EMG signal data*

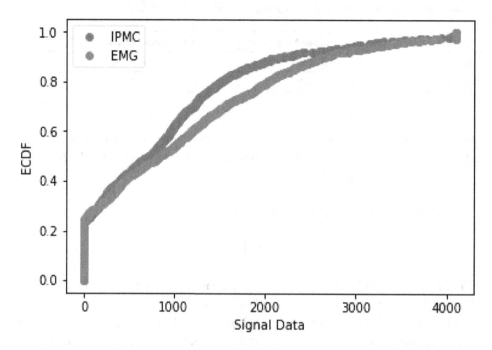

range of values into a series of intervals—and then count how many values fall into each interval. The bins are usually specified as consecutive, non-overlapping intervals of a variable. The bins (intervals) must be adjacent, and are often (but are not required to be) of equal size. (Howitt, 1974; Burke, 1988) In this experiment the Histogram density has been estimated for each dataset:- The height of the bars in the relative frequency histogram denotes the density of data points in the cell that the bar is drawn upon. If a cell centred at x has -

width = w and contains k data points, the height of the bar is:-
$h(x) = k/n \times 1/w$ which is directly proportional to the density of points in the interval.
Data Density = k/ w (4)

## Feature Extraction of Both IPMC and EMG

The following data shows the values of the statistical features for both IPMC and EMG, calculated by mathematical formulation with Python programming language -

*Figure 7. Histogram representation of IPMC and EMG data under relaxed phase of muscle*

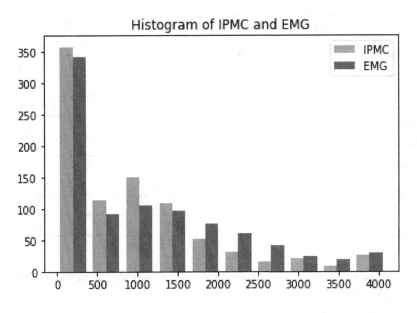

*Figure 8. Histogram representation of IPMC and EMG data under ball grip posture of muscle*

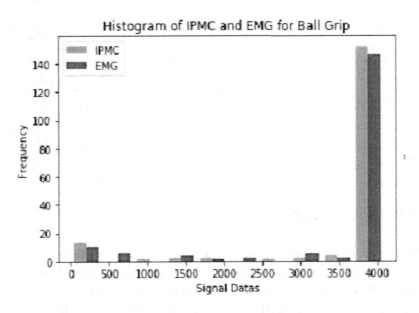

*Table 2. Statistical features during ball gripping activity as detected by IPMC and EMG*

| Statistical Features during Ball Grip as detected by IPMC and EMG | | |
|---|---|---|
| **Features** | **IPMC** | **EMG** |
| Mean | 3693.7 | 3616.26 |
| Median | 4095 | 4095 |
| Variance | 1263615.33 | 1366287.72 |
| Standard Deviation | 1124.1 | 1168.88 |
| Root Mean Square | 3860.96 | 3800.48 |
| Mean Absolute Deviation | 689.2 | 789.21 |
| Skewness | -2.71 | -2.33 |
| Kurtosis | 5.74 | 3.93 |
| Entropy | 0.75 | 0.98 |

*Table 3. Statistical features during normal muscle contraction activity as detected by IPMC and EMG*

| Statistical Features during Muscle Contraction as detected by IPMC and EMG | | |
|---|---|---|
| **Features** | **IPMC** | **EMG** |
| Mean | 908.68 | 1089.6 |
| Median | 716 | 841 |
| Variance | 944185.97 | 1198199.2 |
| Standard Deviation | 971.69 | 1094.62 |
| Root Mean Square | 1330.37 | 1544.5 |
| Mean Absolute Deviation | 748.04 | 904.96 |
| Skewness | 1.37 | 0.92 |
| Kurtosis | 1.65 | 0.06 |
| Entropy | 5.38 | 5.32 |

## Results and Analysis

The below conclusions can be drawn from the above tables of Features data that:-

The datasets of both EMG and IPMC have a low Skewness and Kurtosis, implying that both of these distributions tend to be close to a normal distribution with fewer outliers. It can be inferred that due to the lack of outliers in both the datasets, the reliability of IPMC dataset for modelling prediction analysis can be at par with that of EMG methodology.

The Entropy of both the datasets are almost similar in value suggesting that the decision tree models shall split both the datasets at the same level with equal affinity for both the cases of IPMC and EMG. Since entropy is a measure of how ordered a dataset, the similarity between of IPMC dataset to EMG makes it a probable choice for decision tree algorithms in Machine Learning as much as EMG dataset. The Standard Deviation, Variance and Mean Absolute Variance being less for IPMC with respect to EMG dataset (for both the cases of normal muscular contraction and gripping a ball) implies that the IPMC data is less spread out around the mean and hence more concentrated towards the central tendency, making it a more reliable dataset when compared to the EMG signal data. The distance of each datapoint from its mean (or the central tendency) determines the reliability of the entire dataset as a whole and in case of IPMC - all these mentioned features are lower with respect to EMG, making the data less varied around the mean and hence more consistent when it comes to data modelling for muscle movement or disease prediction with Machine Learning models.

## The K-S Test Interpretation

The K-S test returns a p-value of 2.000041630 in case of normal muscle contraction and 0.972715155 in case of muscle contraction during ball grip (Table 1), which is above the significance level of 5%, that gives a hint about the similarity of data distribution between the EMG signal data and the IPMC signal data for both the cases of muscle contraction – normal as well as ball grip. Hence, we cannot reject the null hypotheses (H0) and it can be a favourable inclination towards the resemblance in the nature of data collected from both IPMC and EMG data.

The D - statistic value of 0.113765642 and 0.050847457 for muscle contraction and ball gripping scenario respectively (Table 1) indicates that the absolute maximum distance between the CDFs of the two functions tends to zero, suggesting the closeness of the probability distributions of IPMC and EMG.

## Histogram Analysis

The Histogram data density comparative graph produced with the Python algorithm shows that for each data interval, the density for IPMC and EMG are near to one another (Fig 5 and Fig 6). The bar graphs point out that except for all the intervals the density for both the datasets are almost similar and alike. The height of bars for every data interval for both the cases of normal muscle contraction as well as ball gripping are almost equivalent for both IPMC and EMG. This makes IPMC a potential alternative for Machine learning decision making models for muscle movement and muscle disease predictability for humans.

## CONCLUSION

In this chapter, the nature of data obtained from EMG electrodes as well as IPMC Strips on two cases, one for normal muscle contraction of the forearm and the other case of gripping a ball have been addressed. The K-S Test carried out on the two pairs of datasets and the results indicate a close similarity between the probability distributions of IPMC and EMG datasets. The Histogram Analysis and the data distribution among the intervals have been very much similar for both IPMC and EMG for both the occasions of muscular contraction. The statistical features computed for each dataset for the two muscle contraction cases indicate that IPMC data distribution has the tendency to be more reliable if fit into Machine Learning models in the future, for being less spread out away from mean. In terms of Entropy, Kurtosis and Skewness both EMG data as well as IPMC have shown equivalent characteristics. Hence data obtained from IPMC has shown considerable potential and reliability to be used as bio sensors to retrieve muscular signals, and there is potential in the data distribution obtained from IPMC to be fit into Machine Learning models for data training purposes in the field of Disease prediction and Muscular motion analyses, in the future.

## REFERENCES

Andersen, L. L., Kjaer, M., Andersen, C. H., Hansen, P. B., Zebis, M. K., Hansen, K., & Sjøgaard, G. (2008). Muscle activation during selected strength exercises in women with chronic neck muscle pain. *Journal of the American Physical Therapy Association*, *88*(6), 703–711. PMID:18339796

Bhattacharya, S., Bepari, B., & Bhaumik, S. (2014). IPMC-Actuated Compliant Mechanism Based Multifunctional. *Multifinger Microgripper*, *42*(3), 312–325.

Brown, S. (2011). Measures of shape: Skewness and kurtosis. Retrieved on August, 20, 2012.

Burke, P, V., & Bullen, L. (1988). *Bertha*. Poff L Kenneth, Frequency Distribution Histograms for the Rapid Analysis of Data; doi:10.1104/pp.87.4.797

Burnett, A., Green, J., Netto, K., & Rodrigues, J. (2007). Examination of emg normalization methods for the study of the posterior and posterolateral neck muscles in healthy controls. *Journal of Electromyography and Kinesiology*, *17*(5), 635–641. doi:10.1016/j.jelekin.2006.06.003 PMID:16899375

Cemil, A., & Orhan, E. (2016) Comparison of Different Time and Frequency Domain Feature Extraction Methods on Elbow Gesture's EMG, ISSN 2411-4138 (Online)

Chai T., & Draxler, R. R. (n.d.). Root mean square error (RMSE) or mean absolute error (MAE)? – Arguments against avoiding RMSE in the literature, doi:10.5194/gmd-7-1247-2014

Chung, C. K., Fung, P. K., Hong, Y. Z., Ju, M. S., Lin, C. C. K., & Wu, T. C. (2005). A novel fabrication of ionic polymer-metal composites (IPMC) actuator with silver nano-powders, 117(2006) 367-375.

Farina, D., Madeleine, P., Graven-Nielsen, T., Merletti, R., & Arendt-Nielsen, L. (2002). Standardising surface electromyogram recordings for assessment of activity and fatigue in the human upper trapezius muscle. *European Journal of Applied Physiology*, *86*(6), 469–478. doi:10.100700421-001-0574-0 PMID:11944093

Schroer, G., & Trenkler, D. (n.d.). Kolmogorov-Smirnov tests two or three samples, doi:10.1016/0167-9473(94)00040-P

Gu, Y., Zhang, Q., & Yu, L. (2018). Some Inequalities Combining Rough and Random Information. *Entropy (Basel, Switzerland)*, *20*(3), 211. doi:10.3390/e20030211

Gudarzi, M., Smolinski, P., & Wang, Q. M. (2017). Compression and Shear Mode Ionic Polymer-metal Composite (IPMC) Pressure Sensors: Sensors and Actuators A, Elsevier, 99–111.

Gurland, J., & Tripathi, R. C. (1971). A Simple Approximation for Unbiased Estimation of the Standard Deviation. *The American Statistician*, *25*(4), 30–32.

Howitt, D., & Cramer, D. (2008). *Introduction to Statistics in Psychology* (4th ed.). Prentice Hall.

Hummel, A., Laubli, T., Pozzo, M., Schenk, P., Spillmann, S., & Klipstein, A. (2005). Relationship between perceived exertion and mean power frequency of the EMG signal from the upper trapezius muscle during isometric shoulder elevation. *European Journal of Applied Physiology*, *95*(4), 321–326. doi:10.100700421-005-0014-7 PMID:16096843

Kocer, B., & Weiland, L. M. (2013). Experimental investigation of the streaming potential hypothesis for ionic polymer transducers in sensing. *Smart Materials and Structures*, *22*(3). doi:10.1088/0964-1726/22/3/035020

Punning, A., Kruusmaa, M., & Aabloo, A. (2007). Surface resistance experiments with IPMC sensors and actuators. Sensors and Actuators. A, Physical, 133, 200–209.

Reaz, M. B. I., Hussain, M. S., & Mohd-Yasin, F. (2006). Techniques of emg signal analysis: detection, processing, classification, and applications, *Biol. Procedures Online, 8*(1), pp. 11-35, doi:10.1251/bpo115

Stephens, M. A. (1974). EDF Statistics for Goodness of Fit and Some Comparisons. *Journal of the American Statistical Association*, *69*(347), 730–737. doi:10.1080/0 1621459.1974.10480196

Zhou, Y., Lei, J., Wang, J., & Cheng, Z. (2012). Analysis and Selection of Features for Gesture Recognition Based on a Micro Wearable Device, IJACSA, 3(1).

# Chapter 2
# Vision and Sensor–Based Human Activity Recognition:
## Challenges Ahead

**Md Atiqur Rahman Ahad**

(iD) https://orcid.org/0000-0001-8355-7004
*University of Dhaka, Bangladesh*

## ABSTRACT

*Human action or activity or behavior analysis, recognition, and understanding are very important research areas in the field of computer vison, internet of things (IoT) sensor-based analysis, human-computer interaction (HCI), affective computing, intelligent system, healthcare facilities, and so on. There is much importance in human action recognition. This chapter introduces the core aspects of human action or activity recognition (HAR). These are split into two different domains: computer vision-based action/activity recognition, action localization, etc.; and wearable IoT sensor-based HAR. Though cameras are also sensors that provide vision-based information, the author puts camera-based or vision-based methods in another category. The chapter introduces core challenges and strategies to move forward.*

## INTRODUCTION

Human action or activity or behavior analysis, recognition, understanding are very important research areas in the field of computer vison, Internet of Things (IoT) sensor-based analysis, human-computer interaction (HCI), affective computing, intelligent system, healthcare facilities, and so on (Ahad et al, 2012; Ahad et al,

DOI: 10.4018/978-1-7998-2584-5.ch002

2011; Ahad et al, 2019). There are lots of importance on human action recognition. For example,

- Video surveillance in various facilities
- Games and interactive systems
- Hospital and medical applications
- Smart-home, rehabilitation centers
- Assisted living
- Context-awareness
- Fall down detection and recognition
- Activity of Daily Living (ADL)
- Entertainment fields as movie, animation, 3D TV
- Intelligent Transport Systems (ITS)
- Robotics and automation
- Abnormal behavior analysis
- Crowd scene analysis
- Affective computing
- Emotion analysis
- Pain analysis
- Gait recognition
- Gait understanding for healthcare applications
- Man-machine interaction
- Gesture analysis
- Scene analysis
- Egocentric applications
- Hand movement understanding
- Sign language recognition

## SENSORS FOR HUMAN ACTIVITY RECOGNITION

In this section, we split the human action or activity recognition approaches into two broad areas, namely – vision-based domain (based on video cameras) and wearable / IoT sensor-based domain (based on wearable sensors having accelerometer, gyroscope, or other sensors). Methodologies and sensors are widely varied in both arenas. There are only a few approaches where these two modalities are blended.

## Vision-Based Domain

More and more applications are enriching due to the advent of different cameras and their modalities. Camera-based data can have the following modalities:

- RGB video data in 3 color channels
- Depth image data (for example, from depth sensors, Kinect sensors, RealSense camera) (Sinz et al, 2004).
- Extracted skeleton data. There are a number of skeleton-based datasets which are extracted from depth image mainly (Pham et al, 2018; Kong et al, 2015; Vemulapalli et al, 2014; Gaglio et al, 2015; Yang et al, 2012; Batabyal et al, 2015; Seidenari et al, 2013). These can be computed or extracted from the following options:
  - Kinect sensor can produce these data (Sell et al, 2014), or
  - We can explore OpenPose method (such as, Body-25, or MPI, or COCO model), or AlphaPose (Cao et al, 2017).

Hence, due to the camera sensors, the scopes are enhanced. There are egocentric cameras that can be placed on forehead or chest or nearby to capture data of any hand movements or frontal view. Due to the miniaturization of sensors with higher accuracy as well as capacity, the results are getting better.

Surveillance camera-based activity understanding is another important research area (Jin et al, 2017). Multi-camera systems turn the action monitoring more challenging. These later two issues will remain very difficult. However, we will shortly notice that for over a decade, almost all works have been done based on non-realistic and simplistic data. These are mostly not based on real action data in our daily lives. Activities are extremely diverse in real-life and very difficult for an intelligent system to understand. In the last few years, a recent trend has been explored where YouTube-based activities are recognized. However, it becomes extremely challenging though more realistic. We will discuss these issues in this chapter.

## Sensor-Based Domain

Apart from the camera-based human action recognition and study, the Internet of Things (IoT) sensor-based wearable (mostly) devices are immensely explored in the ubiquitous research community for human activity recognition (Amiribesheli et al, 2015). The terminology 'human activity recognition' (HAR) is very well-known and widely-used term in sensor-based field. On the other hand, vision-based community does the code action or activity recognition but the seldom coin the term HAR in their works. We will also notice that the diversity of activities in sensor-based domain are limited compare to the vision-based domain.

## NOMENCLATURE OF HUMAN ACTION OR ACTIVITY

Human motion that has some sort of variations in the scene or has any locomotion that a sensor can capture – can be mentioned as an action or an activity (e.g., run, jog, walk, read, cook). Usually, when more than one person are doing something together, it can be termed as interaction (e.g., hugging, handshaking, fighting). Any movement in a scene will ignite the possibility of an action/activity. Postural changes in a meaningful manner can be coined as action or activity. These can vary with time period. For example,

- Someone is 'walking for five minutes' is an action, whereas, someone is walking for few seconds' can be the same action: both are 'walking action or activity'.
- However, if several basic or simple actions are done one after another that can be meaningful as well – then we can call it as a 'complex action or activity' (Brand et al, 1997). One example is cooking activity where we do cutting, cleaning, stirring, putting, frying, moving and so on to cook something. So a cooking activity is comprised of a number of other simpler action or activities. Similarly, any sports can be explained in this manner.
- Finally, if an action is accomplished by more than one person then we can call it as an interaction. Interactions are usually considered between two or more persons. In some cases, interactions can be with objects as well. So, interactions can be split into the following sub-categories:
  ○ Human and human interaction
  ○ Human and static object interaction
  ○ Human and moving object interaction
  ○ Interactions among more than two persons or objects

### Action vs. Activity in Vision/Sensor

Another point is the action or activity. In sensor-based domain, everything is termed as 'activity' in almost all literatures. On the other hand, in vision-based domain – the activity is based on some 'actions', which are based on some

- Basic actions, or
- Movements, or

- Movems, or
- Action snippets, or
- Action primitives, or
- Dynemes, or
- Basic gestures.

These terms are mainly defining the atomic or primitive action units (Fanti et al, 2008; Weiyao et al, 2008; Brann et al, 2007).

In the domain of sensor-based human activity recognition, even simple 'walk' or 'stay', or 'sitting on a chair' are also termed as activities even though these are all basic and simple actions. We need to understand these differences and in the literature, there is no conformity on the nomenclature of action or activity. There are over thousands of research works and papers on these areas, yet the nomenclature is not established and hugely varied from one paper to another. Hence, we need to look into the datasets to get the objective of the method to understand any movement / action / activity / interaction, rather the *adjective* of the classes. In Figure 1, we schematically present a typical example setting for these various options – from basic action to action to activity to interaction. Note that some of these are overlapping from one set to another set. Also, in sensor-based research, 'action' classes are typically coined as 'activity'.

## Human Activity Recognition and Challenges Ahead

Actions are recognized or understood through different strategies where we take the video data or sensor data – then process to extract important features or cues to create smart feature vectors – then these features are exploited to recognize or classify different activity classes by exploiting classifiers. This basic process is similar to any other pattern recognition strategies, e.g., image classification, object classification or recognition (Ahad et al, 2012; Ahad et al, 2011; Ahad et al, 2019). Figure 2 shows a typical flow diagram for human action recognition. The details are varied from methods to methods as well as on the input modality – whether video data or sensor-based data.

However, it is deemed to be really a daunting task to recognize various classes in a smart manner. Some of the challenges in activity recognition are addressed below:

1.  **Real-life Activity Classes:** Real-life actions are very much diverse and have innumerable issues or objects or situations. The no. of classes is massively diverse as well. Therefore, it is really difficult to classify many activity classes by exploiting one method.

*Figure 1. A typical hierarchy of action-activity-interaction*

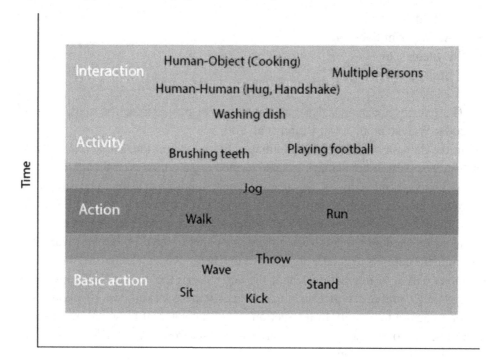

*Figure 2. A system flow diagram for human activity recognition.*

2.  **Variations Per Activity Class:** Each action class can be acted differently. For example, walking towards a camera, from the camera, walking diagonally, walking in uphill or downhill, walking randomly, etc. can produce different types of vision-based cues or information. So, walking patterns become difficult. However, sensor-based cases, an accelerometer can easily collect walking patterns whether the directions are different.

3.  **Similar Activity Classes:** Similar action classes are also present. There are many overlapping between classes by different people. One example of this is walking and jogging. Sometimes, faster walking pattern can be resembled as jogging class. Similarly, jogging and running can confuse each other. Figure 3 depicts a simplistic example of these three classes where the magnitude of them are demonstrated. Note that in few cases, one class is confused by another

*Figure 3. A graph that demonstrates the variations and overlapping of three action classes*

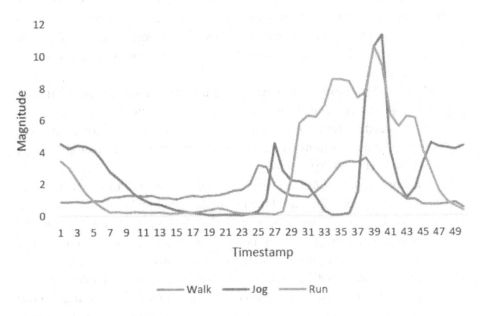

class. The reasons may be due to the data collection error or missing data from the sensor, or variations of speed in different periods.

4. **Continuous vs. Segmented Activity Classes:** One major concern till-to-date (mainly for computer vision domain), each action class is a separate video! So, when we recognize, we input one video for *one* class only to test. However, in real-life, we do actions one after another with varied timing and patterns. From a continued video scene, we need to segment automatically or we need to localize actions then start recognizing process. These issues are extremely difficult and few recent approaches are handling these challenges.

5. **Periodicity in Activity:** Some actions are periodic. Most of the methods cannot decipher the periodicity of any action that has repetitions. For instance, sitting down and standing up and if it is continued, many feature representations mix up with other classes.

6. **Number of Classes:** Most of the methods till to date are handling simple actions or few classes only per each benchmark datasets. Most of the datasets have 6 or 8 or 10 action or activity classes only (e.g., KTH dataset, HASC dataset (Takamichi et al, 2016))! And most of these datasets are created in unrealistic constrained environment – hence, these mostly do not reflect the reality of action variations. Few recent exceptions are some large datasets, which are built from YouTube videos (e.g., UCF101 has 101 classes (Soomro et al,

2018), Kinetics has now 700 classes – having 6,50,000 videos (Kinetics et al, 2019), YouTube-8M has 3862 classes having 5,62,000 videos, Sports-1M has 487 classes (Karpathy et al, 2014). Some of these datasets are getting larger as time passes with new classes and instances. Those recent datasets have even several hundred classes and we need to explore deep learning approaches for these big dataset.

7.   **Motion Information Extraction:** Motion information extraction and further processing is a challenge. There are basically three options or strategies:

   a.   **Localized Motion Cues:** Some methods consider local information where movements or actions are present and extract these for further processing (Laptav et al, 2005).

   b.   **Global Information:** On the other hand, a number of methods including many deep learning-based methods take the global motion information from the video scene (bruhn et al, 2005). This is a challenge. Optical flow can extract any kind of motion in the scene. So, we can consider or highlight the core motion parts for further processing. Figure 4 shows an example of optical flow vectors where a person is moving and the flow vectors demonstrate the core motion direction. Note that optical flow methods produce noisy vectors. In order to achieve more accurate motion vectors (as shown in this image in an idealistic situation), we need to remove outliers by employing different methods, e.g., RANdom SAmple Consensus (RANSAC), PROSAC, LO-RANSAC, ANTSAC (RANSAC with Ant Colony algorithms), RANSAC using a Maximum Likelihood framework (MLESAC), RANSAC using importance sampling (IMPSAC) (Fischler et al, 1981; Torr et al, 2000; Otte et al, 2014; Laptev et al, 2005).

   c.   **Hybrid Approach:** Some approaches are mixing both ideas partially for recognizing various actions (Castrodad et al, 2012).

8.   **Activity With Object Recognition:** Actions and objects are related. If someone is running towards me with a flower – it has a special meaning! If someone is rushing towards me with a knife or something dangerous – then it need to act differently. There is no scope of romanticism here! Therefore, object identification or recognition as well as action understanding will help a lot to understand any realistic situation. In this case, sensor-based domain cannot identify object in a smart manner, whereas, computer vision community has engulfed a great number of development in object recognition and detection.

9.   **Activity With Emotional State:** Action is related to emotion. If the psychology or emotion cannot be understood, then we can misclassify an action just by looking into the pattern or shape of the action. Consider that your good friend jumped on you from the back with a smile and friendly gesture. It is not fighting

*Figure 4. An ideal example of optical flow vector for a running scene*

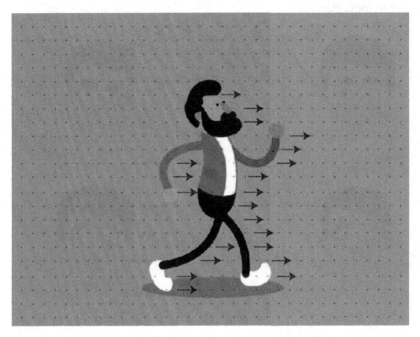

if you look at it and the slapping on the back is not actually an act of anger or fight. But if someone does the similar thing with angry mode, then you will feel different than the 'friendly' situation. Therefore, emotional cues are very important and these are mostly missing so far from the methods on activity recognition. Two domains can have different strategies and these are outlined below:

a.   **Facial Action Coding System:** In vision field, closer cameras can extract facial action units (AU) based on Facial Action Coding System (FACS) from which we can understand the psychological status or mode to some reasonable extent. So, computer vision-based action recognition method with the facial emotional information can help better understanding. Figure 5 depicts an example of four different emotional statuses based on the facial muscle movements in different parts of the face. These constitute different cues of action units and coding through which we can estimate emotional stages. These can be incorporated for understanding human actions.

b.   **Emotional State in Sensor:** The sensor-based activity recognition methods need to find ways in this direction to incorporate human emotional issues. There are a few approaches where different other sensors can accumulate some data to gain information on human mental status. For example, if

25

*Figure 5. Four different emotional states are mentioned based on the variations on facial action movements.*

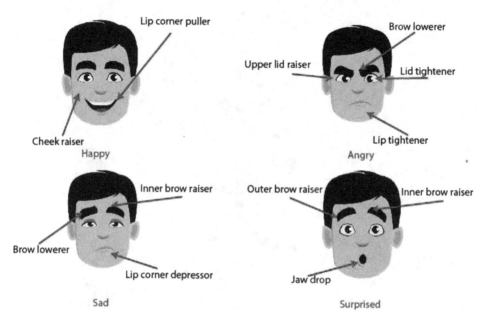

someone is sleepy or not, high blood pressure or not than his/ her usual rate, and so on – these information can be useful to understand an action in a better manner.

10. **Isolated Action to a Meaningful Activity:** Isolated action classes are recognized by different approaches more or less. However, if there are multiple actions one after another – then, can we cluster them into a meaningful action? Situations like Activity of Daily Living (ADL) at home, at elderly support center – these issues are important to understand. There are few works that have explored this issue. This is more realistic indeed.

11. **Illumination Variation:** Vision-based domain, indoor and outdoor make huge difference. Image captures the light and if there are drastic variations in illuminations then the camera sensors may fail to extract proper motion cues. So, the classification system may fail to recognize. Illumination variation is a major challenge. However, sensor-based methods have no issue on illumination variation. If a method needs light sensor, then a simple light sensor can record the luminance and it can assist in understanding action classes.

12. **Camera Views:** There are a number of datasets that are taken not only from frontal view camera but also from multiple directions. Jumping on the floor from side view and frontal view will provide different motion cues or information

by different methods. Hence, it is another major challenge. In reality, there are many surveillance cameras around us and the data they capture from different directions should be assessed smartly to understand an action. Multi-view based human activity recognition is still a major challenge.

13. **Real-Time Recognition:** Real-time assessment is important – especially for falling down recognition cases. But due to the massive data processing and due to the presence of many types of activities, it is difficult to recognize an action in real-time. It is possible to recognize a few simple actions easily by some methods but genuine actions are not possible to recognize in real-time. Yes, we have huge development in terms of GPU and more memories in computers, still the challenge is higher.

a. **Real-Time Issue in Sensor Field:** Real-time based methods are more visible in non-vision fields, and sensor-based approaches are more realistic for a set of activity classes to perform in real-time. The reason is that sensors produce data that are not massive like image or depth image or skeleton data. If you exploit an accelerometer, then it will give you just three values from the three axes of X, Y, and Z, along with the timestamp of each data.

b. **Real-Time Issue in Vision Field:** For a vision-based system, one second can produce 30 images or frames for a 30 fps camera (fps is frame per second). And if the image resolution is relatively higher (as we can notice in many mobile phone cameras, webcams, let alone in commercial video cameras), then we can achieve huge amount of information than we get from wearable sensors.

14. **Issues Related to Subjects:** Apart from some recent YouTube-based very large video datasets for activity recognition, most of the datasets are crafted by young adults as subjects. Therefore, anthropometric variations are little. Some datasets are mostly done by male subjects. In falling down datasets, the subjects are also young adults though the datasets are created for elderly people! It is indeed a major challenge to create datasets from elderly people or hospital patients – because of the fact that we are mostly unable to engage them in dataset collection. Some activities are physically difficult and dangerous too. So, it is another important issue to handle. Few alternatives can be –

a. Developing simulated data from different directions, by many subjects having different sexes, ages, heights, weights, speeds of actions, etc.

b. For activities like falling down in different directions or ways – we can buy mannequin or similar things and make some control systems to handle them.

c. Another option that will be expensive to do is to engage robots for various activities.

*Figure 6. Example of image resolution where lower resolution images has less intra-pixel information and lack of proper edge estimation that hinder to have better classification*

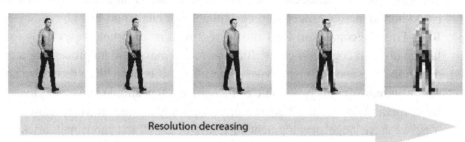

Resolution decreasing

15. **Processing Low-Resolution Video:** Low-resolution images are faster to compute but it lacks sufficient information sometimes for proper recognition. For sensor-based system, there is no worry on this issue. Figure 6 demonstrates an example of an image where the quality of the image reduces drastically due to the decrease in image resolution.

16. **Occlusion Issue:** Occlusion can hinder the performance of recognition. Proper tracking of any target person or object can be useful but it is not done in the typical methods. A moving person can be occluded in various ways, e.g.,
    a.  Occlusion by any static object, e.g., pillars, parked car, table, etc.
    b.  Occlusion by any dynamic object, e.g., by a car, by another person walking next to the target person.
    c.  Self-occlusion by self-body parts, e.g., in sign language case – one hand is occluding another hand
    d.  Self-occlusion by motion where an earlier motion information can be disappeared or occluded by another motion information by the same person in opposite direction. For example, if a person is sitting down and you compute the motion history image (MHI) (Bobick et al, 2001) or optical flow vectors (Yin et al, 2006) then the person is standing up and you compute the same. What will happen? The sitting down motion will be evaporated significantly for these cases and only the late standing up motion information will retain. This is an important issue unless one can segment each basic action (in this case, sitting down or standing up) separately. Some methods will fail to person due this issue of self-occlusion by motion. It is also challenging for repetitive actions.

17. **Variations in Datasets and Associated Issues:** There are about two hundred datasets for the last two decades in video-based action recognition arena. On the other hand, there are over hundred and fifty datasets in sensor-based activity

domain. However, these datasets are massively varied in terms of the following parameters and hence, it becomes difficult to compare important methods and their performances under a single but smart platform. The variables for datasets are –

a. Action classes are varied from one to another by a significant manner.

b. Number of action classes are different as well as the number of subjects.

c. Some datasets have less number of subjects but subjects acted several times to create more instances.

d. Number of sensors or cameras are varied as well. Some datasets have RGB, Depth map data as well as skeleton data, whereas some dataset has only RGB data or depth data only. Using OpenPose, we can create skeleton from RGB data. Regarding sensors, accelerometers are very widely exploited for dataset development. Apart from accelerometer, gyroscope is also employed in some cases. It is found that both accelerometer and gyroscope can provide better recognition results. Only a few datasets, they employed more than two sensors, including audio data, visual data and so on. Environmental sensors are also explored to capture related environmental information. Light sensors, ambient temperature sensors, motion sensors, air quality sensors are some of the important sensors that are used mostly in smart houses and hospitals for healthcare applications and elderly people supports.

e. Indoor and outdoor with huge background variations are present in different datasets. However, with the advent of a number of very large YouTube-based datasets, this background and scene variation issues are gone. But on smaller datasets, these issues remain. On sensor domain, usually, these are less important issues as on-body wearable sensors collect the data only for the person it is using.

f. Ground truths are not available in many datasets. There are some datasets developed using expensive motion capture systems. Those datasets incorporate the respective ground truths for in-depth analysis. Very large datasets do not have ground truth data as these are collected from raw videos from various sources. Contrary to vision-based field, some benchmark datasets integrate ground truth data in sensor-based human activity recognition. Having ground truth data provide the leverage to understand the performance as well as limitations of a method – so that any future research challenge can be unearthed.

## HYBRID APPROACH ON VIDEO AND SENSOR MODALITIES

There is a tremendous lack of combinations of sensor and video-based datasets and methods. A few cases, there are approaches having hybrid dataset from both domains but the datasets and methods are not significantly sophisticated. So there is a dire need for this goal to achieve. These tasks can be done based on any specific applications. It is true that camera has a concern on privacy issue. But depth camera as well as skeleton data provide the scope to hide personal information significantly and we can explore these. There are different kinds of depth sensors from where we can just extract the data. If we do not store the recorded RGB frames and just keep the depth or skeleton data for further processing, then we can easily manage this privacy issue.

Sensors are widely used in the literature and in industry. Due to the proliferation of numerous Internet of Things (IoT) sensors in the human activity analysis, the HAR based methods have been enriching. The academia and industry are engaging various approaches though the success rate is yet to be significant.

## CONCLUSION

In this chapter, we introduce the core aspects of human action or activity recognition (HAR). These are split into two different domains: computer vision-based action/ activity recognition, action localization, etc.; and wearable IoT sensor-based HAR. Though cameras are also sensors that provide vision-based information, we put camera-based or vision-based methods in another category. In this chapter, we introduced a good number of core challenges and some strategies to move forward.

Due to the advent of deep learning-based methods as well as relatively inexpensive computing facilities (thanks to the GPUs and RAMs) than the recent past, we are exploring large datasets and smarter approaches. However, there are numerous constraints and these cannot be evaporated shortly. It is important to cluster some applications and then find strategies for solutions. Industry can play a major role in this regard. There are privacy issues in RGB-based video data collection for activity recognition. Depth images and skeleton data are mitigating the privacy concern by a big margin. Wearable sensor-based domain has several simpler strategies to decipher various activities for a person. The later field is intensifying due to considerable Internet facilities and low-cost sensors. However, there is a huge scope to exploit the important and meaningful cues or strategies of both vision-based and sensor-based domains. Till-to-date, the progress of this hybridization is not much visible in the community. Therefore, we should explore more with the anticipation that human activity recognition will enrich human lives, healthcare, elderly supports, security and related others massively in the near future.

## REFERENCES

Ahad, A., Tan, J., Kim, H., & Ishikawa, S. (2010). Motion history image: Its variants and applications. *Machine Vision and Applications.*

Amiribesheli, M., Benmansour, A., & Bouchachia, A. (2015). A review of smart homes in healthcare. *Journal of Ambient Intelligence and Humanized Computing*, 6(4), 495–517. doi:10.100712652-015-0270-2

Batabyal, T., Chattopadhyay, T., & Mukherjee, D. P. (2015). Action recognition using joint coordinates of 3d skeleton data, in *Proceedings IEEE International Conference on Image Processing (ICIP)*, 10.1109/ICIP.2015.7351578

Bobick, A., & Davis, J. (2001). The recognition of human movement using temporal templates. *IEEE Trans. PAMI*, 23(3), 257–267. doi:10.1109/34.910878

Brand, M., Oliver, N., & Pentland, A. (1997). Coupled hidden Markov models for complex action recognition. *CVPR*, 97, 994.

Brann, D. W., Dhandapani, K., Wakade, C., Mahesh, V. B., & Khan, M. M. (2007). Neurotrophic and neuroprotective actions of estrogen: Basic mechanisms and clinical implications. *Steroids*, 72(5), 381–405. doi:10.1016/j.steroids.2007.02.003 PMID:17379265

Bruhn, A., Weickert, J., & Schnorr, C. (2005). Lucas/Kanade meets Horn/Schunck: Combining local and global optic flow methods. *International Journal of Computer Vision*, 61(3), 211–231. doi:10.1023/B:VISI.0000045324.43199.43

Cao, Z., Simon, T., Wei, S.-E., & Sheikh, Y. (2017). *Realtime multi-person 2d pose estimation using part affinity fields*. CVPR. doi:10.1109/CVPR.2017.143

Castrodad, A., & Sapiro, G. (2012). Sparse modeling of human actions from motion imagery. *IJCV*, 100(1), 1–15. doi:10.100711263-012-0534-7

Cippitelli, E., Gasparrini, S., Gambi, E., & Spinsante, S. (2016). A human activity recognition system using skeleton data from RGB-D sensors. *Computational Intelligence and Neuroscience*, 1–14. doi:10.1155/2016/4351435 PMID:27069469

Devanne, M., Wannous, H., Berretti, S., Pala, P., Daoudi, M., & Bimbo, A. D. (2015). 3-D human action recognition by shape analysis of motion trajectories on riemannian manifold. *IEEE Transactions on Cybernetics, 45*(7), 1340–1352. doi:10.1109/TCYB.2014.2350774 PMID:25216492

El-Ghaish, H., Shoukry, A., & Hussein, M. (2018). CovP3DJ: Skeleton-parts-based-covariance Descriptor for Human Action Recognition, in *Proceedings of the 13th International Joint Conference on Computer Vision, Imaging and Computer Graphics Theory and Applications (VISIGRAPP 2018)*, pp. 343-350. 10.5220/0006625703430350

Fanti, C. (2008) Towards automatic discovery of human movemes. PhD Thesis, California Institute of Technology. Retrieved from http://www.vision.caltech.edu/publications/ phdthesis_fanti.pdf

Fischler, M. A., & Bolles, R. C. (1981). Random sample consensus: A paradigm for model fitting with applications to image analysis and automated cartography. *Communications of the ACM, 24*(6), 381–395. doi:10.1145/358669.358692

Franco, A., Magnani, A., & Maio, D. (2017). Joint Orientations from Skeleton Data for Human Activity Recognition, ICIAP 2017, Part I, LNCS 10484, pp. 152–162. doi:10.1007/978-3-319-68560-1_14

Gaglio, S., Re, G. L., & Morana, M. (2015). Human activity recognition process using 3-D posture data. *IEEE Transactions on Human-Machine Systems, 45*(5), 586–597. doi:10.1109/THMS.2014.2377111

Huynh-The, T., Le, B.-V., & Lee, S. (2016). Describing body-pose feature - poselet - activity relationship using Pachinko allocation model, in *Proceedings 2016 IEEE International Conference on Systems, Man, and Cybernetics (SMC)*, pp. 40–45. 10.1109/SMC.2016.7844218

Jia, C., Kong, Y., Ding, Z., & Fu, Y. (2014). *Latent tensor transfer learning for rgb-d action recognition*. ACM Multimedia. doi:10.1145/2647868.2654928

Jin, C.-B., Li, S., & Kim, H. (2017). Real-Time Action Detection in Video Surveillance using Sub-Action Descriptor with Multi-CNN. *arXiv*.

Karpathy, A., Toderici, G., Shetty, S., Leung, T., Sukthankar, R., & Fei-Fei, L. (2014). Large-scale video classification with convolutional neural networks. In Proceedings of the IEEE conference on Computer Vision and Pattern Recognition (pp. 1725-1732).

Kong, Y., & Fu, Y. (2015). Bilinear heterogeneous information machine for RGB-D action recognition, in *Proceedings 2015 IEEE Conference on Computer Vision and Pattern Recognition (CVPR)*, Boston, MA, 10.1109/CVPR.2015.7298708

Laptev, I. (2005). On space-time interest points. *International Journal of Computer Vision, 64*(2), 107–123. doi:10.100711263-005-1838-7

Li, X., Liao, D., & Zhang, Y. (2017). Mining key skeleton poses with latent SVM for action recognition. *Applied Computational Intelligence and Soft Computing.*

Li, X., Zhang, Y., & Zhang, J. (2018). *Improved Key Poses Model for Skeleton-Based Action Recognition*. Advances in Multimedia Information Processing. doi:10.1007/978-3-319-77383-4_35

Lin, W., Sun, M.-T., Poovandran, R., & Zhang, Z. (2008). Human activity recognition for video surveillance, in *Proceedings 2008 IEEE International Symposium on Circuits and Systems*, 2737-2740. 10.1109/ISCAS.2008.4542023

Ling, J., Tian, L., & Li, C. (2016). 3D Human Activity Recognition Using Skeletal Data from RGBD Sensors, in *Proceedings International Symposium on Visual Computing (ISVC)*, 10.1007/978-3-319-50832-0_14

Liu, A. A., Su, Y. T., Jia, P. P., Gao, Z., Hao, T., & Yang, Z. X. (2015). Multiple/single-view human action recognition via part-induced multitask structural learning. *IEEE Transactions on Cybernetics, 45*(6), 1194–1208. doi:10.1109/TCYB.2014.2347057 PMID:25167566

Liu, Z., Zhang, C., & Tian, Y. (2016). 3D-based deep convolutional neural network for action recognition with depth sequences. *Image and Vision Computing, 55*, 93–100. doi:10.1016/j.imavis.2016.04.004

Md Atiqur Rahman Ahad. (2011). *Computer vision and action recognition: a guide for image processing and computer vision community for action understanding.* Springer Science & Business Media.

Md Atiqur Rahman Ahad. (2012). *Motion history images for action recognition and understanding.* Springer Science & Business Media.

Md Atiqur Rahman Ahad. (2019). *Anindya Das Antar*. Masud Ahmed, IoT Sensor-based Activity Recognition, Springer Nature.

Deepmind.(n.d.). Kinetics dataset. Retrieved from https://deepmind.com/research/open-source/kinetics

Nister, D. (2003). Preemptive RANSAC for live structure and motion estimation. *International Conference on Computer Vision.* 10.1109/ICCV.2003.1238341

Otte, S., Schwanecke, U., & Zell, A. (2014). *ANTSAC: A Generic RANSAC Variant Using Principles of Ant Colony Algorithms.* ICPR.

Pham, H., Khoudour, L., Crouzil, A., Zegers, P., & Velastin, S. A. (2018). *Exploiting deep residual networks for human action recognition from skeletal data* (Vol. 170). Computer Vision and Image Understanding.

Schuldt, C., Laptev, I., & Caputo, B. (2004) Recognizing human actions: A local SVM approach. *International Conference on Pattern Recognition.* 10.1109/ICPR.2004.1334462

Seidenari, L., Varano, V., Berretti, S., Bimbo, A. D., & Pala, P. (2013). Recognizing Actions from Depth Cameras as Weakly Aligned Multi-part Bag-of-Poses, in *Proceedings IEEE Conference on Computer Vision and Pattern Recognition (CVPR) Workshop.* 10.1109/CVPRW.2013.77

Sell, J., & O'Connor, P. (2014). The xbox one system on a chip and kinect sensor. *IEEE Micro, 34*(2), 44–53. doi:10.1109/MM.2014.9

Sinz, F. H., Candela, J. Q., Bakır, G. H., Rasmussen, C. E., & Franz, M. O. (2004). Learning depth from stereo. In *Pattern Recognition* (pp. 245–252). Springer. doi:10.1007/978-3-540-28649-3_30

Soomro, K., Zamir, A. R., & Shah, M. (2018). UCF101: A Dataset of 101 Human Actions. Classes from Videos in The Wild, CoRR.

Toda, T., Inoue, S., & Ueda, N. (2016). Mobile activity recognition through training labels with inaccurate activity segments. In *Proceedings of the 13th International Conference on Mobile and Ubiquitous Systems: Computing, Networking and Services,* pp. 57–64. ACM. 10.1145/2994374.2994378

Torr, P., & Davidson, C. (2000). IMPSAC: A synthesis of importance sampling and random sample consensus to effect multi-scale image matching for small and wide baselines. In *Proceedings European Conference on Computer Vision,* pp. 819–833.

Torr, P., & Zisserman, A. (2000). MLESAC: A new robust estimator with application to estimating image geometry. *Computer Vision and Image Understanding, 78*(1), 138–156. doi:10.1006/cviu.1999.0832

Vemulapalli, R., Arrate, F., & Chellappa, R. (2014). Human Action Recognition by Representing 3D Skeletons as Points in a Lie Group, in *Proceedings 2014 IEEE Conference on Computer Vision and Pattern Recognition*, Columbus, OH, 10.1109/CVPR.2014.82

Yang, X., & Tian, Y. (2014). Super normal vector for activity recognition using depth sequences, in *Proceedings EEE Conference on Computer Vision and Pattern Recognition (CVPR)*, 10.1109/CVPR.2014.108

Yang, X., Zhang, C., & Tian, Y. (2012). *Recognizing actions using depth motion maps-based histograms of oriented gradients*. ACM Multimedia. doi:10.1145/2393347.2396382

Yang, Y., Deng, C., Tao, D., Zhang, S., Liu, W., & Gao, X. (2017). Latent max-margin multitask learning with skelets for 3-D action recognition. *IEEE Transactions on Cybernetics*, 47(2), 439–448. PMID:27046919

Yin, Z., & Collins, R. (2006). Moving object localization in thermal imagery by forward-backward MHI. In *Proceedings IEEE Workshop on Object Tracking and Classification in and Beyond the Visible Spectrum*, 133-140.

Youssef, C. (2016). Spatiotemporal representation of 3d skeleton joints-based action recognition using modified spherical harmonics, Pattern Recogn. Lett. 83.

Chapter 3

# Detection of Epileptiform Seizure From Pre–Ictal Part of Epileptic EEG Recording:
## A Single Blind Study

**Khakon Das**
 https://orcid.org/0000-0001-9183-581X
*RCC Institute of Information Technology, India*

**Shankar Prasad Saha**
*Nil Ratan Sircar Medical College and Hospital, India*

**Kundan Kumar Singh**
*RCC Institute of Information Technology, India*

## ABSTRACT

*Nowadays, the most common neurological disorder is Epilepsy. An epileptic seizure is a sudden synchronous and repetitive discharge from brain cells. The seizure is very dangerous and life-threatening for people affected by Epilepsy, as this may occur anywhere and anytime. The analysis of Electroencephalogram data (EEG) is a difficult task for a neurologist to go through the entire EEG records visually, in consideration with an increasing number of channels and more extended EEG recording. Authors are working to develop a system that gives a warning message so a safety measure can be taken before the seizure occurs. To do that, authors analyze epileptic EEG data in depth to get unique characteristics from EEG data, namely, disrupts background; sharply define components, Electrocerebral negativity, and electrical field. With the consideration of all of the above attributes of Epilepsy, an algorithm is developed, which is able to segment out the susceptible seizure waveform occurrence from EEG recording (onset) in different channels.*

DOI: 10.4018/978-1-7998-2584-5.ch003

## INTRODUCTION

Epilepsy is a mental state in which the human brain does not function properly. Millions of people are affected by this disease (Aarabi A, 2007). An epileptic seizure is a sudden synchronous and repetitive discharge of brain cells (Hanscomb and Hughes, 1995), (Bauquier et. al. 2015), (Chang and Lowenstein, 2003). It characterized by recurrent seizures in which unusual electrical activity in the brain causes the whole body convulsion or loss of consciousness. The occurrence of a seizure is uncertain. Due to the random nature of seizure, it may increase the risk of physical injury. This research says that 4-5% of the global population is suffering from epilepsy out of which one-fourth of epilepsy patients are not getting any treatment due to unavailability of therapy resource (Dreifuss, 1981), (Greene et. al., 2008). The previously artificial neural network was used to implement an automated interpretation of epilepsy in electroencephalography (EEG) (Gwet, 2008), (Das, et. al., 2019), (Frost, 1985). Many methods have described for this purpose, like hyper-clustering in long-term EEG records, which had a concordance rate of 91% with visual interpretation (Harinder et al, 2012). Recently many researches are made to diagnose and offer far better treatment in Seizure disorder. We are unable to completely understand the Molecular and Cellular mechanism which is responsible for developing epilepsy. Epilepsy Syndromes can be differentiated according to the seizure type, the presence or absence of neurologic abnormalities and EEG finding. Epilepsy Syndrome is categorized into two broad categories: partial & generalized (localization related syndrome). Sometimes the insult of one or more than one nervous system of central are responsible for result of partial epilepsies between the occurrence of neurologic insult and appearance of recurrent seizure; this is a slightly interval difference according to clinically reputed survey (Chang and Lowenstein, 2003). In the early era's algorithms, there is low sensitivity and specificity reported, but recent reports have shown sensitivity and specificity of >94% (Lehnertz, 2003), (K. Das, 2020). In Sheng-Fu Liang et al. (2010) describes a systematic evaluation of current approaches to seizure detection in the literature. This evaluation was then used to suggest a reliable, practical epilepsy detection method. The combination of complexity analysis and spectrum analysis on an EEG can perform robust evaluations on the collected data. Principle component analysis (PCA) and genetic algorithms (GAs) were applied to various linear and nonlinear methods. The best linear models resulted from using all of the features without other processing. For the nonlinear models, applying PCA for feature reduction provided better results than applying GAs. The feasibility of executing the proposed methods on a personal computer for on-line processing was also demonstrated. In Bauquier et. al. (2015) the authors developed an algorithm using five GEAR which has been underwent four session for 120 seconds EEG and that EEG recording is been analysed manually and algorithms to calculated Positive Predictive Value (PPV) and Negative Predictive Value (NPV). From the result they have found that automatic algorithms had specificity, sensitivity, PPV and NPV greater than 94% as compare to manual analysis. This provides a good alternative as a method designed to mimic human making in the time domain. For detecting spike-wave discharges (SWDs) with duration >= 1 second and SDWS of >=1 second duration, we detected the reputed SWD frequency range from 7Hz to 11 Hz, was intended to include SWDS ranging from 5Hz to 13 Hz . The longer frequency value is treated as tolerance where sometimes spikes of below threshold resulting in lower spikes count. In the paper describing the EEG of GEARs (Maurescaus et. al., 1992) used 24 minutes recording so that time span can be used to analyse. EEG recording evaluations by two researches are made to establish a baseline range of sensitivity, specificity, PPV and NPV. The comparison between manual investigates and semi- automated SWD detection algorithms resulted in higher sensitivity while compared to the baseline (95% to 96% versus 91%) which retaining a high specificity (96-97%). An automated system can produce an online warning signal to inform health care professional, or it can instruct a treatment device such as electrical simulator to enhance the chance of the patient to recover. Till date, this research is one of the most extensive series that evaluates the preformation of an automated algorithm for detection of epileptiform discharges. A novel mathematical approach is in use for the detection of seizure. This process is practically useful and reliable to point out an epileptic seizure waveform from EEG. The combination of sophisticated analysis and spectrum analysis on an EEG can perform robust evaluations on the collected data (Khakon et. al. 2020).

**Contributions of the paper:** The contributions of the proposed model of epileptic seizure detection are as follows:

1.  First, this proposed work has identified the epileptic seizure waveform (spike only) onset of the EEG signal.
2.  Second contribution is, the identifying of the epileptic seizure waveform using mono-polar montage setup.
3.  Third contribution is to generate a warning message for the patient, currently suffering from epileptic seizure.

There are four distinct sections in this paper. The first section explains the introduction and general information. The second section demonstrates the design methodology of the proposed work. The third section explains about result and discussion and in the fourth section we draw the conclusion of this work.

## DESIGN METHODOLOGY OF PROPOSED WORK

In this system, incorporating the pattern recognition method, different skills have developed, and the information is obtained from EEG related to the human brain, which technically and globally used in various cerebral medical diagnostics. This technology is incorporated in many researches and is increasing day to day. Here the primary aim is to focus on some essential pattern recognition and to improve a future classification of the data (M. B. Westover et. al., 2013), (N. Grogan, 1999), (Faust, 2015). The segmentation and feature extraction is applied here (Oweis and Abdulhay, 2011), (Das. K, 2020), (M. Scherg, 2012). Randomly selecting 150 patients from Neurology OPD in Nil Ratan Sircar Medical College and Hospital, they have provided a clinical evaluation and EEG recording after giving consent to them. Fig. 1 represent a symbolic representation of signal flow; the EEG recording was done using RMS Brain view equipment with 16- channels, the sampling frequency is 256Hz, HFF-70Hz, LFF-0.1Hz. The proposed model considers frequency ranges from 0.1Hz to 70Hz which includes most of the seizure related information (located in <40Hz frequency). The proposed model is also be able to covers the part of higher frequency band the range from 40 Hz to 70Hz. Frequency greater than 70Hz termed high-frequency oscillations (HFOs). High-frequency oscillations can be recorded intracranially at the time of inter-ictal, onset seizure from all over the brain regions. For epilepsy patients, HFOs are being considered as pathologic regardless of the frequency band. It may be difficult to distinguish among the physiologic HFOs, which occur in a similar frequency range. Inter-ictal HFOs are likely to be confined mostly to the seizure onset zone (C. Alvarado-Rojas at. el., 2014). However, the analysis of pre-ictal phase of EEG data is the major concerned area of this research. Visually inspected and segmented without epileptiform discharges of EEG records were exported to .xlsx format. The classification of the EEG data is done using two different interpreters (i.e., AC and BS) are with and without epileptic discharge (Shoeb, 2009), (Bhattacharyy, et. al., 2013), (Temko, 2009). Fig.2 demonstrates the algorithm developed by the author, who is blinded to clinical interpretation. The aim of this algorithm is to detect abrupt changes in amplitude, energy, and power of the input EEG signal as compared to the background and the analysing field of discharge by using the closet neighbour method. The use of slope and direction of change features are focused on this algorithm. The sensitivity and specificity of the algorithm in comparison with the EEG records which were classified unanimously by visual interpretation is very high. As traditional methods are slower than Matlab, so the Matlab is used as a platform to develop the algorithm and to work with the EEG data. Analytically implemented a large number of mathematical functions using the above information, and as it provides instant access to graphics functions; it turns out to be constructive to design the algorithm.

## Algorithm

Here continuous EEG recording is taken and is divided for a particular span of time (10 Sec). Which we called the windows and it is used as an input signal into the current maxima for further calculation.

**Current Maxima** $C_{pmax} = C_{max} = (Max\ (EEG_{(i,j)}) < C_{pmax})$ Where

$$\begin{cases} i = 1\ to\ N\ (number\ of\ channels) \\ j = 1\ to\ CL\ (length\ of\ each\ channel) \\ Cpmax = Large\ positive\ value\ initially \end{cases}$$

Calculate the current maxima value for the input signal windows. It is the local maximum (peak value) of a particular window. The time index of the current maxima position has been used as an input of lower threshold calculation algorithm.

## Lower Threshold

$$\partial\left(\frac{EEG}{Cmax(index)}\right) = \frac{\sum_{\substack{1 \le i \le N \\ j = Cmax(index)}} EEG(i,j)}{N}$$

A local average has been calculated at the time index of the current maxima position of all input channels (EEG Signal). Local threshold value has been used as a binary switch, which is an activation function for the target point selection algorithm.

## Target Point Selection

Using Optimization technique, the local maxima or local minima is calculated at a certain point of a waveform (EEG); for N number of identical channels, we can find the maxima points of the EEG waveforms. Let, a straight line equation be

Ax+By+C=0;

Where the maximum numbers of local maxima, i.e., Current maxima lies in the line. The line will vertically intersect all the EEG channels at same index, containing maximum numbers of points of Current Maxima.

## Segmentation

One segment ($\Delta$i) is selected which is a strict subset of the full EEG waveform frame of the i$^{th}$ channel. This represents the sets and one subset of each set is selected to represent a cluster

Segment($\Delta\_i$) $\subset$ EEG_(i$^{th}$ Channel);

Where i =1, 2, 3, ........N.

## Template Matching

Now split the Segment ($\Delta\_i$) into two subsets of equal length from the center point and termed as background and foreground. The comparison of background with the foreground is performing to analyse the disturbing background, which shows the abnormality and that help the authors to detect seizure.

## FLOWCHART

Figure -1 Explain us that the data sample of EEG recording of different patients from different sources, imported to the system .That data is then analysed and computed to find the current maxima which is a maximum value of a specific window. Here windows are referred to a time span. We calculate for a recording of each window. The computed output (maximum value) is computed to get target point (tp) for suspected seizure detection of different channel. Target point gives us a straight line throughout all channels which intersects the maximum numbers of current maxima point. After this processed data has been passed to the segmentation algorithm, where one segment is selected and store after that delete all identical segments. Again select another segment from the rest number of segments and do the same. Then we do a pattern matching to find out all similar waveform of an epileptic seizure.

## IMPLEMENTATION DETAILS

### Technology (Electroencephalogram)

Electroencephalogram (EEG) device is used to measure and record the electrical activity of the brain. The conventional method to perform the test is done through placing the electrodes along the scalp that will transmit the obtained information

*Figure 1. System flow chart*

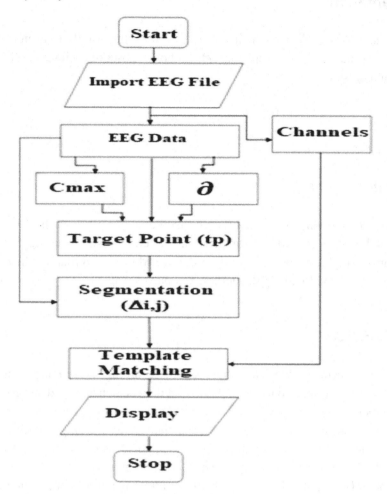

to a recorder machine. With this method is possible to determine the activity on a specific location within the brain and to evaluate brain disorders, is the most common reason to diagnose and monitor seizure disorders.

## PC and Tools (MatLab R2015a)

The algorithm is tested in the Matlab R2015b (64 bit) and Operating System-Windows-10 (64bit), Processor- Intel Core(TM) i7, RAM-8GB. The MATLAB environment allows working interactively with data; keeps track of files and variables, and simplifies basic programming or debugging tasks. It can use in other purposes,

*Figure 2 Segments after Channel Domain Filtration; (a) contains channel 1 to 8 and (b) contains channel 9 to 16.*

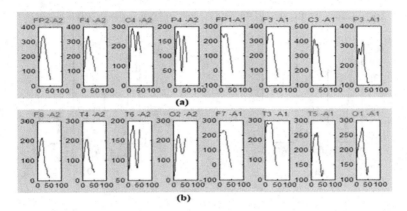

such as simulation, optimization, statistics, or data analysis, and then there is a rapid learning curve for using it in image processing.

## Subject and Dataset Description

Total of 150 subjects with balanced male, female ratio and age range from 18 years to 62 years have participated in this experiment. The dataset is being classified into two categories; seizure and normal after diagnosis by doctors. EEG signal has been captured during this experiment. For each patient, an experiment has been conducted for three days, with an interval of two weeks. The experiment has been divided into three sessions, where the duration of each session is 30 minutes/1800 seconds. The sampling frequency is 256Hz; so, in one session (1800 seconds) maximum $460.8*10^3$ data samples have been collected during the experiment. Total duration of EEG recording is 90 minutes, and within that timestamp, we able to collect $1382.4*10^3$ samples for each patient.

## RESULT AND DISCUSSION

## Output

Figure 2 show all the segments with the individual channel name. In the graph, the amplitude is plotted in the vertical axis (units in microvolt) and Time is plotted horizontally (unit in second where one small division is equal to 0.0039 sec). Filter all affected channel using Domain Matcher Algorithm.

*Figure 3. A Picture of Typical Seizure Sharp of Spike*

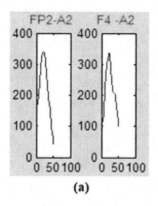
(a)

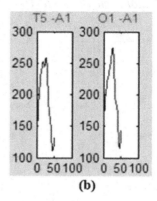
(b)

## Seizure Spike

In the investigation of epilepsy, the better resolution of spikes and sharp waves play a significant role. The duration of a spike is less than 70 ms, whereas spike with waves has duration between 70 ms to 200 ms (Webber, 1994), (Khan, 2012), (Ullah et al 2018). In Figure 3, it is evident that the waves are having small time duration, very close to the recognized criterions of epilepsy.

## RESULT ANALYSIS

Out of the 150 cases, the algorithm correctly classified 139 cases, having a sensitivity of 91.07%. The algorithm showed a specificity of 97.37%. Positive predictive value of the algorithm was 99.03%.

### Sensitivity and Specificity

The calculation of sensitivity and specificity is documented in Table 1.

## DISCUSSION

In this paper, the onset of epileptic seizure detection has been done from the EEG signal using a set of algorithms. Today due to unpredictable and spontaneous occurrence of seizures epilepsy has become a significant burden on our society. There is a need for an automated process for epilepsy detection. That could help

*Table 1. Calculation of sensitivity and specificity*

| Sensitivity and Specificity Calculation | |
|---|---|
| **Positive** | |
| True Positive | 102 |
| False Negative | 10 |
| **Negative** | |
| False Positive | 1 |
| True Negative | 37 |
| **Result** | |
| Sensitivity | 91.07% |
| Specificity | 97.37% |
| Positive Predictive value | 99.03% |
| Negative Predictive value | 78.72% |

epileptologist to determine and diagnose the patients as soon as epileptic seizures arise. Different phases of EEG signals such as normal, pre-ictal, ictal and inte-rictal along with the various patterns related to seizure such as spikes, spikes and waves have been discussed in Ihsan Ullah et al 2018. That information is helpful to design an algorithm and also to design a balanced test dataset.

The proposed model predicts the seizure onset so that health staff or doctors can take the required actions. The comparison of spike background with the foreground is performed to analyse the disturbing background. It has a significant role to determine the abnormality in EEG Signal and that is helpful for the authors to detect a seizure. The proposed model consists of two modules namely pattern matching and feature extraction. It has the ability to identify the epileptic seizure waveform spike onset from the EEG signal and generate a warning message for the patient who currently suffers from an epileptic seizure. That is why it will be supportive for doctors to diagnose the epileptic seizure patients. For evaluating our model, we calculate the sensitivity and specificity.

## CONCLUSION

After applying the proposed method, the result, we got is incredibly positive for advance seizure detection and analysis. This algorithm is tested on 150 numbers of subjects. The sensitivity and specificity reach 91.07% and 97.34%, respectively (Details are in Table 1). The work demonstrates elemental steps to achieve a classification problem. It has the ability to separate normal and epileptic EEG Record. The study evaluated an algorithm of detecting epileptiform discharges, which showed significant agreement with the visual interpretation of neurology experts. At this point, the cases not classified as focal or generalized discharges, which is a part of on-going work. In future, an automated artefact detection and rejection method will be added to this algorithm and will use a larger sample size to emphasize the robustness of the algorithm in future research.

## ACKNOWLEDGMENT

We express our sincere gratitude to Dr. Samarendra Kumar Sharma, Assistant Director of Health Services (MERT) & State Technical Officer-RSBY-WB, Kolkata, India for providing valuable comments throughout this Research work. We have obtained all approvals from an appropriate committee of NRSMC&H, and the consents have been taken regarding the use of the data in our research work. Neither the editors nor the publisher will be responsible for any misuse or misinterpretation of the data.

## REFERENCES

Aarabi, A., Grebe, R., & Wallois, F. (2007). A multistage knowledge-based system for EEG seizure detection in newborn infants. *Clinical Neurophysiology*, *118*(12), 2781–2797. doi:10.1016/j.clinph.2007.08.012 PMID:17905654

Bauquier, S. H., Lai, A., Jiang, J. L., Sui, Y., & Cook, M. J. (2015). Evaluation of an automated spike-and-wave complex detection algorithm in the EEG from a rat model of absence epilepsy. *Neuroscience Bulletin*, *31*(5), 601–610. doi:10.100712264-015-1553-5 PMID:26242485

Bhattacharyya, S., Biswas, A., Mukherjee, J., Majumdar, A. K., Majumdar, B., Mukherjee, S., & Singh, A. K. (2013). Detection of artifacts from high energy bursts in neonatal EEG. *Computers in Biology and Medicine*, *43*(11), 1804–1814. doi:10.1016/j.compbiomed.2013.07.031 PMID:24209926

Chang, B. S., & Lowenstein, D. H. (2003). Epilepsy. *The New England Journal of Medicine*, *349*(13), 1257–1266. doi:10.1056/NEJMra022308 PMID:14507951

Das, K., Chakladar, D. D., Roy, P. P., Chatterjee, A., & Saha, S. P. (2020). Epileptic seizure prediction by the detection of seizure waveform from the pre-ictal phase of eeg signal. Biomedical Signal Processing and Control, DOI: . doi:10.1016/j.bspc.2019.101720

Das, K., Maitra, M., Sharma, P., & Banerjee, M. (2020). Embedded Implementation of Early Started Hybrid Denoising Technique for Medical Images with Optimized Loop. In *Emerging Technology in Modelling and Graphics, Advances in Intelligent Systems and Computing, vol: 937* (pp. 295–308). Springer; doi:10.1007/978-981-13-7403-6_28

Dreifuss, F. E. (1981). Proposal for revised clinical and electroencephalographic classification of epileptic seizures. *Epilepsia, 22*(4), 489–501. doi:10.1111/j.1528-1157.1981.tb06159.x PMID:6790275

Jaseja, H., & Jaseja, B. (2012). EEG spike versus EEG sharp wave: Differential clinical significance in epilepsy Jaseja. *Epilepsy & Behavior, 25*(1), 137. doi:10.1016/j.yebeh.2012.05.023 PMID:22809496

Marescaux, C., Vergnes, M., & Depaulis, A. (1992). Genetic absence epilepsy in rats from Strasbourg—a review. *Journal of Neural Transmission. Supplementum, 35*, 37–69. PMID:1512594

Greene, B. R., Faul, S., Lightbody, G., Korotchikova, I., Marnane, W. P., & Boylan, G. B. (2008). A comparison of quantitative EEG features for neonatal seizure detection. *Clinical Neurophysiology, 119*(6), 1248–1261. doi:10.1016/j.clinph.2008.02.001 PMID:18381249

Gwet, K. L. (2008). Computing inter-rater reliability and its variance in the presence of high agreement. *British Journal of Mathematical & Statistical Psychology, 61*(1), 29–48. doi:10.1348/000711006X126600 PMID:18482474

Hanscomb, A., & Hughes, L. (1995). *Epilepsy*. Family Health Guides. Ward Lock.

James, D. (1985). Automatic recognition and characterization of epileptiform discharges in the human EEG. *Journal of Clinical Neurophysiology, 2*(3), 231–249. doi:10.1097/00004691-198507000-00003 PMID:3916845

Khakon, D., Khorat, D., & Sharma, S. K. (2020). An Embedded System for Gray Matter Segmentation of PET-Image, in *Proceedings of the Global AI Congress 2019 in Advances in Intelligent Systems and Computing book series,* Springer Singapore.

Khan, Y. U., Farooq, O., & Sharma, P. (2012). Automatic detection of seizure onset in pediatric EEG. *International Journal of Embedded Systems and Applications, 2*(3), 81–89. doi:10.5121/ijesa.2012.2309

Lehnertz, K., Mormann, F., Kreuz, T., Andrzejak, R. G., Rieke, C., David, P., & Elger, C. E. (2003). Seizure prediction by nonlinear EEG analysis. *IEEE Engineering in Medicine and Biology Magazine, 22*(1), 57–63. doi:10.1109/MEMB.2003.1191451 PMID:12683064

Liang, S. F., Chang, W. L., & Wang, H. C. (2010). Combination of EEG complexity and spectral analysis for epilepsy diagnosis and seizure detection. *EURASIP Journal on Advances in Signal Processing, 2010*(1), 853434. doi:10.1155/2010/853434

McGrogan, N. (1999), Neural network detection of epileptic seizures in the electroencephalogram. (PhD thesis), Oxford University, UK.

Modur, P. N.Alvarado-Rojas, C. (2014). High frequency oscillations and infraslow activity in epilepsy. *Annals of Indian Academy of Neurology, 17*(5), 99–106. doi:10.4103/0972-2327.128674 PMID:24791097

Oliver Faust, U. R. (2015). Wavelet-based EEG processing for computer-aided seizure detection and epilepsy diagnosis. *Seizure, 26*, 56–64. doi:10.1016/j. seizure.2015.01.012 PMID:25799903

Oweis, R. J., & Abdulhay, E. W. (2011). Seizure classification in EEG signals utilizing Hilbert-Huang transform. *Biomedical Engineering Online, 10*(38), 38. doi:10.1186/1475-925X-10-38 PMID:21609459

Das, K., Maitra, M., Sharma, P., & Banerjee, M. (2019). Early started hybrid denoising technique for medical images. In Recent Trends in Signal and Image Processing. Advances in Intelligent Systems and Computing, vol: 727 (pp. 131–140). Springer Singapore; doi:10.1007/978-981-10-8863-6_14

Scherg, M., & Ebert, A. (2012). Fast evaluation of interictal spikes in long-term EEG by hyper-clustering. *Epilepsia, 53*(7), 1196–1204. doi:10.1111/j.1528-1167.2012.03503.x PMID:22578143

Shoeb, A. H. (2009). Application of machine learning to epileptic seizure onset detection and treatment. (PhD Thesis), Massachusetts Institute of Technology.

Temko, A., Thomas, E., Marnane, W., Lightbody, G., & Boylan, G. (2009). An SVM-based system and its performance for detection of seizures in neonates. Annual International Conference of the IEEE Engineering in Medicine and Biology Society. Minneapolis, MN: Institute of Electrical and Electronics Engineers, pp. 2643–2646.

Ullah, I., Hussain, M., Qazi, E.-H., & Aboalsamh, H. (2018). An automated system for epilepsy detection using eeg brain signals based on deep learning approach. *Expert Systems with Applications, 107*, 61–71. doi:10.1016/j.eswa.2018.04.021

Webber, W. R. S., Wilson, K., Lessera, R. P., & Litt, B. (1994). Practical detection of epileptiform discharges (EDs) in the EEG using an artificial neural network: a comparison of raw and parameterized EEG data, Electroencephalography and Clinical Neurophysiology, 91(3), pp. 194-204, DOI: doi:10.1016/0013-4694(94)90069-8

Westover, M. B., Shafi, M. M., Ching, S. N., Chemali, J. J., Purdon, P. L., Cash, S. S., & Brown, E. N. (2013). Real-time segmentation of burst suppression patterns in critical care EEG monitoring. *Journal of Neuroscience Methods*, *219*(1), 131–141. doi:10.1016/j.jneumeth.2013.07.003 PMID:23891828

# Chapter 4
# Modeling and Control of Electric Linear Actuator for Driving Knee Joint of a Lower Body Exoskeleton

**Ganesh Roy**
*Indian Institute of Engineering Science and Technology, Shibpur, India*

**Hano Jacob Saji**
*Indian Institute of Engineering Science and Technology, Shibpur, India*

**Subir Das**
*Indian Institute of Engineering Science and Technology, Shibpur, India*

**Subhasis Bhaumik**
*Indian Institute of Engineering Science and Technology, Shibpur, India*

## ABSTRACT

*The actuator is an integrated part of every robotic system which can actuate the joint for the necessary movement of the device. Depending on the energy conversion mechanism, the actuators are subdivided into three classes, namely electric, pneumatic, and hydraulic. The electric actuators are very popular in the field of engineering and technology due to their ease of use and low maintenance. In this chapter, an electric linear actuator (Manufactured by TiMOTION, Model: TA1) has been modeled by considering its each and every associated physical parameter and also simulated in MATLAB Simscape to observe its performance. Also, different control actions like PID, LQR, and Sliding mode methods have been studied to select the best control action for the actuator. Finally, as an application of the developed actuator model, a one DOF robotic assistive device called human knee exoskeleton has been designed in the MATLAB Simscape. It has been tested that the knee joint trajectory has been followed by the actuator with suitable control action.*

DOI: 10.4018/978-1-7998-2584-5.ch004

## INTRODUCTION

In a powered exoskeleton, a low to medium range of force and highly precise control action is required to get the human locomotion. Generally, the Pneumatic actuator produces high force with poor controllability and the Hydraulic actuator has an inherent leakage problem. Whereas, the Electric actuators are most popular in the field of assistive robotic devices due to their ease of use and low maintenance compared to the pneumatic and hydraulic actuators. A survey, based on all those issues related to the design and development of a lower limb exoskeleton has been provided by (Aliman, Ramli, & Haris, 2017). The electric linear actuator is a combination of dc motor, gearing system, and lead screw. The rotational motion of the dc motor is converted to a linear one with the help of a lead screw. The linear motion of a human muscle can be easily replicated by this type of electromechanical device, as discussed by (S. Wang, Van Dijk, & Van Der Kooij, 2011). Hence, using the linear actuators, medical rehabilitation devices are being developed by researches like (Ruiz-Rojas, Vazquez-Gonzalez, Alejos-Palomares, Escudero-Uribe, & Mendoza-Vázquez, 2008). The exoskeleton is a device which can perform as an assistive device for an injured or physically weak people to help his/her locomotion. The exoskeleton joints can be easily powered up with the help of a linear actuator. The approach of such design is going on all over the globe during the past few years. In the year of 2004, Jerry E. Pratt et al. described knee exoskeleton based on a series elastic actuator, which can enhance human strength and speed at the time of walking (Pratt, Krupp, Morse, & Collins, 2004). Further development of the same actuator has been done for trajectory generation and load augmentation by (Mazumder et al., 2015). The lower body exoskeleton called BLEEX has been designed using an electric actuator, and comparison with hydraulic actuators have also been discussed by (Adam Zoss & Kazerooni, 2006), (A Zoss, Chu, & Kazerooni, 2006). According to (J. Wang et al., 2018), the comfort issues related to the wearing of the knee exoskeleton has been resolved by utilizing different mechanical design. A Fuzzy PID control scheme has been discussed by (Rezage & Tokhi, 2016) for older people's mobility to control the exoskeleton. The development of knee exoskeleton with linear actuator and its proper control schemes which can control the device smoothly drive is highly challenging. Being motivated by this phenomenon, the present work has been initiated to design a suitable actuator for the electromechanical device.

Simulation is the imitation of a real situation or process in a virtual environment. In the field of engineering and technology, the simulations are frequently used for substituting the physical experimentation and calculating the effect of design or process, as discussed by (Ong, Hicks, & Delp, 2016). The design in the simulation provides an insight view of the real scenario. Modeling and simulation also reduce the risk and cost involved in the practical implementation. Hence, in this work,

*Figure 1. General block diagram of the electric linear actuator*

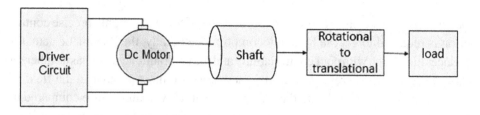

modeling and simulation of the linear actuator have been presented with MATLAB Simscape environment(MathWorks, 2019). Also, three different control schemes viz. PID, LQR, and Sliding mode have been applied over the model for finding the best control strategy of the linear actuator. In addition, a knee joint of a lower-body exoskeleton model has been prepared using the same software toolbox as a real-time application of the designed actuator. It has been presented that the proposed knee exoskeleton can track the human knee joint trajectory successfully.

## MODELING OF LINEAR ACTUATOR

The mathematical model helps to develop the physical system of the linear actuator and its schematic (Nise, 2011). Generally, the electric linear actuator has three parts: a dc motor, which is driven by the motor driver, a motor shaft, and a lead screw. The general block diagram of the electric linear actuator is presented in Figure 1. The motor shaft is coupled with a set of gears to step down the speed for increasing the torque of the motor. The lead screw mechanism is used to exchange the rotating motion into translating motion.

The conversion of electrical energy to mechanical energy is the primary function of an electric motor. Mainly, there are three different types of DC motors available viz. PMDC (Permanent Magnet DC Motor), series and shunt DC motor. The PMDC motor used a permanent magnet for the generation of the magnetic field during the rotation of the armature coil. Instead of the permanent magnet, the series and shunt type dc motor used a coil to generate the electromagnetic field. In the case of shunt dc motor, a field winding is connected across the supply voltage to produce the required field proportional to supply voltage. The field winding is connected in series to the armature conductors in the case of series dc motor. So the field is produced due to the armature current flowing through it. Generally, for any mobile devices like an exoskeleton, PMDC motors are used. Hence, for modeling of PMDC

*Figure 2. DC motor modeling*

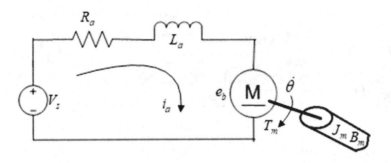

motor, the whole system is divided into two sections: electrical and mechanical. A simplified diagram of the armature controlled PMDC motor is given in Figure 2.

As the PMDC motor used a constant magnetic field, its field distribution is not included in Figure 2. A closed electric loop has been considered for the electrical portion. This loop consists of a dc source voltage $V_s$, a loop inductance of $L_a$, the armature resistance of $R_a$ and a back e.m.f. $e_b$. The current flowing through the armature is $i_a$. By applying KVL in the circuit we have,

$$V_s = i_a R_a + L_a \frac{di_a}{dt} + e_b \tag{1}$$

Since the back e.m.f. is proportional to the angular velocity of the motor. Hence, Eq. (1) can be re-written as

$$V_s = i_a R_a + L_a \frac{di_a}{dt} + K_b \frac{d\theta}{dt} \tag{2}$$

For the modelling of the mechanical portion, let $J_m$ be the moment of inertia of the motor, $\theta$ is the angle of rotation $B_m$ is the damping coefficient and $T_m$ is the developed electromagnetic torque. So the developed torque can be expressed as follows.

$$T_m = K_t \times i_a \tag{3}$$

Where, $K_t$ is the torque constant. Therefore, the following differential equation has been generated from the mechanical section.

*Figure 3. Rotational to translational motion conversion*

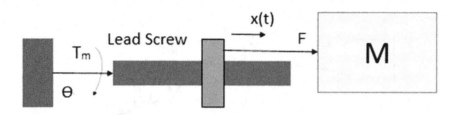

$$K_t i_a = J_m \frac{d^2\theta}{dt^2} + B_m \frac{d\theta}{dt} \tag{4}$$

Hence, the overall transfer function of the dc motor is

$$\frac{\theta(s)}{V_s(s)} = \frac{K_t}{s(L_a s + R_a)(J_m s + B_m) + K_t K_b} \tag{5}$$

Now, a lead screw mechanism is attached with the PMDC motor shaft to convert the rotational motion into translational motion, is shown in Figure 3. A relationship between the shaft angular displacement $\theta(t)$ and the lead linear displacement $x(t)$ is given by the following equation.

$$x(t) = \frac{L}{2\pi}\theta(t) \text{ i.e. } \theta(t) = Px(t) \tag{6}$$

Where, $L$ is the step length of the lead for one full rotation of the screw.

Therefore, the linear displacement is proportional with the angular displacement having the proportionality constant $P = \frac{2\pi}{L}$. Also, if F is the force exerted then the torque, $T_m = \frac{F}{2\pi}$.

Now if all the parts have been combined together an overall block diagram for the electric linear actuator should be represented as the Figure 4.

From Figure 4, the overall transfer function of the linear actuator is calculated as follows.

$$\frac{X(s)}{V_s(s)} = \frac{K_t}{P[s(L_a s + R_a)(J_m s + B_m) + K_t K_b s]} \tag{7}$$

*Figure 4. Overall block diagram for electric linear actuator*

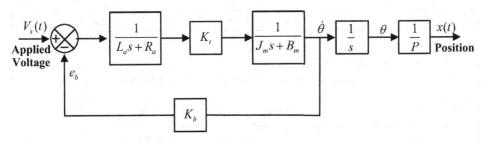

If the three states viz. position, speed and applied current of the linear actuator are, $x_1 = x(t)$, $x_2 = \dfrac{e_b}{k_b p}$, $x_3 = i_a(t)$ and output $y = x_1$ the state space model becomes as follows.

$$\dot{x}_1 = x_2 \tag{8}$$

$$\dot{x}_2 = -\frac{B_m}{J_m} x_2 + \frac{k_t}{p J_m} x_3 \tag{9}$$

$$\dot{x}_3 = -\frac{k_b p}{L_a} x_2 - \frac{R_a}{L_a} x_3 + \frac{1}{L_a} u \tag{10}$$

Hence, in the vector matrix form of the equations (8), (9), (10) becomes as given below.

$$
\begin{bmatrix} \dot{x}_1 \\ \dot{x}_2 \\ \dot{x}_3 \end{bmatrix}
=
\begin{bmatrix}
0 & 1 & 0 \\
0 & -\dfrac{B_m}{J_m} & \dfrac{k_t}{p J_m} \\
0 & -\dfrac{k_b p}{L_a} & -\dfrac{R_a}{L_a}
\end{bmatrix}
\begin{bmatrix} x_1 \\ x_2 \\ x_3 \end{bmatrix}
+
\begin{bmatrix} 0 \\ 0 \\ \dfrac{1}{L_a} \end{bmatrix} u
\tag{11}
$$

*Table 1. Linear actuator parameters*

| Sl. No. | Parameters Name | Value |
|---|---|---|
| 1 | Armature inductance ( $L_a$ ) | $940 \times 10^{-6}$ H |
| 2 | Armature resistance ( $R_a$ ) | 3.9 Ohm |
| 3 | No-load speed | 3500 rpm |
| 4 | Rated speed (at rated load) | 2764 rpm |
| 5 | Rated load (mechanical power) | 23.4 w |
| 6 | Rated DC supply voltage | 24 v |
| 7 | Rotor Inertia ( $J_m$ ) | $10^{-3}$ Kgm² |
| 8 | Rotor damping ( $B_m$ ) | $1.047 \times 10^{-7}$ Nm/(rad/s) |
| 9 | Initial rotor speed | 0 rpm |
| 10 | Back-emf constant ( $K_b$ ) | 0.0274 V/(rad/s) |
| 11 | Torque constant ( $K_t$ ) | $6.876 \times 10^{-4}$ Nm/A |
| 12 | Proportionality constant ( $P$ ) | $5 / (2 \times \pi \times 46)$ |

## SIMULATION OF LINEAR ACTUATOR MODEL

The developed mathematical model of the linear actuator is simulated with the help of MATLAB Simscape toolbox. The developed Simulink model is shown in Figure 5. The parameter values are taken from the datasheet of the TA1 linear actuator which is manufactured by TiMOTION, and it uses a brushed dc motor with a permanent magnet (Timotiom, 2019). The parameters are listed in Table 1.

This model involves two types of energy conversion: electrical to mechanical rotation and mechanical rotational motion to mechanical translational motion. According to Figure 5, the electrical portion of the linear actuator is represented as blue color, whereas the mechanical portion is marked as green. Here two controlled voltage source is used. One is 24V to actuate the dc motor, and another 5V is used for the driver circuit. The driver unit generates PWM based controlled output voltage to switch the H-Bridge. The Wheel and Axle, i.e., lead screw, is used to convert the

*Figure 5. Simulation of the linear actuator using Simscape toolbox in MATLAB*

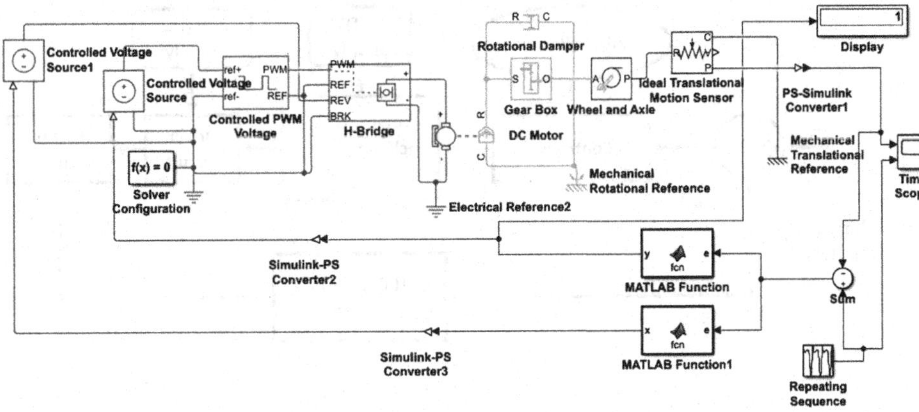

angular motion to a linear one. The linear displacement is easily measured using the built-in translational motion sensor.

## CONTROLLING OF LINEAR ACTUATOR

The electric linear actuator control system for the lower limb extremities has to work in a real-time environment. The closed-loop control system for the linear actuator is depicted in Figure 6. It receives the command from the master controller as the reference input and is required to generate a motion that matches the input signal. In short, it produces a mechanical output from the electrical input, which follows a specific joint trajectory. On the reception of the reference signal, it should generate a control signal using a suitable algorithm in the controller section. This control signal is given to the H-Bridge driver circuit, which in turn drives the linear actuator. The PWM modulation technique is used for generating the required controlled signal. The technique of PWM modulation has been used in the case of a sliding mode control signal in some applications like dual inverter based photovoltaic system (Kumar, Saha, & Dey, 2016). The mechanical load that the linear actuator drive is to be dynamic, and its motion may be visualized in a virtual environment. It would be suitable to develop the model of the linear actuator using MATLAB Simscape toolbox by considering all these facts. In Figure 5, the MATLAB Function is used to develop a control scheme. Three different control action methods have been applied here. The first one is PID (Proportional Integral Derivative) control action, which is described as the following equation.

*Figure 6. Feedback control system for the electric linear actuator*

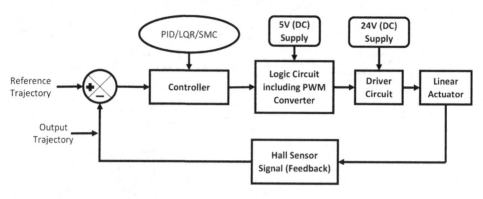

$$x(t) = K_p e(t) + K_i \int e(t)dt + K_d \frac{de(t)}{dt} \qquad (12)$$

Where, $x(t)$ is the linear displacement, $e(t)$ is the error signal, $K_p$, $K_i$ and $K_d$ are the Proportional, Integral and Derivative gains respectively. The constants values have been selected by following the guideline mentioned by (Chattopadhyay, Roy, & Panda, 2011). $K_p = 0.819, K_i = 0.034, K_d = 4.743$.

The second control logic is selected as LQR (Linear Quadratic Regulator) method, as discussed by (Vinodh Kumar & Jerome, 2013). The logic for the control action is as follows.

$$u(t) = -Kx(t) \qquad (13)$$

Where, $u(t)$ is the input to the system, $x(t)$ are the states of the system. Since the present system is a three-state system, the gain matrix $K$ would be the order of $(1 \times 3)$. By considering, $Q = \begin{bmatrix} 5090 & 0 & 0 \\ 0 & 1 & 0 \\ 0 & 0 & 10 \end{bmatrix}$, $R = \begin{bmatrix} 1 \end{bmatrix}$ and obtained gain $K = \begin{bmatrix} 71.344 & 243.809 & 1.121 \end{bmatrix}$.

The third control scheme is Sliding mode control action as first described by (VADIM I. UTKIN, 1977). The control technique is most robust, easily implementable and put up with good accuracy. Several researchers have been focused their research for developing of sliding mode control in the application of inverse dynamics of an under actuated system (Barai, Dey, & Rudra, 2013). The surface discontinuity equation for the controller has been selected as follows.

*Figure 7. Sliding mode control parameters*

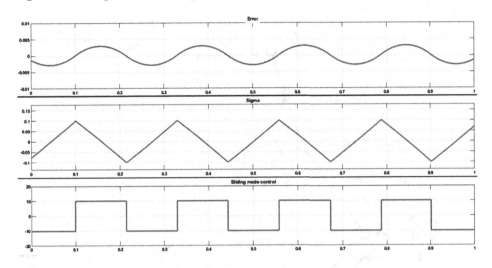

$$\sigma = \dot{e} + c_0 e \qquad (14)$$

Where, $\sigma$ is the sliding surface, $e$ is the error signal, $c_0$ is a constant coefficient considered as a unity. Depending upon the order of the surface equation the constant changes it's value. The next phase is the selection of control action for steering the $\sigma$ variable as an input trajectory. It can be represented by the following equation.

$$u = -U \operatorname{sgn}(\sigma) \qquad (15)$$

Where, $u$ is the control input, $U = 10$. The value of the U variable is considered as the strength of the Signum function.

All the necessary arrangements are depicted in Figure 7.

The obtained response from the three control schemes has been provided in Results and Discussion section.

## APPLICATION OF LINEAR ACTUATOR IN KNEE EXOSKELETON

Two lower limbs support human gait for the necessary locomotion. There are three joints associated with the gait event namely-hip, knee, and ankle. The flexion/extension for the joints is caused by the contraction/extraction of leg muscles. The EMG signal generated in agonist-antagonist muscle pairs, called A-A ratio

*Figure 8. Human lower limb joints and torques*

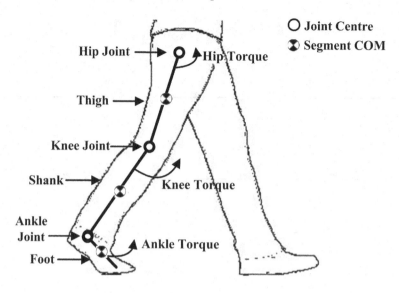

can produce modular movement of lower limb kinematics (Hirai, Matsui, Iimura, Mitsumori, & Miyazaki, 2010). The lower limb inactive peoples are unfortunate to get the advantage of muscle force. An exoskeleton device is used to regenerate the mobility to facilitate those people. And the linear actuator served as an artificial muscle for the robotic device. Figure 8 describes the position of all the necessary arrangement of the human lower limb and the direction of the generated torque. A knee joint mechanism based on a linear actuator has been depicted in Figure 9. Here, the fully extended position of the electric linear actuator is considered as the zero position, and the vertical movement is considered as the positive displacement.

From Figure 9, the relation between the linear motions of the actuator with the knee angle has been derived by the following equation.

$$\theta = \cos^{-1}\left[\frac{a^2 + b^2 + \left(L_f + x\right)}{2ab}\right] \qquad (16)$$

Where, $\theta$ is the knee angle, $a$ is the thigh length, $b$ is the shank length, $L_f$ is the fixed length of the linear actuator and $x$ is the variable stroke length. A knee exoskeleton structure is designed by following a four-bar mechanism with the help of MATLAB Simscape toolbox as given in Figure 10. The corresponding output from the model is a representation of a CAD model as shown in Figure 11.

*Figure 9. Knee joint mechanism*

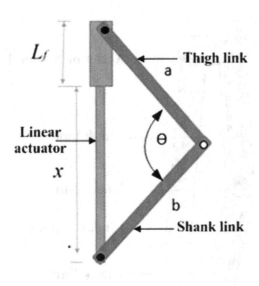

## RESULTS AND DISCUSSION

The overall transfer function of the linear actuator is given in Eq. (7). It is visible from the pole-zero map of Figure 12 that the system is marginally stable due to the presence of a pole at the origin of the s plane. In order to validate the stability of the closed-loop actuator model, the step response of PID, LQR, and Sliding mode control actions have been presented in Figure 13. The corresponding time-domain specification has also been studied and tabulated in Table 2. Through this comparative study, it has been proved that the Sliding mode method provides the best control scheme for controlling the motion of a linear actuator. Further, the knee

*Figure 10. Knee joint exoskeleton with linear actuator*

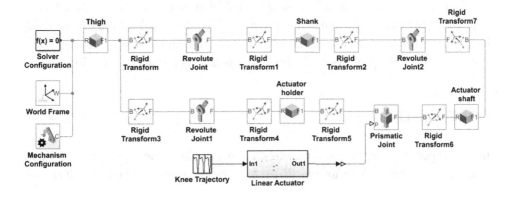

*Figure 11. CAD model of knee exoskeleton*

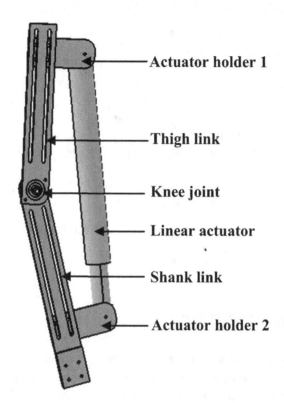

Actuator holder 1

Thigh link

Knee joint

Linear actuator

Shank link

Actuator holder 2

exoskeleton device has also run by the same control action and obtained the total span, or the trajectory is 1.66 milliseconds; it is as shown in Figure 14. The human knee trajectory has been considered from the publication of (Roy, Jacob, Bhatia, & Bhaumik, 2020). Moreover, the linear actuator can follow the reference trajectory very reasonably. There is a slight delay in the output as compared to the reference. This delay is introduced for the smooth operation of the linear actuator, and it is equal to the sampling time. The controlled PWM signals and the associated knee joint trajectory have been depicted in Figure 15. The duty cycle of the PWM signal is controlled by suitable control action. As it is seen from Figure 15, the duty cycle varies at very high speed when the trajectory is having a low range of slope.

## CONCLUSION

In this paper, a linear actuator is modeled analytically. The physical parameters of the linear actuators (Timotiom, 2019) have been adopted from the TiMOTION

*Figure 12. Pole Zero map of the linear actuator transfer function*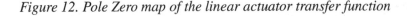

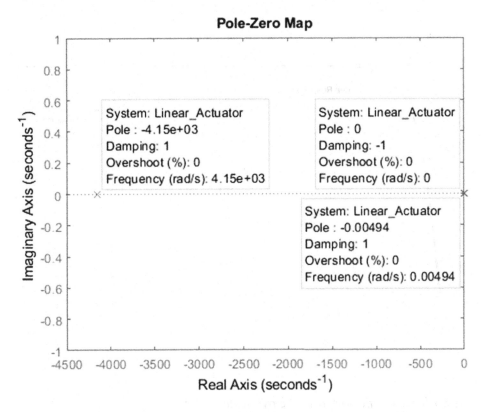

Technology and simulated using MATLAB Simscape environment to promote the real-time properties. The open-loop linear position response becomes marginally stable due to the presence of zero at the origin of the Pole-Zero map, as shown in Figure 12. Hence, an external feedback system is required to stabilize the performance according to the desired specifications. Three different control strategies viz. PID, LQR, and Sliding mode control have been followed to obtain a stabilizing response. After verifying all the time domain specifications, as shown in Figure 13 and Table 2, it is proved that the performance of Sliding mode control action is the best among the others. Finally, as an application of the linear actuator, a knee exoskeleton device has been modeled in the same MATLAB Simscape domain. From Figure 14, it is also shown that the human knee trajectory is well followed by the developed linear actuator with a proper control system. Therefore, with this present study, it is proved that using a linear actuator, a human prosthetic device can be developed to help the lower limb disabled people for necessary locomotion.

*Figure 13. Step response of linear actuator*

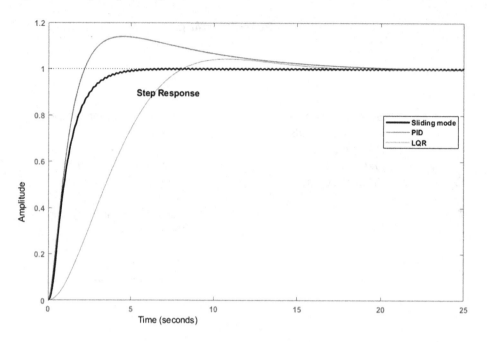

*Figure 14. Knee trajectory tracking by linear actuator*

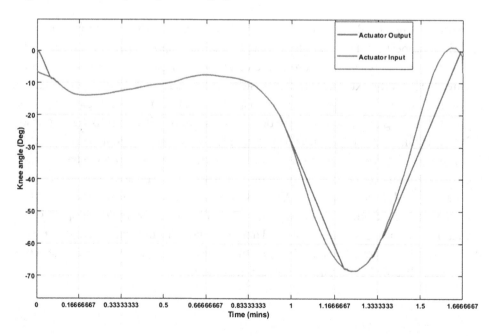

*Figure 15. Controlled PWM Signals with Knee trajectory tracking for linear actuator*

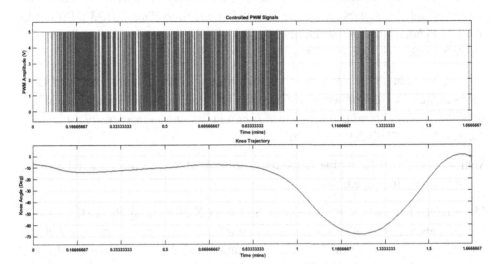

## REFERENCES

Aliman, N., Ramli, R., & Haris, S. M. M. (2017). Design and development of lower limb exoskeletons: A survey. *Robotics and Autonomous Systems*, *95*, 102–116. doi:10.1016/j.robot.2017.05.013

Barai, R. K., Dey, A., & Rudra, S. (2013). Sliding Mode Compensation for Model Uncertainty, Payload Variation and Actuator Dynamics for Inverse Dynamics Velocity Control of Direct Drive Robot Manipulator. *Journal of Control Engineering and Technology*, *3*(4), 203–211.

Chattopadhyay, S., Roy, G., & Panda, M. (2011). Simple Design of a PID Controller and Tuning of Its Parameters Using LabVIEW Software. *Sensors & Transducers Journal*, *129*(6), 69–85.

*Table 2. Time response comparison*

| Control technique | Overshoot (%) | Rise time (Sec) | Settling time (Sec) |
|---|---|---|---|
| Sliding mode | 0 | 2.4 | 4.8 |
| LQR | 4.32 | 5.23 | 14.5 |
| PID | 13.9 | 1.5 | 15.8 |

Hirai, H., Matsui, K., Iimura, T., Mitsumori, K., & Miyazaki, F. (2010). Modular control of limb kinematics during human walking. In *Proceedings 2010 3rd IEEE RAS and EMBS International Conference on Biomedical Robotics and Biomechatronics, BioRob 2010*, 716–721. 10.1109/BIOROB.2010.5628042

Kumar, N., Saha, T. K., & Dey, J. (2016). Sliding-Mode Control of PWM Dual Inverter-Based Grid-Connected PV System: Modeling and Performance Analysis. *IEEE Journal of Emerging and Selected Topics in Power Electronics, 4*(2), 435–444. doi:10.1109/JESTPE.2015.2497900

MathWorks. (2019). Simscape. Retrieved October 3, 2019, from https://in.mathworks.com/products/simscape.html

Mazumder, O., Lenka, P. K., Kundu, A. S., Gupta, K., Chattaraj, R., & Bhaumik, S. (2015). Development of series elastic actuator based myoelectric knee exoskeleton for trajectory generation and load augmentation. *ACM International Conference Proceeding Series*. 10.1145/2783449.2783472

Nise, N. S. (2011). *Control System Engineering* (6th ed.). Hoboken, NJ: John Wiley & Sons.

Ong, C. F., Hicks, J. L., & Delp, S. L. (2016). Simulation-Based Design for Wearable Robotic Systems: An Optimization Framework for Enhancing a Standing Long Jump. *IEEE Transactions on Biomedical Engineering, 63*(5), 894–903. doi:10.1109/TBME.2015.2463077 PMID:26258930

Pratt, J. E., Krupp, B. T., Morse, C. J., & Collins, S. H. (2004). The RoboKnee: An exoskeleton for enhancing strength and endurance during walking. *Proceedings - IEEE International Conference on Robotics and Automation*, 2430–2435.

Rezage, G. A. L., & Tokhi, M. O. (2016). Fuzzy PID Control of Lower Limb Exoskeleton for Elderly Mobility. In *Proceedings 2016 IEEE International Conference on Automation, Quality and Testing, Robotics (AQTR)*, 1–6. 10.1109/AQTR.2016.7501310

Roy, G., Jacob, T., Bhatia, D., & Bhaumik, S. (2020). Optical Marker- and Vision-Based Human Gait Biomechanical Analysis. In S. Bhattacharyya, D. Konar, P. J. C. Kar, & K. Sharma (Eds.), Hybrid Machine Intelligence for Medical Image Analysis. Studies in Computational Intelligence, vol. 841. Springer, Singapore (pp. 275–291). doi:10.1007/978-981-13-8930-6_11

Ruiz-Rojas, E. D., Vazquez-Gonzalez, J. L., Alejos-Palomares, R., Escudero-Uribe, A. Z., & Mendoza-Vázquez, J. R. (2008). Mathematical model of a linear electric actuator with prosthesis applications. In *Proceedings - 18th International Conference on Electronics, Communications, and Computers, CONIELECOMP 2008*, 182–186. 10.1109/CONIELECOMP.2008.29

Timotiom. (2019). TA1. Retrieved September 21, 2019 from https://www.timotion.com/_upload/files/datasheet_ta1-ac_en.pdf

Utkin, V. (1977). Variable Structure Systems with Sliding Modes. *IEEE Transactions on Automatic Control*, 22(2), 212–222. doi:10.1109/TAC.1977.1101446

Vinodh Kumar, E., & Jerome, J. (2013). Robust LQR controller design for stabilizing and trajectory tracking of inverted pendulum. *Procedia Engineering*, 64, 169–178. doi:10.1016/j.proeng.2013.09.088

Wang, J., Li, X., Huang, T. H., Yu, S., Li, Y., Chen, T., ... Su, H. (2018). Comfort-Centered Design of a Lightweight and Backdrivable Knee Exoskeleton. *IEEE Robotics and Automation Letters*, 3(4), 4265–4272. doi:10.1109/LRA.2018.2864352

Wang, S., Van Dijk, W., & Van Der Kooij, H. (2011). Spring uses in exoskeleton actuation design. In *Proceedings IEEE International Conference on Rehabilitation Robotics*, 1–6. 10.1109/ICORR.2011.5975471

Zoss, A., Chu, A., & Kazerooni, H. (2006). Biomechanical Design of the Berkeley Lower Extremity Exoskeleton (BLEEX). *IEEE/ASME Transactions on Mechatronics*, 11(2), 128–138. doi:10.1109/TMECH.2006.871087

Zoss, A., & Kazerooni, H. (2006). Design of an electrically actuated lower extremity exoskeleton. *Advanced Robotics*, 20(9), 967–988. doi:10.1163/156855306778394030

# Chapter 5
# S–ADALINE:
## A System for Harmonic Detection and Electrical Power Measurement

**Soumyajit Goswami**

 https://orcid.org/0000-0001-8911-9603
*IBM India Pvt. Ltd., India*

**Arghya Sarkar**
*MCKV Institute of Engineering, India*

**Samarjit Sengupta**
*University of Calcutta, India*

## ABSTRACT

*In this chapter, the design and implementation of the self-synchronized adaptive linear neural (S-ADALINE) network approach for harmonic detection and the measurement of electrical power components (active power, reactive power, apparent power, power factor, etc.) at non-sinusoidal state have been discussed. A brief of the importance of electrical power measurement has been specified in Section 2. Section 3 is to discuss on the modern techniques of power measurement. The use of ADALINE style for harmonic estimation has been reflected in Section 4. In Section 5, harmonic tracking using S-ADALINE has been presented. Section 6 has been utilized to compare between ADALINE and S-ADALINE. In Section 7, S-ADALINE based power components measurement has been enlightened. A set of simulation tests in terms of accuracy, speed, and convergence of the S-ADALINE has been performed in MATLAB and deliberated in Section 8. The developed prototype is presented in Section 9 with experimental results.*

DOI: 10.4018/978-1-7998-2584-5.ch005

## INTRODUCTION

Voltage and current waveforms, in essence power waveforms, are pure sinusoidal in nature for an ideal power system. However, under diverse surroundings, voltage and current waveforms become distorted and origins harmonics and/or inter-harmonics. This makes difficult to measure different power components, such as active, reactive and apparent power, accurately. In this chapter, the design and implementation of the two stage self-synchronized adaptive linear neural (S-ADALINE) network based novel approach for harmonic detection and the measurement of electrical power components under non-sinusoidal condition have been discussed.

In modern electrical systems, voltages and especially currents become less sinusoidal and periodical due to the large number of domestic and industrial non-linear loads. Harmonics can cause signal interference, over voltages and circuit breaker failure, as well as equipment heating, malfunction and damage. It is difficult to measure the electrical power components at the present of harmonics. The standard measuring equipment do not comply with any valid definition in this non-sinusoidal situation, which exhibit large errors (Goswami, S., Sarkar, A. & Sengupta, S (2016). *Sensors and Applications in Measuring and Automation Control Systems*: International Frequency Sensor Association Publishing). To overcome these problems, many modern methods available in literature, such as, Fourier Transform based assessment (Su, T. et al (2018) and Goswami, S., Sarkar, A., & Sengupta (2019)), Wavelet Transform based assessment (Apetrei, V. et al (2014) and Filote, C. et al (2014)), Adaptive Linear Neuron (ADALINE) based assessment in Dash, P. K. et al (1996), Newton type algorithm in Terzija, V. V. et al (2007), time domain technique (Aiello, M. et al (2005) and Cataliotti, A. et al (2004)), DAQ-based sampling wattmeter (Islam, M. et al (2014) and Cataliotti, A. et al (2015)), FPGA-based assessment (Cardenas, A. et al (2010) and Cardenas, A. et al (2012)), microcontroller-based assessment in Srividyadevi, P. (2013) etc. Authors have elaborated those methods and their consequences in Goswami, S., Sarkar, A. & Sengupta, S (2016). *Sensors and Applications in Measuring and Automation Control Systems*: International Frequency Sensor Association Publishing. In this chapter, the drawbacks of conventional ADALINE to measure the power components are deliberated. To overcome those drawbacks, S-ADALINE algorithm has been established by the authors. Harmonic detection and power components measurement using the established S-ADALINE have been presented here.

# HARMONIC ESTIMATION USING CONVENTIONAL ADALINE

Mathematical model and analysis can be done for relatively simple systems. More complex systems cannot be managed by conventional mathematical and analytical methods. Soft computing came into the picture to cope up this problem. It deals with imprecision, vagueness, partial truth and approximation to achieve controllability, robustness and minimum solution cost. The applications of Soft computing have two main benefits. First, it can solve nonlinear problems, in which mathematical models are not available and possible. Second, it familiarizes the human knowledge such as cognition, recognition, understanding, learning and others into the field of computing. The basic methods of soft computing are Fuzzy Logic (FL), Neural Networks (NN), Genetic Algorithms (GA), Support Vector Machines (SVM), Machine Learning (ML) and Probabilistic Reasoning (PR). These methods are not originated from classical models. The conventional adaptive linear neuron (ADALINE) is a typical supervised learning mechanism which has been discussed in below subsections.

## Conventional ADALINE Structure

The ADALINE is a two-layered feed-forward perceptron, having multiple input units and a single output unit as per Dash, P. K. et al (1996). The ADALINE is described as a combinational circuit that accepts several inputs and produces one output which is a linear combination of these inputs. An ADALINE in block diagram form is depicted in Figure 1.

The input vector $X_A[n] = [x_1[n] \ x_2[n] \ .... \ x_{H-1}[n] \ x_H[n]]^{Tr}$ at any sample instant $n$, is multiplied by the adjustable weighting vector $W_A[n] = [w_1[n] \ w_2[n] \ ...... \ w_{H-1}[n] \ w_H[n]]$, and then summed to produce the estimated signal $\hat{y}[n] = W_A[n] X_A[n]$. $Tr$ is the transpose of a vector. After the initial random estimation, an adaptive algorithm updates the weight vector $W_A[n]$ of the ADALINE network so that the output $\hat{y}[n]$ ultimately reaches to desired signal $y[n]$. The weight up gradation rule, also known as modified Widro–Hoff delta rule is given by:

$$W_A[n+1] = W_A[n] + \frac{\alpha_{wh} e_{wh}[n] p_{wh}[n]}{\lambda_{wh} + (X_A[n])^{Tr} p_{wh}[n]} \tag{5.1}$$

where $p_{wh}[n] = \text{sgn}(X[n])$, $e_{wh}[n] = y[n] - \hat{y}[n]$ is the prediction error, at sample instant $n$, respectively, $\lambda_{wh}$ is a small constant term. The learning parameter $\alpha_{wh}$ is adapted recursively in the following way:

*Figure 1. Adaptive linear neuron (ADALINE)*

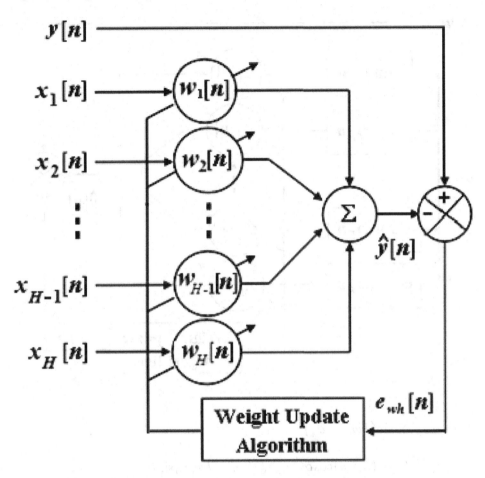

$$\alpha_{wh}[n+1] = \mu_{wh}\alpha_{wh}[n] + \gamma_{wh}\left|e_{wh}[n]\right|^{2} \tag{5.2}$$

where $\mu_{wh}$ and $\gamma_{wh}$ are constant terms.

## Application of Conventional ADALINE as Harmonic Detector

The use of this architecture for harmonic estimation is depicted in Figure 2.

If, the discrete time input signal (voltage or current) contains a finite number of significant harmonics with maximum order $M_s$, then at any sample instant $n$, it may be represented by Fourier series of the form

*Figure 2. ADALINE as a harmonic estimator*

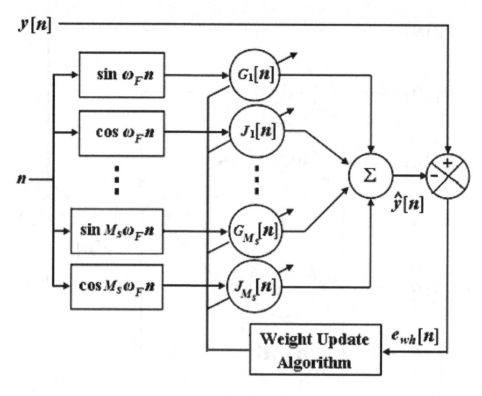

$$s[n] = \sqrt{2} \sum_{h=1}^{M_s} S_h \sin\left(h\omega_F n + \alpha_h\right)$$

$$= \sum_{h=1}^{M_s} \sqrt{2} S_h \sin\left(h\omega_F n\right)\cos\alpha_h + \sum_{h=1}^{M_s} \sqrt{2} S_h \cos\left(h\omega_F n\right)\sin\alpha_h \qquad (5.3)$$

$$= \sum_{h=1}^{M_s} E_h \sin\left(h\omega_F n\right) + \sum_{h=1}^{M_s} F_h \cos\left(h\omega_F n\right)$$

where $E_h = \sqrt{2} S_h \cos\alpha_h$, $F_h = \sqrt{2} S_h \sin\alpha_h$, $\omega_F$ is the fundamental angular frequency, $S_h$ are the rms values and $\alpha_h$ are the phase angles, at voltage harmonic $h$. Rearrangement of (5.3) in a matrix form gives

$$s[n] = W_{AH}[n] x_{AH}[n] \qquad (5.4)$$

where,

$$W_{AH}[n] = [E_1 \quad F_1 \quad E_2 \quad F_2 \quad \cdots\cdots \quad E_{M_s} \quad F_{M_s}] \qquad (5.5)$$

and

$$x_{AH}[n] = [\sin\omega_F n \quad \cos\omega_F n \quad \sin 2\omega_F n \quad \cos 2\omega_F n \cdots\cdots \sin M_s\omega_F n \quad \cos M_s\omega_F n]^{Tr}$$

(5.6)

In the literature (Dash, P. K. (1997) and Dash, P. K. (1998)), $\omega_F$ is assumed to be known in advance. In this situation, $x_{AH}[n]$ is known quantity and used as an input vector of Figure 2 and its desired output $y[n]$ is set to be equal to the actual distorted signal $s[n]$. After the initial random estimation, the adjustable weighting vector

$$W_{Ad}[n] = [G_1 \quad J_1 \quad G_2 \quad J_2 \quad \cdots\cdots \quad G_{M_s} \quad J_{M_s}]$$

updates using modified Widro–Hoff delta rule. Perfect tracking is attained when the tracking error $e_{wh}[n]$ is brought to zero. Then $W_{Ad}[n] = W_{AH}[n]$ and, rms magnitudes and phases of the harmonics ($S_h$ and $\alpha_h$, $h = 1, 2, ..., M_s$) can be readily calculated from the elements of $W_{Ad}$, as (Dash, P. K. (1997) and Dash, P. K. (1998)).

$$S_h = \sqrt{\frac{W_{Ad}^2(2h-1) + W_{Ad}^2(2h)}{2}}$$

(5.7)

$$\alpha_h = \tan^{-1}\left\{\frac{W_{Ad}(2h)}{W_{Ad}(2h-1)}\right\}$$

(5.8)

where $W_{Ad}(h)$ indicates $h^{th}$ element of $W_{Ad}$ vector.

## Drawbacks of Conventional ADALINE Structure for Harmonic Estimation

Conventional ADALINE has been proven to be an efficient harmonic detection approach and provides good accuracy and convergence speed in tracking the harmonic components due to its simple structure and characteristic of supervised learning mechanism. Moreover, it is adaptive in nature and can estimate the amplitude and phase angle variations of the harmonic components. However, the conventional ADALINE structure suffers from the following drawbacks:

- It works well at fixed frequency system but utterly fails at off-nominal frequency conditions stated by Sarkar, A., & Sengupta, S. (2009).

- Chang, G. W. et al (2008) states the convergence speed is very slow, even though, the steepest descent method based modified Widrow–Hoff weight updating rule provides guaranteed convergence.

A modification or upgradation is required, which diminishes the above-mentioned downsides.

## HARMONIC DETECTION WITH SELF-SYNCHRONIZED ADALINE (S-ADALINE)

To overcome the drawbacks of conventional ADALINE structure and a Self-synchronize ADALINE (S-ADALINE) network is proposed by Sarkar, A. et al (2011), which depends on the Levenberg gradient descent (LGD) method based parameter updating rule and is capable of handling both nominal and off-nominal frequency conditions. The LGD is a combination of the steepest descent and the Gauss-Newton method. When the present solution is far away from the exact one, it performs like steepest descent method and offers slow, but guaranteed convergence. On the other hand, when the current solution becomes close to the correct solution, it turns out to Gauss-Newton method and converges rapidly.

If, the discrete time input signal $y[n]$ with the fundamental angular frequency comprises a finite number of significant harmonics with maximum order $M$, then at any sample instant $n$, it can be represented as:

$$
\begin{aligned}
y[n] &= \sum_{k=1}^{M} Y_k \sin\left(k\omega_r n + \alpha_k\right) \\
&= \sum_{k=1}^{M} Y_k \sin\left(k\omega_r n\right)\cos\alpha_k + \sum_{k=1}^{M} Y_k \cos\left(k\omega_r n\right)\sin\alpha_k \\
&= \sum_{k=1}^{M} G_k \sin\left(k\omega_r n\right) + \sum_{k=1}^{M} H_k \cos\left(k\omega_r n\right)
\end{aligned}
\tag{5.9}
$$

where $Y_k$ and $\alpha_k$ are the amplitudes and phase angles of $k^{th}$ harmonic, respectively, $G_k = Y_k \cos\alpha_k$ and $H_k = Y_k \sin\alpha_k$.

By reordering of (5.9) in matrix form:

$$
y[n] = \left(W[n]\right)^{Tr} x[n]
\tag{5.10}
$$

where

*Figure 3. Architecture of the S-ADALINE*

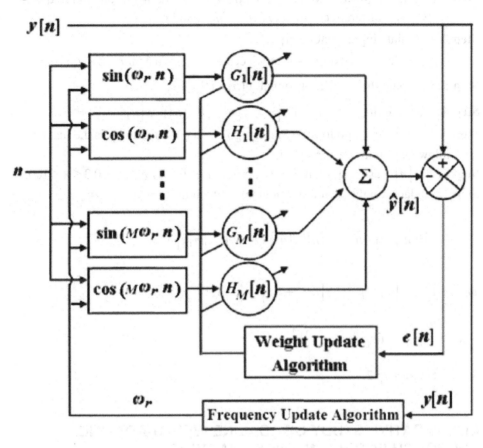

$$W[n] = [G_1 \quad H_1 \quad G_2 \quad H_2 \quad \cdots \quad G_M \quad H_M]^{Tr} \tag{5.11}$$

and

$$x[n] = [\sin\omega_r n \quad \cos\omega_r n \quad \sin 2\omega_r n \quad \cos 2\omega_r n \cdots \sin M\omega_r n \quad \cos M\omega_r n]^{Tr} \tag{5.12}$$

Tr indicates transpose of a vector quantity.

The S-ADALINE network can be applied to track the weighting vector $W[n]$ and $\omega_r$ adaptively. The overall architecture of the S-ADALINE network for harmonic detection has been presented in Figure 3. The S-ADALINE based harmonic estimation steps are given below:

**Step 1:** Initialize adjustable weighting vector $W_A[0]$, fundamental angular frequency $\omega_r[0]$, and different constants $\lambda$, $\eta_{lmw}$, $\eta_{lmf}$, and r.

**Step 2:** Calculate input vector x[n] as

$$x[n] = \left[\sin\omega_r n \quad \cos\omega_r n \quad \sin 2\omega_r n \quad \cos 2\omega_r n \cdots \sin M\omega_r n \quad \cos M\omega_r n\right]^{Tr}$$

**Step 3:** Compute the estimation signal $\hat{y}[n] = \left(W_A[n]\right)^{Tr} x[n]$

**Step 4:** Estimate the error signal $e[n] = y[n] - \left(W_A[n]\right)^{Tr} x[n]$

**Step 5:** If $e[n] < e_{nom}$, go to **Step 8**, if not go to **Step 6.** Here, $e_{nom}$ is the maximum allowable limit of error signal.

**Step 6:** If $e[n] > e[n-1]$, then $\lambda > \lambda r$, otherwise $\lambda > \lambda / r$ Limit $0.3 \leq \lambda \leq 100$.

**Step 7:** Update weight vector and fundamental angular frequency as:

$$W_A[n+1] = W_A[n] + \eta_{lmw}\left(x[n]\left(x[n]\right)^{Tr} + \lambda I\right)^{-1} e[n]x[n] \tag{5.13}$$

$$\omega_r[n+1] = \omega_r[n] + \eta_{lmf}\left(\left(S[n]\right)^2 + \lambda I\right)^{-1} e[n]S[n]$$

where, $S[n] = -\partial e[n]\left(\partial\omega_r[n]\right)^{-1}$ (5.14)

Step 8. Go to Step 2.

## COMPARATIVE STUDY OF ADALINE WITH S-ADALINE APPROACH FOR HARMONICS TRACKING

A set of simulation tests have been performed by Goswami S. (2013) in MATLAB environment to compare the performance of the conventional ADALINE and S-ADALINE network. The updating of the S-ADALINE network has been carried out considering the following initial values: $W$ = random numbers, $\lambda = 100$, $\eta_{lmw}$ = 0.4, $\eta_{lmf}$ = 1.6, $r = 0.89$, $\omega_r$ = nominal system angular frequency, weight upgradation stops when $e[n]$ £ 0.0001. The sampling rate is taken as 6.4 kHz based on a 50Hz system. For a fair comparison, weights of the S-ADALINE networks have also been updated using same factors as that of conventional ADALINE.

### Static Test

The following input signal has been processed:

$$y(t) = 1.5\sin\left(\omega_r t + 29.3^\circ\right) + 0.5\sin\left(3\omega_r t + 141.6^\circ\right) +$$
$$0.1\sin\left(5\omega_r t + 66.2^\circ\right) + 0.017\sin\left(9\omega_r t - 99.4^\circ\right)$$

(5.15)

The evaluated converged results for fundamental frequency $\omega_r = 50$ Hz and $\omega_r = 48$ Hz have been presented in Table 5.1. In both the cases the sampling frequency is kept constant at 6.4 kHz. From the table, it has been observed that both S-ADALINE and the conventional ADALINE provide high accuracy at nominal system frequency (50 Hz). However, the S-ADALINE provides faster convergence than the ADALINE at 50 Hz, as depicted in Figure 4.

At off-nominal frequency condition (48 Hz), the conventional ADALINE network fails to converge and shows oscillating estimations as presented in Figure 5, whereas S-ADALINE provides stable and accurate measurement without any extra computational complexity.

Noise Test A Gaussian noise with signal to noise ratio equal to 20 dB is added to the measured samples of the waveform given by (5.15). Figure 6 displays the results of estimation of the amplitude of the fundamental, third and fifth harmonic using both the approaches. From figures it has been observed that the S-ADALINE has better noise rejection capability than the conventional structure.

## Dynamic Test

In this test, the performance of the S-ADALINE is evaluated at the time-varying conditions. In the period from $t = 0$ to 0.15s, the test signal was as given by (5.16).

*Figure 4. Error signal comparison of conventional ADALINE and S-ADALINE at nominal frequency condition (50 Hz)*

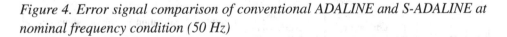

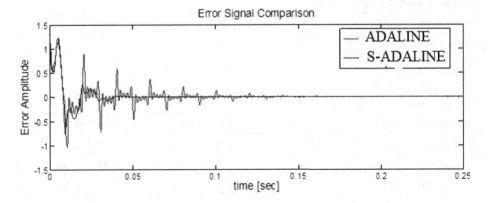

*Figure 5. Error signal of the conventional ADALINE at off-nominal frequency (48 Hz)*

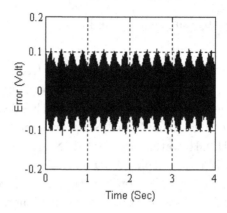

$$y(t) = \sin\left(\omega_r t + 29.3^\circ\right) + 0.5\sin\left(5\omega_r t + 81.6^\circ\right) \tag{5.16}$$

At $t = 2$s, the input signal is instantaneously changed to (5.17). At the same time, the fundamental frequency is also changed from 50 Hz (nominal) to 48 Hz (off-nominal).

*Table 1. harmonic detection with the S-ADALINE Networks and the Conventional ADALINE Networks*

| | S-ADALINE | | Conventional ADALINE | |
|---|---|---|---|---|
| | Percent Error in amplitude estimation | Percent Error in phase estimation | Percent Error in amplitude estimation | Percent Error in phase estimation |
| **Input fundamental frequency = 50 Hz** | | | | |
| **Fundamental** | 0.001 | 0.001 | 0.005 | 0.005 |
| **3rd Harmonic** | 0.001 | 0.002 | 0.005 | 0.006 |
| **5th Harmonic** | 0.002 | 0.002 | 0.006 | 0.005 |
| **9th Harmonic** | 0.001 | 0.001 | 0.005 | 0.005 |
| **Input fundamental frequency = 48 Hz** | | | | |
| **Fundamental** | 0.001 | 0.001 | Not Converged | Not Converged |
| **3rd Harmonic** | 0.003 | 0.003 | Not Converged | Not Converged |
| **5th Harmonic** | 0.002 | 0.002 | Not Converged | Not Converged |
| **9th Harmonic** | 0.001 | 0.001 | Not Converged | Not Converged |

*Figure 6. Estimation of the fundamental, third and fifth harmonic amplitude in the presence of noise using S-ADALINE and conventional ADALINE*

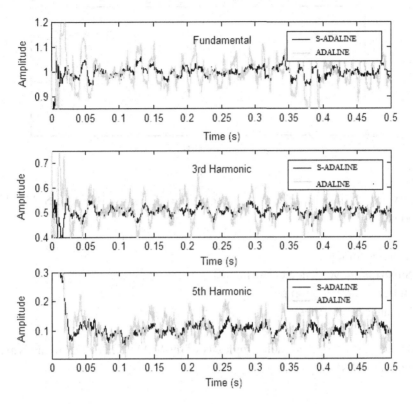

$$y(t) = 1.4\sin\left(\omega_r t + 50°\right) + 0.1\sin\left(5\omega_r t - 66.2°\right) \qquad (5.17)$$

The Figure 7 shows that the S-ADALINE tracks the frequency accurately, but the conventional ADALINE fails to do so.

## Computational Complexities

Computational load of the S-ADALINE is greater than the conventional ADALINE. Frequency estimation algorithm and inversion of the matrix mainly influence the computational complexities of S-ADALINE. The execution time of the S-ADALINE program is 0.183016 seconds in an Intel Pentium 4 CPU B940 @ 2 GHz laptop whereas the time is 0.055803 seconds for the Conventional ADALINE.

This section presents a comparative study of two adaptive algorithms, the conventional ADALINE and the S-ADALINE network to estimate harmonic components of the measured power signal. By observing the simulation results, it

*Figure 7. Estimated frequency comparison of conventional ADALINE and S-ADALINE*

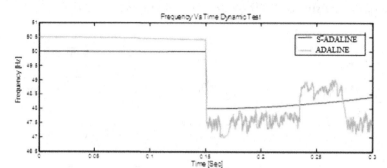

is observed that in comparison to the conventional ADALINE, the S-ADALINE method shows

- More accuracy
- Superior convergence performance
- Better noise rejection property
- Enhanced robustness against parameter changes.

However, the computational complexity of the S-ADALINE technique is greater than the ADALINE approaches.

## S-ADALINE BASED POWER COMPONENT MEASUREMENT ALGORITHM

By observing the ample advantage of S-ADALINE approach in harmonic estimation, attempt has been taken to extend the application of this unique approach in the field of power component measurement. This section delivers single-phase power components' definitions limited to the IEEE Standard 1459–2010 (Mar. 2010) and its reformulation in S-ADALINE domain. The basic assumption is that power system signals have been uniformly sampled at sampling frequency $f_s$, greater than the Nyquist rate, so that aliasing of spectra does not happen.

### Derivation of Power Components

At steady state situations, the non-sinusoidal instantaneous voltage, $v$, and current, $i$, of fundamental angular frequency $\omega$ can be presented as,

$$v = v_1 + v_K$$
$$= \sqrt{2}V_1 \sin(\omega t + \alpha_1) + \sqrt{2} \sum_{\substack{k \neq 1}}^{M_v} V_k \sin(k\omega t + \alpha_k) \tag{5.18}$$
$$= \sum_{k=1}^{M_v} A_k \sin(k\omega t) + \sum_{k=1}^{M_v} B_k \cos(k\omega t)$$

$$i = i_1 + i_K$$
$$= \sqrt{2}I_1 \sin(\omega t + \beta_1) + \sqrt{2} \sum_{\substack{k \neq 1}}^{M_i} I_k \sin(k\omega t + \beta_k) \tag{5.19}$$
$$= \sum_{k=1}^{M_i} C_k \sin(k\omega t) + \sum_{k=1}^{Mi} D_k \cos(k\omega t)$$

where $A_k = \sqrt{2}V_k \cos\alpha_k$ $\tag{5.20}$

$B_k = \sqrt{2}V_k \sin\alpha_k$ $\tag{5.21}$

$C_k = \sqrt{2}I_k \cos\beta_k$ $\tag{5.22}$

$D_k = \sqrt{2}I_k \sin\beta_k$ $\tag{5.23}$

$\alpha_1, \beta_1$ correspond to the fundamental voltage and current phase angles respectively, while $\alpha_k$ and $\beta_k$ represent the harmonic voltage and current phase angle respectively, at $k^{th}$ harmonic. $v_1$, $i_1$ represent the power system frequency components, and $v_H$, $i_H$ represent the harmonic components. Goswami S., Sarkar A., & Sengupta S. (2017) have established the below mentioned derivations of power components.

## RMS Calculation

The RMS values of the non-sinusoidal voltage signals with period $T$ is

$$V = \sqrt{\frac{1}{hT} \int_{\tau}^{\tau+hT} v^2 \, dt} = \sqrt{\sum_{k=1}^{M_v} V_k^2} \tag{5.24}$$

where $h$ is a positive integer number. Using (5.18) and (5.19), it can be shown that,

$$V = \sqrt{\frac{1}{2} \sum_{k=1}^{M_v} (A_k^2 + B_k^2)} \tag{5.25}$$

Similarly, the expressions of rms value of distorted current signal is

$$I = \sqrt{\frac{1}{hT} \int_{\tau}^{\tau+hT} i^2 dt} = \sqrt{\sum_{k=1}^{M_i} I_k^2} = \sqrt{\frac{1}{2} \sum_{k=1}^{M_i} (C_k^2 + D_k^2)}$$ (5.26)

## Total Harmonic Distortion

The total harmonic distortion of the voltage is given by

$$THD_v = \frac{V_K}{V_1} = \frac{\sqrt{\sum_{k \neq 1}^{M_v} (A_k^2 + B_k^2)}}{\sqrt{(A_1^2 + B_1^2)}}$$ (5.27)

The total harmonic distortion of the current is represented as

$$THD_i = \frac{I_K}{I_1} = \frac{\sqrt{\sum_{k \neq 1}^{M_i} (C_k^2 + D_k^2)}}{\sqrt{(C_1^2 + D_1^2)}}$$ (5.28)

## Active Power

The total active power $P$, fundamental active power $P_1$ and harmonic active power $P_H$ can be derived as

$$P = \frac{1}{hT} \int_{\tau}^{\tau+hT} vi \, dt = \sum_k V_k I_k \cos\theta_k = \frac{1}{2} \sum_k (A_k C_k + B_k D_k)$$ (5.29)

$$P_1 = \frac{1}{hT} \int_{\tau}^{\tau+hT} v_1 i_1 \, dt = V_1 I_1 \cos\theta_1 = \frac{1}{2} (A_1 C_1 + B_1 D_1)$$ (5.30)

$$P_H = V_0 I_0 + \sum_{k \neq 1} V_k I_k \cos\theta_k = \frac{1}{2} \sum_{k \neq 1} (A_k C_k + B_k D_k)$$ (5.31)

## Reactive Power

The total reactive power $Q_B$, fundamental reactive power $Q_I$ and harmonic reactive power $Q_H$ can be obtained as

$$Q_B = \frac{\omega_k}{hT}\int_{\tau}^{\tau+hT} i_k [\int v_k ]dt = \sum_k V_k I_k \sin\theta_k = \frac{1}{2}\sum_k (B_k C_k - A_k D_k) \tag{5.32}$$

$$Q_1 = \frac{\omega_1}{hT}\int_{\tau}^{\tau+hT} i_1 \left[\int v_1 dt \right]dt = V_1 I_1 \sin\theta_1 = \frac{1}{2}(B_1 C_1 - A_1 D_1) \tag{5.33}$$

$$Q_H = V_0 I_0 + \sum_{k\neq1} V_k I_k \sin\theta_k = \frac{1}{2}\sum_{k\neq1}(B_k C_k - A_k D_k) \tag{5.34}$$

## Apparent Power

The total apparent power $S$, fundamental apparent power $S_1$, harmonic apparent power $S_N$, current distortion power $D_1$, voltage distortion power $D_V$, harmonic apparent power $S_H$ and harmonic distortion power $D_H$ can be demarcated as

$$S = VI = \frac{1}{2}\sqrt{\sum_k (A_k^2 + B_k^2)\sum_k (C_k^2 + D_k^2)} \tag{5.35}$$

$$S_1 = V_1 I_1 = \frac{1}{2}\sqrt{(A_1^2 + B_1^2)(C_1^2 + D_1^2)} \tag{5.36}$$

$$S_N = \sqrt{S^2 - S_1^2} = \frac{1}{2}\sqrt{\sum_k (A_k^2 + B_k^2)\sum_k (C_k^2 + D_k^2) - (A_1^2 + B_1^2)(C_1^2 + D_1^2)} \tag{5.37}$$

$$D_I = V_1 I_H = \frac{1}{2}\sqrt{(A_1^2 + B_1^2)\sum_{k\neq1}^{M_I}(C_k^2 + D_k^2)} \tag{5.38}$$

$$D_V = V_H I_1 = \frac{1}{2}\sqrt{(C_1^2 + D_1^2)\sum_{k\neq1}^{M_v}(A_k^2 + B_k^2)} \tag{5.39}$$

$$S_H = V_H I_H = \frac{1}{2}\sqrt{\sum_{k \neq 1}^{M_v}\left(A_k^2 + B_k^2\right)\sum_{k \neq 1}^{M_i}\left(C_k^2 + D_k^2\right)} \qquad (5.40)$$

$$D_H = \sqrt{S_H^2 - P_H^2} = \frac{1}{2}\sqrt{\left(\sum_{k \neq 1}^{Mv}\left(A_k^2 + B_k^2\right)\sum_{k \neq 1}^{M_i}\left(C_k^2 + D_k^2\right)\right)^2 - \left(\sum_{k \neq 1}\left(A_k C_k + B_k D_k\right)\right)^2} \qquad (5.41)$$

## Power Factor

The fundamental power factor $PF_1$ and total power factor $PF$ are represented as

$$PF_1 = \frac{P_1}{S_1} = \frac{\left(A_1 C_1 + B_1 D_1\right)}{\sqrt{\left(A_1^2 + B_1^2\right)\left(C_1^2 + D_1^2\right)}} \qquad (5.42)$$

$$PF = \frac{P}{S} = \frac{\sum_k \left(A_k C_k + B_k D_k\right)}{\sqrt{\sum_k\left(A_k^2 + B_k^2\right)\sum_k\left(C_k^2 + D_k^2\right)}} \qquad (5.43)$$

## Block Diagram of S-ADALINE Based Power Component Measurement Unit

The basic block diagram (Goswami S., Sarkar A., & Sengupta S. (2017)) of the power component measurement algorithm has been presented in Figure 8, in which, S-ADALINE Network 1 and S-ADALINE Network 2 are used to process the scaled down voltage signal $v[n]$ and current signal $i[n]$, respectively. The sampling instant, $n$, along with estimated angular frequencies and previous knowledge of harmonic orders generate input vectors $x_v[n]$ and $x_i[n]$ which are fed to S-ADALINE Network 1 and S-ADALINE Network 2, respectively. S-ADALINE Network 1 tracks $A_k$, $B_k$ using $x_v[n]$ and weight up-gradation rule, whereas S-ADALINE Network 2 tracks $C_k$, $D_k$ from $x_i[n]$. The power components have been obtained using equations (5.18) - (5.43) based upon the information of converged $A_k$, $B_k$, $C_k$ and $D_k$.

*Figure 8. Block diagram of S-ADALINE based power component measurement unit*

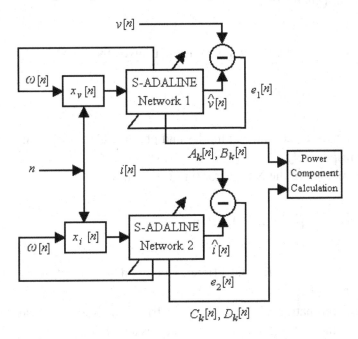

## PERFORMANCE EVALUATION USING SIMULATION

To compare the performance of the established algorithm with the conventional ADALINE (Dash, P. K. et al (1996)) and Newton-Type Algorithm (NTA) (Terzija, V. V. et al (2007)), simulation tests have been performed in MATLAB environment. Primarily, the harmonic tracking capabilities of NTA, conventional ADALINE and S-ADALINE are examined. Then, the accuracy, speed and convergence of the power components estimation algorithms are experimented under steady-state, dynamic and noisy conditions.

### Harmonic Detection using Newton-Type Algorithm (NTA)

NTA belongs to the family of non-recursive nonlinear estimators. Brief description of the NTA based harmonic tracking procedure has been presented below.

If, the discrete time input signal $y[n]$ with the fundamental angular frequency $\omega_r$ contains a finite number of significant harmonics with maximum order $M$, then at any sample instant $n$, it can be represented

$$y[n] = \sum_{k=1}^{M} Y_k \sin\left(k\omega_r n + \alpha_k\right) \tag{5.44}$$

A suitable vector of unknown parameters is given by,

$$x[n] = \left[\omega_r, Y_1, Y_2, \cdots, Y_M, \ \alpha_1, \alpha_2, \cdots, \alpha_M\right]^{Tr} \tag{5.45}$$

where $Y_k$ and $\alpha_k$ are the amplitudes and phase angles of $k^{th}$ harmonic ($k = 1$, ......., $M$), respectively.

The key relation of the NTA algorithm is as below,

$$x[n+1] = x[n] + \left(J[n]\left(J[n]\right)^{Tr}\right)^{-1}\left(J[n]\right)^{Tr} e[n] \tag{5.46}$$

Where, error signal $e[n]$ is the difference between the desired signal $y[n]$ and the estimated signal $\hat{y}[n]$.

The Jacobian matrix $J$ is an ($N$ X $n$) matrix, and its elements are the partial derivatives of the signal (5.46). If $j$ is denoted as an arbitrary row of the Jacobian,

$$j = \left[j_1, j_2, j_3, \cdots, j_{2+2M}\right]^{Tr} \tag{5.47}$$

$$j_1 = \frac{\delta y[n]}{\delta \omega_r} = \sum_{k=1}^{M} Y_k k n \cos(k\omega_r n + \alpha_k) \tag{5.48}$$

$$j_{2+k} = \frac{\delta y[n]}{\delta Y_k} = \sin(kwn + \alpha_k) \tag{5.49}$$

$$j_{2+M+k} = \frac{\delta y[n]}{\delta \alpha_k} = Y_k \cos(kwn + \alpha_k) \tag{5.50}$$

Figure 9 represents the block diagram of NTA based power components estimation. The main drawback of this approach is, it requires the right choice of the sampling frequency, the length of the data window and the initial guess for the vector of the unknown parameters.

*Figure 9. Block diagram of NTA based power component measurement unit*

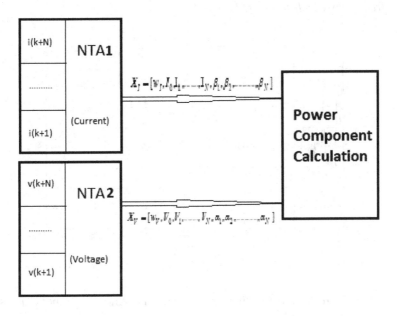

## Signal Tracking Capability

The S-ADALINE network has been updated by considering the following initial values: $W_A$ = random numbers, $\lambda$=100, $\eta_{lmw}$ =0.4, $\eta_{lmf}$ =1.6, $r$= 0.89, $\omega_r$ = nominal system angular frequency, weight up-gradation runs until $e[n]$ £ 0.0001. The FFT has been utilized to obtain the initial values of the unknown parameters of the NTA. The sampling rate is taken as 6.4 kHz based on a 50Hz system.

To test the harmonic tracking capability of this adaptive algorithms at nominal frequency condition (fundamental frequency = 50 Hz), a signal of known harmonic is taken for estimation. The sample waveform is presented as:

$$y(t) = \sin\left(\omega_0 t + 29.3^\circ\right) + 0.5\sin\left(3\omega_0 t + 81.6^\circ\right) + 0.1\sin\left(5\omega_0 t - 66.2^\circ\right) \qquad (5.51)$$

The estimation errors in signal tracking for three different algorithms (Conventional ADALINE, NTA and S-ADALINE) have been shown in Fig. 5.10 which shows the S-ADALINE provides faster response than conventional ADALINE and NTA. Theoretically it is true for conventional ADALINE, but surprisingly NTA techniques shows slower convergence than the S-ADALINE. This is basically due to larger value of learning parameter $\eta_{lmf}$ (in NTA $\eta_{lmw} = \eta_{lmf} = 1$). Moreover, NTA doesn't converge fully and shows small oscillations around steady state value.

*Figure 10. Error comparison of conventional ADALINE, NTA and S-ADALINE at nominal frequency condition (50 Hz)*

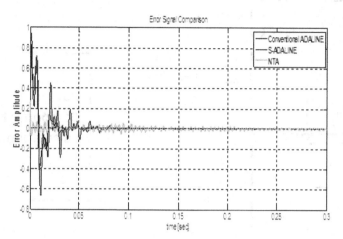

The estimated amplitude and phase angle of each harmonic component at steady state have been presented in Table 2, which indicates that the accuracies of all the methods except NTA are very high and almost same at nominal frequency.

The same waveform is used in off-nominal condition (48 Hz) for the estimation of errors, which have been shown in Figure 11. However, in that case the error of conventional ADALINE is omitted, as it is well-known that conventional ADALINE fails to converge at off-nominal frequency condition.

As expected, the S-ADALINE provides better accuracy and faster convergence than the NTA based approach and NTA again exhibits large convergence time.

## Static Test

The input voltage and current signals used for experiment are given below:

$$v(t)=\sqrt{2}\left[1.0\sin\left(2\pi ft\right)+0.03\sin\left(6\pi ft+135^{\circ}\right)+0.01\sin\left(10\pi ft+150^{\circ}\right)+0.01\sin\left(14\pi ft+140^{\circ}\right)\right] \tag{5.52}$$

$$i(t)=\sqrt{2}\left[1.0\sin\left(2\pi ft+10^{\circ}\right)+0.3\sin\left(6\pi f+150^{\circ}\right)+0.2\sin\left(10\pi ft+135^{\circ}\right)+0.1\sin\left(14\pi ft-22.5^{\circ}\right)\right] \tag{5.53}$$

The estimated power components at nominal frequency (f=50 Hz) are presented in Table 5.3 which reveals that the developed method provides much better accuracy (percent errors is of the order of $10^{-12\%}$) than NTA (percent errors is of the order of $10^{-2\%}$).

*Table 2. Test conditions and % error in amplitude and phase characterization*

| | Conventional ADALINE | | NTA | | S-ADALINE | |
|---|---|---|---|---|---|---|
| | % Error in Amplitude Est. | % Error in Phase Est. | % Error in Amplitude Est. | % Error in Phase Est. | % Error in Amplitude Est. | % Error in Phase Est. |
| **Fundamental** | $1 X 10^{-4}$ | $1 X 10^{-4}$ | $2 X 10^{-2}$ | $3 X 10^{-2}$ | $1 X 10^{-4}$ | $1 X 10^{-4}$ |
| **3$^{rd}$Harmonic** | $2 X 10^{-4}$ | $3 X 10^{-4}$ | $1 X 10^{-1}$ | $2 X 10^{-1}$ | $2 X 10^{-4}$ | $3 X 10^{-4}$ |
| **5$^{th}$Harmonic** | $3 X 10^{-3}$ | $3 X 10^{-3}$ | $2 X 10^{-1}$ | $2 X 10^{-1}$ | $3 X 10^{-3}$ | $3 X 10^{-3}$ |

*Figure 11. Error comparison of NTA and S-ADALINE at off-nominal frequency (48 Hz)*

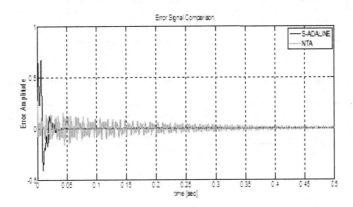

Active power, reactive power and apparent power components at nominal frequency ($f$=50 Hz) are calculated for the input voltage and current signals (5.52) and (5.53). Error to calculate power components for NTA and S-ADALINE are presented in Figure 12. From those power components, Power Factor is also calculated and the error in Power Factor is presented in Table 4 which reveals that the S-ADALINE offers better accuracy than conventional ADALINE and Newton-Type Algorithm.

## Dynamic Test

Additional investigations have been taken place to test the performance of the considering algorithms at dynamic condition. In the period from $t = 0$ to 0.15s, the used test signal is given by (5.54).

*Table 3. Power Components Assessment at Nominal Frequency*

| | | IEEE Standard | S-ADALINE based Definitions | | NTA based Definitions | |
|---|---|---|---|---|---|---|
| | | | Measured Values | % error | Measured Values | % error |
| **RMS** | $V_1$ | 1.0000 | 1.0000 | -0.0005 | 1.0000 | -0.0025 |
| | $V_{rms}$ | 1.0005 | 1.0005 | -0.0003 | 1.0006 | -0.0045 |
| | $I_1$ | 1.0000 | 1.0000 | -0.0004 | 1.0001 | -0.0057 |
| | $I_{rms}$ | 1.0677 | 1.0676 | 0.0013 | 1.0678 | -0.0053 |
| **Active power** | $P_1$ | 0.9848 | 0.9848 | -0.0007 | 0.9849 | -0.0108 |
| | $P$ | 0.9945 | 0.9946 | -0.0015 | 0.9946 | -0.0117 |
| **Reactive power** | $Q_1$ | -0.1736 | -0.1736 | 0.0009 | -0.1736 | 0.0047 |
| | $Q_B$ | -0.17516 | -0.17518 | -0.0037 | -0.1752 | 0.0077 |
| **Apparent power** | $S_1$ | 1.0000 | 1.0000 | -0.0017 | 1.0001 | -0.0098 |
| | $S$ | 1.0683 | 1.0683 | -0.0005 | 1.0684 | -0.0089 |
| | $S_N$ | 0.3758 | 0.3759 | -0.0102 | 0.3759 | -0.0104 |

*Table 4. Test Conditions and % Error in Power Factor Characterization*

| | Conventional ADALINE | NTA | S-ADALINE |
|---|---|---|---|
| **% Error in Power Factor** | 0.366639910113800 | 0.748367617575003 | 0.025018494189220 |

$$y(t) = \sin\left(\omega_0 t + 29.3^\circ\right) + 0.5\sin\left(5\omega_0 t + 81.6^\circ\right) \tag{5.54}$$

At $t = 0.15$s, the input signal is rapidly altered to (5.55). At the same time, the fundamental frequency is also changed from 50 Hz (nominal) to 48 Hz (off-nominal).

$$y(t) = 1.4\sin\left(\omega_0 t + 50^\circ\right) + 0.1\sin\left(5\omega_0 t - 66.2^\circ\right) \tag{5.55}$$

The frequency estimation of the S-ADALINE provides high accuracy and fast convergence compared to the NTA as depicted in Figure 13.

## Noise Test

The same input signals (5.54) and (5.55) with the superimposed zero-mean white noise has been utilized as input test signals. A range from a highly noisy signal

*Figure 12. Absolute % errors in power components estimation under off-nominal frequency*

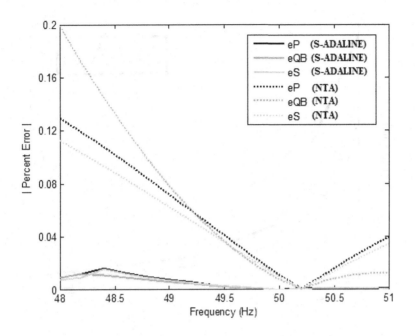

*Figure 13. Estimated frequency comparison of NTA and S-ADALINE*

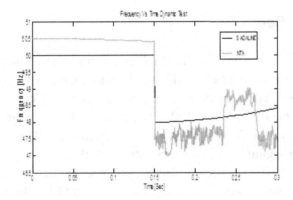

(SNR=20 dB) to a low noisy signal (SNR=60 dB) is covered and, in each case, the steady-state error is measured using the established algorithm; and compared with the NTA based technique. As shown in Figure 14, error drops from SNR=20 dB to SNR=60 dB rapidly and S-ADALINE delivers better immunity to noise than NTA.

*Figure 14. Absolute maximum steady-state errors in active power estimation in terms of SNR*

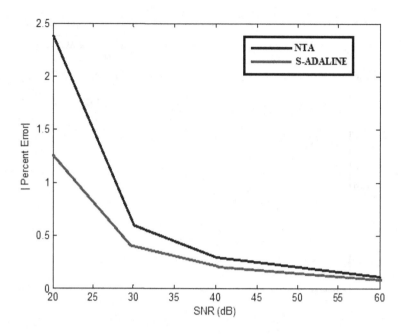

## PC-BASED INSTRUMENT DEVELOPMENT

### Experimental Setup

To establish the viability of the S-ADALINE algorithm in a real-time environment, it has been experimented physically with the laboratory setup by Goswami S., Sarkar A., & Sengupta S. (2017). The developed rapid prototyping system has been shown in Fig. 5.15, in which the programmable ac power source/power analyzer (PS/PA) Agilent 6812B (750 VA, 300 V, 6.5 A, rms. voltage (35 - 100 Hz) accuracy: 0.03% + 100mV) (User's Guide AC Power Solutions Agilent Models 6811B, 6812B, and 6813B (Sep. 2004)) has been utilized to generate required waveforms. RS 232 bus connects computer (Dual Core Intel Pentium D 3.4 GHz CPU) and PS/PA for signal control.

The measurement system uses a Hall-effect voltage sensor (LEM LV25-P with a 40-μs response time and 0.8% accuracy) for the accommodation of voltage signal from PS/PA to the floating-point controller-board dSPACE DS1103 DSP (four A/D channels—12-b resolution, four A/D channels—14-b resolution, eight A/D channels—12-b resolution, six incremental encoder channels, and a complete subsystem for digital I/O). The established strategy is implemented on the DSP system using the

*Figure 15. Laboratory test setup for the amplitude tracking*

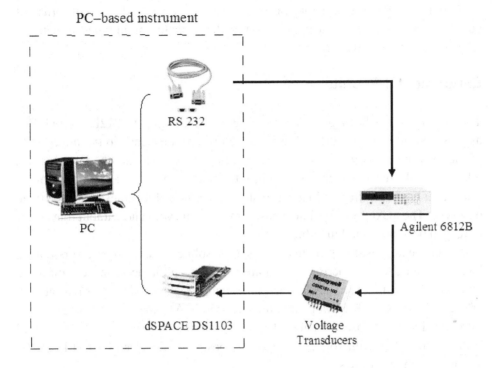

SIMULINK (toolbox of MATLAB) software package. The sampling time is set to 200 μs. The A/D conversion was performed by means of a 14-b analog-to-digital converter (ADC). Single computer has been utilized to control both the wave form generation and measuring procedure.

## Third-Order Iterative Matrix Inversion Method

The computational complexities and response time of the S-ADALINE are primarily influenced by inversion of the Hessian matrix ($H[n] = x[n](x[n])^{Tr} + \lambda I$). To reduce the computational burden in real time implementation, the third-Order Iterative method, as presented by Li, H. B. et al (2011) has been utilized here.

If, $A = [a_{i,j}]_{NXN}$ is an iterative matrix with real or complex elements and the initial guess $V_0$ satisfies $\| I - AV_0 \| < 1$, then with third convergence order,

$$A^{-1} \simeq V_{n+1} = V_n(3I - AV_n(3I - AV_n)) \tag{5.56}$$

Where, $I$ is the Identity matrix and iteration number $n = 0, 1, 2, ....$

This is an effective tool for constructing iterative methods of high order of convergence to calculate matrix inversion mathematically for all types of matrices (especially for ill-conditioned).

## Experimental Results

The test signal has been generated by programming Agilent 6812B through PC, as presented in (5.54) and (5.55). Since, the primary influence to the uncertainty of the instrument is due to the transducers, in order to evaluate the uncertainties related only the measurement algorithm, at the first stage of the experimentation no transducer has been utilized. In the next stage, the effect of the transducers has been observed. The maximum absolute measurement errors with and without transducer have also been presented in Table 5.

Experimental results show that the peak absolute measurement errors during "without transducer" experimentation are very low and in accordance with those obtained by simulations. The accuracies are mainly influenced by the bit limitation effect of the software/hardware implementation unit. As expected, the uncertainties introduced by the transducers are relatively predominant. However, the PC-based instrumental setup with voltage transducer does not still exceed Class-I limits ($\pm$ 1% of the nominal values).

## CONCLUSION

In this chapter, an overview of several classical methods applicable for electrical power measurement in the presence of harmonics and/or inter-harmonics have been discussed. At the same time, problems associated with classical methods and to overcome those, different modern technologies with their pros and cons are presented

*Table 5. Accuracy characterization of S-ADALINE*

| Power Components | Maximum Absolute Measurement % Errors (without transducer) | Maximum Absolute Measurement % Errors (with transducer) |
|---|---|---|
| Active Power | $4 X 10^{-3}$ | $8 X 10^{-2}$ |
| Reactive Power | $1 X 10^{-3}$ | $3 X 10^{-2}$ |
| Apparent Power | $3 X 10^{-3}$ | $7 X 10^{-2}$ |

for power components measurement. A modified algorithm for the digital metering of power components according to IEEE Standard 1459-2010 is presented with detail experiments. It is based on the application of the S-ADALINE, which is an improved approach for real time implementation of the ADALINE. The S-ADALINE is able to synchronize itself with system frequency and can estimate the spectrum at the exact harmonic order of interest. The obtained results confirm an advantage in improved accuracy, better immunity to noise, and faster convergence than the conventional ADALINE and NTA approaches. A simple laboratory implementation, based on MATLAB and the prototype hardware, confirms the feasibility of the proposed algorithm for real-time applications.

## REFERENCES

Agilent Technologies, User's Guide AC. (2004). *Power Solutions Agilent Models 6811B, 6812B, and 6813B.*

Aiello, M., Cataliotti, A., Cosentino, V., & Nuccio, S. (2005). A self-synchronizing instrument for harmonic source detection in power systems. *IEEE Transactions on Instrumentation and Measurement, 54*(1), 15–23. doi:10.1109/TIM.2004.834600

Apetrei, V., Filote, C., & Graur, A. (2014, March). Harmonic analysis based on Discrete Wavelet Transform in electric power systems. In *Proceedings of the 2014 Ninth International Conference on Ecological Vehicles and Renewable Energies (EVER)* (pp. 1-8). IEEE.

Cardenas, A., Guzman, C., & Agbossou, K. (2010, July). Real-time evaluation of power quality using FPGA based measurement system. In *Proceedings 2010 IEEE International Symposium on Industrial Electronics* (pp. 2777-2782). IEEE. 10.1109/ISIE.2010.5636556

Cardenas, A., Guzman, C., & Agbossou, K. (2012). Development of a FPGA based real-time power analysis and control for distributed generation interface. *IEEE Transactions on Power Systems, 27*(3), 1343–1353. doi:10.1109/TPWRS.2012.2186468

Cataliotti, A., Cosentino, V., Di Cara, D., Lipari, A., & Nuccio, S. (2015). A DAQ-based sampling wattmeter for IEEE Std. 1459-2010 powers measurements. Uncertainty evaluation in nonsinusoidal conditions. *Measurement, 61*, 27–38. doi:10.1016/j.measurement.2014.10.033

Cataliotti, A., Cosentino, V., & Nuccio, S. (2004, May). A time domain approach for IEEE Std 1459-2000 powers measurement in distorted and unbalanced power systems. In *Proceedings of the 21st IEEE Instrumentation and Measurement Technology Conference (IEEE Cat. No. 04CH37510)* (Vol. 2, pp. 1388-1393). IEEE. 10.1109/IMTC.2004.1351325

Chang, G. W., Chen, C. I., Huang, B. C., & Liang, Q. W. (2008, September). A comparative study of two weights updating approaches used in ADALINE for harmonics tracking. In *Proceedings 2008 13th International Conference on Harmonics and Quality of Power* (pp. 1-5). IEEE. 10.1109/ICHQP.2008.4668760

Dash, P. K., Panda, S. K., Liew, A. C., Mishra, B., & Jena, R. K. (1998). A new approach to monitoring electric power quality. *Electric Power Systems Research, 46*(1), 11–20. doi:10.1016/S0378-7796(98)00015-7

Dash, P. K., Panda, S. K., Mishra, B., & Swain, D. P. (1997). Fast estimation of voltage and current phasors in power networks using an adaptive neural network. *IEEE Transactions on Power Systems, 12*(4), 1494–1499. doi:10.1109/59.627847

Dash, P. K., Swain, D. P., Liew, A. C., & Rahman, S. (1996). An adaptive linear combiner for on-line tracking of power system harmonics. *IEEE Transactions on Power Systems, 11*(4), 1730–1735. doi:10.1109/59.544635

Filote, C., Apetrei, V., & Graur, A. (2014, September). Topologies of three-phase rectifier with near sinusoidal input currents—A comparative analysis of power quality indices using FFT and DWT. In *Proceedings 2014 16th International Power Electronics and Motion Control Conference and Exposition* (pp. 731-736). IEEE.

Goswami, S. (2013). A Comparative Study of the ADALINE Method with S-ADALINE Approach for Harmonics Tracking. In Proceedings of Recent Development in Electrical, Electronics & Engineering Physics (RDE3P-2013), 94–97.

Goswami, S., & Sarkar, A., & Sengupta (2019, August), S. Digital Metering of Electrical Power Components Using Adaptive Non-Uniform Discrete Short Time Fourier Transform. *International Journal of Emerging Electric Power Systems, 20*(4).

Goswami, S., Sarkar, A., & Sengupta, S. (2017). Power Components Measurement Using S-ADALINE. *International Journal of Engineering Innovation & Research, 6*(3), 120–126.

Goswami, S., Sarkar, A., & Sengupta, S. (2016). Electrical Power and Energy Measurement Under Non-sinusoidal Condition, in S. L. Sergey, & Y. Yurish (Ed.), *Sensors and Applications in Measuring and Automation Control Systems, 19, pp. 369–382*, International Frequency Sensor Association (IFSA) Publishing, Retrieved from http://www.sensorsportal.com/HTML/BOOKSTORE/Advance_in_Sensors_Vol_4.htm

Islam, M., Mohammadpour, H. A., Ghaderi, A., Brice, C. W., & Shin, Y. J. (2014). Time-frequency-based instantaneous power components for transient disturbances according to IEEE standard 1459. *IEEE Transactions on Power Delivery, 30*(3), 1288–1297. doi:10.1109/TPWRD.2014.2361203

Langella, R., & Testa, A. (2010). IEEE standard definitions for the measurement of electric power quantities under sinusoidal, non sinusoidal, balanced, or unbalanced conditions, IEEE Standard 1459-2010.

Li, H. B., Huang, T. Z., Zhang, Y., Liu, X. P., & Gu, T. X. (2011). Chebyshev-type methods and preconditioning techniques. *Applied Mathematics and Computation, 218*(2), 260–270. doi:10.1016/j.amc.2011.05.036

Sarkar, A., Choudhury, S. R., & Sengupta, S. (2011). A self-synchronized ADALINE network for on-line tracking of power system harmonics. *Measurement, 44*(4), 784–790. doi:10.1016/j.measurement.2011.01.009

Sarkar, A., & Sengupta, S. (2009). On-line tracking of single-phase reactive power in non-sinusoidal conditions using S-ADALINE networks. *Measurement, 42*(4), 559–569. doi:10.1016/j.measurement.2008.10.001

Srividyadevi, P., Pusphalatha, D. V., & Sharma, P. M. (2013). Measurement of power and energy using arduino. *Research Journal of Engineering Sciences, 2278*, 9472.

Su, T., Yang, M., Jin, T., & Flesch, R. C. C. (2018). Power harmonic and interharmonic detection method in renewable power based on Nuttall double-window all-phase FFT algorithm. *IET Renewable Power Generation, 12*(8), 953–961. doi:10.1049/iet-rpg.2017.0115

Terzija, V. V., Stanojevic, V., Popov, M., & Van der Sluis, L. (2007). Digital metering of power components according to IEEE standard 1459-2000 using the Newton-type algorithm. *IEEE Transactions on Instrumentation and Measurement, 56*(6), 2717–2724. doi:10.1109/TIM.2007.908235

# Chapter 6
# Characteristics of Ionic Polymer Metal Composite (IPMC) as EMG Sensor

**Srijan Bhattacharya**
iD https://orcid.org/0000-0002-5405-2231
*RCC Institute of Information Technology, India*

**Suvojit Sinha**
iD https://orcid.org/0000-0001-9266-0812
*RCC Institute of Information Technology, India*

**Satwik Halder**
*RCC Institute of Information Technology, India*

**Saheli Banerjee**
*RCC Institute of Information Technology, India*

**Ankana Sadhu**
*RCC Institute of Information Technology, India*

**Sankita Kundu**
*RCC Institute of Information Technology, India*

**Saurav Banerjee**
*RCC Institute of Information Technology, India*

**Bikash Bepari**
*Haldia Institute of Technology, India*

**Subhasis Bhaumik**
*Indian Institute of Engineering Science and Technology, India*

## ABSTRACT

*The following chapter is a comparative study of signals obtained using Electromyogram sensors and Ionic Polymer Metal Composite (IPMC) sensors. This chapter studies in detail the behavior of the electromechanical sensor, i.e., IPMC as an EMG sensor. The former being an electromechanical sensor picks up the electrochemical gradient due to flow of ions through the axon ends released within the muscle which ultimately causes the muscle contraction, and also detects the mechanical tension created because of muscle contraction. EMG sensors are an electrical sensor that is able to detect voltage changes due to electrochemical changes under our skin due to voluntary muscle movements. During the relaxed phase, both the sensors stay stagnant at different reference voltage levels, and shows variation in voltages only during the instants of contraction. The characteristic obtained by plotting the experimental readings are compared in the chapter.*

DOI: 10.4018/978-1-7998-2584-5.ch006

## INTRODUCTION

IPMC is becoming a suitable popular material among engineers and scientists because of its inherent characteristics of low activation voltage, large bending strain, which can be used as both sensors and actuators. Ionic polymer-metal composites are composed of a per- fluorinated ionomer membrane usually Nafion® or Flemion® plated on both faces with a noble metal such as gold or platinum or nickel and neutralized with a certain quantity of counter ions that provide equity for the electrical charge of anions that are covalently fixed to the backbone ionomer (Sai Nemat Nasser,2006) Ionic polymer-metal composite (IPMC) sensors typically are in the shape of beams, and only provide response to stimuli acting perpendicular to the beam plane (Hong Lei, 2016). For a better review of IPMC as electromechanical sensor, the charge current generation mechanisms due to external pressure in both compression and shear modes can be observed and identified using streaming potential hypothesis. Ionic polymer metal composite (IPMC) has high potential as an artificial muscle which can be driven by a low voltage range between -3 to +3 V. During actuation of an IPMC, an EMG signal can be measured in electric potential which is produced by voluntary contraction of muscle fiber (Mohammad Gudarzi, 2017). The electrolyte that flows in the channels are oriented in different directions within the IPMC, the EDL formed on the metallic phase of the electrode is distributed which results generation of streaming potential. Moreover, the sensing signal is generated in the electrode region. IPMC is similar to piezoelectric sensors which generates potential which is proportional to the applied force (R. K Jain, 2010). The performance of IPMC depends on its dimensions and also the electrode plating[6]whether it is nickel, gold or platinum (Kiwon Park, 2013). IPMC is an EAP material that bends in response to an electrical activation and because of the price efficiency and open-loop control, ionic polymer-metal composite (IPMC) actuators is one of the prime attractions in several biomedical and robotic applications. It is a soft and nontoxic hydrophilic material, making it eligible for application in medical domain. Previously, IPMC Sensor has shown satisfactory results for finger movements, acquiring senses from neural damaged areas. The biggest advantage to this sensor is, it does not require any external source to work and can be moulded in a simple mechanical structure (Narihiro, 2006). Distributed actuation found in animal muscular systems is one of the main reasons of flexibility, high efficiency, and large energy density (Qingsong, 2018). Thus, the biomimetic actuators or artificial muscles with large displacements have drawn great attention in research and industrial application development. The research work in artificial muscle field, exhibiting the mathematical analysis of a muscle, the software simulation, the comparative study with the natural muscles is implemented[11] (Mirna, 2014). Electromyography (EMG) is a process to measure the electric voltage generated due to muscle contraction (Amrutha, 2017). EMG signals can be recorded from muscle using either by intra-muscular EMG (highly accurate detail at muscle fiber level) or surface EMG (basic characteristics i.e. amplitude and shape). Amplitude of surface EMG signals are very low and are easily influenced by external noise, thus to reduce external influences differential configuration is used where the noise is cancelled to some extent owing to the high CMRR of instrumentational amplifier (Beneteau, 2014). Physical signal namely electromyography and skin conductance can be taken into effect[13]for measuring muscle activity and at the same time can be correlated with the precise measuring instrumentation applications (Arturo). Moreover, the working of the EMG which is mainly controlled by the nervous system depends on the muscle physiological properties, which can be further extended and can be correlated with the properties of the IPMC. Primarily the EMG signals are procured from the electrodes directly over the skin, then the signal consisting of all the muscle fiber action potential from underneath the skin, but it fail to detect highly precise values or data coming from the muscle fiber itself, which can be overcome by implementing IPMC sensor and using amplifiers along with it which will be discussed further in this paper (Reaz, 2006; Ambily,2017).Moreover, if compared with IPMC, the EMG sensor are meant to record the electrical signals that emanate the body muscles, and in extension to that IPMC records the electrical manifestation of neuromuscular activation that is being generated during muscle contraction and relaxation (Raut, 2015). Furthermore in detail study it was found that, many muscles can go through several abnormalities such as inflammation of muscle which are quite capable of interrupting the normal output of the EMG Sensor and also can damage it (Hemu, 2015). EMG is an electrical discloser of neuromuscular activation which allows making different physiological process to develop force(Angkoon, 2009). But, they are very sensitive to noise, so a significant quite[15] place is required to work with them (Jonghwa, 2008). So, EMG's are used, for the examination of the nervous system and to measure the electrical pulse signals, some of its tests includes nerve conduction studies, and muscle needle examination (Mohammad, 2010). After processing of Electromyogram signals it can be used for control signal for a robotic arm (Chris, 2008).Mechanomyography is a method for logging and predicting mechanical activity in the muscle that is contracting (Waqas, 2009). Ionic polymer metal composites (IPMCs) are advanced resources fitting to the grade of ionic electroactive polymers (Barbar, 2004). Low actuation bandwidth of these materials is due to low speed of sound.

## BASIC ARCHITECTURE

The authors obtain output voltages from the instrumentational amplifier that is used to amplify the input voltage from the EMG sensor. The current to voltage converter is used to amplify and stabilize the output voltage from the IPMC. Both the output voltages are fed into the LabView software as input and the waveform is observed and the data is collected for a full resolution of +/-10V (Fig. 1)

*Figure 1. Basic architecture of the setup used*

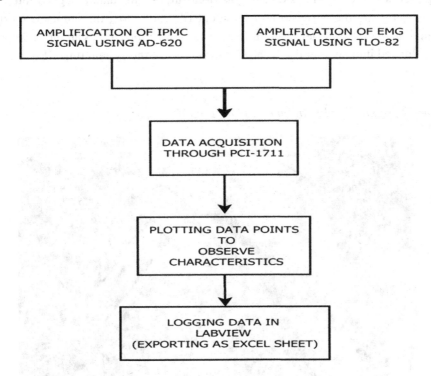

## Experimental Setup

The subject contracts his muscle. The analog circuits for amplification of the sensor voltages are shown in the above Figure 2.Three electrodes of the Electromyogram sensor has been used, Two, on the bicep muscles for differential input voltage into the instrumentational amplifier, and one on the elbow as the reference potential. The IPMC is place on the bicep muscle, the same area where the EMG electrodes are placed, and the voltage generated due to the pressure and the electrochemical change created due to voluntary muscle activity has been fed into the current to voltage converter circuit. The given circuit also assists to amplify the voltage which is inputted into the PCI-1711 data acquisition card and the data is logged into the excel sheet using the Write to Measurement file. Similarly, the output from the instrumentational amplifier is fed into the data acquisition card as an input and the data is logged into another excel sheet with respect to the system time. (Figure 2)

*Figure 2. Signal Amplification and Data Loging*

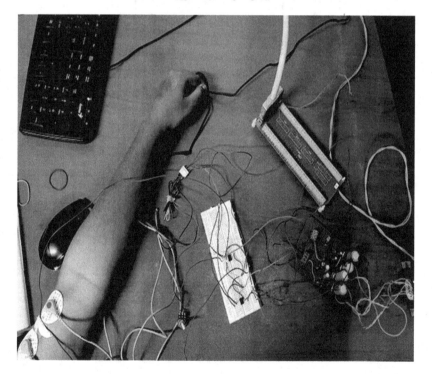

*Figure 3. Lab-view circuit setup*

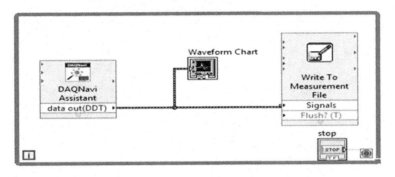

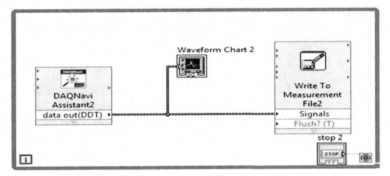

Data Acquisition tool is used to retrieve the data from the respective sensors. The Write to Measurement File tool has been implemented to log the data into an excel files sheet. The waveform chart has been employed to observe the signal being generated from the sensors. Two circuits have been drawn for both the sensors (EMG and IPMC) and inserted within an infinite while loop (Fig. 3). "Write to Measurement File" tool of Lab View 2015, was used for data logging for both EMG sensor and IPMC sensor. Also, it is observed a distinct similarity between the characteristics of the two sensors for the working interval and also for the instants when both the sensors remain ideal. The next set of observations is taken with greater amplitude gain and shows complete stagnant behavior during the period of no muscle activity. Just when the subject contracts his muscles, both the sensors show exact similar characteristic changes.

*Figure 4. Characteristics analysis of EMG and IPMC signals*

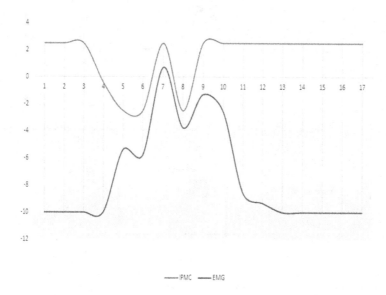

Characteristics Analysis of EMG and IPMC signals

In Fig. 4 the IPMC signal changes from 2.498V as per data and EMG signal rises from -10V which are set as standard. As the contraction is provided both the sensors show very similar behavior. The points (1-4) were in relaxed state and points (5-10) was the period of time during which muscle activity was provided by the subject, after that again relaxed conditions was given. Since EMG is more sensitive than IPMC it takes time to return to the constant voltage of -10V unlike IPMC which immediately returns to the constant voltage of 2.498V.

The authors observe the characteristics in Fig. 5, that when the relaxed condition was provided i.e. from points (1-4) they show constant voltages of 2.4987V (IPMC) and -10V (EMG). For points (5-10) a contraction was provided by the subject and a series of peak was observed for both the cases. Again, the subject provides no muscle activity i.e. points (10-18) and the authors observe similar pattern as points (1-4). For points (19-43) continuous contraction -relaxation and again contraction was provided by the subject. The points 22 and 34 were observed to be of inverted characteristics and the contradictory behavior is assumed to be due to noise in either of the circuits

*Figure 5. Characteristics analysis of EMG and IPMC signals*

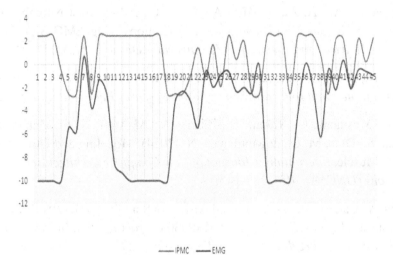

## CONCLUSION

The characteristics obtained from IPMC were found to be analogous to that obtained from EMG electrode. Thus, it can be inferred from the above observation that IPMC, here, behaves as a sensor thus detecting the electrochemical signal produced during muscle movement. The different magnitude of voltage generated due to varying amount of applied pressure is detected by the IPMC strip. The amplified output generates the characteristics showing the different extent to which muscle has contracted. Since here it behaves as a pressure sensor, the magnitude and pattern of the characteristics can be further studied individually for different objects. This application of IPMC can also be put into use along with machine learning to detect various neuromuscular diseases.

## ACKNOWLEDGMENT

The authors thankfully acknowledges the financial support provided by The Institution of Engineers (India) for carrying out Research & Development work in this subject

# REFERENCES

Akle, B., & Leo, D. J. (2004). Electromechanical transduction in multilayer ionic transducers. *Institute of Physics Publishing Smart Materials and Structures, 13*(5), 1081–1089. doi:10.1088/0964-1726/13/5/014

Al-Faiz, M. Z., Ali, A. A., & Miry, A. H. (2010). A k-Nearest Neighbor Based Algorithm for Human Arm Movements Recognition Using EMG Signals, Iraq. *Journal of Electrical and Electronics Engineering (Oradea), 6*(2), 158–166.

Amrutha, N., & Arul, V. H. (2017). A Review On Noises in EMG Signal and its Removal. *International Journal of Scientific and Research Publications, 7*(5), 23–27.

Atieh, M., Mustapha, O., Tahini, H., Zibara, A., Al Awar, N. F., Marak, R. A., Eljammal, S., Diab, M. O., & Moubayed, N. (2014). Modeling and Utilization Of An IPMC Muscle, *International Journal of New Computer Architectures and their Applications (IJNCAA), 4*(3), 137-145.

Beneteau, A., Caterina, G. D., Petropoulakis, L., & Soraghan, J. J. (2014). Low-cost wireless surface EMG sensor using the MSP430 microcontroller, In *Proceedings of the 6th European Embedded Design in Education and Research,* 264-268.

Bonomo, C., Fortuna, L., Giannone, P., & Graziani, S. (2005). A method to characterize the deformation of an IPMC sensing membrane. *Sensors and Actuators. A, Physical, 123–124*, 146–154. doi:10.1016/j.sna.2005.03.012

Farooq, H., & Sharma, S. (2015). A Review paper on EMG Signal and its Classification Techniques. *International Journal of Emerging Research Management & Technology, 4*(4).

Francis, A., Mohan, N., & Roy, R. (2017). Multi-Tasking EMG Controlled Robotic Arm. *International Journal of Advanced Research in Computer and Communication Engineering, 6*(4), 108–111.

Gudarzi, M., Smolinski, P., & Wang, Q.-M. (2017). Compression and shear mode ionic polymer-metal composite (IPMC) pressure sensors, *Sensors and Actuators A 260,* Elsevier, 99–111.

He, Q., Vokoun, D., & Shen, Q. (2018). Biomimetic Actuation and Artificial Muscle Applied Bionics and Biomechanics Volume. *Article ID, 4617460*, 1–2.

Park, K., Lee, B., Kim, H. M., Choi, K. S., Hwang, G., Byun, G. S., & Lee, H. K. (2013). IPMC Based Biosensor for the Detection of Biceps Brachii Muscle Movements. *International Journal of Electrochemical Science,* (8), 4098–4109.

Jain, R. K., Datta, S., Majumder, S., Mukherjee, S., Sadhu, D., Samanta, S., & Banerjee, K. (2010). Bio-mimetic Behaviour of IPMC Artificial Muscle Using EMG Signal, In *Proceedings International Conference on Advances in Recent Technologies in Communication and Computing*, 186-190. 10.1109/ARTCom.2010.49

Kamamichi, N., Yamakita, M., Asaka, K., & Luo, Z.-W. (2006). A Snake-like Swimming Robot Using IPMC Actuator/Sensor, In *Proceedings of the IEEE International Conference on Robotics and Automation*, pp. 1812-1817, Orlando, FL.

Kim, J., Mastnik, S., & André, E. (2008). EMG-based Hand Gesture Recognition for Realtime Biosignal Interfacing, In *IUI '08 Proceedings of the 13th International Conference on Intelligent User Interfaces*, 30-39.

Lughmani, W. A., Jho, J. Y., Lee, J. Y., & Rhee, K. (2009). Modeling of Bending Behavior of IPMC Beams Using Concentrated Ion Boundary Layer. *International Journal of Precision Engineering and Management, 10*(5), 131–139. doi:10.100712541-009-0104-2

Murphy, C., Campbell, N., Caulfield, B., & Ward, T. (2008). Micro electro-mechanical, systems-based sensor for mechanomyography, In 19th International Conference BIOSIGNAL, Brno, Czech Republic.

Nakasone, A., Prendinger, H., & Ishizuka, M. (2005, September). Emotion recognition from electromyography and skin conductance. In *Proc. of the 5th International Workshop on Biosignal Interpretation* (pp. 219-222), Retrieved from http://www.miv.t.u-tokyo.ac.jp/papers/arturo-BSI-05.pdf,1-4

Nasser, S., Zamani, S., & Tor, Y. (2006). Effect of solvents on the chemical and physical properties of ionic polymer-metal composites. *Journal of Applied Physics, 99,* pp. 104902-1 to 104902-17.

Phinyomark, A., Limsakul, C., & Phukpattaranont, P. (2009). A Novel Feature Extraction for Robust EMG Pattern Recognition. *Journal of Computers, 1*(1), 71–80.

Raut, R., & Gurjar, A. A. (2015). Bio-Medical (EMG) Signal Analysis and Feature Extraction using Wavelet Transform, *Journal of Engineering Research and Application,* 17-19.

Reaz, M. B. I., Hussain, M. S., & Yasin, F. M. (2006). Techniques of EMG signal analysis: Detection, processing, classification, and applications. *Biological Procedures Online, 8*(1), 11–35. doi:10.1251/bpo115 PMID:16799694

# Chapter 7
# Electronic Tongue for Tea Quality Assessment:
## Advanced Signal Processing Techniques for Estimation of Thearubigin and Theaflavin

**Pradip Saha**
*Heritage Institute of Technology, India*

**Bipan Tudu**
*Jadavpur University, India*

**Santanu Ghorai**
iD https://orcid.org/0000-0003-0301-4849
*Heritage Institute of Technology, India*

**Rajib Bandyopadhyay**
iD https://orcid.org/0000-0003-1655-9899
*Jadavpur University, India*

**Nabarun Bhattacharyya**
*Centre for the Development of Advanced Computing, Kolkata, India*

## ABSTRACT

*Biochemical means of tea quality evaluation is quite accurate, but it requires very costly instruments and takes a long time to conduct the experiment. Researches show that thearubigin (TR) and theaflavin (TF) are the two most important biochemical compounds present in tea liquor on which liquor characteristics of black CTC tea depends. Consequently, this fact may be the basis of determining tea quality by assessment of TR and TF via electronic tongue (ET) response. This technique is free from subjective factors. In literature, there are only two research works using this technique so more research work is required to address the problem. This chapter proposes a modeling technique of ET response using sparse decomposition technique to estimate TR and TF content in a given tea sample. For each tea sample, sparse model coefficients obtained from the ET response is considered as a characteristic attribute of it. Experimental results using dissimilar regression models show high prediction accuracies which justify the efficacy of the proposed method.*

DOI: 10.4018/978-1-7998-2584-5.ch007

chemical transformations during the processing stages. Finished tea is manufactured from tea leaves in such a way so that it can preserve liquor characteristic. There are various stages of tea processing, such as plucking, withering, cut-tear-curl, fermentation or oxidation, etc. Among these, the most crucial phase is fermentation as proper fermentation of tea leafs can enhance the taste and aroma of finished tea. Thearubigin (TR) and theaflavin (TF) (Robertson, 1992; Mahanta, 1988) are two such compounds produced during the fermentation stage where enzymic oxidation occurs with the presence of two enzymes such as polyphenol oxidase (PPO) and peroxidise (PO). TF comprises of about 0.5–2% of dry weight whereas TR constitutes about 6–18% of dry weight depending on the tea processing parameters such as temperature, pH, humidity, etc. TR and TF are mostly responsible for two important taste characteristics of tea liquor such as, strength and briskness (Robertson, 1992; Mahanta, 1988;Robertson, 1983). Table 1 represents some important biochemical compounds and their contribution to the taste of tea. The presence of TR imparts liquor color and thickness (mouth feel sensation) while TF contributes to the brightness and briskness of the tea liquor (Robertson, 1983). In (Ngurea, Wanyokob, Mahungua, &Mahungua, 2009; Obandaa, Owuora, Mang'okab, &Kavoi, 2004), human tasters and spectrophotometric analysis confirmed that TR amount improves mouth-feel sensation but degrades the liquor color and taste while TF content improves liquor brightness.

A number of research studies (Ngurea et al., 2009; Obandaa et al., 2004; Wright, Mphangwe, Nyirenda, & Apostolides, 2002; Hazarika et al., 2002) validate that contribution of TR and TF, in the midst of a number of bio-chemical compounds, is the most towards the finished tea qualities, such as briskness, brightness, strength and mouth-feel perception. Thus, prediction of TR and TF content can be the basis of tea quality assessment. For this purpose, bio-chemical method can be used to estimate the contents of TR and TF using spectrophotometry, high performance liquid chromatography, and gas chromatography, etc. Though this method is very accurate, but at the same time very expensive regarding to time and cost, and requires expert man power. On the other hand, quality evaluation of tea can also be carried out by the organoleptic senses of human "Tasters Panel". As humans are involved in this method, it is highly biased and thus, the method has limited accuracy as well as less reproducibility. In view of the above difficulties of biochemical and organoleptic methods, usage of artificial gadgets like electronic nose (Dutta, Kashwan, Bhuyan, Hines, & Gardner, 2003; Bhattacharyya et al., 2008; Baietto, & Wilson,

*Table 1. Biochemical constituent in black tea*

| Compounds | Taste |
|---|---|
| Theaflavin | Astringent |
| Thearubigin | Ashy and slight astringent |
| Polyphenol | Astringent |
| Amino acids | Brothy |
| Caffeine | Bitter |

2015; Wilson, 2013) and electronic tongue (Palit et al., 2010; Saha, Ghorai, Tudu, Bandyopadhyay, & Bhattacharyya, 2014; Saha, Ghorai, Tudu, Bandyopadhyay, & Bhattacharyya,2016) has increased in recent years for tea quality assessment. These instruments are calibrated by establishing a correlation between its outputs and grades of tea allotted by human tea analysts. Thus, this method is not totally free from human intervention. With the intension of making this device free from human involvement, an alternative methodology is to build association between ET signal and the responsible constituents, such as TR and TF, for the taste of tea measured by bio-chemical technique. Assessment of tea grades by this approach may be considered as highly efficient as in this application there is no score provided by human being as well as it eliminates the use of expensive biochemical instruments and saves large time to conduct the experiment. The main challenge in this technique is the processing of high-dimensional ET signal to extract relevant features for establishing correlation with the TR and TF concentrations.

## BACKGROUND

Almost a decade ago researchers have started investigation about the role of bio-chemical constituents that are responsible for different tea taste. However, most of the techniques follow bio-chemical means. Extraction of TF and TR using high performance liquid chromatography was proposed by Robertson & Bendall, 1983. Hall & Robertso, (1988) employed NIR spectroscopy for estimation of the constituent TF. In (Degenhardt, Engelhardt, Wendt, & Winterhalter, 2000; Degenhardt, Engelhardt, Lakenbrink, & Winterhalter, 2000; Wang et al., 2008), TR, TF and catechins were separated using high speed countercurrent chromatography. In (Zabadaj et al., 2017), a hybrid ET (hET) coupled with PLS analysis was compared with HPLC coupled with PLS method for the monitoring of yeast fermentation where hET-PLS performs better than HPLC-PLS method. Nandy-Chatterjee et al. (2017) proposed molecular imprinted polymer electrode for detecting total TF in tea samples using cyclic voltammetry and differential pulse voltammetry where they obtained a prediction accuracy of 94%. From literature survey, it is clear that most of the methods proposed are based on estimation of the contents of TR and TF using expensive analytical apparatuses which take time to conduct experiment and the process is quite complicated too. Ghosh et al. (2012) succeeded to determine TF and TR with the help of voltammetric type ET using 6th level discrete wavelet transform (DWT) coefficients with Haar wavelet. Saha et al. (2017) proposed a regression framework for tea quality assessment by which they estimated TF and TR concentrations in tea samples using voltammetric ET signals. To accomplish this, fusion of singular value decomposition (SVD) based feature, discrete cosine transform (DCT) based feature, and features using Stockwell transform (ST) was employed for improved performance. This method is complex and time consuming to test a tea sample as it requires a trained regression model based on the fusion of three different features and still there are possibilities to improve the accuracy.

## CONTRIBUTION TO THE CHAPTER

Previous literature survey shows that there are only two research works, Ghosh et al., 2012, and Saha et al., 2017, on estimation TF and TR concentrations of black tea with the analysis of ET output. This fact motivated the authors to explore suitable methods to address this problem. Two previous methods employed mainly DWT and combination of DCT, Stockwell transform (ST) and SVD for feature extraction along with regression algorithms like SVR, PLSR, ANN, VVRKFA, etc. All of these methods were used mainly to reduce the dimensionality of the ET response. However, there is no such attempt of ET signal to address the problem. In this chapter, the authors have addressed the problem by modeling the ET signal dynamics using sparse modeling technique (Chen & Donoho, 1999; Donoho et al.,2006; Candès, Romberg, & Tao, 2006). Each of the ET response is approximated by a sparse linear combination of non-orthogonal basis vectors. The goal is to represent each ET signal in a composite manner with smallest set of atoms from a learned dictionary. This model has advantages, like it is very robust to redundancy and noise since it selects very few among all of the basis vectors. This fact motivated the authors to investigate its usefulness for tea quality estimation. The objectives of this research work are as follows:

1.    To establish the effectiveness of the sparse model coefficients as characteristic features for estimating TR and TF content in tea samples by three different regressors, namely artificial neural network (ANN), support vector regression (SVR) and vector valued regularized kernel function approximation (VVRKFA).
2.    To explore the consequences of dictionary size and sparsity variation on prediction accuracy.

The present model based TR and TF prediction method is very simple, fast and accurate. Effectiveness of the suggested model-based technique for quality estimation of black tea is ensured by very low RMSE in a number of experiments compared to the other two existing methods in literature.

## PROPOSED METHOD

The suggested model-based TR and TF concentration prediction technique of tea samples is illustrated by block diagram in Fig. 1. It has two stages of conducting the experiment- training and testing. During training, TR and TF concentrations are determined by the conventional spectrophotometric analysis and at the same time ET response of these tea samples are recorded. A customary voltametric electronic tongue response is shown in fig.2. Interpretation of TR and TF from ET response is very difficult as it is a mixture of responses of a number of electrodes (Ivarsson, Holmin, Höjer, Krantz-Rülcker, & Winquist, 2001). The signal consists of large number of sampled values and thus the interpretation of TR and TF from it is a demanding task. So, interpretation of ET signal requires proficient methods for a sound addressing of this problem. So, to interpret the ET signal properly, the authors recommend use of sparse modeling techniques to model the dynamics of ET response.

The entire training samples are used to learn the dictionary with normalized columns and the corresponding sparse coefficients are considered as the characteristic features of the corresponding ET signal. Regression model is trained to establish a correlation between these characteristic features and the content of TR, TF and TR/TF ratio of the known tea samples. In order to test an unknown sample, learned dictionary is used to model the test samples with minimum number of dictionary atoms and the corresponding sparse coefficients are used for training of regression model to correlate the signal with the concentration of TR, TF and TR/TF ratio.

*Figure 1. Block diagram representation of the proposed method*

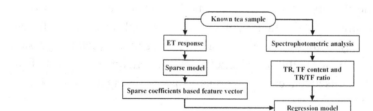

*Figure 2. Typical response of custom-built voltammetric ET.*

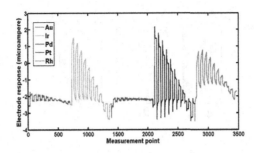

## Feature Extraction Method

### Sparse Model of Signal

Performance of any model-based system depends on how accurately the original signal is being reconstructed. Sparse decomposition is widely used in many signal processing applications such as signal separation, denoising, coding, image inpainting, etc., (Starck, Elad, & Donoho, 2005; Li, Cichocki, & Amari, 2004; Olshausen, Sallee, & Lewicki, 2001; Elad & Aharon, 2006). In the sparse model, a signal is embodied sparsely by combining linearly a least number of atoms or elementary signals from a pre-specified dictionary. Let, a signal be represented as $\phi_i \in \mathbb{R}^p$ and the entire data set $\Phi = (\phi_1, \phi_2, \ldots, \phi_k) \in \mathbb{R}^{p \times k}$. The sparse model can be represented as

$$\Phi = DX \qquad s.t. \ \left\| \Phi - DX \right\|_F \le \varepsilon, \tag{1}$$

where $D = (D_1, D_2, \ldots, D_d) \in \mathbb{R}^{p \times d}$ is a dictionary contains $d$ atoms, $X = (x_1, x_2, \ldots, x_k) \in \mathbb{R}^{d \times k}$ contains the sparse coefficient vectors that represents model coefficients and contains only few nonzero elements, $\varepsilon$ represents maximal allowed representation error and $\left\| \bullet \right\|_F$ is the Frobenius norm. The goal is to find a linear combination of a minimum number of atoms from the dictionary $D$ that is infinitely close to the original signal $\phi$, as explained in the fig. 3. The dictionary $D$ may be over complete (when $d > k$), under complete (when $d < k$) or complete (when $d = k$) (Mallat and Zhang, 1993).

In this application, the second option holds good. The sparse learning tries to find both the dictionary $D$ and sparse coefficient $X$ simultaneously from the given signal matrix $\Phi$. The sparsest solution of $X$ is obtained by minimizing the following objective function:

*Figure 3.Graphical representation of sparse model.*

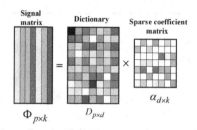

$$\min_{D,X} \left\| \Phi - DX \right\|_F^2 \quad \text{subject to } \forall i, \left\| x_i \right\|_0 \leq n \tag{2}$$

where, $n$ is the sparsity limit. There are many methods to solve the problem (2) as discussed by Zhang, Xu, Yang, Li, & Zhang, 2015. Among them, the well-known methods are OMP (Mallat et al., 1993; Zhang et al., 2015; Tropp & Gilbert, 2007), method of optimal directions (MODs) (Engan, Skretting, & Håkon-Husøy, 2007), and K-SVD (Aharon, Elad, & Bruckstein, 2006; Rubinstein, Peleg, & Elad, 2013), etc. In all these methods, the main purpose is to find the solution of (2) in an efficient way. For example, MOD algorithm (Engan et al., 2007) finds optimal $D$ for a fixed $X$ by minimizing (2) w.r.t. $D$ as

$$\widehat{D} = \text{Arg} \min_D \left\| \Phi - DX \right\|_F^2 = \Phi X^T (XX^T)^{-1} = \Phi X \ . \tag{3}$$

K-SVD method (Aharon, Elad, & Bruckstein, 2006; Aharon et al., 2013) solves this problem in two stages- sparse coding stage that finds optimal $X$ assuming known $D$ and dictionary update stage that update $D$ assuming known values of $X$. In this chapter, the authors have used the improved method to both of these MOD and K-SVD technique suggested by (Smith & Elad, 2013) which solves following problem:

$$\{\widehat{D}, \widehat{X}\} = \text{Arg} \min_{D,X} \left\| \Phi - DX \right\|_F^2 \quad \text{s.t. } X \odot M = 0 \tag{4}$$

where, $M$ is a mask matrix containing zeros and ones and $X \odot M$ is the Schur multiplication between two matrices of the same size. Since (4) is a non-convex problem, MOD approach is followed to solve it by fixing $X$ and minimizing $\left\| \Phi - DX \right\|_F^2$ with respect to $D$ followed by updating $X$ for a fixed $D$ and solving

$$\widehat{X} = \underset{X}{\text{Arg min}} \left\| \Phi - DX \right\|_F^2 \quad \text{s.t. } X \odot M = 0 . \tag{5}$$

A closed form solution of (5) is obtained simply by updating only the supports of each column of $X$ and keeping the zeros unchanged. The obtained sparse coefficient vectors $\widehat{x}$ are taken as the features of the corresponding signals and are used to train a regression model.

## Regression Models

The correlation between TR and TF concentration and the extracted features from sparse model coefficients is established with regression or function approximation models. To ensure the capability of the features for addressing this problem, the authors have employed three regression algorithms, which are described below in brief.

## Support Vector Regression

Support vector machine (SVM) (Vapnik et al., 1998) algorithm is a state of the art binary classification technique that classifies patterns of two classes with maximum margin of separation between them. Support vector regression (SVR) (Smola & Schölkopf, 2004) is based on SVM algorithm (Vapnik et al., 1998) that can be applied for regression or fitting a function. SVR is a widely used efficient technique in many applications for the purpose of fitting data. SVR uses kernel trick to map the training patterns in the feature space where it pursuits a linear hyper surface for fitting nonlinear data set. This surface obtained in the high dimensional space is equivalent to the nonlinear surface in input space. The quadratic objective function (Smola et al., 2004) of SVR consists of an $\varepsilon$ –insensitive loss function and thus SVR allows a minute inaccuracy to fit the patterns during the training process. The trained function obtained by learning process is employed for the prediction of TR, TF or TR/TF ratio of the unknown samples. The details about formulation of SVR may be obtained in (Smola et al., 2004).

## VVRKFA

Vector valued regularized kernel function approximation (VVRKFA) (Ghorai, Mukherjee, & Dutta, 2010; Ghorai, Mukherjee, & Dutta, 2012) is a recently developed algorithm based on the function approximation or regression method. It also uses kernel trick to map all the training samples into feature space whose dimension is equal to the number samples in the training set. A regression function is then fitted to the target values of the corresponding patterns in low dimensional input space using those mapped features. For classification by VVRKFA, the targets are vectors of class labels. In this research work, the authors have used VVRKFA as a regressor with considering the targets as continuous values in one dimension. In practical, content of TR, TF and TR/TF ratio are separately considered as targets. More detail about VVRKFA algorithm may be found in (Ghorai, Mukherjee, & Dutta, 2012).

## ANN

Artificial neural network (ANN) (Haykin et al., 2001) is a well-recognized competent algorithm for classification and regression problems which is based on the empirical risk minimization (ERM) principle, where sum squared error between the predicted and target output is minimized. During the training of NN, the objective is to learn a weight vector $w$ that minimizes the sum squared error and this is usually done by gradient descent procedure. Practically, most of the data sets are not linear and thus multilayer perceptron is used where a number of hidden layers are used in between input and output layer. A multilayer perceptron (MLP) is a feed forward neural network where output of every node is feeding the input to everynode in the next above layer. Each of the nodes in all the layers except input layer employs a nonlinear function. A sigmoid function is considered among the different types of activation function as it is not only differentiable but its differentiation is of very simple. The details about the formulation of this method may be obtained in (Haykin et al., 2001).

## EXPERIMENTAL SETUP

The authors have performed experimentation with 46 different kinds of black tea. Some of these tea samples were collected during April-May and rest during September-October season by Tea Research Association, Tocklai, India. These tea samples were treated with optimized processing parameters by a controlled environmental atmosphere. Thus, there will be a proper variation of TR and TF content among all the samples. Spectrophotometric analysis was carried out to evaluate the actual content of TR or TF of the tea samples.

### TR and TF Prediction by Spectrophotometry

The authors prepared tea liquor of each sample for determining TR and TF concentration by spectrophotometric analysis (Saha et al., 2017). To prepare liquor of a tea sample 6 g of tea leaves is soaked in 250 ml boiling water and kept it for ten minutes in a covered thermos. The combination is then passed through a filter to obtain the liquor only and brought it at room temperature. 6 ml of this filtered liquor is then mixed with equal volume of 1% (w/v) di-sodium hydrogen phosphate and 10 ml of ethyl acetate. The mixture is brewed suitably for one minute. By draining out the heavy layer from this blend only the left over is which contains mainly TR and TF. The collected mixture is dissolved in 5 ml of ethyl acetate.

Finally, this ethyl acetate combination is used to prepare both sample solutions and reference solutions which are required for spectrophotometric analysis. Absorbance data for reference solution and sample solution were collected separately from spectrophotometer where collected absorbance data for reference solution is required to set the reference point of the spectrophotometer "Cary 50 Conc. UV-VIS Spectrophotometer". Different steps are followed for the preparation of sample solutions and reference solutions. They are:

**N1:** 10 ml ethyl acetate extract mixed with 15 ml methanol.
**N2:** 1 ml water extract of tea sample mixed with 1 ml of 10% (w/v) oxalic acid, 8 ml water and 15 ml methanol.
**M1:** 10 ml ethyl acetate extract mixed with 15 ml methanol.
**M2:** 9 ml water and 1 ml of 10% (w/v) oxalic acid mixed with 15 ml methanol.

The collected absorbance readings from the used spectrophotometer for the prepared sample solutions are:

**R1:** Collected absorbance value using solution N1 at 380 nm with respect to the reference solution M1.
**R2:** Collected absorbance value using solution N2 at 460 nm with respect to the reference solution M2.

Finally, the content of TR and TF of all the tea samples are evaluated by the using following relations (Ullah, Gogoi, & Baruah, 1984):

$$\%TR = 7.06 \times (4R_2 - R_1) \tag{6}$$

$$\%TF = 2.23 \times R_1 \tag{7}$$

Four replicate measurements are made for each tea samples to take into account the uncertainty in the measurement of TR and TF by the spectrophotometer. Average of these four readings is used as the true value of TR and TF content of the corresponding tea sample. The authors have established correlation between

*Figure 4. A picture of the customized ET system used for experiment*

sparse model coefficients and these true values of TR and TF by means of regression algorithms.

## Electronic Tongue Setup

The authors have built up an electronic tongue (ET) in their LAB as shown in fig. 4 for the collection of electronic responses of all the samples.

The detail of the customized ET presented by the authors in (Palit et al., 2010; Ghosh et al., 2012; Saha et al., 2017). Fig. 2 demonstrates a characteristic response of voltammetric ET using LAPV method where 694 sampled values of output from each electrode were captured. In this way, one ET signal contains 3470 sampled values considering five electrodes.

## Preparation of Tea Sample for Electronic Tongue

To prepare tea liquor, 1g dry tea samples is infused in 200 ml de-ionized boiled water. This blend is kept for five minutes and brewed up properly for uniform mixing of tea extract with water. Infused tea leaves are then filtered out from the mixture and collected tea liquor samples is allowed to cool down to 25-28°C (Ghosh et al., 2012). This cooled tea liquor is used as the sample to test by ET for its characteristic response.

## RESULTS AND ANALYSIS

The authors employed a LAPV based voltammetric ET to test 46 different tea samples. The details about all the samples are presented in table 2 (Saha et al., 2017). The contents of TR and TF in the samples are determined by spectrophotometric analysis. Tea samples collected over first season having higher TR and TF content and thus their quality in terms of briskness and brightness is better than that of

*Table 2. Details of collected tea sample*

| Seasons | Number of tea samples | Range of TR content (%) | Range of TF content (%) | Range of quality scores |
|---------|----------------------|------------------------|------------------------|------------------------|
| April-May | 19 | 13.11 -19.67 | 0.77 - 2.67 | 6 - 10 |
| Sept.-Oct. | 27 | 10.1 -15.6 | 0.94 - 1.40 | 5 - 8 |

second season's tea samples. For each of 46 different tea samples, the ET experiment is repeated 38 times. As a result, the experiment is carried on $46 \times 38 = 1748$ signals with the dimension of each signal being 3470.

## Experimental Procedure

Training and testing samples are selected randomly from the total of 1748 samples with a ratio of 7:3. During raining, all the training samples are used to learn the dictionary with normalized columns using K-SVD method and the coefficient vectors are used to develop three regression models with respect to spectrophotometric TR, TF and TR/TF values of all the training samples. The learned dictionary is used to model each test samples with minimum number of dictionary atoms and the corresponding coefficient vectors are considered as feature vectors for prediction of TR, TF, and TR/TF ratio by the trained regression model. The dictionary size $d$ is varied between 10 and 50 with 10 incremental steps and sparsity is varied from 50% to 90% with 10% incremental steps. For example, if it is consider a sparse model to represent the response of ET system with sparsity 60% and dictionary size 10, the feature vector dimension will be 10 among which there are 4 non-zero model coefficients as shown in fig. 5(a), while fig. 5(b) shows how closely the proposed sparse model with sparsity 60% and dictionary size 10 can represent the ET response for a test sample. The observed RMSE of the reconstructed ET signal is obtained as $4.83 \times 10^{-4}$ by the above specified sparse model for LAPV data. The efficacy of the suggested technique is evaluated using SVR, VVRKFA and artificial ANN. VVRKFA and SVR algorithms are implemented by using a Gaussian kernel. ANN model is realized by a three layer network consisting of an input layer, one hidden layer and an output layer. These layers contain neurons same as the number of features, ten and one, respectively. Initially, weights of all neurons in the ANN model are selected randomly. For SVR and VVRKFA models, the optimum Gaussian kernel and regularization parameters are selected from the sets. $\{10^i \mid i = -9, -8, ...., 8, 9\}$ and $\{2^i \mid i = -10, -9, ..., 9, 10\}$, respectively, by tuning method with the division of training data into training and tuning in 4:1 ratio. Final model is trained with selected optimal parameters considering entire training set while evaluation of performance

*Figure 5. Learned sparse model with (a) model coefficients and (b) original Vs. predicted response for a test sample*

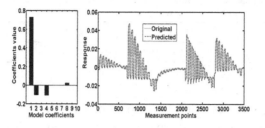

is carried out on test set. The authors have conducted the experiments fifty times with permuting the data randomly and average of the results are reported along with standard deviations.

## Experimental Results

Experimental results of the proposed sparse model with varying dictionary size and sparsity on LAPV data set is shown in table 3. This table demonstrates performances of three different regression techniques for five different dictionary sizes starting from 10 for the prediction of concentration of TR, TF, and TR/TF ratio in tea samples using proposed method. From table 3, it is observed that all the three learning methods provide very low RMSE using the coefficients of all forms of sparse model. Thus, the proposed method is extremely competent to address the prediction problem.

*Table 3. Model performance (RMSE) for different dictionary size and sparsityon LAPV data set*

| Dictionary size | Sparsity (%) | Average percentage of RMSE (± Standard deviation) | | | | | | | | |
|---|---|---|---|---|---|---|---|---|---|---|
| | | TF | | | TR | | | TR by TF | | |
| | | SVR | VVRKFA | ANN | SVR | VVRKFA | ANN | SVR | VVRKFA | ANN |
| 10 | 50 | 0.16 (0.02)) | 0.75 (0.06) | 0.58 (0.07) | 0.14 (0.05) | 0.57 (0.06) | 0.24 (0.02) | 0.21 (0.02) | 0.72 (0.06) | 0.61 (0.07) |
| | 60 | **0.15** (0.04) | 0.77 (0.07) | 0.58 (0.05) | 0.13 (0.06) | 0.71 (0.08) | 0.24 (0.03) | 0.20 (0.04) | 0.85 (0.07) | 0.60 (0.04) |
| | 70 | 0.16 (0.02) | 0.79 (0.09) | 0.58 (0.07) | 0.14 (0.03) | 0.72 (0.06) | 0.25 (0.02) | 0.22 (0.03) | 0.86 (0.07) | 0.62 (0.06) |
| | 80 | 0.20 (0.03) | 0.56 (0.07) | 0.59 (0.06) | 0.16 (0.07) | 0.47 (0.06) | 0.24 (0.02) | 0.31 (0.05) | 0.66 (0.05) | 0.62 (0.08) |
| | 90 | 0.29 (0.06) | 0.61 (0.05) | 0.60 (0.07) | 0.20 (0.06) | 0.56 (0.07) | 0.23 (0.03) | 0.43 (0.06) | 0.71 (0.09) | 0.59 (0.07) |

*continues on following page*

## Table 3. Continued

| Dictionary size | Sparsity (%) | Average percentage of RMSE (± Standard deviation) | | | | | | | | |
|---|---|---|---|---|---|---|---|---|---|---|
| | | TF | | | TR | | | TR by TF | | |
| | | SVR | VVRKFA | ANN | SVR | VVRKFA | ANN | SVR | VVRKFA | ANN |
| 20 | 50 | 0.22 (0.02) | 0.78 (0.04) | 0.58 (0.03) | 0.14 (0.03) | 0.70 (0.08) | 0.25 (0.04) | 0.23 (0.05) | 0.86 (0.08) | 0.60 (0.05) |
| | 60 | 0.20 (0.07) | 0.56 (0.07) | 0.55 (0.04) | **0.12** (0.04) | 0.46 (0.03) | 0.25 (0.05) | 0.20 (0.04) | 0.64 (0.07) | 0.60 (0.04) |
| | 70 | 0.18 (0.04) | 0.54 (0.08) | 0.58 (0.07) | 0.14 (0.03) | 0.44 (0.06) | 0.24 (0.03) | 0.21 (0.03) | 0.63 (0.05) | 0.61 (0.08) |
| | 80 | 0.16 (0.02) | 0.66 (0.07) | 0.60 (0.08) | 0.13 (0.05) | 0.59 (0.07) | 0.22 (0.04) | **0.17** (0.05) | 0.75 (0.06) | 0.60 (0.07) |
| | 90 | 0.17 (0.02) | 0.74 (0.09) | 0.61 (0.07) | 0.15 (0.08) | 0.68 (0.08) | 0.25 (0.03) | 0.25 (0.08) | 0.84 (0.07) | 0.59 (0.06) |
| 30 | 50 | 0.27 (0.04) | 0.53 (0.06) | 0.57 (0.03) | 0.14 (0.07) | 0.41 (0.06) | 0.23 (0.03) | 0.27 (0.02) | 0.67 (0.04) | 0.58 (0.05) |
| | 60 | 0.26 (0.05) | 0.73 (0.07) | 0.59 (0.04) | 0.14 (0.03) | 0.65 (0.07) | 0.24 (0.04) | 0.25 (0.04) | 0.77 (0.05) | 0.59 (0.04) |
| | 70 | 0.25 (0.04) | 1.27 (0.08) | 0.58 (0.07) | 0.14 (0.05) | 1.25 (0.08) | 0.25 (0.05) | 0.27 (0.03) | 1.29 (0.09) | 0.60 (0.03) |
| | 80 | 0.20 (0.07) | 0.70 (0.07) | 0.58 (0.08) | 0.13 (0.02) | 0.61 (0.08) | 0.24 (0.03) | 0.21 (0.02) | 0.77 (0.08) | 0.61 (0.04) |
| | 90 | 0.18 (0.04) | 0.53 (0.08) | 0.59 (0.06) | 0.14 (0.03) | 0.43 (0.06) | 0.21 (0.02) | 0.22 (0.02) | 0.61 (0.05) | 0.57 (0.04) |
| 40 | 50 | 0.32 (0.07) | 0.83 (0.07) | 0.57 (0.06) | 0.16 (0.06) | 0.79 (0.09) | 0.26 (0.04) | 0.31 (0.05) | 0.92 (0.07) | 0.64 (0.05) |
| | 60 | 0.32 (0.05) | 0.44 (0.06) | 0.59 (0.07) | 0.15 (0.06) | 0.32 (0.05) | 0.25 (0.02) | 0.30 (0.04) | 0.54 (0.03) | 0.62 (0.07) |
| | 70 | 0.27 (0.04) | 0.72 (0.09) | 0.60 (0.09) | 0.15 (0.07) | 0.65 (0.08) | 0.23 (0.03) | 0.27 (0.02) | 0.78 (0.06) | 0.59 (0.06) |
| | 80 | 0.22 (0.04) | 0.63 (0.07) | 0.62 (0.08) | 0.13 (0.03) | 0.53 (0.06) | 0.24 (0.02) | 0.22 (0.01) | 0.70 (0.05) | 0.59 (0.06) |
| | 90 | 0.17 (0.03) | 0.52 (0.06) | 0.60 (0.07) | 0.13 (0.02) | 0.42 (0.06) | 0.25 (0.04) | 0.18 (0.02) | 0.60 (0.04) | 0.59 (0.04) |
| 50 | 50 | 0.36 (0.02) | 0.56 (0.07) | 0.58 (0.06) | 0.16 (0.03) | 0.47 (0.05) | 0.24 (0.03) | 0.34 (0.07) | 0.65 (0.04) | 0.61 (0.07) |
| | 60 | 0.34 (0.07) | 0.71 (0.08) | 0.58 (0.07) | 0.16 (0.05) | 0.62 (0.06) | 0.23 (0.02) | 0.35 (0.05) | 0.79 (0.05) | 0.60 (0.05) |
| | 70 | 0.35 (0.05) | 0.75 (0.06) | 0.58 (0.04) | 0.16 (0.04) | 0.68 (0.07) | 0.23 (0.03) | 0.33 (0.05) | 0.82 (0.09) | 0.69 (0.04) |
| | 80 | 0.30 (0.06) | 0.59 (0.07) | 0.59 (0.08) | 0.15 (0.02) | 0.650 (0.06) | 0.24 (0.03) | 0.29 (0.04) | 0.69 (0.05) | 0.60 (0.07) |
| | 90 | 0.35 (0.07) | 0.66 (0.08) | 0.61 (0.07) | 0.16 (0.03) | 0.66 (0.08) | 0.25 (0.02) | 0.29 (0.02) | 0.75 (0.06) | 0.84 (0.07) |

Different regression methods provide the lowest RMSE with different model specifications. Among the three regression models, SVR model provides the lowest RMSE of 0.15% to predict TF using the model coefficients with dictionary size 10 and sparsity 60%. For TR prediction it provides 0.12% by the coefficients of a model with dictionary size 20 and sparsity 60%, and 0.17% using model coefficients with dictionary size 20 and sparsity 80%, for TR/TF ratio. These values are made bold in the table 3. There are many other combinations of dictionary size and sparsity for which almost similar values of RMSE are obtained. For VVRKFA and ANN models, slightly higher RMSE values are obtained for all such combinations of dictionary size and sparsity. Thus, SVR model provides better performance compared to VVRKFA and ANN models. But, high accuracy of all the three regression techniques substantiates the effectiveness of the sparse model coefficients as features to establish the correlation between these with TR and TF contents in tea.

## Analysis

The results of table 3 may be used to study the effect of sparsity and dictionary size on prediction error. Fig. 6 (a) shows the effect of dictionary size on prediction RMSE of TR using SVR for five different sparsity level starting from 50%. From this fig., it is observed that performances of the models are better for dictionary size in the range 20 to 40 for different sparsity levels. On the other hand, fig. 6(b) shows effect of TR prediction RMSE on sparsity using SVR size 20 performs better than others for different sparsity levels. For better perception of the effect of variation of dictionary size and sparsity on prediction RMSE, authors have shown the error surface for different combinations of those two parameters on a two dimensional grid points in fig. 7. This fig. shows the TR prediction RMSE for variation of both

*Figure 6. SVR model performance (RMSE) for TR prediction with the variation of -(a) dictionary size with sparsity as a parameter and (b) sparsity with dictionary size as a parameter*

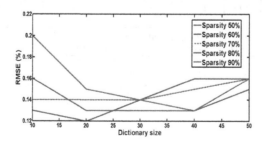

*Figure 7. TR prediction RMSE with the variation of sparsity (%) and dictionary size*

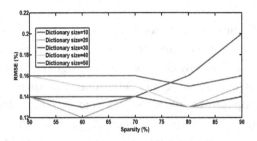

dictionary size and sparsity by SVR method. This shows that model with dictionary size 20 and 60% sparsity performs better for TR prediction. Similarly, it can be developed best models to predict TF and TR/TF ratio.

## Comparison of Results

Authors have compared performance of this method with other two methods available in the literature on TF and TR estimation of tea samples, namely 6th level DWT features using Haar wavelet (Ghosh et al., 2012) and fusion of three transformed features, like discrete cosine transform (DCT), Stockwell transform (ST) and singular value decomposition (SVD) (Saha et al., 2017) of ET response. With the purpose of comparing feature set quality, the authors have conducted the experiment under the similar settings by SVR method. Mean percentage RMSE is compared for all the methods. The results are provided in table 4. It reveals that the performance of the proposed sparse model-based method provides the lowest RMSE of 0.15% for TF, 0.12% for TR and 0.17% for TR/TF prediction, respectively, among the three methods. This fact confirms the effectiveness of the proposed method.

*Table 4. Performance comparisons with other existing methods*

| Feature extraction methods | Average % of RMSE ($\pm$ std.) on | | |
|---|---|---|---|
| | TF | TR | TR by TF |
| Discrete wavelet transform at 6th level with Haar wavelet (Ghosh et al., 2012) | 5.03 (0.44) | 4.01 (0.11) | 5.84 (0.60) |
| Fusion of three different features (Saha et al., 2017) | 6.08 (0.40) | 3.05 (0.28) | 4.61 (0.72) |
| Proposed sparse model coefficients | **0.15 (0.04)** | **0.12 (0.04)** | **0.17 (0.05)** |

# CONCLUSION

In this chapter, the authors have addressed the technique of determining the concentration of bio-chemical compounds, such as thearubigin (TR) and theaflavin (TF) in black tea samples by using electronic tongue signals. TR and TF contribute to the taste of tea. Usually, these values are determined by expensive chromatography experiments. The proposed technique shows sparse model representation of ET signal can determine these values very accurately. This method is efficient both in terms of extraction of features and performance compared to the two existing methods, (Ghosh et al., 2012) and (Saha et al., 2017), present in literature to address this problem. This method may be improved further if some closed form technique is developed to find optimal dictionary size, sparsity level and parameters of the regression technique for minimum RMSE. The only limitation of all these three methods is that it requires the use of chromatograph initially to get the amount of TR and TF contents in the tea for establishing the correlation between these and ET response. Once this correlation is established, all future estimation of TR and TF does not require the use of costly chromatograph instruments. In this way, it will be very useful in tea processing industries by eliminating human tasters as well as costly instruments. This technique may also be useful for ET signal processing in other applications.

# REFERENCES

Aharon, M., Elad, M., & Bruckstein, A. (2006). K-SVD: An algorithm for designing over complete dictionaries for sparse representation. *IEEE Transactions on Signal Processing*, *54*(11), 4311–4322. doi:10.1109/TSP.2006.881199

Baietto, M., & Wilson, A. D. (2015). Electronic-Nose Applications for Fruit Identification, Ripeness and Quality Grading. *Sensors (Basel)*, *15*(1), 899–931. doi:10.3390150100899 PMID:25569761

Bhattacharyya, N., Bandyopadhyay, R., Bhuyan, M., Tudu, B., Ghosh, D., & Jana, A. (2008). Electronic nose for black tea classification and correlation of measurements with "Tea Taster" marks. *IEEE Transactions on Instrumentation and Measurement*, *57*(7), 1313–1321. doi:10.1109/TIM.2008.917189

Candès, E. J., Romberg, J., & Tao, T. (2006). Robust uncertainty principles: Exact signal reconstruction from highly incomplete frequency information. *IEEE Transactions on Information Theory*, *52*(2), 489–509. doi:10.1109/TIT.2005.862083

Chen, S., Donoho, D. L., & Saunders, M. A. (1999). Atomic decomposition by basis pursuit. *SIAM Journal on Scientific Computing*, *20*(1), 33–61. doi:10.1137/S1064827596304010

Degenhardt, A., Engelhardt, U. H., Lakenbrink, C., & Winterhalter, P. (2000). Preparative separation of polyphenols from tea by high-speed counter current chromatography. *Journal of Agricultural and Food Chemistry*, *48*(8), 3425–3430. doi:10.1021/jf0000833 PMID:10956128

Degenhardt, A., Engelhardt, U. H., Wendt, A. S., & Winterhalter, P. (2000). Isolation of black tea pigments using high-speed counter current chromatography and studies on properties of black tea polymers. *Journal of Agricultural and Food Chemistry*, *48*(11), 5200–5205. doi:10.1021/jf000757+ PMID:11087459

Donoho, D. L. (2006). Compressed sensing. *IEEE Transactions on Information Theory*, *52*(4), 1289–1306. doi:10.1109/TIT.2006.871582

Dutta, R., Kashwan, K. R., Bhuyan, M., Hines, E. L., & Gardner, J. W. (2003). Electronic nose-based tea quality standardization. *Neural Networks*, *16*(5-6), 847–853. doi:10.1016/S0893-6080(03)00092-3 PMID:12850043

Elad, M., & Aharon, M. (2006). Image denoising via learned dictionaries and sparse representation. In *Proceedings of CVPR '06 Proceedings of the 2006 IEEE Computer Society Conference on Computer Vision and Pattern Recognition* (vol. 1, pp. 895-900). Washington, DC: IEEE Computer Society. 10.1109/CVPR.2006.142

Engan, K., Skretting, K., & Husøy, J. H. (2007). Family of iterative LS-based dictionary learning algorithms, ILS-DLA, for sparse signal representation. *Digital Signal Processing*, *17*(1), 32–49. doi:10.1016/j.dsp.2006.02.002

Ghorai, S., Mukherjee, A., & Dutta, P. K. (2010). Discriminant analysis for fast multiclass data classification through regularized kernel function approximation. *IEEE Transactions on Neural Networks*, *21*(6), 1020–1029. doi:10.1109/TNN.2010.2046646 PMID:20421179

Ghorai, S., Mukherjee, A., & Dutta, P. K. (2012). *Advances in Proximal Kernel Classifiers*. Germany: LAP LAMBERT Academic Publishing.

Ghosh, A., Tudu, B., Tamuly, P., Bhattacharyya, N., & Bandyopadhyay, R. (2012). Prediction of theaflavin and thearubigin content in black tea using a voltammetric electronic tongue. *Chemometrics and Intelligent Laboratory Systems*, *116*(7), 57–66. doi:10.1016/j.chemolab.2012.04.010

Hall, M. N., Robertso, A., & Scotter, C. N. G. (1988). Near-infrared reflectance prediction of quality, theaflavin content and moisture content of black tea. *Food Chemistry, 27*(1), 61–75. doi:10.1016/0308-8146(88)90036-2

Haykin, S. (2001). *Neural Networks – A Comprehensive Foundation* (2nd ed.). London, UK: Pearson Education.

Hazarika, M., Goswami, M. R., Tamuly, P., Sabhapondit, S., Baruah, S., & Gogoi, M. N. (2002).Quality measurement in tea- biochemist's view. *Two and a bud, 49*, 3-8.

Ivarsson, P., Holmin, S., Höjer, N. E., Krantz-Rülcker, C., & Winquist, F. (2001). Discrimination of tea by means of a voltametric electronic tongue and different applied waveforms. *Sensors and Actuators. B, Chemical, 76*(1-3), 449–454. doi:10.1016/S0925-4005(01)00583-4

Li, Y., Cichocki, A., & Amari, S. (2004). Analysis of sparse representation and blind source separation. *Neural Computation, 16*(6), 1193–1234. doi:10.1162/089976604773717586 PMID:15130247

Mahanta, P. K. (1988). Colour and flavor characteristics of made tea. In H. F. Linskens, & J. F. Jackson (Eds.), *Modern method of plant analysis* (pp. 221–295). Berlin, Germany: Springer-Verlag.

Mallat, S. G., & Zhang, Z. (1993). Matching pursuits with time frequency dictionaries. *IEEE Transactions on Signal Processing, 41*(12), 3397–3415. doi:10.1109/78.258082

Nandy Chatterjee, T., Banerjee Roy, R., Tudu, B., Pramanik, P., Deka, H., Tamuly, P., & Bandyopadhyay, R. (2017). Detection of theaflavins in black tea using a molecular imprinted polyacrylamide-graphite nanocomposite electrode. *Sensors and Actuators. B, Chemical, 246*(7), 840–847.

Ngurea, F. M., Wanyokob, J. K., Mahungua, S. M., & Mahungua, A. A. (2009, July). Catechins depletion patterns in relation to theaflavin and thearubigins formation. *Food Chemistry, 115*(1), 8–14. doi:10.1016/j.foodchem.2008.10.006

Obandaa, M., Owuora, P. O., Mang'okab, R., & Kavoi, M. M. (2004). Changes in thearubigin fractions and theaflavin levels due to variations in processing conditions and their influence on black tea liquor brightness and total colour. *Food Chemistry, 85*(2), 163–173. doi:10.1016/S0308-8146(02)00183-8

Olshausen, B., Sallee, P., & Lewicki, M. (2001). Learning sparse image codes using a wavelet pyramid architecture. In *NIPS'00 Proceedings of the 13th International Conference on Neural Information Processing Systems*, (pp. 887–893). Denver, CO: MIT Press. Cambridge, MA.

Palit, M., Tudu, B., Dutta, P. K., Dutta, A., Jana, A., Roy, J. K., ... Chatterjee, A. (2010). Classification of black tea taste and correlation with tea taster's mark using voltammetric electronic tongue. *IEEE Transactions on Instrumentation and Measurement, 59*(8), 2230–2239. doi:10.1109/TIM.2009.2032883

Robertson, A. (1983). Effects of physical and chemical conditions on the in vitro oxidation of tea leaf catechins. *Phytochemistry, 22*(4), 897–903. doi:10.1016/0031-9422(83)85018-3

Robertson, A. (1992). The chemistry and biochemistry of black tea production, the non-volatiles. In K. C. Wilson, & M. N. Clifford (Eds.), *Tea: Cultivation to consumption* (pp. 555–601). London, UK: Chapman and Hall. doi:10.1007/978-94-011-2326-6_17

Robertson, A., & Bendall, D. S. (1983). Production and HPLC analysis of black tea theaflavins and thearubigins during in vitro oxidation. *Phytochemistry, 22*(4), 883–887. doi:10.1016/0031-9422(83)85016-X

Rubinstein, R., Peleg, T., & Elad, M. (2013). Analysis K-SVD: A dictionary learning algorithm for the analysis sparse model. *IEEE Transactions on Signal Processing, 61*(3), 661–667. doi:10.1109/TSP.2012.2226445

Saha, P., Ghorai, S., Tudu, B., Bandyopadhyay, R., & Bhattacharyya, N. (2014). A novel method of black tea quality prediction using electronic tongue Signals. *IEEE Transactions on Instrumentation and Measurement, 63*(10), 2472–2479. doi:10.1109/TIM.2014.2310615

Saha, P., Ghorai, S., Tudu, B., Bandyopadhyay, R., & Bhattacharyya, N. (2016). Tea Quality Prediction by Autoregressive Modelling of Electronic Tongue Signals. *IEEE Sensors Journal, 16*(11), 4470–4477. doi:10.1109/JSEN.2016.2544979

Saha, P., Ghorai, S., Tudu, B., Bandyopadhyay, R., & Bhattacharyya, N. (2017). Feature fusion for prediction of theaflavin and thearubigin in tea using electronic tongue. *IEEE Transactions on Instrumentation and Measurement, 66*(7), 1703–1710. doi:10.1109/TIM.2017.2672458

Smith, N. L., & Elad, M. (2013). Improving Dictionary Learning: Multiple dictionary Updates and Coefficient Reuse. *IEEE Signal Processing Letters, 20*(1), 79–82. doi:10.1109/LSP.2012.2229976

Smola, A. J., & Schölkopf, B. (2004). A tutorial on support vector regression. *Statistics and Computing, 14*(3), 199–222. doi:10.1023/B:STCO.0000035301.49549.88

Starck, J., Elad, M., & Donoho, D. (2005). Image decomposition via the combination of sparse representation and a variational approach. *IEEE Transactions on Image Processing*, *14*(10), 1570–1582. doi:10.1109/TIP.2005.852206 PMID:16238062

Tropp, A. J., & Gilbert, A. C. (2007). Signal recovery from random measurements via orthogonal matching pursuit. *IEEE Transactions on Information Theory*, *53*(12), 4655–4666. doi:10.1109/TIT.2007.909108

Ullah, M. R., Gogoi, N., & Baruah, D. (1984). The effect of withering on fermentation of tea leaf and development of liquor characters of black tea. *Journal of the Science of Food and Agriculture*, *35*(10), 1142–1147. doi:10.1002/jsfa.2740351014

Vapnik, V. N. (1998). *The Nature of Statistical Learning Theory*. New York: John Wiley & Sons.

Wang, K., Liu, Z., Huang, J., Dong, X., Song, L., Pana, Y., & Liu, F. (2008). Preparative isolation and purification of theaflavins and catechins by high-speed counter current chromatography. *Journal of Chromatography. B, Analytical Technologies in the Biomedical and Life Sciences*, *867*(2), 282–286. doi:10.1016/j. jchromb.2008.04.005 PMID:18436487

Wilson, A. D. (2013). Diverse Applications of Electronic-Nose Technologies in Agriculture and Forestry. *Sensors (Basel)*, *13*(2), 2295–2348. doi:10.3390130202295 PMID:23396191

Wright, L. P., Mphangwe, N. K., Nyirenda, H., & Apostolides, Z. (2002). Analysis of the theaflavin composition in black tea (Camellia sinesis) predicting the quality of black tea produced in Central and Southern Africa. *Journal of the Science of Food and Agriculture*, *82*(5), 517–525. doi:10.1002/jsfa.1074

Zabadaj, M., Ufnalska, I., Chreptowicz, K., Mierzejewska, J., Wróblewski, W., & Ciosek-Skibińska, P. (2017). Performance of hybrid electronic tongue and HPLC coupled with chemometric analysis for the monitoring of yeast biotransformation. *Chemometrics and Intelligent Laboratory Systems*, *157*(8), 69–77. doi:10.1016/j. chemolab.2017.05.003

Zhang, Z., Xu, Y., Yang, J., Li, X., & Zhang, D. (2015). A survey of sparse representation: Algorithms and applications. *IEEE Access: Practical Innovations, Open Solutions*, *3*(5), 490–530. doi:10.1109/ACCESS.2015.2430359

# Chapter 8
# Measurement of Junction Depth in Sub-Micron Device Using SIMS Technique for Performance Estimation in RF Range

**Arpan Deyasi**
*RCC Institute of Information Technology, India*

**Pampa Debnath**
*RCC Institute of Information Technology, India*

## ABSTRACT

*This chapter shows the measurement procedure of junction depth using SIMS method with detailed experimental procedure, and the result is verified by theoretical computation. SIMS profile is analytically characterized by Pearson's distribution function, and all the results together established the fact that the device can be utilized for operating as a diode in RF range; where ion dose is considered as a variable parameter with ion energy. Implanted impurity distribution profile is obtained as a function of depletion width from which junction depth can be evaluated. Straggle parameters and projected range profile near the ion energy range is computed for which depth is evaluated, and skewness & kurtosis are estimated to get a theoretical knowledge of all the moments assuming the Pearson IV distribution. Results suggest that distribution of atoms may be considered as Gaussian in nature.*

DOI: 10.4018/978-1-7998-2584-5.ch008

## INTRODUCTION

Present research of nanoelectronic device fabrication is one of the promising fields for the experimental as well as for theoretical device researchers in order to explore novel electronic and photonic properties of the low-dimensional devices compared to their bulk counterparts. With shrinking dimension of electronic and optoelectronic devices in the last two decades following Moore's law, novel complex multi-layer structures are designed to serve specific applications. Due to lowering of device size in sub-micrometer region, quantum confinement effect starts to dominate, which leads to several novel structures, nomenclature as quantum well (Uomi 2019; Amargianitakis *et. al.* 2019), wire (Yakimenko *et. al.* 2019; Kerner 2018), dot (Chinnathambi & Shirahata 2019; Lu *et. al.* 2019) etc. Owing to equivalence of device dimension with de-Broglie wavelength, carrier motions are confined in different directions leads to internment. Thanks to the acquaintance with the existing fabrication methodologies for these submicron devices, complex geometrical structures proposed by theoretical workers, are now practically realizable (Chen *et. al.* 2019; Drouin *et. al.* 2017; Yang *et. al.* 2018), where quantum phenomena dominate their behavior under the presence of various external excitations (Sadeghzadeh & Rezapour 2016; Wulf *et. al.* 2017). Properties of these low-dimensional devices critically depend on layer widths, whose growth can precisely be monitored during fabrication process (Franckié *et. al.* 2019; Su *et. al.* 2018; Molla *et. al.* 2019). Recent developments of fabrication technology lead to successful physical manifestation of several nanoelectronic devices (Meel *et. al.* 2018; Giraud *et. al.* 2018; Karmakar 2019), many of which has arbitrary potential distributions (Abdolkader *et. al.* 2018; Lin *et. al.* 2018) leading to controlled electron flow in desired directions. Shape of the potential in a composite heterostructure depends on the individual material properties, along with the junctions formed. Surface potential at junctions can greatly be affected due to electrical and mechanical dissimilarities between two layers, and with change of layer thickness in either side of the junction guided to a change of the electrical properties. Researches are carried out so far (Androulidakis *et. al.* 2018; Liao *et. al.* 2017) in this regard, which reveals the importance of fabrication procedure and its measurement.

The expected properties for specific applications, as computed by different numerical methods (Deyasi & Sarkar 2018; Quhe *et. al.* 2018), or by analytical means (Stepnicki *et. al.* 2015; Pal & Sarkar 2014), can be matched with experimental outputs, where accuracy of fabrication instruments or characterization tools and their handling are near-perfect, and here lies the importance of understanding the behavior of electrons and their internal distributions in the device. Since the devices are in sub-micron level, so any minute fluctuation in the carrier distributions leads to a radical change from the expected outcome. Henceforth, precise measurement of carrier distributions play a crucial role in shaping the device performance, and modern instruments is therefore required prior to packaging the product for internal analysis.

As the progress of technology in semiconductor device demands the complex nature under different external conditions, so growth of various heterostructure comes into the mainstream research (Zheng *et. al.* 2019) where quantum confinement plays a leading role in designing the future roadmap. In heterostructure devices, utmost accuracy is taken for the layer thickness and its spreading in the undesired region, as tolerance for these cases will be minutely small. But after fabrication, measurement of carrier distribution becomes important not only in the desired location, but also in the nearby vicinity; where density of states of the unwanted elements in a measurable and significant value can adversely affect the performance of device. Several experimental techniques are improvised in this regard to measure the carrier density for quantum devices, and can play a pivotal role in tailoring the procedure of fabrication from their outcome, if undesired allocations are detected. A detailed review on the experimental works of quantum devices exposes that the formation of heterostructure makes pivotal role in tailoring the electrical or mechanical properties of the device; and to control the growth process minutely; several experimental techniques are realized. Among them, molecular beam epitaxy (MBE), chemical vapor deposition (CVD), metallo-organic chemical vapor deposition (MOCVD) etc to name a few. The choice of these various methods are basically the requirement-dependent growth control and MBE is far superior compared to the other techniques reported so far (Pelzel 2013). Since junction width is inversely related to the frequency of operation of the device, hence nanoelectronic devices are claimed as superior candidates for working in RF range (Galal & Hesselbach 2018; Bozzi *et. al.* 2015) and beyond. This fact also underlines the feature that very minute fluctuation in junction depth or layer width ultimately makes a major noticeable fluctuation in the operating frequency. Therefore models developed/proposed by theoretical researchers should be near accurately realized by experimental workers with tolerable error in picometer dimension during the growth process. A precise measurement unit is henceforth required before packaging of the structure for application purpose.

One of the most important measurements in this regard is to measure the junction depth, where external doping is made by either diffusion or ion implantation methodologies. Though diffusion is a very lost procedure, but for sub-micron or nanometric devices, this technique is not at all suitable due to lower accuracy. Hence ion implantation becomes the widely accepted techniques for doping, and be implemented by Molecular Beam Epitaxy [MBE], Chemical Vapor Deposition [CVD], or MOCVD etc. After the doping upto desired depth, it becomes the duty of the researchers to measure the junction depth and its extent in the desired as well as neighborhood regions. Among the different methods, Secondary Ion Mass Spectrometry [SIMS] is one of the extensively established techniques for the much-said purpose. In the present proposal, we have briefly discussed the junction depth for fabrication of a microwave device by SIMS technique, and results are analyzed in the light of device performance. Investigation contains detailed understanding of the instrument, and its potential applications for measurement of the Ka-band device, where we have clearly established the fact that a slight change from the predicted value impacts a large shift from operation.

In the present chapter, we have showed the measurement procedure of junction depth using SIMS method with detailed experimental procedure, and the result is verified by theoretical computation. SIMS profile is analytically characterized by Pearson's distribution function, and all the results together established the fact that the device can be utilized for operating as a diode in RF range; where ion dose is considered as a variable parameter with ion energy. Implanted impurity distribution profile is obtained as a function of depletion width from which junction depth can be evaluated. Straggle parameters and projected range profile near the ion energy range is computed for which depth is evaluated, and skewness & kurtosis are estimated to get a theoretical knowledge of all the moments assuming the Pearson IV distribution. Results suggest that distribution of atoms may be considered as Gaussian in nature.

## LITERATURE REVIEW

Since the discovery of diffusion process as a uniform and controllable mechanism to introduce dopant into semiconductors, it has grown to be the principal low-cost doping technology. The microscopic mechanism of boron diffusion in Si has been a subject of extensive theoretical and experimental research for past few years (Watkins 1975; Sadigh *et. al.* 1999; Bennett & Parish 1975). An inclusive acquaintance of the atomic level transfer and transport mechanism of impurity carriers through diffusion route is required to tailor the doping profile (Salvador *et. al.* 2006) and corresponding, junction depth. Researchers also established the importance of temperature dependence of diffusivity for the process (Panda *et. al.* 1994), which was first reported after detailed work, carried on different crystal orientation (Masetti *et. al.* 1976). Crystal orientation of the wafer is established as an important factor as earlier reported by different group of experimental workers (Allen & Anand 1971; Fair 1975) which help to get knowledge about density of defect states before initiation of experimental works.

Boron diffusion during predeposition and drive-in steps are already analyzed by extremely resolute SIMS depth profiling (Masetti *et. al.* 1976) much earlier, as it is one of the most widely used technique for analysis of semiconductor process control, composition and contamination showed in a survey (Bilgera *et. al.* 1985; Cyr *et. al.* 2001). In the last decade, several workers investigated experimentally the process of B diffusion in Si (Bennett & Parish 1975; Cyr *et. al.* 2001; Lee *et. al.* 2008) along with other types of impurities. If the source is a localized one, then SIMS provides superior precision than earlier reported literatures (Bevan & Townsend 1972). Importance of SEM for measurement of diffusion length is also emphasized by another group (Ioannou & Davidson 1979) for junction fabrication. A measurement of impurity profile for B, P and As (Davies 1970) also helps to determine the maximum normalized ion count ratio. This pioneering work leads the investigation of junction depth of boron in Si over a finite energy level and ion dose, which is in quite good agreement with theoretical predictions. A comparative analysis of boron implantation in both amorphous and polycrystalline Si is carried out to determine the concentration profiles (Hofker *et. al.* 1974; Hofker *et. al.* 1975). This work was later extended (Hobler *et. al.* 1987) considering the spatial moments for 2-D distribution; whereas researchers also approximated the profiles for low-energy impurities only (Obradovic 1997).

The Pearson family of distributions was developed to approximate all unimodal distributions. The Pearson Type IV distribution allows for varying degrees of skewness and kurtosis, and so is ideally suited for distributions of interest is often asymmetric with extensive tails. Its algorithm is used to describe ion implanted depth distributions in various literatures (Hobler *et. al.* 1987; Obradovic 1997). Pearson algorithms are used (Ashworth *et. al.* 2007) to describe a statistical distribution in terms of four central moments, $\mu$, $\sigma$, $\gamma$ and $\beta$, based on a modified or skewed Gaussian distribution. Physically based Monte Carlo calculation is utilized to compute ion trajectories (Jahanshah *et. al.* 2007) for calculation of final distribution of stopped particles. Lateral standard deviation and lateral kurtosis are established as a function of depth (Hobler *et. al.* 1987) using 2-D Monte-Carlo simulations. Depth-dependent lateral distribution using symmetrical Pearson curves are analytically derived (Ashworth *et. al.* 1990) for the moment surfaces.

Depth resolution, sensitivity and dynamic range for depth profiling and penetration using SIMS technique is characterized (Magee & Honig 1982) in presence of atomic mixing effects. Resolution takes an important aspect when ultra-shallow depth profiling is performed for ULSI fabrication, and comparative study is performed (Budrevich & Hunter 1998) with deep profiling as already carried out. For small depth measurement, highly sensitive TOF-SIMS is utilized (Iltgen *et. al.* 1998) which becomes essential for DRAM and other memory device characterization. Subsequently core-shell structure is characterized (Verlinden *et. al.* 1999) for sub-micron structure measurement. Comparative study is also carried out with carrier illumination technique (Borden 2001) in connection with source/drain profiling for NMOS/PMOS processes. Apart from nanometric depth measurement, impurity traces are also determined (van Lierde *et. al.* 2002), and two major techniques e.g. Rutherford Backscattering Spectrometry (RBS) and x-ray diffraction (XRD) data are correlated with the major and minor components determination. Following ITRS, the technique is used for 90 nm technology node (Anderle *et. al.* 2003) for quantification and depth calculation. Profile shape for boron ion distribution is recently measured (Magee *et. al.* 2007). With newly additive features, the apparatus is now-a-days used to calibrate junction depth for less than 50 nm devices (Whitby *et. al.* 2012) which is also useful to extract roughness information. Detailed diffusivity analysis of boron in Si and Ge is investigated (Mirabella *et. al.* 2013) where Fermi level position is also considered along with various chemical effects like precipitation. Here effects of ion energy, sixe of device, presence of point defects are all included for depth measurement. Work is recently further extended on the source type for diffusion (Singha & Solanki 2016) which greatly affects the device performance. Specific resistivity of the wafer material is also taken into consideration (Lee *et. al.* 2016), and corresponding relation is experimentally established. These works are effectively revealing the importance of the boron diffusion analysis in context of junction analysis from device fabrication point-of-view, and thus satisfied the present work.

## OBJECTIVE

The present chapter contains the estimation of junction depth both from theoretical perspective as well as from practical fabrication methodologies. The computational result is verified with experimental findings, and the result are in very close agreement. Henceforth, the present work shows the accuracy for junction depth measurement,and corresponding RF parameter dependence on it; as a little deviation will cause a large error in estimating device properties. Both type of measurement are graphically displayed, and resemblance suggests the importance of fabrication technique and corresponding key parameter dependence. The fabrication procedure is also theoretically analyzed to study the characteristic parameters, which basically signifies the importance of fabrication techniques as mentioned in the next section of this chapter.

## JUNCTION FORMATION

For the present work, we have considered the starting material as $nn^+$ Si wafer with <111> orientation. Our end target is to make it a read diode, i.e., $p^+nn^+$ structure, for the purpose of microwave operation, and henceforth, boron-nitride (BN) is used to diffuse boron (B) atoms in the wafer under consideration. As per convention, the present diffusion process is a two-step journey: [i] predeposition, [ii] drive-in. But the initial problem is related with the source of boron. As the material boron nitride is chemically inert, it should be turned on in $O_2$-riched atmosphere around 950þC. This helps to form $B_2O_3$ on the top surface of BN solid substance (Deyasi & Bhattacharyya 2014; Deyasi 2007).

For predeposition, it is customary to fix the temperature of central zone of the diffusion furnace. For the present set-up, we kept it around 975þC for almost 20 minutes. This ensures deposition of B atoms and insertion upto a very small depth within the Si surface. After predeposition, temperature is raised owing to the requirement of further penetration of the deposited atoms on the surface. So temperature is set at a higher value around 1100þC, and kept for 45 minutes. In this case, both temperature and time is adjusted in order to provide the required junction depth (Deyasi & Bhattacharyya 2014; Deyasi & Banerjee 2010). While diffusion process, specially while drive-in is going on, there is a possibility of back-diffusion; and in order to prevent it, IOLAR grade nitrogen is flown throughout the time of diffusion to create an inert atmosphere around the diffusion zone. Along with nitrogen, a flow of IOLAR oxygen is allowed to prevent silicide formation.

## THEORETICAL FOUNDATION

### Diffusion Analysis

The ultimate goal of diffusion studies is to calculate the electrical characteristics of a semiconductor device from the processing parameters. Calculation of design frequency for Si p+nn+ diode requires solution for dopant profiles following either a predeposition or a drive-in or a combination of both, and the impurity profiles introduced during any one of the process can be obtained by solving Fick's law of diffusion (Deyasi & Bhattacharyya 2014). Assuming D is independent of impurity concentration distribution, one obtains for 1-D problem under consideration

$$\partial C / \partial t = D(\partial^2 C / \partial z^2) \tag{1}$$

which is Fick's 2nd law of diffusion.

In predeposition, the concentration $C_0$ is called background concentration, which actually gives the dopant present at the surface of wafer, and a uniform and reproducible amount of dopant enters the crystal lattice. Then junction depth under this condition $z_{j1}$ denotes the depth at which the dopant concentration $C(z,t)$ becomes numerically equal to the background doping $C_B$. So, we get

$$C_B / C_0 = erfc[z_{j1} / 2\sqrt{D_1 \tau_1}] \tag{2}$$

where $C_0$ is The solid solubility of dopant in Si at predeposition temperature, $D_1$ is diffusion constant of dopant at predeposition temperature, $\tau_1$ is predeposition time.

Again, for practical consideration, diffusion length for drive-in is very large compared to that obtained under predeposition condition, so extent of penetration of predeposited profile may not be significant while measuring the junction depth, and can mathematically be represented by delta-function. Subject to this approximation, dopant profile for drive-in can be expressed as-

$$C_B = [(Q / \sqrt{\pi D_2 \tau_2}) \exp(-z_{j2}^2 / 4D_2 \tau_2)] \tag{3}$$

where $Q$ represents the total dopant amount during predeposition within that time $\tau_1$, $D_2$ is diffusion constant of dopant at drive-in temperature, $\tau_2$ is drive-in time.

The RF frequency for oscillation is given by

$$f = 0.37 v_S / W \tag{4}$$

where $v_s$ is the saturated carrier drift velocity for that substrate material, and $W$ can be obtained from a knowledge of predeposition and drive-in process.

Using the data for fabrication, junction depth can theoretically be obtained as 0.938 μm and corresponding frequency spectrum for operation is 27.47 GHz to 38.7 GHz, which speaks in favor of Ka-band operation (Deyasi & Bhattacharyya 2014).

## Ion Implantation Analysis

Far from the mask edge, the lateral motion can be ignored and n (z), the ion concentration at depth $x$, can be written as:

$$n(z) = \frac{\phi}{2\pi\sigma_P} \exp\left[\frac{-(z - R_p)^2}{2\sigma_P^2}\right] \tag{5}$$

where $R_p$ is the projected range, and $\sigma_p$ is the standard deviation. If the total implanted dose is $\Phi$, integrating gives an expression for longitudinal straggle

$$\sigma_P = \sqrt{\frac{m_2}{\phi}} \tag{6}$$

The i-th central moments of the probability density function n(z) are defined by:

$$m_i = \frac{1}{\phi} \int_{-\infty}^{\infty} (z - R_P)^i n(z) dz \tag{7}$$

with the consideration of the mean value of the distribution. Skewness and kurtosis are respectively computed from third and fourth order moments as-

$$y = {m_3} \Big/ {\sigma_P^3} \tag{8}$$

$$\beta = {m_4} \Big/ {\sigma_P^4} \tag{9}$$

## RESULTS FOR JUNCTION DEPTH

SIMS analysis was carried out on $p^+nn^+$ wafer, which is nothing but Read type SDR structure. From this analysis, boron doping profile is obtained (Deyasi & Bhattacharyya 2014). The junction depth has been determined when the external doping concentration becomes equal to the background concentration (Deyasi & Bhattacharyya 2014; Deyasi 2007). In this regard, note has to be taken of the fact that the boron analysis has been made by bombarding the sample with a beam of $O_2$ ions, whereas in the previous P analysis, the bombardment has been done by Cs ions. This has been done since Phosphorous has a very poor ionization cross-section with the oxygen ion, while Boron has a poor ionization cross-section with Cs. Fig 1, Fig 2, Fig 3 and Fig 4 denote different ion concentrations present in that sample.

With reference to Figure 1-4, junction depth is easily calculated. It is found that The junction depth is approximately 0.91978 μm. The maximum normalized ion count ratio for B/Si is $2.34 \times 10^{-3}$. Peak boron concentration is obtained to be $3 \times 10^{24}$ atoms/m$^3$.

*Figure 1. Boron concentration profile with penetration depth obtained from SIMS analysis*
Source: Deyasi & Bhattacharyya 2014

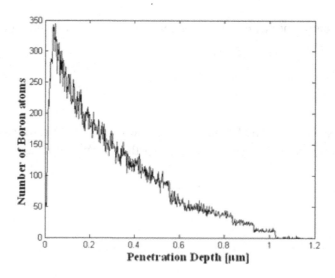

*Figure 2. Phosphorous concentration profile with penetration depth obtained from SIMS analysis*
Source: Deyasi & Bhattacharyya 2014

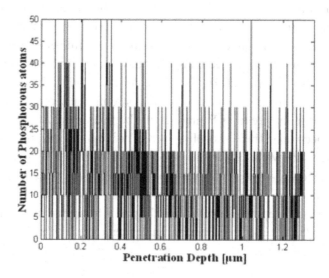

*Figure 3. Silicon concentration profile with penetration depth obtained from SIMS analysis*
Source: Deyasi & Bhattacharyya 2014

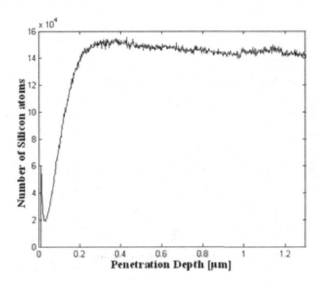

*Figure 4. Arsenic concentration profile with penetration depth obtained from SIMS analysis*
Source: Deyasi & Bhattacharyya 2014

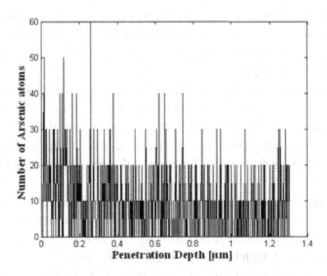

*Figure 5. Comparative study of Boron and Phosphorous profile with penetration depth obtained from SIMS analysis which provides junction depth*
Source: Deyasi 2007

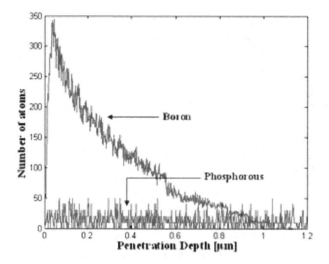

## ANALYSIS OF ION IMPLANTATION METHOD

Statistical distribution of implanted atoms along the axis of interface (longitudinal), and perpendicular of that axis (lateral) are plotted as a function of ion energy, and particular interest is in the lower region of the profile (less than MeV), as junction depth matches with the projected range in that assortment. The value of ion energy as approximated is 400 KeV.

It can be noted that initially, for very low ion energy, longitudinal distribution predominates, but with increase of input, lateral distribution starts to play. The lateral moments are function of depth and energy as well as the vertical moments is function of energy only. This suggests that atoms with higher energy distributed themselves more along the normal direction of the axis, which doesn't contribute to the depth profile.

The third and fourth normalized moments can be found out from the knowledge of ion dose, longitudinal straggle, and the concentration profile. As the energy is increased, the profile become more negatively skewed and deviates more significantly from a true Gaussian, which is not in our range of interest.

Also, Kurtosis reaches its Gaussian value, which is 3, at lower ion energy values (200 KeV). In higher energy values, skewness increases rapidly along negative axis.

*Figure 6. Profile of projected range with ion energy*
Source: Deyasi 2010

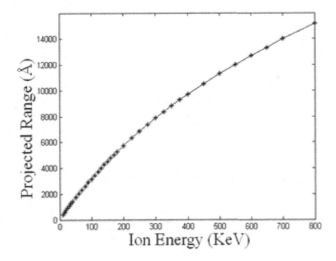

*Figure 7. Profiles of longitudinal and lateral straggles with ion energy*
Source: Deyasi 2010

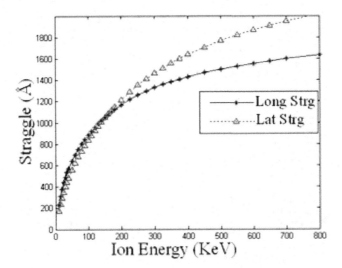

*Figure 8. Variation of skewness with ion energy*
Source: Deyasi 2010

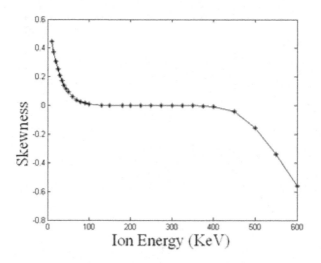

*Figure 9. Variation of kurtosis with ion energy*
Source: Deyasi 2010

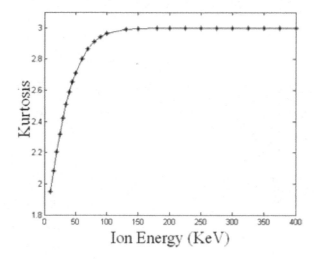

## CONCLUSION

A detailed study on junction depth measurement and corresponding process analysis is hereby presented where the total design is based around 34 GHz (Ka-band), i.e. RF range. Read type diode structure is considered for the analysis, where process is minutely controlled to obtain pre-estimated junction depth as it is the most responsible parameter for determining operating frequency range of the diode. Experimental result and theoretical computation differ less than 1.94%, which speaks the accuracy of fabrication and characterization procedure. Though diffusion technique is used to prepare the diode, but ion implantation technique is later utilized for verification and characterization of the process. This alternative technique is far better and accurate than the diffusion, and therefore a vis-a-vis study clearly reveals the accuracy of the employed procedure. The theoretical comparison is carried out by Pearson-IV distribution. Skewness and kurtosis are computed considering ion dose as a variable parameter, where it is generally considered as constant in earlier works, and calculated from equilibrium surface concentration. Here choice of the centre frequency is primarily based on the making of Read type SDR diode, and all theoretical and experimental procedure is centred around that data. The atomic distribution may be considered as Gaussian, as kurtosis gets a value of 3 in the energy range where junction depth is evaluated. Results give the importance of the present analysis, and also of modification required when devices are designed at millimeterwave frequency region.

## REFERENCES

Abdolkader, T. M., Shaker, A., & Alahmadi, A. N. M. (2018). Numerical simulation of tunneling through arbitrary potential barriers applied on MIM and MIIM rectenna diodes. *European Journal of Physics*, *39*(4). doi:10.1088/1361-6404/aab5cf

Allen, W. G., & Anand, K. V. (1971). Orientation dependence of the diffusion of boron in silicon. *Solid-State Electronics*, *14*(5), 397–406. doi:10.1016/0038-1101(71)90190-0

Amargianitakis, E. A., Miziou, F., Androulidaki, M., Tsagaraki, K., Kostopoulos, A., Konstantinidis, G., Delamadeleine, E., Monroy, E., & Pelekanos, N. T. (2019). Improved GaN Quantum Well Microcavities for Robust Room Temperature Polaritonics. *Physica Status Solidi B: Advances in Physics of Semiconductors, 256*(6).

Anderle, M., Barozzi, M., Bersani, M., Giubertoni, D., & Lazzeri, P. (2003). Ultra shallow depth profiling by secondary ion mass spectrometry techniques. In *Proceedings International Conference on Characterization and Metrology for ULSI Technology*. 10.1063/1.1622547

Androulidakis, C., Zhang, K., Robertson, M., & Tawfick, S. (2018). Tailoring the mechanical properties of 2D materials and heterostructures, *2D Materials, 5*(3).

Ashworth, D. G., Bowyer, M. D. J., & Oven, R. (2007, October). Representation of Ion Implantation Distributions in Two and Three Dimensions. In *Proceedings of the 7th WSEAS International Conference on Wavelet Analysis & Multirate Systems*, France. Academic Press.

Ashworth, D. G., Oven, R., & Mundin, B. (1990). Representation of ion implantation profiles by Pearson frequency distribution curves. *Journal of Physics. D, Applied Physics, 23*(7), 870–876. doi:10.1088/0022-3727/23/7/018

Bennett, R. J., & Parish, C. (1975). Determination of diffusion, partition and sticking coefficients for boron, phosphorous and antimony in silicon. *Solid-State Electronics, 18*(10), 833–838. doi:10.1016/0038-1101(75)90003-9

Bevan, O. J., & Townsend, W. G. (1972). A method of measuring the diffusion of boron into silicon from a localized surface source. *Journal of Physics. E, Scientific Instruments, 5*(7), 704–706. doi:10.1088/0022-3735/5/7/029

Bilgera, G., Nebela, C. E., Bauera, G. H., & Mohring, H. D. (1985). Boron diffusion in amorphous silicon analyzed by SIMS and temperature dependent conductivity. *Journal of Non-Crystalline Solids, 77-78*(1-2), 503–506. doi:10.1016/0022-3093(85)90708-2

Borden, P. (2001). Junction Depth Measurement using Carrier Illumination. *AIP Conference Proceedings, 550*, 175–180. doi:10.1063/1.1354393

Bozzi, M., Pierantoni, L., & Bellucci, S. (2015). Applications of graphene at microwave frequencies. *Wuxiandian Gongcheng, 24*(3), 661–669.

Budrevich, A., & Hunter, J. (1998). Metrology Aspects of SIMS Depth Profiling for Advanced ULSI Processes. *AIP Conference Proceedings, 449*, 169–181.

Chen, S., Kim, S. P., Chen, W., Yuan, J., Bashir, R., Lou, J., ... King, W. P. (2019). Monolayer MoS2 Nanoribbon Transistors Fabricated by Scanning Probe Lithography. *Nano Letters, 19*(3), 2092–2098. doi:10.1021/acs.nanolett.9b00271 PMID:30808165

Chinnathambi, S., & Shirahata, N. (2019). Recent advances on fluorescent biomarkers of near-infrared quantum dots for *in vitro* and *in vivo* imaging. *Science and Technology of Advanced Materials, 20*(1), 337–355. doi:10.1080/14686996.2 019.1590731 PMID:31068983

Cyr, H. F. S., Noshkina, E., Stevie, F., Chow, L., Richardson, K., & Zhou, D. (2001). Secondary ion mass spectrometry characterization of the diffusion properties of 17 elements implanted into silicon. *Journal of Vacuum Science & Technology. B, Microelectronics and Nanometer Structures: Processing, Measurement, and Phenomena: An Official Journal of the American Vacuum Society, 19*(5), 1769–1774. doi:10.1116/1.1396638

Davies, D. E. (1970). The implanted profiles of boron, phosphorous and arsenic in silicon from junction depth measurements. *Solid-State Electronics, 13*(2), 229–232. doi:10.1016/0038-1101(70)90055-9

Deyasi, A. (2010). Numerical Analysis of Moment Parameters for Ion Implantation of Boron in n-Si Designed for SDR IMPATT Structure in Ka-Band. *International Journal BITM Transaction on EECC, 2,* 23–29.

Deyasi, A. (2007, January). Junction Depth Estimation of Si p+nn+ diode Designed at Ka-Band for IMPATT. In *Proceedings International Conference in Emerging Trends in Electrical Engineering,* pp. 52-53.

Deyasi, A., & Banerjee, J. P. (2010, February). Investigation of Junction Depth for Boron Implantation in Silicon Designed for IMPATT Structure at Ka-Band. In *Proceedings National Conference on Electrical, Power Engineering, Electronics & Computer,* pp. 122-125. Academic Press.

Deyasi, A., & Bhattacharyya, S. (2014). Investigating Penetration Depth of Boron into P-Doped Silicon by Diffusion Process For p+nn+ SDR IMPATT Structure at Ka-Band. *Journal of the Association of Engineers, 83*(3-4), 18–24. doi:10.22485/ jaei/2013/v83/i3-4/119923

Deyasi, A., & Sarkar, A. (2018). Analytical computation of electrical parameters in GAAQWT and CNTFET using NEGF Method. *International Journal of Electronics, 105*(issue: 12), 2144–2159. doi:10.1080/00207217.2018.1494339

Drouin, D., Droulers, G., Labalette, M., Sang, B. L., Harvey-Collard, P., Souifi, A., ... Ecoffey, S. (2017). A Fabrication Process for Emerging Nanoelectronic Devices Based on Oxide Tunnel Junctions. *Journal of Nanomaterials.* doi:10.1155/2017/8613571

Fair, R. B. (1975). Boron diffusion in silicon: Concentration and orientation dependence, background effects and profile estimation. *Journal of the Electrochemical Society, 122*(6), 800–805. doi:10.1149/1.2134326

Franckié, M., Bosco, L., Beck, M., Mavrona, E., & Faist, J. (2019). Optimization and fabrication of two-quantum well THz QCLs operating above 200 K. In *Proceedings 2019 Conference on Lasers and Electro-Optics (CLEO)* (pp. 1-2). IEEE.

Galal, A., & Hesselbach, X. (2018). Nano-networks communication architecture: Modeling and functions. *Nano Communication Networks, 17*, 45–62. doi:10.1016/j.nancom.2018.07.001

Giraud, P., Hou, B., Pak, S., Sohn, J. I., Morris, S., Cha, S. N., & Kim, J. M. (2018). Field effect transistors and phototransistors based upon p-type solution-processed PbS nanowires. *Nanotechnology, 29*(7). doi:10.1088/1361-6528/aaa2e6 PMID:29324436

Hobler, G., Langer, E., & Selberherr, S. (1987). Two-dimensional modeling of ion implantation with spatial moments. *Solid-State Electronics, 30*(4), 445–455. doi:10.1016/0038-1101(87)90175-4

Hofker, W. K., Oostheok, D. P., Koeman, N. J., & De Grefte, H. A. M. (1975). Concentration profiles of boron implantations in amorphous and polycrystalline silicon. *Radiation Effects, 24*(4), 223–231. doi:10.1080/00337577508240811

Hofker, W. K., Werner, H. W., Oostheok, D. P., & Koeman, N. J. (1974). Boron implantation in silicon: A comparison of charge carrier and boron concentration profiles. *Applied Physics (Berlin), 4*(2), 125–133. doi:10.1007/BF00884267

Iltgen, K., MacDonald, B., Brox, O., Bennlnghoven, A., Weiss, C., Hossain, T., & Zschech, E. (1998). Ultra-shallow junction depth profile analysis using TOF-SIMS and TXRF. *AIP Conference Proceedings, 449*, 777–781.

Ioannou, D. E., & Davidson, S. M. (1979). Diffusion length evaluation of boron-implanted silicon using the SEM-EBIC/ Schottky diode technique. *Journal of Physics. D, Applied Physics, 12*(8), 1339–1344. doi:10.1088/0022-3727/12/8/014

Jahanshah, F., Sopian, K., Abdullah, H., Ahmad, I., Othman, M. Y., & Zaidi, S. H. (2007, October). Investigation on ion implantation models impact on i-v curve and thin film solar cell efficiency. In *Proceedings of the 7th WSEAS International Conference on Wavelet Analysis & Multirate Systems,* France. Academic Press.

Karmakar, S. (2019). Design of Multi-state DRAM Using Quantum Dot Gate Non-volatile Memory (QDNVM). *Silicon, 11*(2), 869–877. doi:10.100712633-018-9879-z

Kerner, J. (2018). On pairs of interacting electrons in a quantum wire. *Journal of Mathematical Physics, §§§*, 59.

Lee, J. C., Won, J., Chung, Y., Lee, H., Lee, E., Kang, D., ... Kim, J. (2008). Investigations of semiconductor devices using SIMS; diffusion, contamination, process control. *Applied Surface Science, 255*(4), 1395–1399. doi:10.1016/j. apsusc.2008.06.129

Lee, W. J., Choi, C. J., Park, G. C., & Yang, O. B. (2016). Characterization of boron diffusion phenomena according to the specific resistivity of n-type Si wafer. *Journal of Nanoscience and Nanotechnology, 16*(2), 1665–1668. doi:10.1166/ jnn.2016.11945 PMID:27433642

Liao, Z., Gauquelin, N., Green, R. J., Macke, S., Gonnissen, J., Thomas, S., ... Rijnders, G. (2017). Thickness dependent properties in oxide heterostructures driven by structurally induced metal–oxygen hybridization variations. *Advanced Functional Materials, 27*(17). doi:10.1002/adfm.201606717

Lin, Z., Wang, Z., Yuan, G., & Leburton, J. P. (2018). Numerov Schrödinger solver with complex potential boundaries for open multilayer heterojunction systems. *Journal of the Optical Society of America. B, Optical Physics, 35*(7), 1578–1584. doi:10.1364/JOSAB.35.001578

Lu, J., Wang, R., Ren, J., Kulkarni, M., & Jiang, J. H. (2019). Quantum-dot circuit-QED thermoelectric diodes and transistors. *Physical Review B: Condensed Matter and Materials Physics, 99*(3). doi:10.1103/PhysRevB.99.035129

Magee, C. W., Hockett, R. S., Biiyiiklimanli, T. H., Abdelrehim, I., & Marino, J. W. (2007). SIMS analyses of ultra-low energy B ion implants in Si: Evaluation of profile shape and dose accuracy. *AIP Conference Proceedings, 931*, 142–145. doi:10.1063/1.2799359

Magee, C. W., & Honig, R. E. (1982). Depth profiling by SIMS-depth resolution, dynamic range and sensitivity. *Surface and Interface Analysis, 4*(2), 35–41. doi:10.1002ia.740040202

Masetti, G., Solmi, S., & Soncini, G. (1976). Temperature dependence of boron diffusion in <111>, <110> and <100> silicon. *Solid-State Electronics, 19*(6), 545–546. doi:10.1016/0038-1101(76)90020-4

Meel, K., Mahala, P., & Singh, S. (2018). Design and fabrication of multi quantum well based GaN/InGaN blue LED. *IOP Conference Series. Materials Science and Engineering, 331*(1). doi:10.1088/1757-899X/331/1/012008

Mirabella, S., De Salvador, D., Napolitani, E., Bruno, E., & Priolo, F. (2013). Mechanisms of boron diffusion in silicon and germanium. *Journal of Applied Physics, 113*(3). doi:10.1063/1.4763353

Molla, M. Z., Zhigunov, D., Noda, S., & Samukawa, S. (2019). Structural optimization and quantum size effect of Si-nanocrystals in SiC interlayer fabricated with bio-template. *Materials Research Express, 6*(6). doi:10.1088/2053-1591/ab102a

Obradovic, B. J. (1997, October). Low energy model for ion implantation of As & B in <100> single-crystal silicon, In *Proceedings of SPIE 1997 Symposium on Microelectronic Manufacturing, Device technology*. Academic Press.

Pal, A., & Sarkar, A. (2014). Analytical study of Dual Material Surrounding Gate MOSFET to suppress short-channel effects (SCEs). *Engineering Science and Technology, an International Journal, 17*(4), pp. 205-212.

Panda, A. K., Dash, G. N., & Pati, S. P. (1994). Effect of the diffusion impurity profile on the microwave properties of silicon $p^+nn^+$ IMPATT diodes. *Semiconductor Science and Technology, 9*(3), 241–248. doi:10.1088/0268-1242/9/3/002

Pelzel, R. (2013). A Comparison of MOVPE and MBE growth technologies for III-V epitaxial structures. In *Proceedings CS MANTECH Conference*, pp. 105-108. New Orleans, LA. Academic Press.

Quhe, R., Li, Q., Zhang, Q., Wang, Y., Zhang, H., Li, J., ... Lu, J. (2018). Simulations of quantum transport in sub-5-nm monolayer phosphorene transistors. *Physical Review Applied, 10*(2). doi:10.1103/PhysRevApplied.10.024022

Sadeghzadeh, S., & Rezapour, N. (2016). The mechanical design of graphene nanodiodes and nanotransistors: Geometry, temperature and strain effects. *RSC Advances, 6*(89), 86324–86333. doi:10.1039/C6RA18191K

Sadigh, B., Lenosky, T. J., Theiss, S. K., Caturla, M. J., de la Rubia, T. D., & Foad, M. A. (1999). Mechanism of boron diffusion in silicon: An *ab initio* and kinetic Monte Carlo study. *Physical Review Letters, 83*(21), 4341–4344. doi:10.1103/PhysRevLett.83.4341

Salvador, D. D., Napolitani, E., Mirabella, S., Bisognin, G., Impellizzeri, G., Carnera, A., & Priolo, F. (2006). Atomistic mechanism of boron diffusion in silicon. *Physical Review Letters, 97*(25). doi:10.1103/PhysRevLett.97.255902 PMID:17280368

Singha, B., & Solanki, C. S. (2016). Boric acid solution concentration influencing p-type emitter formation in n-type crystalline Si solar cells. In *Proceedings IOP Conf. Series: Materials Science and Engineering*, vol. 149. 10.1088/1757-899X/149/1/012174

Stepnicki, P., Pietka, B., Morier-Genoud, F., Deveaud, B., & Matuszewski, M. (2015). Analytical method for determining quantum well exciton properties in a magnetic field. *Physical Review B: Condensed Matter and Materials Physics*, *91*(19). doi:10.1103/PhysRevB.91.195302

Su, Q., Zou, R., Su, Y., & Fan, S. (2018). Morphology control and growth mechanism study of quantum-sized ZnS nanocrystals from single-source precursors. *Journal of Nanoscience and Nanotechnology*, *18*(10), 6850–6858. doi:10.1166/jnn.2018.15516 PMID:29954502

Uomi, K. (2018). "Ultra high-speed quantum-well semiconductor lasers", OSA Technical Digest: Optical Fiber Communication Conference, M2F.1, 2019. Academic Press.

van Lierde, P., Tian, C., Rothman, B., & Hockett, R. A. (2002). Quantitative Secondary Ion Mass Spectrometry (SIMS) of III-V Materials. In *Material Res. Society Symposium Proceeding*, vol. 692, H9.40, pp. 543-548. 10.1117/12.467668

Verlinden, G., Gijbels, R., & Geuens, I. (1999). Quantitative secondary ion mass spectrometry depth profiling of surface layers of cubic silver halide microcrystals. *Journal of the American Society for Mass Spectrometry*, *10*(10), 1016–1027. doi:10.1016/S1044-0305(99)00064-1

Watkins, G. D. (1975). Defects in irradiated silicon: EPR and electron-nuclear double resonance of interstitial boron. *Physical Review B: Condensed Matter and Materials Physics*, *12*(12), 5824–5839. doi:10.1103/PhysRevB.12.5824

Whitby, J. A., Östlund, F., Horvath, P., Gabureac, M., Riesterer, J. L., Utke, I., ... Michler, J. (2012). High spatial resolution time-of-flight secondary ion mass spectrometry for the masses: A novel orthogonal ToF FIB-SIMS instrument with in situ AFM. *Advances in Materials Science and Engineering*, *2012*, 180437. doi:10.1155/2012/180437

Wulf, U., Kučera, J., Richter, H., Horstmann, M., Wiatr, M., & Höntschel, J. (2017). Channel Engineering for Nanotransistors in a Semiempirical Quantum Transport Model. *Mathematics*, *5*(4), 68. doi:10.3390/math5040068

Yakimenko, I. P., Yakimenko, I. I., & Berggren, K. F. (2019). Basic modeling of effects of geometry and magnetic field for quantum wires injecting electrons into a two-dimensional electron reservoir. *Journal of Physics Condensed Matter*, *31*(34).

Yang, X., Gao, A., Wang, Y., & Li, T. (2018). Wafer-level and highly controllable fabricated silicon nanowire transistor arrays on (111) silicon-on-insulator (SOI) wafers for highly sensitive detection in liquid and gaseous environments. *Nano Research*, *11*(3), 1520–1529. doi:10.100712274-017-1768-z

Zheng, W., Zheng, B., Yan, C., Liu, Y., Sun, X., Qi, Z., ... Pan, A. (2019). Direct vapor growth of 2D vertical heterostructures with tunable band alignments and interfacial charge transfer behaviors. *Advancement of Science*, *6*(7). PMID:30989032

Chapter 9

# Wireless Medicine Searching System Using GSM Modem in Smart City

**Mandakinee Bandopadhyay**
*Asansol Engineering College, India*

**Subrata Chattopadhyay**
*National Institute of Technical Teachers' Training and Research, Kolkata, India*

## ABSTRACT

*With the development of mobile communication technologies and the popularity of relating devices, GSM network-based intelligent systems have been used more and more widely. Most existing intelligent systems have built on mobile platforms, but those systems don't provide any facility that could save time and energy. But people suffer from lack of time and energy to buy essential needs like medicine, etc. and they like to communicate to the supplier to get confirmation instantly before leaving home or office to collect the same. So, in society, it needs to give alignment without going on field. This chapter copes this problem using wireless database searching scheme using GSM technology, which is very useful in smart cities, where cell phone is an essential part of living. The system receives information from outsiders and customers through GSM modem database searches of all the suppliers connected in a common server and sends the result through short messages independently to the customer showing the availability.*

DOI: 10.4018/978-1-7998-2584-5.ch009

# INTRODUCTION

The wireless data services associated with communication industry becomes flourishing day by day (Pahlavan & Levesque, (1994); Zheng, Lee & Lee, (2007); Jamil, (2008); Cao, (2009); Wang, (2010); Figueiredo, Riberio, & Conforti, (2011). Many academicians as well as industry personnel have come forward to develop the wireless network area and also making it more and more popular. Point-to-point access employs a basic client-server model, where the server is responsible for processing a query and returning the result to the client via a dedicated point-to- point channel (Hu, Lee & Lee, (1999); Zheng, Lee & Lee, (2007)). Wireless data services and systems represent a rapidly growing and increasingly important segment of the communications industry. While the wireless data industry is becoming increasingly diverse and fragmented, one can identify a few mainstreams, which relate directly to users' requirement for data services (Pahlavan & Levesque, (1994); Jamil, (2008); Cao, (2009); Wang, (2010); Haifeng, (2010); Hu, Lee & Lee, (1999)). With the widespread deployment of wireless networks and the fast growing popularity of smart mobile devices, there has been an increasing interest in wireless data services from both industrial and academic communities in recent years. Point-to-point access employs a basic client-server model, where the server is responsible for processing a query and returning the result to the client via a dedicated point-to-point channel (Zheng, Lee & Lee, (2007); Figueiredo, Riberio, & Conforti, (2011)). For instance, in search of a medicine people must go to the medicine shop nearby and if it is unavailable they search to the other shop. But in an emergency situation, it is a bit difficult and also the condition of the patient deteriorate. Even, the customer can get the conformation via email or phone calls for the required medicine, but it is dependent on the staff and customer must wait for reply.

The advancement of mobile computing technologies in recent years has contributed to the growth of smart cities. Though internet may be indispensable today, but still it is not that friendly for many of the users. But nowadays, most of the users know to operate the mobile phones and write messages. For this simplicity, the Global System for Mobile communication (GSM) digital wireless network has been developed (Haifeng, (2010); Ansari, Navada, Agarwal, Patil & Sonkamble, (2011)). It may be used to transmit data at rates of 9600 bits/s. From anywhere people can get the valuable information about any medicine from the common server with the name and address of a store. SMS messages can be sent between users or to and from an application, which gives service development an extra flexibility that encourages innovation (Hansen, (2001); Ansari, Navada, Agarwal, Patil & Sonkamble, (2011)). Basically it interacts between medicine shop server and external world. It is low cost, user-friendly and convenient for secondary development.

In order to overcome this problem, a wireless medicine database searching scheme has been developed. People can get the valuable information from anywhere about any medicine and its availability from any shop.

In the present chapter, an attempt has been made to establish a communication between customer and medicine shopkeeper using wireless data services through SMS alert.

In this present chapter, a smart city is divided into many blocks or zones. All the medicine shop of each blocks are connected with main server, which is containing message receiving and sending circuitry through GSM modem. The details of medicine will be updated by the individual shops through their computer and internet. Whenever people search for a particular medicine, they get reply through SMS mentioning the availability, name of the shop along with its address of that said medicine. This system will take couple of seconds to reply back to the customer through SMS.

## METHOD OF APPROACH

The aim of the investigation is to get useful information about the availability of any medicine in any medicine store through wireless database connection from the common server of the medicine stores, where all the medicine shops of each block of a SMART city is connected. A block diagram of this system is given in Figure 1. The scheme is divided into basic three functional modules each of the module provides a different interface and feature implementation.

### Functional Module Design

The main goal of this scheme was to get useful information about any medicine wirelessly from a common server of all the medicine shop. A block diagram of this scheme is given in Figure 1. The scheme will be divided into three functional modules, and each can provide a different interface and feature implementation.

GSM module provides a standard serial interface, which uses AT command to communicate between a mobile platform and a Data Terminal Equipment (DTE). Therefore, we can use AT command through serial port to control GSM modem and achieve its receiving and sending short messages.

The switching circuit provides different role to maintain the communication between GSM module and Microcontroller unit (MCU) or MCU and common server. Two control pins from MCU are connected to the switching circuit to control the switching functionalities.

*Figure 1. Block diagram of the system*

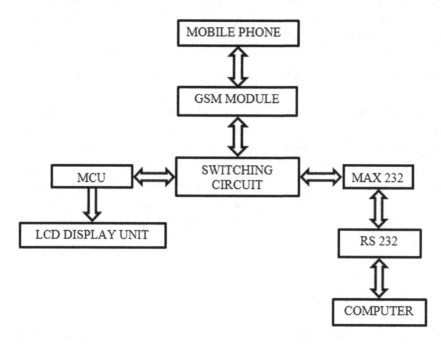

MCU (basically ATMEGA32A) is mainly responsible for coding, which controls the total flow of different modules to make other modules manage their own processes. It also maintains two control pins, which are responsible for communication between GSM module and computer. This module extracts the message content and sends to the computer through switching circuit. Then receives result from computer and sends back to the user through GSM module as shown in Figure 2.

Computer is used as a search engine, which includes common database server and a java application. Database contains name of the medicines and its, quantity available in medicine shops with their address. The application receives query from MCU through RS232 serial port using DB9 female connector, searches in database and sends back the result to the MCU. MAX232 is used to communicate between MCU and RS232 serial port to convert from/to TTL voltage level to/from RS232 voltage levels.

LCD display unit is connected with MCU and shows the status of different data transferring stages.

*Figure 2. GSM module*

## System Software Architecture Design

System software architecture design includes mainly MCU functions and computer functions.

## MCU Functions

MCU functional diagram is shown in Figure 3. MCU functions include message content, mobile no. and data and time extraction, check whether the message is received from an mobile number, which is updated in data base or not.

If yes then go for database updating otherwise go for database searching. In case of database searching, MCU is connected to the computer through switching circuit, then sends the message content to the computer and waiting for the searching result. After receiving the result from the computer, MCU will be connected to the GSM module and sends the result to the users' mobile through the GSM module. These functions have been implemented using C programming.

For debugging AVR software the AVR Studio 4 have been used as an Integrated Development Environment. The AVR Studio allows chip simulation and in-circuit emulation for the AVR family of microcontrollers. The AVR Studio uses a COF object file for simulation. This file is created with through the C compiler by selecting COF as the output file type.

*Figure 3. Flow chart of MCU function*

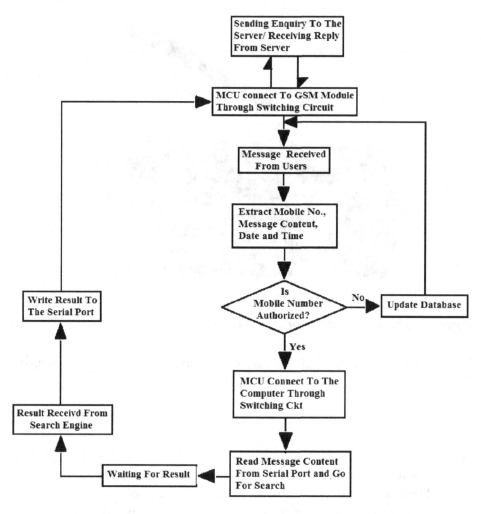

## Computer Functions

Computer functions include mainly database searching and updating. After reading data through serial port, searching is being done and the results are to be written to the serial port. These functions have been developed using Java programming. The Flow Chart of Computer Function is shown in Figure 4.

Basically, the JAVA application of the system is always running condition. When data comes through the serial port, searching will be done by the application and send the result through serial port to the microcontroller. To run JAVA application

*Figure 4. Flow Chart of computer function program*

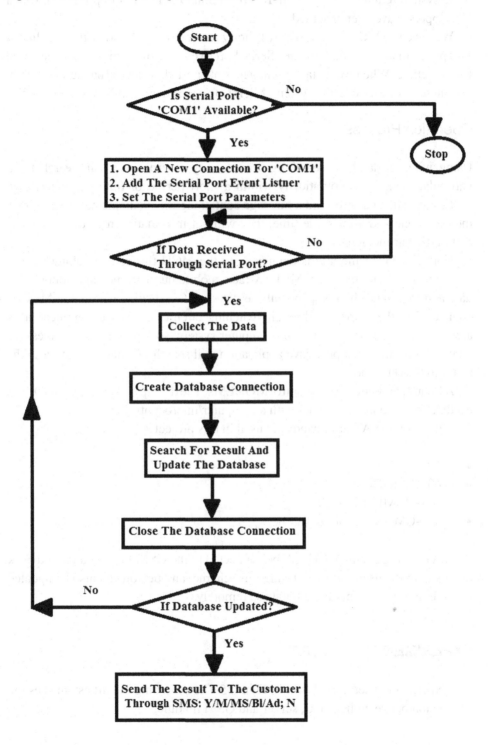

some system requirements (like JDK 6 from Sun/Oracle and Eclipse IDE for Java Developers) have been installed.

We have used RXTX Serial port Library to access serial port with Java. In our Java program we have implemented Serial Port Event Listener and override the Serial Event method. Whenever data is coming in serial port, this method has automatically executed. For designing the system, Microsoft office access 2007has been used.

## Operation Process

Using wireless database searching scheme, any external user can search for a particular medicine automatically within a short period of time from anywhere of the city. They have to send a message containing the medicine name from their mobile phone and after some time, they will get information regarding status of that particular medicine.

Normally GSM module is connected to the MCU through switching circuit. After receiving any message, MCU extracts mobile number, message content and date and time, and then displays all the data in LCD display unit. Then MCU is connected to the computer through switching circuit. As the java application is always in running condition in the computer system, so after reading the message content from the serial port, java application will search in database and write the result to the serial port.

AT commands are used to control MODEMs. The dial up and wireless MODEMs need AT commands to interact with a computer/microcontroller

The following AT commands are used in this project

- AT
- AT+CMGF=1
- AT+CNMI=1,2,0,0,0
- AT+CMGS="Mobile Number"

After getting result, MCU will be connected to the GSM module and send back the result to the users' mobile. Using this scheme, any person can also be updated through their mobile no in the database remotely.

## EXPERIMENTAL RESULT

The experimental setup is shown in Figure 5.The switching circuit establishes the connection between the MCU, server and GSM module.

*Figure 5. Front view of experimental set-up*

The database has been designed in Microsoft Office Access 2007 as shown in Figure 6. The medicine details such as availability of requested medicine, name of medicine, name of available shop, location of the shop along its details address are mentioned in table form. The abbreviations used in the table are listed below:

- Y-Available
- M- Medicine
- MS- Medicine Shop
- Bl-Block
- Ad-Address
- N-Not Available

In this present investigation, we have chosen 4 numbers of medicines, 4 nos. of Block for a SMART City and each Block is having 4 numbers of Medicine Shop. Different circumstances are illustrated here. The database is containing the information like availability of requested medicine, medicine ID, name of medicine, name of medicine shop, block and particular address of the shop. In the database, we can see that, medicine M1 is available in the shop no 1 and 13, medicine M2 is available in shop no 6 and 14, medicine M3 is available in shop no 3,7,11 and medicine M4 is not at all available in any shop.

When any customer will request for any medicine to the server through SMS, he/she will receive a reply message from the server mentioning the availability of the medicine, shop no, block no and address.

After switching on the system, LCD display will initialize, baud rate and input-output pins are set up, that are a part of the primary settings. During this period, LCD module displays the message "INITIALIZING…" which is shown in Figure

*Figure 6. Database Design in MS Access 2007*

| ID | Field1 | Field2 | Field3 | Field4 | Field5 | Field6 | Field7 | Add New Field |
|----|--------|--------|--------|--------|--------|--------|--------|---------------|
| 2 | Medicine Id | Medicine Name | Medicine Shop | Block | Address | Quantity | Availability | |
| 3 | 2001 | M1 | MS1 | Bl1 | Ad1 | 05 | Y | |
| 4 | 2002 | M2 | MS2 | Bl1 | Ad2 | 00 | N | |
| 5 | 2003 | M3 | MS3 | Bl1 | Ad3 | 09 | Y | |
| 6 | 2004 | M4 | MS4 | Bl1 | Ad4 | 00 | N | |
| 7 | 2001 | M1 | MS5 | Bl2 | Ad5 | 00 | N | |
| 8 | 2002 | M2 | MS6 | Bl2 | Ad6 | 10 | Y | |
| 9 | 2003 | M3 | MS7 | Bl2 | Ad7 | 09 | Y | |
| 10 | 2004 | M4 | MS8 | Bl2 | Ad8 | 00 | N | |
| 11 | 2001 | M1 | MS9 | Bl3 | Ad9 | 00 | N | |
| 12 | 2002 | M2 | MS10 | Bl3 | Ad10 | 00 | N | |
| 13 | 2003 | M3 | MS11 | Bl3 | Ad11 | 06 | Y | |
| 14 | 2004 | M4 | MS12 | Bl3 | Ad12 | 00 | N | |
| 15 | 2001 | M1 | MS13 | Bl4 | Ad13 | 06 | Y | |
| 16 | 2002 | M2 | MS14 | Bl4 | Ad14 | 05 | Y | |
| 17 | 2003 | M3 | MS15 | Bl4 | Ad15 | 00 | N | |
| 18 | 2004 | M4 | MS16 | Bl4 | Ad16 | 00 | N | |
| * | (New) | | | | | | | |

7. After completing these tasks, "READY......" is exhibited, this is shown in Figure 8. Then the content of SMS is sent to the computer and the status will be shown in Figure 9. After that, the computer sends the response to the user mobile.

The status and useful information received from computer through mobile against different SMS of medicine name by different customer are shown in Figures 10 – 13.

## CONCLUSION

Nowadays, the database is more and more widely used, but the research combining it with message system is still limited. This Database system (DBS) is connected with mobile phone; hence the medicine user can get useful information rapidly.

*Figure 7. Display after powered on*

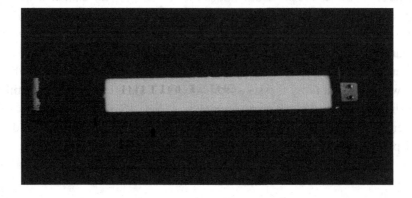

*Figure 8. Display after initializing*

*Figure 9. Data sending to the PC*

On an average, it only takes 1-2 minutes (depending upon size of the database and length of the title) to received and send a return message, that is, the DBS has a higher efficiency of delivering the information.

From the experimental study, a good repeatability has been observed in the proposed system. The GSM module finds the transmitter (users' mobile) output and the useful information is returned back to the user's mobile according to their medicine queries quite satisfactorily. The designed circuit saves energy and valuable time. It works automatically without any involvement of manpower.

There are several opportunities for improving on the work presented here. During searching functionality (from receiving message to transmitting message) if the GSM module is receiving any new message, the new message is wasted because at that time microcontroller is being connected to the computer. In future work, a queue can be implemented in the system, which stores the new messages and after completion of the current cycle, the next message will come from the queue.

*Figure 10. Status of medicine M1*

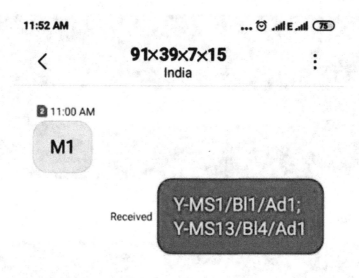

*Figure 11. Status of medicine M2*

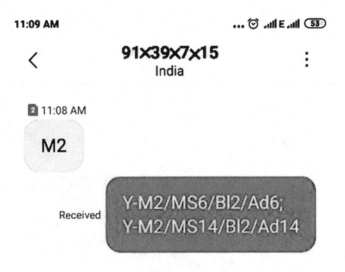

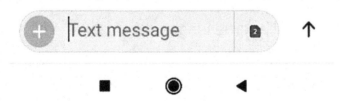

*Figure 12. Status of medicine M3*

*Figure 13. Status of medicine M4*

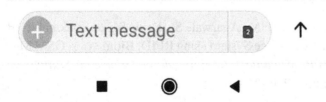

## DISCUSSION

The most advantage of this system is that, it works automatically after receiving the message from the customer, without any involvement of any other system as well as manpower. The system is cost-effective and the design is very simple.

When the system is powered on, it would take few seconds to get started properly, otherwise some problem like character missing, blank screen, may occur. It is to be noted the after every restart of PC the software application should be run manually.

The design has a good flexibility and can be implemented in different organizations regarding part-searching facility, library, banking sectors etc. So, people can easily avoid the queue at the counters and save their valuable time and energy. Hence the developed automation system may be treated as a low cost reliable and user-friendly system.

## FUTURE SCOPE

There are several scopes for improving on the work presented here. If the GSM module receives any new message, during any running cycle, the new message becomes wasted as no two different instruction can run simultaneously due to the microcontroller is connected to the computer at that time.

In future work, a queue might be implemented in the system, which may store the new messages and it will be received to the receiver after completion of the current cycle. Another system could be implemented that, in the unavailability of the prescribed medicine a tentative date for availability of that particular medicine or the name of some alternate medicine with same composition is sent back through SMS automatically within a short time period. In the present work, a prototype of the system has been designed with limited number of medicine shops but in future it can be implemented with cloud computing and big data for large scale application.

## REFERENCES

Ansari, A. N., Navada, A., Agarwal, S., Patil, S., & Sonkamble, B. A. (2011). Automation of Attendance System using RFID, Biometrics, GSM Modem with Net Framework. In *Proceedings International Conference on Multimedia Technology [ICMT 2011]*, pp. 2976-2979.

Cao, S. (2009). GSM Modem-based Mobile Auxiliary Learning System. In *Proceedings International Conference on Computational Intelligence and Software Engineering [CISE 2009]*, pp. 1-4.

Figueiredo, R. C., Riberio, A. M. O., Arthur, R., & Conforti, E. (2011). *Remote SMS Instrumentation Supervision and Control Using LabVIEW, Practical Application and Solutions Using Labview Software* (pp. 317–342). PA: Intechopen.

Haifeng, C. (2010). SQL-based Educational Management System Design. In *Proceedings 2nd International Conference on Computer Engineering and Technology [ICCET 2010]*, pp. v3 (441-445).

Hansen, M. S., & Dørup, J. (2001). Wireless access to a pharmaceutical database: A demonstrator for data driven Wireless Application Protocol applications in medical information processing. *Journal of Medical Internet Research, 3*(1), e4. doi:10.2196/jmir.3.1.e4 PMID:11720946

Hu, Q., Lee, D. L., & Lee, W. C. (1999). Performance Evaluation of a Wireless Hierarchical Data Dissemination System. In Proceedings IEEE International Conference on Mobile Computing and Networking, pp. 163-173. doi:10.1145/313451.313528

Jamil, T. (2008). Design and Implementation of a Wireless Automatic Meter Reading System. In *Proceedings of the World Congress on Engineering [WCE 2008]*, vol. I, UK.

Pahlavan, K., & Levesque, A. H. (1994). Wireless Data Communications. *Proceedings of the IEEE, 82*(9), 1398–1430. doi:10.1109/5.317085

Wang, N. (2010). Material Information Management System Design in Enterprise. In *Proceedings of 2nd International Conference on Computer and Automation Engineering [ICCAE 2010]*, pp. 521-525. 10.1109/ICCAE.2010.5451597

Zheng, B., Lee, W. C., & Lee, D. L. (2007). On Searching Continuous k Nearest Neighbours in Wireless Data Broadcast Systems. *IEEE Transactions on Mobile Computing, 6*(7), 748–761. doi:10.1109/TMC.2007.1004

# Chapter 10
# Instrumentation and Automation Grounding

**Shreem Ghosh**
*Johnson Controls Inc, India*

**Arijit Ghosh**
*RCC Institute of Information Technology, India*

## ABSTRACT

*In any electrical or electronic systems, unwanted signals known as noise signals are encountered which interact with the true signal and thus affecting signal quality. Noise may enter into a device or system in many forms and have a different order of impacts. Prevention and elimination of noise had attained paramount importance to ensure signal fidelity. This chapter presents a comprehensive analysis on elimination of noise by electronic grounding of instrumentation and automation systems as well as various engineering considerations for the same.*

## INTRODUCTION

Noise can be defined as an unwanted random signal which interferes with the desired signal to distort its quality. Our subject of interest in this paper is electrical noise. As is evident that noise need to be prevented to enter into the system and if already present need to be eliminated. For this we need to analyse the various sources of noise, the types of noise, the impact it creates on the main signal and the mechanism by which we can eliminate the noise and maintain signal fidelity. Noise may be internally generated within the system i.e., within the circuit when we call it internal noise or the source may be external when we call it an external noise (Attri, R. K.,

DOI: 10.4018/978-1-7998-2584-5.ch010

1998). The sources of internal noise may be Thermal noise, Shot noise, etc. which may be defined as below.

1.  Thermal Noise is generated as a statistical random kinetic motion of electron due to thermal energy. This sets up a noise voltage whose time integral over a long period is however zero. This random voltage depicts as a random noise.
2.  Shot noise is characterised by random arrival of electron across junctions like P-N junctions in a semiconductor circuit.
3.  Transit Time Noise is due to the different time taken by the charge carriers to travel from input to output terminals. This is particularly significant at high frequency signal.
4.  Flicker noise also known as (1/f) noise is a type of low frequency noise, which is generated mainly in DC electronic circuits due to variation in either base current or junction temperature in BJTs or MOSFETs resulting in variation of resistanceand hence voltage or current fluctuations in the circuit.

Principle external noise is classified as Atmospheric, Solar/Cosmic Noise and machine made noise which may be described as below.

1.  Atmospheric noise arises due to lightning discharge in the atmosphere while the solar and cosmic noises are emitted as electrical energy due to very high temperature of the Sun or stars.
2.  Machine made noise is generated by electrical machines,high voltage lines, fluorescent lights, etc.

Next it is important to study the impact of noise on the basic signal. The impact of noise is analysed by Signal to Noise ratio (S/N). The noise appears in a current carrying conductor in common mode or differential mode. The nature of noise pickup is different and so is the methodology of elimination. Based on the nature of noise pick up, noise in a circuit is classified as Common Mode Noise and Differential Mode Noise.

1.  In Differential mode noise for a dual input system, noise voltage is picked by the two inputs having voltage at same magnitude but with 180° out of phase. As a result the differential mode signal flows through the load. In a twisted pair cable the direction of current at the adjacent wires are opposite and they cancel out the magnetic field (Pfeiffer, C. John).
2.  Common mode noise for a two-input system is classified by that noise which generates same voltage at the two terminals resulting in zero differential voltage across the terminal. However, the common mode current flows to the ground

coupled with the stray capacitance between the current carrying conductors and ground. This results in generation of electromagnetic radiation. In a twisted pair cable the current in the adjacent twisted pair flows in the same direction adding positively the magnetic field. This results in generation of electromagnetic noise.

While there are many techniques, which eliminate noise pick up in Electronic devices and current carrying conductors, this paper will address the methodology adopted in grounding procedure abiding various codes and standards and various industrial procedures which have been successfully adopted leading to successful elimination of noise in an integrated Instrumentation and Automation system which are geographically distributed in a Plant (Klipec, E. B.) and (Shah, J. S).

## ELECTRONIC GROUND

Electrical/electronic ground is a conceptual medium, which at any point of time may act as an infinite source or sink for electrical charges without any rise or fall of its own potential. Earth's surface is considered to act as an Electrical/ Electronic ground. This capability of earth to source and sink electrical charges are successfully utilised for elimination of electronic noise internally generated in electronic circuit or network or from external pick up. However to convert earth surface to an ideal earthing medium, certain engineering techniques need to be adopted. Also there should be a systematic approach for connecting the circuit, the instrument chassis and other components in the network following isolation as required in the system. The electronic grounding scheme for the instrumentation and automation system consists of the following components:

1. Grounding points for instrumentation system
2. Connection with earth pits
3. Earth pits

The different grounding points in a typical instrumentation and automation system can be explained through Figure 1 presented herewith. A study of the diagram reveals that virtually there are two grounding points viz. Electrical Ground or also called as Plant Earth and the other Instrumentation Ground or designated Electronic Earth. Although both are connected to mother earth and virtually interconnected, separate electronic earth is practiced to protect flow of high current discharge in electrical ground to have any impact on the electronic circuit of Instrumentation and Automation system. In the diagram shown below it may be noted that while the

*Figure 1. Different grounding points in a typical instrumentation and automation system*

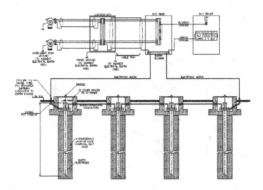

body of the field instruments or field Junction Box or the Cabinet housing of the electronic hardware and the cable tray are connected directly to the nearest electrical earth pit, the electronic earth is connected to the cable screen and the Electronic card rack or Chassis which are in contact with the reference electronic circuit earth. Thus we see that any point which may come in contact with human touch and not connected to electronic circuit earth are connected to the electrical earth pit. However electronic circuit reference earth and free pick up charges along the screen of the signal carrying cables are connected to the Electronic earth.

While the requirement of Electronic earth is established, it is important to define the ideal specification requirement of such ground and the constructional and topological aspects. It is evident that ideally the earth pit resistance as seen by an electronic circuit should be zero, but in practice the same cannot be achieved. In industry, electronic circuits are designed with due consideration of the practical ground resistance limitation and in field engineering practices as followed by reputed Control system manufacturers, the ground resistance has been accepted between 0.5 to 1 Ohm. With this value, projects are in successful operation. The basic construction of Earth Pit to maintain earth resistance within the stipulated limits is shown in Figure 2. It essentially consists of an earth pit about 3-3.5 meters in depth containing a hollow GI pipe embedded in a uniform and homogeneous mixture of coke or charcoal, salt and sand. Often Bentonite mixture is also introduced to ensure an ideal almost zero resistance earth path. At the top, the pipe bolting arrangements with the terminal strip are provided. Also a funnel with wire mesh is connected to the pipe top for occasional introduction of water or electrolyte to ensure minimum resistance to the ground. Connection to the ground pit as per IS: 3043 -2001 is shown in Figure 2, Detail A.

*Figure 2. A typical schematic diagram of a single earth pit electrode*

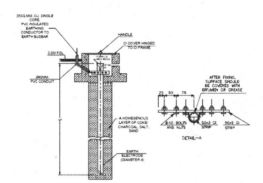

Sometimes due to high soil resistivity at a location, a single earth pit often fails to maintain the desired earth resistance and as a result, more no. of earth pits are constructed and connected in various topologiesas shown in Figure 3 based on mathematical calculations considering the local earth soil resistivity to achieve the desired result. Often it is required to construct deep excavated earth pit called deep bored pit as high as 15 -20 meters depth which become essential to achieve the desired ground resistance path .This is specifically applicable to rocky soil, where the earth resistivity value is typically 700 Ohm meter and higher.

## METHODOLOGY FOR SELECTION OF ELECTRONIC EARTHING SCHEME

In accordance with IEEE 1050-2004, IEEE Std. 80 – 2000 and standard industry practices, the I&C signal ground cables are generally separated from the electrical equipment safety ground cables in order to minimise the EMI coupling from electrical equipment which may have high levels of EMI that could interfere or damage sensitive electronic instruments and automation system. In order to obtain the desired earth pit resistance, initially resistance of a single earth pit is calculated based on the Earth Resistivity Test (ERT) report obtained from the soil survey of the area. If the required pit resistance is not achieved, more than one earth pits are considered which are connected together through buried horizontal conductors or strips and subsequently the equivalent earth resistance is calculated (Liptak, G. Bela) and (Patranabis, D). As a standard practice a maximum of 4-5 earth pits are generally considered for electronic earthing in various topologies. In case the desired resistance value is not achieved, then the earth pits are treated by adding different materials like charcoal, bentonite, salt, etc. to achieve the desired low resistance. If

*Figure 3. Different topologies for interconnection of earth pit electrodes*

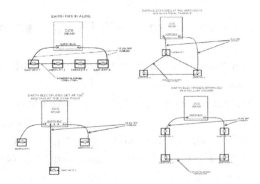

the required earth pit resistance is still not obtained, as a standard practice deep bore type earthing scheme is considered. In general practice, the maximum allowable earth pit resistance for electronic earthing is governed by the industry practices and as provided by the Automation manufacturers as per their system requirements (Yen-Lung, K) and (Whitlock, B).

## EARTH PIT RESISTANCE CALCULATION

### Earth pit Resistance for a Single Electrode

In accordance with BS 7430-2011 standard, the earth resistancefor a single rod electrode as indicated in Figure 2 can be given by equation(1).

$$R = \frac{p}{2\pi L}\left[\bullet \ln(8L/d) - 1\right] \tag{1}$$

where,
R is the resistance of the electrode in ohms ($\Omega$)
$\rho$ is the resistivity of soil, in ohm metres ($\Omega$ m)
L is the length of the electrode, in metres (m)
d is the diameter of the rod, in metres (m)
It is known that the resistivity of soil varies based on any of the following factors:

1. Depth from the soil surface
2. Type and concentration of soluble chemicals in the soil
3. Moisture content in the soil

4.   Soil temperature

## Earth pit Resistance for 'n' no. Earth Electrodes in Parallel

In case of electronic earthing, if the earth pit resistance is still high considering a single earth pit electrode, then a combination of earth pit electrodes in a line are considered which are interconnected together by horizontal buried strips/round electrodes for further reducing the equivalent earth pit resistance. A typical scheme for 'n' number of earth electrodes connected in parallel using buried horizontal strips or conductors is shown in Figure 4. In accordance with BS 7430-2011 standard, the equivalent earth pit resistance for 'n' number of vertical buried rod electrodes can be given by equation (2).

$$R_n = R\frac{[1 + \lambda a]}{n} \tag{2}$$

where,

$$a = \frac{\rho}{2\,\pi Rs} \tag{3}$$

$R$ = Single rod resistance in isolation, $\Omega$

s = Rod spacing, m

$\rho$ = Soil resistivity, $\Omega$ m

$\lambda$ = multiplying factor

n = number of electrodes

The multiplying factor '$\lambda$' is related to the number of parallel electrodes (n) in a line and is indicated in Table 1.

The equation (2) gives the equivalent resistance obtained when 'n' number of electrodes is vertically buried in a line, however the equivalent earth resistance can be further lowered by connecting the horizontal buried strips or electrodes with the vertically buried electrodes as indicated in Figure 4.

*Table 1. Multiplying factors for vertical parallel electrodes arranged in a line*

| No. of electrodes (n) | 2 | 3 | 4 | 5 | 6 | 7 | 8 | 9 | 10 |
|---|---|---|---|---|---|---|---|---|---|
| Multiplying Factor (λ) | 1.00 | 1.66 | 2.15 | 2.54 | 2.87 | 3.15 | 3.39 | 3.61 | 3.81 |

*Figure 4. Typical schematic diagram of 'n' number of earth electrodes connected together by buried horizontal electrodes*

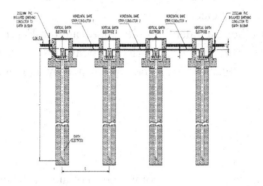

Let us consider the equivalent resistance of 'n' number of vertical electrodes be $R_n$ and let the resistance of each identical buried horizontal strip or electrode be $R_h$, then it can be represented by an equivalent circuit as shown in Figure 5.

## Resistance of a Buried Horizontal Conductor

In accordance with IS 3043 standard, the equivalent resistance for a buried horizontal conductor or strip can be given by equation (4)

*Figure 5. Equivalent circuit diagram for 'n' number vertical earth electrodes connected in parallel and interconnected by horizontal buried strips*

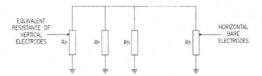

$$R_h = \frac{100\rho}{2\pi S}[ln(2S^2 / wt)] \tag{4}$$

where,

$\rho$ = Soil resistivity, $\Omega$ m

S = Length of strip or conductor in cm

w = Depth of burial of the horizontal electrode in cm

t = Width (in case of strip) or twice the diameter (for conductors) in cm

Equivalent earth pit resistance for multiple vertical earth electrodes with interconnected horizontal electrodes

In accordance to the equivalent circuit as indicated in Figure 4, the equivalent earth pit resistance for 'n' number of buried vertical earth electrodes connected by buried horizontal earth electrodes can be represented by equation (5).

$$R = \frac{R_n\left[R_h / (n-1)\right]}{R_n + \left[R_h / (n-1)\right]} \tag{5}$$

Generally in industrial projects a combination of any of the earth pit topologies are adopted considering the local soil resistivity. However treated earth pit and maintenance of earth pit by periodically adding electrolyte from top ensures a very stable ground and hence a stable reference ground potential and an easy ground path to electronic noise pick up.

## CONCLUSION

Earthing of circuits are the most important criteria to achieve reference working voltage and also to eliminate various external noise signals in Instrumentation and Automation system (Elavsky, T) and (Kanetkar, R.V). Hence under all practical conditions design and implementation of a reliable, maintainable and stable earth pit considering the local soil characteristics are done abiding various reference codes and standards and industrial standard practices.An incorrect grounding will always create a permanent problem to the maintenance team and hence highest consideration need to be given during the design and engineering stage of a project.

# REFERENCES

Attri, R. K. (1998). Various noise sources & noise reduction techniques in instrumentation. In Instrumentation Design Series (Electronics), Paper No. 1, June 1998.

Klipec, E. B. (1967). Reducing Electrical Noise in Instrument Circuits. In Vol. IGA -3, No. 2 MAR/APR 1967. doi:10.1109/TIGA.1967.4180749

Liptak, B. G. (2018). Instrument Engineers Handbook Volume II: Process Control and Optimization, CRC Press.

Patranabis, D. (1976). *Principles of industrial instrumentation* (3rd ed.). Tata McGraw Hill Education Pvt. Ltd.

Pfeiffer, C. J. (2001). *Principles of Electrical Grounding.* Pfeiffer Engineering Co.

Shah, J. S. (2001). Field Wiring and Noise Considerations for Analog Signals 340224C-01, Application Note 025 National Instruments Corporation, July, 2001. BS:7430:2011, "Code of practice for protective earthing of electrical installations". IS:3043 -2001, "Code of practice for earthing". IEEE Std 1050 – 2004, "IEEE guide for Instrumentation and Control Equipment Grounding in Generating Stations". IEEE Std. 80 – 2000, "IEEE guide for safety in AC Substation Grounding".

Whitlock, B. (2016). Understanding, Finding, & Eliminating Ground Loops, CEDIA Class EST016.

Yen-Lung, K. (n.d.). Considerations for Instrument Grounding, Application Note. *Agilent Technologies Taiwan.*

Elavsky, T. (n.d.). A Condensed Guide to Automation Control System Specification, Design, & Installation: White Paper, Automation Direct.

Kanetkar, R. V. (n.d.). AR/01-Grounding and Earthing of Distributed Control Systems and Power Electronic Systems. *Asia Power Quality Initiative.*

Chapter 11

# Spray Pyrolysis Thin Film Deposition Technique for Micro–Sensors and Devices

**Monoj Kumar Singha**
https://orcid.org/0000-0003-3838-9229
*Indian Institute of Science, India*

**Vineet Rojwal**
*Indian Institute of Science, India*

## ABSTRACT

*Thin film is used for sensing and electronic devices applications. Various techniques are used for thin film deposition. This chapter presents the Spray pyrolysis deposition technique used for the growth of thin films sensing and device material. Spray pyrolysis is an inexpensive method to grow good crystalline thin film compared to other thin film deposition techniques. The chapter gives an overview of the spray process used for thin film deposition. Basic setup for this process is explained. Parameters affecting the deposition process is explained, as are the various spray methods. Finally, some examples of spray pyrolysis in different applications like a gas sensor, UV photodetector, solar cell, photocatalysis, and supercapacitor are discussed.*

## INTRODUCTION

Sensing films are a necessary part of sensors and electronic devices. Sensing films as a form of thin films are used heavily for the last 100 years because of their properties,

DOI: 10.4018/978-1-7998-2584-5.ch011

technical value, and sensing performance. They have a huge range of applications, ranging from micrometer to a few square meters on the outer surface of window glasses to microsensors and devices. But thin film technology has progressed rapidly since the last 4-5 decades which in turn progress the research on microsensors and devices. Last 2-3 decades microsensors and device research gain attention to the researchers due to the advancement of fabrication technology. Different techniques like metalorganic chemical vapor deposition (MOCVD) (Myong, Baik, Lee, Cho, & Lim, 1997; Vispute et al., 1998), molecular beam epitaxy (MBE) (Look et al., 2002), radiofrequency magnetron sputtering (Chitanu & Ionita, 2010), pulsed laser deposition (PLD) (Wisz, Virt, Sagan, Potera, & Yavorskyi, 2017), sputtering (Van de Pol, Blom, & Popma, 1991), sol-gel process (Znaidi, Illia, Benyahia, Sanchez, & Kanaev, 2003), hydrothermal (Wang, Xie, Yan, & Duan, 2011) and spray pyrolysis (Nunes, Fernandes, Fortunato, Vilarinho, & Martins, 1999) are used for thin film deposition. These thin films can be grown on any substrate such as glass, polyamide, silicon, stainless steel etc. Various techniques have been studied to find the most reliable and inexpensive way to produce such thin films for sensing applications.

Spray pyrolysis is an inexpensive method compare to other available thin film deposition techniques. Spray technique is an established and widely used thin film technology. It is a one form of chemical vapor deposition which is successfully used to develop solar cells and various oxide-based materials (Ayouchi et al., 2003; Miki-Yoshida & Andrade, 1993; Nunes et al., 1999; Subbaramaiah & Raja, 1994). In this method, two significant advantages are: deposition happens at atmospheric pressure with a large deposition area and it is an inexpensive and fast deposition method. This is a fairly simple method because of the use of a vacuum free framework, whereas basic thin film deposition setups such as Sputtering, CVD, Evaporation, Ablation laser, etc. require vacuum environment for depositing the thin films.

Pyrolysis stands for decomposition at high temperature i.e. under the influence of heat (high temperature)/thermal treatment materials decomposed and it changes its chemical composition. In spray pyrolysis deposition techniques, fine droplets (size of 1-30 μm) are first generated from the precursor solution. Then these streams of droplets containing metal salts are showered onto a heated substrate to develop a solid/porous thin film. Subsequently, the property of the utilized solution and the thermodynamic at the interface of droplets and substrate are key parameters controlling the spray process and the properties of the deposited film. Important deposition parameter such as precursor molarity, flow rate, doping concentration, substrate temperature and properties of the substrate. In this chapter, we will discuss spray pyrolysis, its fundamentals and advantages, different types of spray pyrolysis and finally the application of spray pyrolysis in different sensors and devices.

First work on chemical spray pyrolysis happened on cadmium sulfide (CdS) thin-film solar cell (Chamberlin & Skarman, 1966). After that Researchers made extraordinary efforts to make chemical spray pyrolysis techniques better over about three decades for preparation of the thin film. Subsequently, the spray pyrolysis apparatus is very simple to handle and has good productivity in large scale production for the formation of thin films of metal oxides and metal composite. It has several advantages.

1.    In this system, doping of films is extremely easy, by adding any element into spray solution in any desired proportion.
2.    This technique does not need any high-quality substrate or target, which makes it very economical to be scaled up for industrial applications and not even require vacuum at any stage
3.    By changing the system parameters thickness of the films and deposition rate can be controlled effectively. This feature makes it a better technique than other chemical deposition such as a sol-gel method of deposition.
4.    Establishment of spray pyrolysis setup in the laboratory for thin film development can be easily and would be at low cost compared to other deposition techniques.
5.    Spray thin film formation can be operated at a moderate temperature and developed on various substrate materials.
6.    Large surface area deposition is easily possible with reproducibility.
7.    By varying the spray solvents composition during the deposition process, it may be used to develop multi-layered thin films or films with composition gradients throughout the whole thickness.
8.    Batch production of the thin film is possible.
9.    Developed films are quiet compact and uniform through which reliable kinetic data can be obtained on the film surface.
10.   The different nanostructured based thin film can easily be prepared in a large area. So shape, size, composition, and phase of the film can be easily altered using this method.

## MECHANISM OF SPRAY PYROLYSIS

Decomposition of precursor materials is the basic and fundamental aspects of any spray pyrolysis technique. Pyrolysis happens at the presence of heated substrates. Here we will discuss the total set up for spray pyrolysis. Any spray pyrolysis system has five parts. It consists of precursor solution, atomizer, spray (a stream of droplets), substrate and hot plate. Atomizer is used to atomize the precursor solution into fine streams of droplets. The generation of droplets happens with the help of either air/nitrogen gas or using ultrasonic waves. Most of the cases air is used to generate it. The solution of the metal salt is prepared and kept in the atomizer place. Then atomizer either by air or ultrasonic wave generates the droplets. These droplets then carried by nitrogen gas or air to the heated substrate. A substrate is kept on a heater which is controlled by an external controller for precise temperature. A thermocouple is attached to measure the temperature of the substrate and the feedback temperature control algorithm is used for getting precise temperature during the deposition process. Now uniform and large area of the coating can be achieved by controlling the nozzle or substrate or both. Even film is deposited on a large area ($10 \times 10$ cm$^2$) by using X-Y movement of the nozzle (Pommier, Gril, & Marucchi, 1981). The geometry of the nozzle of the spray plays a crucial role in droplet size and distribution of droplets from the jet on the substrate. The researcher has to change the geometry of the spray nozzle for uniform thin film deposition. Some researcher has done few modifications regarding nozzle such as swinging rotating sprayer resulted in inhomogeneous films with reproducible properties (Kulaszewicz, 1980). Some more modified version of Spray generator has been designed such as using an ultrasonic sprayer to produce aerosol (Dutta, Perrin, Emeraud, Laurent, & Smith, 1995), upward and downward spray mechanism (Arya, 1986) and rotating sprayer for the spray action (Unaogu & Okeke, 1990). Lang's formula is used to measure the size of the droplets generated by ultrasonic vibrations and is given by following formula (Gottlieb, Koropecki, Arce, Crisalle, & Ferron, 1991):

$$d = k\left(\frac{8\pi\sigma}{\rho f}\right)$$

where $d$ is the diameter of the droplets, $\sigma$ is the surface tension, $\rho$ the density of the precursor, $f$ the frequency of vibration and $k$ a constant that depends on the system used. If the frequency of the vibrator increases, droplet size decreases. Some researchers have obtained a uniform distribution of 1-3 μm droplet sizes using a 2.1 MHz ultrasonic generator.

To obtain a fine quality thin film, a spray pyrolysis system must have good solvents and metal salts. Because they need to decompose completely during the process and must produce volatile compounds so that no external defects should not be there in the films. A good crystalline thin film will be produced only when droplets evaporate completely on the surface and forms a crystalline film whereas by products or excess solvents should come out as a vapor phase. This is a heterogeneous process. On the other hand, if the products and by products both are in the vapor phase, then films will not be good. They will make a powdery or amorphous film. This process is known as a homogeneous process. So a heterogeneous process is desirable for the spray pyrolysis based thin film deposition techniques.

There are two main challenges in spray pyrolysis in the deposition of films.

*Figure 1. Schematic diagram of spray pyrolysis system and process flow*

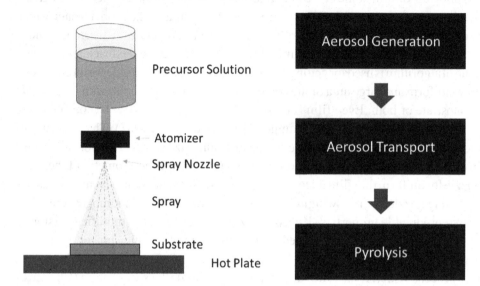

1.   Fine droplets preparation.
2.   It should be uniformly distributed.
3.   decomposition of droplets on a heated substrate

The atomization process is dependent on the atomizer. In general, most of the cases pneumatic system is used as an atomizer. But it has some problems like non-uniform distribution of droplets and it depends on nozzle size. In other cases, the ultrasonic wave is used as an atomizer which produces a very fine stream of droplets. As a consequence, some new or modified version atomization techniques had been developed recently and are being used efficiently for thin film preparation.

## FORMATION OF PARTICLE MORPHOLOGY IN THIN-FILM

During the atomization process, it produces micron or sub-micron sizes of droplets with high purity. Spraying this droplet on a heated substrate give narrow size distribution of particles without aggregates and large quantities in a large area. While droplets tend to form a crust near its surface during the diffusion drying stage at the presence of heating substrate or near to heating substrate. This lead to hollow or fragmented particles. Again forming crust decreases the evaporation rate of the solvent which leads to a sudden rise in temperature and partial pressure inside the droplet. Different morphology of the films obtained when the pressure inside the droplet is sufficiently high. So this process of diffusion drying after forming a crust shell is the main reason for the different morphology of the films. Similarly, high concentrated solution tries to make irregular shapes due to more pressure inside the droplets and reduce the distance between the nozzle to substrate leads to high partial pressure inside the droplets.

Two different groups (Vigui and Spitz, and Siefert) have proposed the model for particle deposition based on substrate temperature and droplet size. These model clearly explain whether a film will be crystalline or amorphous in nature. Figure 2 shows a schematic of this model. This is subdivided into 4 process steps based on droplet sizes: large droplets, medium-size droplets, smaller droplets, and very smaller droplets. When larger droplets are used, they will not be able to vaporize completely on the heated substrate. So these droplets, when fall on the heated substrate, it will form an amorphous film after decomposition. When medium-size droplets are used, solvents will evaporate completely before the heated substrate and left with amorphous salt only. This amorphous salt then decomposed into desired films and by-products will leave as a vapor form. Solvents from the smaller droplets vaporize fast before reaching the heated substrate which left the only salt. So they went to decomposed just before the heated substrate and thin film are formed on the substrate. Finally, when very small droplets are used, solvents quickly evaporate much before the heated substrate and they start to decompose during the vapor state before the heated substrate. So this type of smaller deposition is not good for films because it will produce powdery film and most of the material is wasted due to adhesion issues. This problem can be solved by varying the distance between the nozzle and the heated substrate.

## PARAMETER FOR SPRAY PYROLYSIS DEPOSITION CHARACTERISTICS FEATURES

There are different parameters which affect the film deposition using spray pyrolysis. These parameters include substrate temperature, substrate selection, carrier gas pressure, the distance between nozzle and substrate, the concentration of the solutions. Optimizing these parameters will give a good crystalline film. The growth rate of the films depends on all of it.

### Carrier Gas Pressure

Carrier gas pressure is used for the atomization process of solution into fine particles. Higher pressure results in increased fine particles that can cause the mist of the particles. By adjusting the pressure, we can obtain the desired size but to

*Figure 2. Mechanism for particle formation in spray pyrolysis*

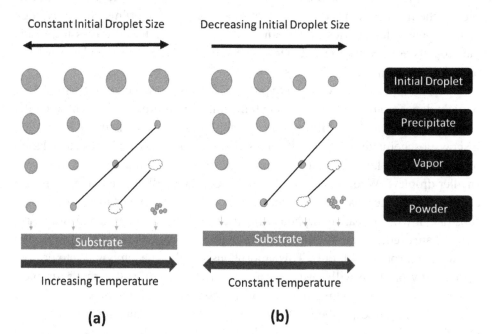

have uniformity in the size Carrier gas pressure also affects the substrate surface temperature and hence it has to be optimized. This is true when we are using a conventional spray pyrolysis system where air/nitrogen pressure is used to generate the mist. But it is not true when we are using ultrasonic as atomizer where ultrasonic wave is used to generate the stream of droplets. Then external nitrogen gas or air is used to carry the droplets on to the heated substrate.

## Nozzle-Substrate Distance

Another important parameter for spray deposition is nozzle to substrate distance. Many reports suggested that distance between the nozzle to substrate is almost 28-30 cm apart. But in our cases, deposition of ZnO on a glass substrate, we have varied the distance as low as 3 cm to 0.8 cm. We get different morphologies like microflowers, nanoflakes, nanorods, thin film of the ZnO material. But in this case, probable nozzle diameter plays an important role. The nozzle diameter is 1.2 cm for our cases. Most of the conventional spray pyrolysis setup has nozzle diameter of 1 mm and they have used air pressure to generate the droplets. In this case, closing the distance between substrate and nozzle, the temperature of the substrate surface reduces which leads to powdery depositions. Another thing is that the spray deposition area reduces when the distance is shorter. So it will not able to cover the full substrate for deposition. The area of spray deposition is increased as this distance increases but not continuously. The flow rate and compressed gas pressure also affect the deposition area along with this parameter. So nozzle to substrate distance plays a crucial role for the morphology of the films.

## Substrate Temperature

Pyrolysis happened on a heated substrate. So substrate temperature plays a crucial role in film deposition. Also, solvent evaporation happened at an elevated temperature so the substrate temperature has the most significant effect on film quality. Many researchers first optimized the substrate temperature for film deposition and they investigated the role of the substrate temperature on film formation and microstructure. Films grown at a lower temperature are generally amorphous in nature whereas films deposited at higher temperatures are polycrystalline in nature (J.-C. Manifacier, Szepessy, Bresse, Perotin, & Stuck, 1979; Maudes & Rodriguez, 1980; Viguie & Spitz, 1975). So there is a requirement of optimum temperature at which crystalline films should be formed. It should retain its electrical, optical, material and mechanical properties. There are other issues of adhesion of films to the substrate if the deposition temperature is low. Films are then peeled off from the substrate. And they form powdery and amorphous films. Again at high substrate temperature cations react with oxygen to form the corresponding oxides. In that case, desired films are not grown instead of oxide films will grow. This is generally very important for solar cell applications where earth-abundant materials (Cu, Zn, Sn. S, Se, Cd etc.) are used for making sensing films.

## Substrates Selection

In general neutral surfaces do not participate in pyrolytic reactions. Thus the selection of substrate is limited to glass, quartz, ceramics, coated oxide/nitride/carbide, Ge, Si, ITO, etc. But recently oxide materials also deposited on polymer substrate also. But the growth of film in a certain direction requires some ions on the substrate which are available on the glass substrate. Sometimes, oxide films on silicon cause etching and usual deposition of a coherent film on a metallic substrate are difficult. Most of the substrates do not react chemically but they may contain some incorporated earth ions in films or removable alkali. Especially glass substrate contains ions like $Ca^{2+}$ and $Li^+$ or $Si^{4+}$. These ions are either as substitutions or interstitial defects in the substrate which increase the substrate temperature during thermal heating. So substrate nature is an essential parameter, particularly for glass, for the diffusion of the alkali ions (J. C. Manifacier, Fillard, & Bind, 1981). The amorphous nature of the substrate (glass) mainly produces favourable growth of thin films; where the crystalline nature (Si) can cause epitaxial growth.

## Precursor Solutions

Precursor solutions are other important parameters for the growth of thin films. Mainly metal salts of nitrate, chloride, acetate and sulfate are used for metal and metal oxides source. Besides some organic compounds of metals are used for the source also. It is always preferable to have nitrate, chloride and acetate metal salt for film deposition. Thermodynamics of the decomposition of salts plays a crucial role here for depositing the films (Aranovich, Ortiz, & Bube, 1979). Mostly water is used as a solvent but in some cases, organic solvents like ethanol, methanol, IPA, and acetones are also used. The concentration of the solution plays a crucial role here. If a high concentration of the solution is used, then it will deposit powdery films. Because the high concentration of solution contains more salts which may not be decomposed completely at that substrate temperature and will have adhesion issues. Besides, it will block the nozzle for conventional spray systems when it uses low flow rate. Again at low concentration of the solution, films will not be deposited entirely on the substrate. So porous pin hole thin films will be deposited on the substrate. So proper concentration of the solution required for the growth of the films. Besides other parameters like nozzle diameter, type of carrier gas, flow rate, time of deposition and volume of the solution also affect the film quality. The film's texture, transparency, and thickness are controlled by controlling these parameters.

After optimizing all the parameters, a fine optimized film is obtained for sensing and device applications. Here we will discuss the growth rate of film in keeping the metal oxide and earth-abundant materials. Growth rate and morphology of the film depends on chemical used as a precursor, solution concentration, substrate temperature, size of droplets while atomizing and other various parameters.

Organometallic compounds are also used due to the low-temperature decomposition. Moreover, the high vapor pressure of compounds allows for using vapor transport rather than liquid transport (Kane, Schweizer, & Kern, 1976; Korzo & Chernyaev, 1973; Korzo & Ryabova, 1967). Researchers have discussed that growth rate and mechanism as a function of precursor molarities (Maudes & Rodriguez, 1980). Furthermore, in case of transparent oxide film thickness increases with time of deposition, molarity of the solution and growth of film depends on substrate temperature (Song, Shigesato, Yasui, Ow-Yang, & Paine, 1998; Vink, Walrave, Daams, Baarslag, & Van den Meerakker, 1995; Yi, SHIGEsAo, Yasui, & Takaki, 1995). At low-temperature spray deposition, growth rate depends on adsorption, surface diffusion desorption and chemical reaction, etc. Which control the kinetics reaction and the molecules are accumulated on the surface of the substrate. But at high temperatures, a molecules do not break down on the substrate due to fast activation process. The growth rate depends on the droplet size too, as the droplet decomposition is a temperature-dependent process. If the size of the droplets is large, the heat absorbed from the environment is not sufficient to evaporate the solvents completely along the substrate and negatively affect the kinetics of the reaction (Bryant, 1977; Siefert, 1984). This will produce powdery films.

## TYPES OF PYROLYSIS TECHNIQUES

Spray pyrolysis techniques for thin film deposition can be classified based on (i) atomization process and (ii) precursor reaction process.

In the atomization process, it is mainly three types and they are pneumatic (pressure-driven gas flow), ultrasonic and electrostatic spray pyrolysis. Whereas precursor reaction-based spray pyrolysis is classified as tubular reactor spray pyrolysis (SP), emulsion combustion spray pyrolysis (ECSP), vapor flame reactor(VFSP) and flam spray pyrolysis (FSP).

### Precursor Reaction is Driven Spray Pyrolysis

Here the source of energy for precursor reaction is the important part of film deposition. Externally heating element is used to heat the precursor solution. Controlling heat is difficult for achieving good crystalline film. For example, when you are using flame spray pyrolysis where flame is used to heat the substrate, it is very difficult to achieve uniform heating throughout the heating zone. Besides droplets will evaporate at a different rate at different regions. So it is difficult to get uniform crystalline films and require specific solvents.

### Ultrasonic Nebulizer Atomization

An ultrasonic frequency is used to atomize the precursor solutions. Micron and sub-micron size droplets are generated uniformly using ultrasonic waves. (Huang, Tao, & Lee, 1997). Ultrasonic wave first makes the fine stream of droplets which later carried by external gases such as air or nitrogen through the pipe onto a heated substrate. There they pyrolyzed and crystalline thin films are formed on the heated substrate. This method provides better coverage of the films on the substrate. It has several advantages like droplet sizes can be varied by changing the frequency. Besides gas flow is required only to carry the aerosol. So uniform droplets are carried throughout the process.

## Electrostatic Spray Pyrolysis

The electric field is created between nozzle and substrate for generating the droplets. It requires a very high voltage (>10 kV). When a high positive voltage is applied then spray is generated and droplets move toward the hot substrate under electrostatic force. When droplets reach the hotplate, then pyrolysis takes place near the substrate surface. The distance between the nozzle and the substrate is kept very low (6 mm). The advantage of this method is the control of morphology (dense or porous) of the film by simply adjusting the timing of deposition (Chen, Buysman, Kelder, & Schoonman, 1995).

## Nebulized Spray Pyrolysis

This method is the common spray pyrolysis method where air pressure is used as an atomizer to produce fine droplets of the solutions. These methods need many accessories. Fine droplet size is produced when the nebulizer size is reduced. Controlling air pressure for different solutions is a must and flow rate depends on the air pressure. The disadvantage of this process is that it is not able to produce uniform droplets compare to the ultrasonic nebulizer.

## Other Spray Pyrolysis

Other spray pyrolysis techniques use the above-mentioned principle but slightly modified way. Some researchers have used perfumed bottle spray pyrolysis techniques. It is the simpler and most inexpensive way to deposit desired sensing films. In this process, a simple perfume bottle is purchased from the market. Then the precursor solution is filled in the bottle. After that spray the solution on heated substrate and obtain desired materials. The most disadvantages are that it is manually handling so precision is less and there is a chance of growing non-uniform film on the substrate. Some researchers have also used the heated substrate upwards and the stream of droplets will flow from downwards to upwards. This is good for nano-morphology based thin film deposition. It has a smooth surface, good equal size distribution of droplets and have reduced flow rate.

## APPLICATION OF SPRAY PYROLYSIS

Spray pyrolysis is used for depositing materials for different applications like gas sensors, supercapacitors, solar cells, photocatalysis, photodetector etc. Here we will discuss very briefly the application of spray pyrolysis.

## Gas Sensor Application

Metal oxides based semiconductors are used for gas sensor applications due to its easy fabrication. Based on their nature, they are classified as p-type and n-type semiconductors. ZnO, CuO, $SnO_2$, $WO_3$, $Fe_2O_3$, $Cr_2O_3$, $MoO_3$, $MnO_2$ are the oxide materials used for gas sensing applications. J. M. Patil has synthesized nanocrystalline $WO_3$ thin film of different thickness on a glass substrate by varying deposition time (J. M. Patil, 2016). They have sensed $H_2S$ gas at 50 $^0$C with a sensitivity of 789 and response and recovery time of 6s and 13 s respectively. The deposition temperature for $WO_3$ thin film was 350 $^0$C, nozzle to substrate distance was kept 30 cm for the 0.05M concentration of the solution. An ultrathin 50 nm and 100 nm $SnO_2$ was deposited on Si substrate using spray pyrolysis for humidity and 5 ppm carbon monoxide detection by Tischner group (Tischner, Maier, Stepper, & Köck, 2008). L.F. da Silva et al. have synthesized ZnO-$SnO_2$ heterojunction. This heterostructure was used to sense ozone and they have detected as low as 20 ppb ozone in the presence of UV light at room temperature (da Silva et al., 2017). Cobalt doped ZnO was synthesized by Onfore group for the ozone sensor (Onofre et al., 2019). Similarly, L. A. Patil group has doped $TiO_2$ film with Pt for hydrogen gas detection (L. A. Patil, Suryawanshi, Pathan, & Patil, 2014). Reduced graphene oxide was also deposited using spray pyrolysis (Slobodian, 2019). O.M. Slobodian et. al have detected VOCs using reduced graphene oxide. Zheng Jiao group has deposited ITO thin films using ultrasonic spray pyrolysis for $NO_2$ sensing. They have got a linear response of NO2 for 10-500 ppm gas at 180 $^0$C (Jiao, Wu, Qin, Lu, & Gu, 2003). Core-shell ZnO/NiO heterojunction was prepared by G. lu group using ultrasonic spray pyrolysis. They have tested the core-shell structure for ethanol detection (F. Liu et al., 2016). V. 1. Krivetsky group have deposited Au loaded nanocrystalline $SnO_2$ using flame spray pyrolysis. They have detected 10 ppm CO gas at 300 $^0$C (Yuliarto, Gumilar, Zulhendri, Nugraha, & Septiani, 2017). Umarji group have deposited chromium oxide thin film for ethanol sensor using ultrasonic spray pyrolysis (Kamble & Umarji, 2012).

## UV Detector

Metal oxides are also used for UV detection applications. Mostly ZnO or doped ZnO is used for UV detector. In some cases, $TiO_2$ is also used for UV detector application. S.I. Inamdar et. Al has deposited ZnO using a spray pyrolysis method. They have obtained visible blind UV detector with photo rise and fall time of 12 s and 9 s respectively (S. I. Inamdar, Ganbavle, & Rajpure, 2014). Han-Yin Liu has deposited $TiO_2$ for a UV detector by ultrasonic spray pyrolysis. These detectors have good rise and fall time of 5 s and 12 s respectively with UV to visible rejection ratio of $2.1 \times 10^5$ at 5V (H. Y. Liu, Hong, Sun, Wei, & Yu, 2016). Similarly, H. Liu group also synthesized the rutile phase of $TiO_2$ for UV detector applications (H. Y. Liu, Lin, Sun, Wei, & Yu, 2017). A. Mortezaal group deposited Al-doped ZnO (AZO) using spray pyrolysis on a p-type Si (p-Si) wafer. These AZO and heterostructures of AZO/p-Si were used for UV photodetector (Shasti, Mortezaali, & Dariani, 2015). Similarly, Makram A Fakhri group also deposited Al-doped ZnO for UV detector application (Ibraheam, Rzaij, Fakhri, & Abdulwahhab, 2019). N. M. Abd-Alghafour group have made $V_2O_5$ heterojunction photodiode on Si substrate for visible light detection. The device has shown good sensitivity of 2016 at 3v bias voltage under the 560 nm visible light irradiation (Abd-Alghafour, Ahmed, Hassan, & Bououdina, 2016). Umarji group have also synthesized $VO_2$ thin film using ultrasonic nebulizer spray pyrolysis with aqueous combustion mixture for IR photodetector application with a high photodetector gain of $9.99 \times 10^3$ under the illumination of 1064 nm laser (Tadeo, Mukhokosi, Krupanidhi, & Umarji, 2019). Inamdar has again studied the effect of the ZnO buffer layer on Al-doped and undoped ZnO thin films for UV detector response. All the films were grown using spray pyrolysis (S. Inamdar, Ganbavle, Shaikh, & Rajpure, 2015). R. A. Ismail et al have synthesized $In_2S_3$/Si heterojunction for visible photodiode application (Ismail, Habubi, & Abbod, 2016).

## Photocatalysis

Photocatalysis is used for removing dyes, heavy metal from the sewages, wastewater before discharging it to the environment like sea, river, lake. If the dyes are not treated well, it will pollute the drinking water source and create unbalance in environmental ecology. Mostly $TiO_2$ is used for photocatalysis application. But presently other materials like ZnO is also used for photocatalysis application also. V. Mata et al have used ZnO thin film for methylene blue (MB) degradation. They have degraded 99% MB in 3hr (Mata, Maldonado, & de la Luz Olvera, 2018). Our group have studied ZnO microflower for MB degradation also (Singha, Patra, Rojwal, Deepa, & Kumar, 2019). Spherical core-shell Ag/ZnO nanocomposites were synthesized by I. M. Fernandez group to remove 93% MB from the solution which is almost double when bare ZnO is used (Muñoz-Fernandez, Alkan, Milošević, Rabanal, & Friedrich, 2019). Nitrogen-doped $TiO_2$ was synthesized using co-spray pyrolysis by N. P. Van group (Van & Ngan, 2013). A. Duta group deposited $TiO_2$ thin film using spray pyrolysis for wastewater treatment by removing methyl orange (MO) and MB from the solution under the presence of UV light (Andronic, Manolache, & Duta, 2007). Not only thin film but mesoporous $TiO_2$ microspheres were also synthesized by Jaehyung Choi group for photocatalytic activity. Similarly I. Dundar et. Al has used spray pyrolyzed $TiO_2$ for self-cleaning applications (Choi, Yoo, & Kim, 2018; Ibrahim Dundar, Marina Krichevskaya, Atanas Katerski, & Ilona Oja Acik, 2019).

This transparent $TiO_2$ was deposited on window glass for air purification application and they degraded 80% methyl tert-butyl ether (MTBE). Thickness of the film was varied between 13-35 nm. Flame spray pyrolysis was used to synthesized pure and Ce doped TiO2 which are used for hydrogen production under the presence of solar light and removing dyes from waste water (Mikaeili, Topcu, Jodhani, & Gouma, 2018). Composite of reduced graphene oxide and $TiO_2$ was prepared using the USP method by Lee group (Park et al., 2018). These composite enhance photocataltic behavior and increase the MB degradation rate. Multi heterojunction of $TiO_2$-$WO_3$-pt microsphere and WO3 nanosheets were synthesized by the USP method by Zheng group. They have shown that the addition of these Pt into the heterostructure improves the degradation performance. They have degraded gaseous acetaldehyde and isopropyl alcohol from the solution (Zheng et al., 2016). Another group like Alex et. Al has synthesized $MoO_3$ thin film using the USP method. They have degraded 0.5mM of rhodamine-B dyes under 2 hrs light illumination from the solution. Photodegradation efficiency was found at 91% (Alex et al., 2019). $BiVO_4$ powder was synthesized by USP for visible-light photocatalyst (Dunkle, Helmich, & Suslick, 2009).

## Supercapacitor

The supercapacitor is used in electric vehicles, starting power of fuel cells and other applications. The supercapacitor has advantages like long cycle life, high power density, and high specific capacitances. Many metal oxide, reduced graphene oxide are used for supercapacitor applications. Here we will give some examples of these materials synthesized by spray pyrolysis for supercapacitor application. C. d. Lokhande group synthesized $Co_3O_4$ thin films for supercapacitor applications. They have obtained a specific capacitance of 74 F/g. The same group have deposited nickel cobalt oxide ($NiCo_2O_4$) for supercapacitor application. They showed that their material can have a high specific capacitance of 752 G/g with excellent cycle stability over 1000 cycles (Deokate, Kalubarme, Park, & Lokhande, 2017; Shinde, Mahadik, Gujar, & Lokhande, 2006). Abhijit A. Yadav et. Al has deposited the rhombohedral (hematite) crystal structure of $Fe_2O_3$. The maximum specific capacitance of 451 F/g with specific energy and specific power of 45 Wh/kg and 1.25KW/kg at 4A/g is obtained from their study (Yadav, Deshmukh, Deshmukh, Patil, & Chavan, 2016). $CoFe_2O_4$-Graphene Composites were synthesized by Jang group for supercapacitor applications. They have synthesized these nanocomposite in nanoparticles form and obtained specific capacitance of 253 F/g (Lee, Chang, & Jang, 2019). Other oxides like $SnO_2$ and $V_2O_5$ nanowires also synthesized by spray pyrolysis method for supercapacitor applications (Yadav, 2016; Zhou et al., 2018). Carbon is known as a good supercapacitor material. Carbon microspheres were synthesized by K.S.Suslick group. These microspheres are porous in nature and thus have a high gravimetric capacitance of 360 F/g (Kim, Fortunato, Xu, Bang, Suslick, 2011).

## Solar Cell

Due to the use of earth-abundant material for solar cell applications, many researchers have used spray pyrolysis to grow solar cell absorber material. In fact, first spray pyrolysis system was used for solar cell applications. Our group has expertise in spray pyrolysis for deposition of solar absorber layer. M. Pavan et al have deposited $TiO_2/Cu_2O$ heterojunction for solar cell application on FTO coated glass slides. Very few studies on oxide-based solar cells are found in the literature (Pavan et al., 2015). M. h. Sayed et al have deposited earth-abundant material $Cu_2SnS_3$ (CTS) thin film on Mo coated glass substrates at 350 $^0$C. They achieved a maximum efficiency of 2.28% when they removed the shunt path (Sayed, Robert, Dale, & Gütay, 2019). Our group also studied CTS and $Cu_2ZnSnS_4$ (CZTS) thin film for solar cell applications (Prabhakar & Nagaraju, 2010). Recently $Cu_2CdSnS_4$ (CCTS) thin film also deposited by low-cost spray pyrolysis method. It is showing the efficiency of 1.14%. Polycrystalline copper sulfide (CuxS) thin film for possible application as a solar absorber material was also deposited using the USP method at different temperatures (Firat, Yildirim, Erturk, & Peksoz, 2017; Tombak, Kilicoglu, & Ocak, 2020). TiO2 as a blocking film in dye-sensitized and perovskite solar cells was synthesized by Krysa group (Krýsová, Krýsa, & Kavan, 2018). Ikeda group have deposited Cu(In,Ga)(S,Se)2 thin film solar cells using spray pyrolysis by varying the sulfur source. They got good results and efficiency of 8.7% was found from their cells. The same group has shown the CZTS solar cell efficiency of 5.8% (Masaaki et al., 2015; Nguyen et al., 2015). Ito group also studies CZTS solar film. They achieved 1.7% efficiency. K G Deepa and S. Guitouni also deposited CZTS thin film by USP method (Deepa, Sajeesh, & Jampana, 2018; Guitouni, Khammar, Messaoudi, Attaf, & Aida, 2016; Kitagawa, Ito, Nguyen, & Nishino, 2013). 8.6% efficiency of a solar cell by CZTSSe Solar Cells is shown from the Gerardo Larramona group (Larramona et al., 2014). Recently our group has deposited CTS thin film for solar cell absorber layer (Rahaman, Sunil, Singha, Ghosh, 2019).

## CONCLUSION

This chapter describes very extensive research on spray pyrolysis method, technique. It is a single-step deposition/synthesis method to deposit or synthesize binary, ternary or more complex compounds. It is a versatile technique that gives not only a thin film but also a different nanostructured based thin film. Due to the presence of nanostructures in the film, it increases the efficiency of the sensors. Different nanostructures like nanorods, microflowers, thin film, the core-shell structure obtained from this method. These structures are then used for different applications like gas sensors, photocatalysis, solar cells, supercapacitor, UV detector, piezogenerator. Spray pyrolysis is an inexpensive method to deposit thin film sensing and devices materials. It can deposit materials on a variety of substrates. The literature on chemical Spray pyrolysis technology reveals that it really offers an attractive way to deposit a variety of thin-film/ powder formed materials for different industrial applications. Experimental view, instrumental specifications, and methodology for these techniques explained in detail. All these SP techniques have their own unique way of depositing materials on the substrates, and thus have their advantages, disadvantages, and limitations in industrial applications. A suitable coating method can be selected as required by the desired physical and chemical properties of the film or coating for the desired application purpose.

Presently many industries are supplying the spray pyrolysis setup to deposit thin film for R&D laboratory, university, but it still lacks for industrial deposition method. Challenges still exist in precisely controlled SP techniques regarding the properties of the target material. As it requires many optimization to grow the doped or undoped, functionalize materials. So in future many mathematical models, relationships between parameters can be created for the beter and controlled deposition process with the help of material characterization techniques. Also in future commercial hybrid structures, flexible electronics, sensors and devices can be made easily in large scale using spray pyrolysis techniques.. In addition, harmful gases like NOX, HCl, NH3, SOX are emitted during pyrolysis process due to decomposition of metal salts, additives. So a separate exhaust gas system require to take out the gases from the experimental site. "

# REFERENCES

Abd-Alghafour, N. M., Ahmed, N. M., Hassan, Z., & Bououdina, M. (2016). High-performance p–n heterojunction photodetectors based on V2O5nanorods by spray pyrolysis. *Applied Physics. A, Materials Science & Processing, 122*(9), 1–9. doi:10.100700339-016-0346-7

Alex, K. V., Jayakrishnan, A. R., Ajeesh Kumar, S., Ibrahim, A. S., Kamakshi, K., Silva, J. P. B., ... Gomes, M. J. M. (2019). Substrate temperature induced effect on microstructure, optical and photocatalytic activity of ultrasonic spray pyrolysis deposited MoO 3 thin films. *Materials Research Express, 6*(6). doi:10.1088/2053-1591/ab0f7a

Andronic, L., Manolache, S., & Duta, A. (2007). TiO2 thin films prepared by spray pyrolysis deposition (SPD) and their photocatalytic activities. *Journal of Optoelectronics and Advanced Materials, 9*(5), 1403–1406.

Aranovich, J., Ortiz, A., & Bube, R. H. (1979). Optical and electrical properties of ZnO films prepared by spray pyrolysis for solar cell applications. *Journal of Vacuum Science and Technology, 16*(4), 994–1003. doi:10.1116/1.570167

Arya, S. P. S. (1986). Study of Upward and Downward Sprayed Fluorine-Doped Tin Oxide Films. *Crystal Research and Technology, 21*(3), K38–K42. doi:10.1002/crat.2170210322

Ayouchi, R., Leinen, D., Martın, F., Gabas, M., Dalchiele, E., & Ramos-Barrado, J. R. (2003). Preparation and characterization of transparent ZnO thin films obtained by spray pyrolysis. *Thin Solid Films, 426*(1–2), 68–77. doi:10.1016/S0040-6090(02)01331-7

Bryant, W. A. (1977). The fundamentals of chemical vapour deposition. *Journal of Materials Science, 12*(7), 1285–1306. doi:10.1007/BF00540843

Chamberlin, R. R., & Skarman, J. S. (1966). Chemical spray deposition process for inorganic films. *Journal of the Electrochemical Society, 113*(1), 86–89. doi:10.1149/1.2423871

Chen, C. H., Buysman, A. A. J., Kelder, E. M., & Schoonman, J. (1995). Fabrication of LiCoO2 thin film cathodes for rechargeable lithium battery by electrostatic spray pyrolysis. *Solid State Ionics, 80*(1–2), 1–4. doi:10.1016/0167-2738(95)00140-2

Chitanu, E., & Ionita, G. (2010). Obtaining thin layers of ZnO with magnetron sputtering method. *International Journal of Computers, 4*(4), 243–250.

Choi, J., Yoo, K. S., & Kim, J. (2018). Spray pyrolysis synthesis of mesoporous TiO2 microspheres and their post modification for improved photocatalytic activity. *Korean Journal of Chemical Engineering, 35*(12), 2480–2486. doi:10.100711814-018-0176-8

da Silva, L. F., M'Peko, J. C., Catto, A. C., Bernardini, S., Mastelaro, V. R., Aguir, K., ... Longo, E. (2017). UV-enhanced ozone gas sensing response of ZnO-SnO2 heterojunctions at room temperature. *Sensors and Actuators. B, Chemical, 240*, 573–579. doi:10.1016/j.snb.2016.08.158

Deepa, K. G., Sajeesh, T. H., & Jampana, N. (2018). Opto-Electronic Properties of Cu2ZnSnS4 Thin Films Grown by Ultrasonic Spray Pyrolysis. *Journal of Electronic Materials, 47*(1), 530–535. doi:10.100711664-017-5803-3

Deokate, R. J., Kalubarme, R. S., Park, C. J., & Lokhande, C. D. (2017). Simple Synthesis of NiCo2O4 thin films using Spray Pyrolysis for electrochemical supercapacitor application: A Novel approach. *Electrochimica Acta, 224*, 378–385. doi:10.1016/j.electacta.2016.12.034

Dundar, I., Krichevskaya, M., Katerski, A., & Acik, I. O. (2019). TiO2 thin films by ultrasonic spray pyrolysis as photocatalytic material for air purification. *Royal Society Open Science, 6*(2). doi:10.1098/rsos.181578 PMID:30891278

Dunkle, S. S., Helmich, R. J., & Suslick, K. S. (2009). BiVO 4as a visible-light photocatalyst prepared by ultrasonic spray pyrolysis. *The Journal of Physical Chemistry C, 113*(28), 11980–11983. doi:10.1021/jp903757x

Dutta, J., Perrin, J., Emeraud, T., Laurent, J.-M., & Smith, A. (1995). Pyrosol deposition of fluorine-doped tin dioxide thin films. *Journal of Materials Science, 30*(1), 53–62. doi:10.1007/BF00352131

Firat, Y. E., Yildirim, H., Erturk, K., & Peksoz, A. (2017). Sulphide Thin Films for Solar Cell Applications, *2017*.

Gottlieb, B., Koropecki, R., Arce, R., Crisalle, R., & Ferron, J. (1991). Characterization of fluorine-doped tin oxide produced by the pyrosol method. *Thin Solid Films, 199*(1), 13–21. doi:10.1016/0040-6090(91)90047-2

Guitouni, S., Khammar, M., Messaoudi, M., Attaf, N., & Aida, M. S. (2016). Electrical properties of Cu4ZnSnS2/ZnS heterojunction prepared by ultrasonic spray pyrolysis. *Journal of Semiconductors, 37*(12), 0–4. doi:10.1088/1674-4926/37/12/122001

Huang, C. S., Tao, C. S., & Lee, C. H. (1997). Nebulized Spray Deposition of Pb (Zr, Ti) O 3 Thin Films. *Journal of the Electrochemical Society, 144*(10), 3556–3561. doi:10.1149/1.1838047

Ibraheam, A. S., Rzaij, J. M., Fakhri, M. A., & Abdulwahhab, A. W. (2019). Structural, optical and electrical investigations of Al:ZnO nanostructures as UV photodetector synthesized by spray pyrolysis technique. *Materials Research Express, 6*(5). doi:10.1088/2053-1591/ab06d4

Inamdar, S., Ganbavle, V., Shaikh, S., & Rajpure, K. (2015). Effect of the buffer layer on the metal-semiconductor-metal UV photodetector based on Al-doped and undoped ZnO thin films with different device structures. *Physica Status Solidi (A). Applications and Materials Science, 212*(8), 1704–1712. doi:10.1002/pssa.201431850

Inamdar, S. I., Ganbavle, V. V., & Rajpure, K. Y. (2014). ZnO based visible-blind UV photodetector by spray pyrolysis. *Superlattices and Microstructures*, *76*, 253–263. doi:10.1016/j.spmi.2014.09.041

Ismail, R. A., Habubi, N. F., & Abbod, M. M. (2016). Preparation of high-sensitivity In2S3/Si heterojunction photodetector by chemical spray pyrolysis. *Optical and Quantum Electronics*, *48*(10), 1–14. doi:10.100711082-016-0725-5

Jiao, Z., Wu, M., Qin, Z., Lu, M., & Gu, J. (2003). The NO2 sensing ITO thin films prepared by ultrasonic spray pyrolysis. *Sensors (Basel)*, *3*(8), 285–289. doi:10.339030800285

Kamble, V. B., & Umarji, A. M. (2012). Chromium oxide thin films by ultrasonic nebulized spray pyrolysis of aqueous combustion mixture for gas sensing application. *Proceedings - ISPTS-1, 1st International Symposium on Physics and Technology of Sensors*, 181–184. 10.1109/ISPTS.2012.6260915

Kane, J., Schweizer, H. P., & Kern, W. (1976). Chemical Vapor Deposition of Antimony-Doped Tin Oxide Films Formed from Dibutyl Tin Diacetate. *Journal of the Electrochemical Society*, *123*(2), 270–277. doi:10.1149/1.2132802

Kim, H., Fortunato, M. E., Xu, H., Bang, J. H., & Suslick, K. S. (2011). Carbon Microspheres as Supercapacitors. *The Journal of Physical Chemistry C*, *115*(42), 20481–20486. doi:10.1021/jp207135g

Kitagawa, N., Ito, S., Nguyen, D.-C., & Nishino, H. (2013). Copper Zinc Sulfur Compound Solar Cells Fabricated by Spray Pyrolysis Deposition for Solar Cells. *Natural Resources*, *4*(01), 142–145. doi:10.4236/nr.2013.41A018

Korzo, V. F., & Chernyaev, V. N. (1973). Electrophysical properties of indium oxide pyrolytic films with disordered structure. *Physica Status Solidi. A, Applied Research*, *20*(2), 695–705. doi:10.1002/pssa.2210200232

Korzo, V. F., & Ryabova, L. A. (1967). *Conductivity of Thin Indium Oxide Films*. USSR: SOVIET PHYSICS SOLID STATE.

Krýsová, H., Krýsa, J., & Kavan, L. (2018). Semi-automatic spray pyrolysis deposition of thin, transparent, titania films as blocking layers for dye-sensitized and perovskite solar cells. *Beilstein Journal of Nanotechnology*, *9*(1), 1135–1145. doi:10.3762/bjnano.9.105 PMID:29719764

Kulaszewicz, S. (1980). Electrical, optical and structural properties of SnO2: Sb films deposited by hydrolysis. *Thin Solid Films*, *74*(2), 211–218. doi:10.1016/0040-6090(80)90083-8

Larramona, G., Bourdais, S., Jacob, A., Choné, C., Muto, T., Cuccaro, Y., ... Dennler, G. (2014). 8.6% Efficient CZTSSe solar cells sprayed from water-ethanol CZTS colloidal solutions. *The Journal of Physical Chemistry Letters, 5*(21), 3763–3767. doi:10.1021/jz501864a PMID:26278747

Lee, C., Chang, H., & Jang, H. D. (2019). Preparation of CoFe 2 O 4 -graphene composites using aerosol spray pyrolysis for supercapacitors application. *Aerosol and Air Quality Research, 19*(3), 443–448. doi:10.4209/aaqr.2018.10.0372

Liu, F., Lu, G., Li, D., Zhang, Y., Liu, D., Yao, S., ... Wang, B. (2016). Hierarchical core/shell ZnO/NiO nanoheterojunctions synthesized by ultrasonic spray pyrolysis and their gas-sensing performance. *CrystEngComm, 18*(41), 8101–8107. doi:10.1039/C6CE01621A

Liu, H. Y., Hong, S. H., Sun, W. C., Wei, S. Y., & Yu, S. M. (2016). TiO2-based metal-semiconductor-metal ultraviolet photodetectors deposited by ultrasonic spray pyrolysis technique. *IEEE Transactions on Electron Devices, 63*(1), 79–85. doi:10.1109/TED.2015.2436701

Liu, H. Y., Lin, W. H., Sun, W. C., Wei, S. Y., & Yu, S. M. (2017). A study of ultrasonic spray pyrolysis deposited rutile-TiO2-based metal-semiconductor-metal ultraviolet photodetector. *Materials Science in Semiconductor Processing, 57*(August 2016), 90–94. doi:10.1016/j.mssp.2016.10.005

Look, D. C., Reynolds, D. C., Litton, C. W., Jones, R. L., Eason, D. B., & Cantwell, G. (2002). Characterization of homoepitaxial p-type ZnO grown by molecular beam epitaxy. *Applied Physics Letters, 81*(10), 1830–1832. doi:10.1063/1.1504875

Manifacier, J. C., Fillard, J. P., & Bind, J. M. (1981). Deposition of In2O3 SnO2 layers on glass substrates using a spraying method. *Thin Solid Films, 77*(1–3), 67–80. doi:10.1016/0040-6090(81)90361-8

Manifacier, J.-C., Szepessy, L., Bresse, J. F., Perotin, M., & Stuck, R. (1979). In2O3:(Sn) and SnO2:(F) films—Application to solar energy conversion; part 1— Preparation and characterization. *Materials Research Bulletin, 14*(1), 109–119. doi:10.1016/0025-5408(79)90238-1

Masaaki, K., Wilman, S., Toshiyuki, H., Yasuhiro, N., Takashi, H., & Shigeru, I. (2015). Fabrication of Cu(In,Ga)(S,Se) 2 thin film solar cells via spray pyrolysis of thiourea and 1-methylthiourea-based aqueous precursor solution. *Japanese Journal of Applied Physics, 54*(9). doi:10.7567/JJAP.54.091203

Mata, V., Maldonado, A., & de la Luz Olvera, M. (2018). Deposition of ZnO thin films by ultrasonic spray pyrolysis technique. Effect of the milling speed and time and its application in photocatalysis. *Materials Science in Semiconductor Processing, 75*(November 2017), 288–295. doi:10.1016/j.mssp.2017.11.038

Maudes, J. S., & Rodriguez, T. (1980). Sprayed SnO2 films: Growth mechanism and film structure characterization. *Thin Solid Films, 69*(2), 183–189. doi:10.1016/0040-6090(80)90035-8

Mikaeili, F., Topcu, S., Jodhani, G., & Gouma, P.-I. (2018). Flame-Sprayed Pure and Ce-Doped TiO2 Photocatalysts. *Catalysts, 8*(9), 342. doi:10.3390/catal8090342

Miki-Yoshida, M., & Andrade, E. (1993). Growth and structure of tin dioxide thin films obtained by an improved spray pyrohydrolysis technique. *Thin Solid Films, 224*(1), 87–96. doi:10.1016/0040-6090(93)90463-Y

Muñoz-Fernandez, L., Alkan, G., Milošević, O., Rabanal, M. E., & Friedrich, B. (2019). Synthesis and characterisation of spherical core-shell Ag/ZnO nanocomposites using single and two – steps ultrasonic spray pyrolysis (USP). *Catalysis Today, 321–322*(November 2017), 26–33. doi:10.1016/j.cattod.2017.11.029

Myong, S. Y., Baik, S. J., Lee, C. H., Cho, W. Y., & Lim, K. S. (1997). Extremely transparent and conductive ZnO: Al thin films prepared by photo-assisted metalorganic chemical vapor deposition (photo-MOCVD) using AlCl3 (6H2O) as new doping material. *Japanese Journal of Applied Physics, 36*(Part 2, No. 8B8B), L1078–L1081. doi:10.1143/JJAP.36.L1078

Nguyen, T. H., Septina, W., Fujikawa, S., Jiang, F., Harada, T., & Ikeda, S. (2015). Cu$_2$ZnSnS$_4$ thin film solar cells with 5.8% conversion efficiency obtained by a facile spray pyrolysis technique. *RSC Advances, 5*(95), 77565–77571. doi:10.1039/C5RA13000J

Nunes, P., Fernandes, B., Fortunato, E., Vilarinho, P., & Martins, R. (1999). Performances presented by zinc oxide thin films deposited by spray pyrolysis. *Thin Solid Films, 337*(1–2), 176–179. doi:10.1016/S0040-6090(98)01394-7

Onofre, Y. J., Catto, A. C., Bernardini, S., Fiorido, T., Aguir, K., Longo, E., ... de Godoy, M. P. F. (2019). Highly selective ozone gas sensor based on nanocrystalline Zn 0.95 Co 0.05 O thin film obtained via spray pyrolysis technique. *Applied Surface Science, 478*(January), 347–354. doi:10.1016/j.apsusc.2019.01.197

Park, J. A., Yang, B., Lee, J., Kim, I. G., Kim, J. H., Choi, J. W., ... Lee, S. H. (2018). Ultrasonic spray pyrolysis synthesis of reduced graphene oxide/anatase TiO 2 composite and its application in the photocatalytic degradation of methylene blue in water. *Chemosphere*, *191*, 738–746. doi:10.1016/j.chemosphere.2017.10.094 PMID:29078195

Patil, J. M. (2016). Low-operable and Low-ppm H2S Gas Sensing Performance of Nanocrystalline WO3 Thin Films. *Journal of Nanoscience and Technology*, *2*(24), 197–200. Retrieved from http://jacsdirectory.com/journal-of-nanoscience-and-technology/admin/issues/20161230144337_2-4-05 JNST16044 published.pdf

Patil, L. A., Suryawanshi, D. N., Pathan, I. G., & Patil, D. G. (2014). Nanocrystalline Pt-doped TiO 2 thin films prepared by spray pyrolysis, *37*(3), 425–432.

Pavan, M., Rühle, S., Ginsburg, A., Keller, D. A., Barad, H. N., Sberna, P. M., ... Fortunato, E. (2015). TiO2/Cu2O all-oxide heterojunction solar cells produced by spray pyrolysis. *Solar Energy Materials and Solar Cells*, *132*, 549–556. doi:10.1016/j.solmat.2014.10.005

Pommier, R., Gril, C., & Marucchi, J. (1981). Sprayed films of indium tin oxide and fluorine-doped tin oxide of large surface area. *Thin Solid Films*, *77*(1–3), 91–98. doi:10.1016/0040-6090(81)90363-1

Prabhakar, T., & Nagaraju, J. (2010). Ultrasonic spray pyrolysis of CZTS solar cell absorber layers and characterization studies. In *Conference Record of the IEEE Photovoltaic Specialists Conference*, 1964–1969. doi:10.1109/PVSC.2010.5616709

Raham, S., Sunil, M. A., Singha, M. K., & Ghosh, K. (2019, August). Temperature dependent growth of $Cu_2SnS_3$ thin films using ultrasonic spray pyrolysis for solar cell absorber layer and photocatalytic application. *Materials Research Express*, *6*(10). doi:10.1088/2053-1591/ab3928

Sayed, M. H., Robert, E. V. C., Dale, P. J., & Gütay, L. (2019). Cu2SnS3 based thin film solar cells from chemical spray pyrolysis. *Thin Solid Films, 669*(October 2018), 436–439. doi:10.1016/j.tsf.2018.11.002

Shasti, M., Mortezaali, A., & Dariani, R. S. (2015). Comparison of carrier transport mechanism under UV/Vis illumination in an AZO photodetector and an AZO/p-Si heterojunction photodiode produced by spray pyrolysis. *Journal of Applied Physics*, *117*(2). doi:10.1063/1.4905416

Shinde, V. R., Mahadik, S. B., Gujar, T. P., & Lokhande, C. D. (2006). Supercapacitive cobalt oxide (Co 3 O 4) thin films by spray pyrolysis. *Applied Surface Science*, *252*(20), 7487–7492. doi:10.1016/j.apsusc.2005.09.004

Siefert, W. (1984). Properties of thin In2O3 and SnO2 films prepared by corona spray pyrolysis, and a discussion of the spray pyrolysis process. *Thin Solid Films*, *120*(4), 275–282. doi:10.1016/0040-6090(84)90242-6

Singha, M. K., Patra, A., Rojwal, V., Deepa, K. G., & Kumar, D. (2019). Ultrasonic spray pyrolysis deposited ZnO thin film for photocatalytic activity, *030023*(March). doi:10.1063/1.5093841

Slobodian, O. M. (2019). Reduced graphene oxide obtained using the spray pyrolysis technique for gas sensing. *Semiconductor Physics. Quantum Electronics & Optoelectronics*, *22*(1), 98–103. doi:10.15407pqeo22.01.098

Song, P. K., Shigesato, Y., Yasui, I., Ow-Yang, C. W., & Paine, D. C. (1998). Study on crystallinity of tin-doped indium oxide films deposited by dc magnetron sputtering. *Japanese Journal of Applied Physics*, *37*(Part 1, No. 4A4R), 1870–1876. doi:10.1143/JJAP.37.1870

Subbaramaiah, K., & Raja, V. S. (1994). Preparation and characterization of all spray-deposited p-CuIn (S0. 5Se0. 5) 2/n-CdZnS: In thin film solar cells. *Solar Energy Materials and Solar Cells*, *32*(1), 1–6. doi:10.1016/0927-0248(94)90250-X

Tadeo, I. J., Mukhokosi, E. P., Krupanidhi, S. B., & Umarji, A. M. (2019). Low-cost VO2(M1) thin films synthesized by ultrasonic nebulized spray pyrolysis of an aqueous combustion mixture for IR photodetection. *RSC Advances*, *9*(18), 9983–9992. doi:10.1039/C9RA00189A

Tischner, A., Maier, T., Stepper, C., & Köck, A. (2008). Ultrathin SnO2 gas sensors fabricated by spray pyrolysis for the detection of humidity and carbon monoxide. *Sensors and Actuators. B, Chemical*, *134*(2), 796–802. doi:10.1016/j.snb.2008.06.032

Tombak, A., Kilicoglu, T., & Ocak, Y. S. (2020). Solar cells fabricated by spray pyrolysis deposited Cu2CdSnS4 thin films. *Renewable Energy*, *146*, 1465–1470. doi:10.1016/j.renene.2019.07.057

Unaogu, A. L., & Okeke, C. E. (1990). Characterization of antimony-doped tin oxide films prepared by spray pyrolysis. *Solar Energy Materials*, *20*(1–2), 29–36. doi:10.1016/0165-1633(90)90014-R

Van, N. P., & Ngan, P. H. (2013). Use of co-spray pyrolysis for synthesizing nitrogen-doped TiO2 films. *Bulletin of Materials Science*, *36*(5), 827–831. doi:10.100712034-013-0534-4

Van de Pol, F. C. M., Blom, F. R., & Popma, T. J. A. (1991). Rf planar magnetron sputtered ZnO films I: Structural properties. *Thin Solid Films, 204*(2), 349–364. doi:10.1016/0040-6090(91)90074-8

Viguie, J. C., & Spitz, J. (1975). Chemical vapor deposition at low temperatures. *Journal of the Electrochemical Society, 122*(4), 585–588. doi:10.1149/1.2134266

Vink, T. J., Walrave, W., Daams, J. L. C., Baarslag, P. C., & Van den Meerakker, J. (1995). On the homogeneity of sputter-deposited ITO films Part I. Stress and microstructure. *Thin Solid Films, 266*(2), 145–151. doi:10.1016/0040-6090(95)06818-X

Vispute, R. D., Talyansky, V., Choopun, S., Sharma, R. P., Venkatesan, T., He, M., ... Li, Y. X. (1998). Heteroepitaxy of ZnO on GaN and its implications for fabrication of hybrid optoelectronic devices. *Applied Physics Letters, 73*(3), 348–350. doi:10.1063/1.121830

Wang, H., Xie, J., Yan, K., & Duan, M. (2011). Growth mechanism of different morphologies of ZnO crystals prepared by hydrothermal method. *Journal of Materials Science and Technology, 27*(2), 153–158. doi:10.1016/S1005-0302(11)60041-8

Wisz, G., Virt, I., Sagan, P., Potera, P., & Yavorskyi, R. (2017). Structural, Optical and Electrical Properties of Zinc Oxide Layers Produced by Pulsed Laser Deposition Method. *Nanoscale Research Letters, 12*(1), 253. doi:10.118611671-017-2033-9 PMID:28381074

Yadav, A. A. (2016). SnO2 thin film electrodes deposited by spray pyrolysis for electrochemical supercapacitor applications. *Journal of Materials Science Materials in Electronics, 27*(2), 1866–1872. doi:10.100710854-015-3965-4

Yadav, A. A., Deshmukh, T. B., Deshmukh, R. V., Patil, D. D., & Chavan, U. J. (2016). Electrochemical supercapacitive performance of Hematite α-Fe2O3 thin films prepared by spray pyrolysis from non-aqueous medium. *Thin Solid Films, 616*, 351–358. doi:10.1016/j.tsf.2016.08.062

Yi, C. H., Shigesato, Y., Yasui, I., & Takaki, S. (1995). Microstructure of Low-Resistivity Tin-Doped Indium Oxide Films Deposited. *Japanese Journal of Applied Physics, 34*(Part 2, No. 2B2B Pt 2), L244–L247. doi:10.1143/JJAP.34.L244

Yuliarto, B., Gumilar, G., Zulhendri, D. W., Nugraha, & Septiani, N. L. W. (2017). Preparation of SnO2 thin film nanostructure for CO gas sensor using ultrasonic spray pyrolysis and chemical bath deposition technique. *Acta Physica Polonica A, 131*(3), 534–538. doi:10.12693/APhysPolA.131.534

Zheng, H., Wang, C., Zhang, X., Kong, L., Li, Y., Liu, Y., & Liu, Y. (2016). Ultrasonic spray pyrolysis assembly of a TiO2-WO3-Pt multi-heterojunction microsphere photocatalyst using highly crystalline WO3 nanosheets: Less is better. *New Journal of Chemistry*, *40*(4), 3225–3232. doi:10.1039/C5NJ02981C

Zhou, W., Mao, Y., Tang, M., Long, L., Chen, H., Li, Y., & Jia, C. (2018). Facile Synthesis of Tremella-Like V 2 O 5 Microspheres and Their Application as Cathode Materials in Lithium Ion Batteries. *Journal of Nanoscience and Nanotechnology*, *19*(1), 194–198. doi:10.1166/jnn.2019.16457 PMID:30327022

Znaidi, L., Illia, G. S., Benyahia, S., Sanchez, C., & Kanaev, A. V. (2003). Oriented ZnO thin films synthesis by sol–gel process for laser application. *Thin Solid Films*, *428*(1–2), 257–262. doi:10.1016/S0040-6090(02)01219-1

# Chapter 12
# Characteristic Behavior of PVDF–Compliant Structure as an End Effector Using Creo Element/Pro Release 5.0

**Neeta Sahay**
*National Institute of Technical Teachers' Training and Research, Kolkata, India*

**Subrata Chattopadhyay**
*National Institute of Technical Teachers' Training and Research, Kolkata, India*

## ABSTRACT

*The tremendous area of application of microprocessors and microcontrollers has exhausted the demand for polymers as sensors among the fastest growing technologies of the $18 billion sensor market worldwide. This chapter presents the study of characteristic behavior of a compliance structure made of PVDF (Poly Vinylidene Fluoride) material which is acting as an actuator and sensor, too. The inverse piezoelectric nature of PVDF has been used to produce the required amount of force by applying the voltage at a specific point at the base of the structure which is generating the opening and closing of the end effector. The displacement of the tip of the end effector can be sensed by generated voltage of piezoelectric effect of PVDF.*

DOI: 10.4018/978-1-7998-2584-5.ch012

## INTRODUCTION

A highly non-reactive thermoplastic fluoropolymer called polyvinylidene fluoride or polyvinylidene difluoride (PVDF) which is typically a semi-crystalline polymer and approximately 50% amorphous is produced by the polymerization of vinylidene difluoride. Due to of its low density (1.78 g/cm$^3$) and availability as piping products, sheet, tubing, films, plate and an insulator, PVDF can be injected, molded or welded which can be commonly used in the chemical, semiconductor, medical and defense industries, as well as in lithium-ion batteries (J. Inderherbergh. (2017)). The polar polymers such as PVDF can be transformed into piezoelectric elements by orienting the molecular dipoles in the same direction by subjecting appropriate films to an intense electric field (L. M. Lediaev. (2006)). This polarization is thermodynamically stable up to about 90°C.

The high permittivity, dielectric strength and low dissipation factor of PVDF shows to be very useful as a dielectric compared to other polymers and other piezoelectric materials. Generally, as shown in figure 1, PVDF's α-phase occurs in a trans-gauche-trans-gauche (TGTG) formation as discussed by Arshad et. al. (A. N. Arshad, M. H. M. Wahid, M. Rusop, W. H. A. Majid, R. H. Y. Subban & M. D. Rozan. (2019); D. M. Esterly. (2002); S. Lee. (2011)), shown in figure.1. It is a combination of helical and planar zigzag structure. Each G or G– bond represents a 60° or –60° angle respectively from the plane of the last bond. The β-phase of PVDF consists a planar zigzag or TT, where T represents a trans-bond that remains in the same plane as the carbon backbone (L. Ruan, X. Yao, Y. Chang, L. Zhou, G. Qin & X Zhang. (2018)). The β-phase has actually more intermolecular stability due to the van der Waals forces acting between the atoms along the carbon backbone and between the molecules of the polymer because of all the trans-structure of β-phase forces the fluorine atoms along the carbon backbone to come closer together and overlap their van der Waals radii. While the α-phase is required on an intramolecular basis.

Among the other applications of PVDF, one of the most required application is as micro grippers used for manipulation of micro-objects in microassembly and microsurgery where the micro-grippers act as end-effectors manipulating objects directly (W. Aia & Q. Xu. (2014)). Grasping and manipulating small or micro-objects in biology and biotechnology require compliance design which provides simple, single-structured element and adds less complexity in manufacturing and operation of the micro grippers.

In this chapter the properties and characteristics of PVDF as an inverse piezoelectric element has been discussed. This PVDF can also be act as a sensor and actuator to form an end effector of compliant structure which has been designed and analyzed with Creo Element/ Pro Release 5.0 software. Then frequency response study of

*Figure 1. Chemical Structure of α-PVDF (left) and β-PVDF (right)*

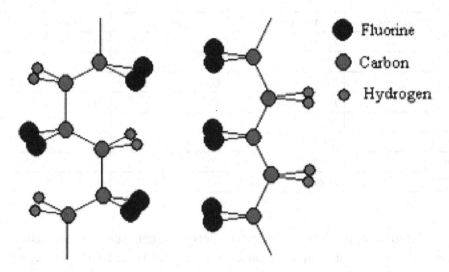

PVDF as a sensor is carried out by Bode diagram. The result of the analysis is discussed at the end of the chapter as a conclusion.

## CHARACTERISTICS PROPERTIES OF PVDF FILMS

The PVDF possessing piezoelectric properties (B. Zaarour, L. Zhu & X. Jin. (2019)) available as film is determined by the coefficients "d" obtained by measuring the density of charge (Coulomb/m²) appearing on the surface of the film i.e in direction 3 (thickness) by applying a mechanical stress of 1 Newton/m².

The relationships between applied forces and the charge generation depend upon the piezoelectric properties of the material; the size and shape of the sample; and the direction of the mechanical and electrical actuation. The polar, or 3 axis, is considered parallel to the direction of polarization within the material. The subscript 5 is used in the second place when the mechanical stress or strain is shear. Therefore $d_{33}$ is used when the force is in the direction 3 (along the polarization axis) and the charge is collected on the same surface on which the force is impressed. When the force is applied at right angles to the polarization axis and the charge is collected on the same surface as before, $d_{31}$ applies. The coefficients "d" can also be expressed in Coulomb/Newton (C/N). The subscripts in $d_{15}$ indicate that the applied mechanical stress is shear and the charge is collected on electrodes which are at right angles to the original poling electrodes. Below in table 1, the different types of PVDF depending upon their availability in terms of thickness and composition is given.

*Table 1. Types of PVDF (available thickness)*

| Composition | Thickness (µm) | (pC/N) | Tolerance % |
|---|---|---|---|
| 75/25 | 12 5% | 16 | 20 |
| 75/25 | 255% | 15 | 20 |
| 75/25 | 505% | 15 | 20 |
| 75/25 | 1105% | 15 | 20 |
| 70/30 | 2010% | -20 | 10 |
| 70/30 | 2510% | -20 | 10 |
| 70/30 | 4010% | -20 | 10 |
| 77/23 | 610% | -19 | 10 |

The availability of PVDF piezoelectric films represents a unique combination of properties such as wide frequency range of about 0.001 Hz to $10^9$ Hz, vast dynamic range from $10^{-8}$ to $10^6$ psi, low acoustic impedance i.e. close match to water, human tissue and adhesive systems, high elastic compliance, high output voltage (10 times higher than piezoceramics for the same input force), high dielectric strength withstanding strong fields (75V/µm) where most piezoceramic materials depolarize, high mechanical strength and impact resistance ($10^9$—$10^{10}$ Pascal modulus), high stability against moisture (<0.02% moisture absorption), most chemicals, oxidants, and intense ultraviolet and nuclear radiation, can be fabricated into unusual designs, can be glued with commercial adhesives etc.

## PVDF END- EFFECTOR DESIGN

The end-effector using PVDF is shown in figure 2 which has been designed using Pro Release 5.0 software. Figure 2 gives the major driving dimensions where all the dimensions are in mm and figure 3 shows the 3-dimensional view having 1mm thickness.

## RESPONSE OF PVDF SENSOR

The voltage output E(s) of a PVDF gripper due to an applied force $F(s)$ in Laplace domain can be written as (J. Sirohi & I. Chopra.(2000); C. K. M. Fung, I. Elhaj, W. J. Lil & N. Xi. (2002); P. Benech, E. Chamberod & C. Monllor. (1996)),

*Figure 2. Design of end effector (All the dimensions*

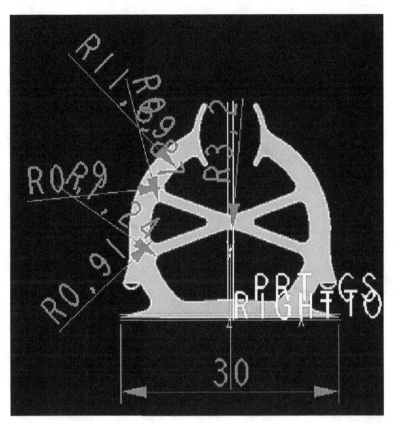

$$\frac{E(s)}{F(s)} = \frac{d_{33}}{A\varepsilon_{33}^T / h} \frac{\tau s}{\left(1 + \tau s\right)} \qquad (1)$$

$$\frac{E(s)}{F(s)} = \frac{A\tau s}{\left(1 + \tau s\right)} \qquad (2)$$

Where,

$A$ : Constant gain of the system $= \dfrac{d_{33}}{a\varepsilon_{33}^T / h}$

$a$ : Area of the gripper through which force is applied (m²)

$t$ : Thickness of the plate (m)

$\varepsilon_{33}^T$ : Mechanical strain in 3-direction due to tensile stress ($T$) in the 3-direction (Fm⁻¹) (PVDF normal dielectric

*Figure 3. Design of end effector (3D view)*
are in mm(Top view))

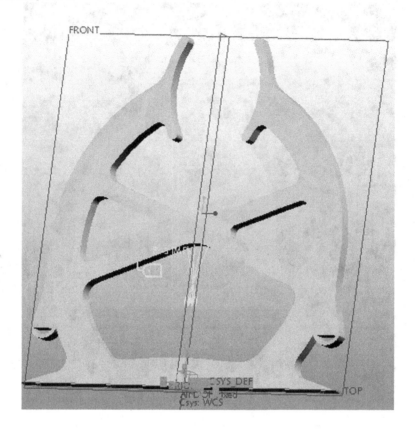

constant)

$\tau$ : Time constant of PVDF sensor and

$= \dfrac{\rho h C_p}{a} = R_p C_p$ ; In which, $R_p = \dfrac{\rho h}{a}$ represents the resistance of PVDF sensor,

$\rho$ and $C_p$ are the resistivity

and capacitance of PVDF material measured in $\Omega$m and F.

$d_{33}$ : PVDF normal piezoelectric constant $(CN^{-1})$

$h$ : Distance through which the force to be transmitted (m)

The polymer considered for this study is PVDF-1000 with a thickness 1mm. Hence, for this study,

$d_{33} = 33\text{pC/N} = 33\text{x } 10^{-12} \text{ C/N}$

$h = 20.0420\text{mm} = 20.0420\text{x}10^{-3}\text{m}$

$\varepsilon_{33}^{T} = 7.4 \text{ F/m}$

$a = 2.25\text{mm}^2 = 2.25 \times 10^{-6} \text{ m}^2$ [Computed according to design]

$\rho = 2 \times 10^{14} \ \Omega\text{-cm} = 2 \times 10^{12} \ \Omega\text{-m}$

$A = 39.72 \times 10^{-9} \ \text{V/N}$

$$\tau = \frac{\rho h C_p}{a} = \rho \, \varepsilon, \ [\text{as } C_p = \frac{\varepsilon \, a}{h}] = 14.8 \times 10^{12} \ \text{sec}$$

eq-(2) can be written as

$$\frac{F(s)}{E(s)} = \frac{1 + \tau s}{A \tau s} \tag{3}$$

The frequency response curve using bode diagram is given in figure 3 in the frequency range of interest from $10^{-12}$ to $10^{-9}$ rad/sec.

From frequency response analysis as shown in figure 4, it is evident that the gain and phase angle is almost constant over the frequency range of $\omega > 10^{-11}$ rad/sec.

*Figure 4. Frequency response of PVDF sensor*

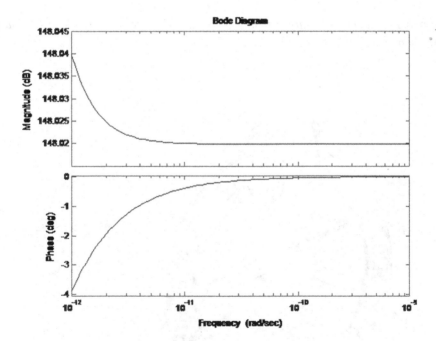

*Figure 5. Stress distribution in MPa. Maximum stress has been evaluated as 16.34MPa*

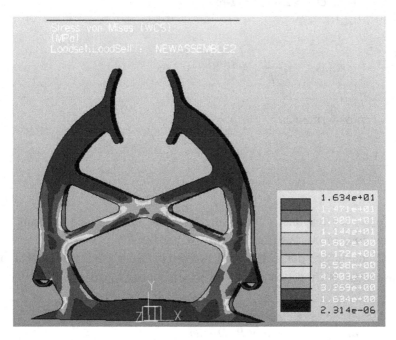

*Figure 6. Displacement analysis in mm. Maximum displacement has been evaluated by 0.106mm*

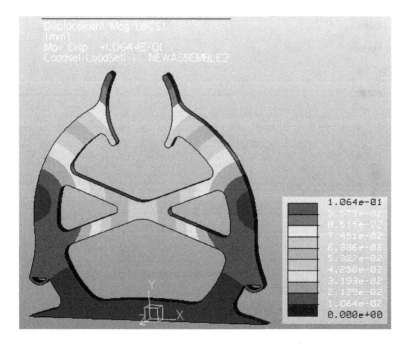

## STRESS AND DISPLACEMENT ANALYSIS

The above design shown in figure 2 has been analyzed with Creo Element/ Pro Release 5.0 software. The end effector has been subjected to the stress of 3MPa in the (–ve) z-direction at the center indicated in figure 3. The corresponding result of stress distribution and displacement has been analyzed and presented in figure 5 and figure 6 respectively.

## CONCLUSION

From the above results and discussions, it is shown that the gain and phase is constant over the frequency range > $10^{-11}$ rad/sec. Therefore, it can be concluded that it can give response in terms of stress for constant input voltage by inverse piezoelectric effect and the signal can be converted almost in unattenuated form. Moreover the maximum stress obtained from stress analysis is within the tensile stress at yield which is 60MPa and maximum displacement obtained from displacement analysis is also in the measurable range .So if the required amount of voltage will be applied at the micro gripper, the voltage will be converted into stress that will be transmitted over the body and will cause the deflection at the tip of the gripper. Therefore the opening and closing can be controlled by controlling the applied voltage at the specific position and direction of the end effector. Moreover as the gripper is miniaturized in size and the force exerted by polymer microgripper is very less, it can be applied for manipulating micro particles and micro components in micro assembly.

## REFERENCES

Aia, W., & Xu, Q. (2014). Overview of flexure-based compliant microgrippers. *Advances in Robotics Research, 1*(1). 001-019. DOI: . doi:10.12989/arr.2014.1.1.001

Arshad, A. N., Wahid, M. H. M., Rusop, M., Majid, W. H. A., Subban, R. H. Y., & Rozan, M. D. (2019). Dielectric and Structural Properties of Poly(vinylidene fluoride) (PVDF) and Poly(vinylidene fluoride-trifluoroethylene) (PVDFTrFE) Filled with Magnesium Oxide Nanofillers. *Journal of Nanomaterials, 2019*, 1–12. doi:10.1155/2019/5961563

Benech, P., Chamberod, E., & Monllor, C. (1996). Acceleration Measurement Using PVDF. IEEE Transactions On Ultrasonics, Ferroelectrics, and Frequency Control, 43(5). doi:10.1109/58.535484

Esterly, D. M. (2002). *Manufacturing of Poly (vinylidene fluoride) and Evaluation of its Mechanical Properties*. Blacksburg, VA: Virginia Polytechnic Institute and State University.

Fung, C. K. M., Elhaj, I., Lil, W. J., & Xi, N. (2002). A 2-D PVDF Force Manipulation Sensing System for Micro and Micro-assembly. In *Proceedings of the 2002 IEEE*. 10.1109/ROBOT.2002.1014754

Inderherbergh, J. (2017). Polyvinylidene Fluoride (PVDF) Appearance, General Properties and Processing. *Journal Ferroelectrics.*, *115*. doi:10.1080/00150193.1 991.11876614

Lediaev, L. M. (2006). *Modeling Piezoelectric PVDF Sheets with Conductive Polymer Electrodes*. Bozeman, MT: Montana State University.

Lee, S. (2011). Crystal Structure and Thermal Properties of Poly(vinylidene fluoridehexafluoropropylene) Films Prepared by Various Processing Conditions. *Fibers and Polymers*, *12*(8), 1030–1036. doi:10.100712221-011-1030-3

Ruan, L., Yao, X., Chang, Y., Zhou, L., Qin, G., & Zhang, X. (2018). Properties and Applications of the β Phase Poly (vinylidene fluoride). *Polymers*, *10*(3), 228. doi:10.3390/polym10030228 PMID:30966263

Sirohi, J., & Chopra, I. (2000). *Fundamental Understanding of Piezoelectric Strain Sensors*. College Park, MD: University of Maryland.

Zaarour, B., Zhu, L., & Jin, X. (2019). Controlling The Surface Structure, Mechanical Properties, Crystallinity, and Piezoelectric Properties of Electrospun PVDF Nanofibers by Maneuvering Molecular Weight. Journal. *Soft Materials*, *17*(2), 181–189. doi:10.1080/1539445X.2019.1582542

Chapter 13

# An Expert System–Based Automation in Indian Traction System for a One Way Single Platform Station by Introducing PLC

**Eshan Samanta**
https://orcid.org/0000-0003-1599-520X
*Global Institute of Science and Technology, India*

**Arif Ahmed**
https://orcid.org/0000-0003-0706-2565
*University of Tromsø, Norway*

**Debnarayan Khatua**
*Global Institute of Science and Technology, India*

## ABSTRACT

*Nowadays, it is very often that some portion of the Indian traction system is still suffering from a single line railway transportation. This in turn creates a havoc disturbance in maintaining the proper sequence of traction control system. Also, passengers are taking risk to catch the train which is already in motion but no such action has been taken to eliminate these consequences. It has been found that more or less various works have been done on Automation in Railway Crossing Gate using Microcontroller and IR Sensor. Thus, it is often decided to develop an idea for*

DOI: 10.4018/978-1-7998-2584-5.ch013

*the Indian traction system to ensure better controlling action by introducing Limit Switches as Tactile Sensors and by introducing HMI using PLC. The purpose here to take control over various controlling domains, including Railway crossing gate are as follows: Track signal, crossing level signal, alarm notification, and platform edge fence. The proper sequencing needs to be operated via a 128 I/O module with 2 KB memory size small PLC kit.*

## INTRODUCTION

The most important part of the transportation system in the present world is now a days the one and only traction system. In India some portion of the country is still suffering from deficit security system and the result is unnecessary death due to unavoidable accident. Many areas are not so well furnished due to single track communication system. The lack of spaces are not supporting government to set a double track railway communication system for a reliable and fast communication process. The accident prone the passengers' inrushes while the train is in motion. For upgrading the security system of traction system to reduce the accidental issues (Dhande and Pacharaney (2017); Reddy, Kavati, Rao, and Kumar (2017); Sharad, Sivakumar, and Ananthanarayanan (2016)) some of the articles have been published on security system associated with railway automated level crossing gate based on IoT. Priyanka et. al. (Priyanka, Saranya, Shanmathi, and Baranikumar (2015)) have shown a method to control unmanned railway crossing gate control with database collection and fixed RF tags on each level crossing to communicate with each other, in order to gather the details about the level crossing, train location, train timings and density of vehicles passing the level crossing. Dewangan et. al. (Dewangan, Gupta, and Patel (2012a,b)) has promoted a technique on frequency modulation based railway gate control and they have also introduced micro-controller based railway gate control conception as well. Many articles presented the security enhancement procedures (Al-Zuhairi (2013); Banuchandar, Kaliraj, Balasubramanian, Deepa, and Thamilarasi (2012); Pwint, Tun, and Tun (2014)) by introducing a IR sensor operated micro-controller based railway gate control. In all the cited articles one particular focused point is level crossing gate. The purpose is to reduce accidental issues occurring since early times. Apart from level crossing gate there are many other portion exist with high risk factor of accident but these articles have not discussed about the following. Younis et. al. (Younis and Frey (2006)) has shown a method of implementing PLC in developing automation setup for industrial purposes. This idea of implementing PLC has given a direction to develop multiple domain controlling concepts. In this paper a discussion is made on the best way to ensure automation in traction system by introducing a centralized controller PLC is the best one to follow as its scanning technology is very fast to accommodate with any kind of on off logic circuitry. Apart from this it is also quite affordable to follow up one time investment with full time reliable services. In this controlling portion the programming language followed up in PLC programming is ladder logic diagram indeed to make it easier to understand by any of the operator just to maintain a consistent cycle for each and every execution.

This paper has six main contributions: 1. Comparison presented between Conventional circuit and Ladder logic, 2. Safety fence controller along the platform, 3. Signal controller of road vehicles, 4. Signal controller of Train, 5. Alarm notification to update status of the train, 6. Level crossing gate controller.

These entire different tasks have been performed by introducing PLC as automated system. The rest of the paper presents the entire work under section 3, section 4.1, section 4.2, section 4.3, section 5 and concluded the same with proper correlated simulation outcomes.

## BLOCK DIAGRAM OF AUTOMATION SYSTEM

In Figure 1 a general block diagram is presented. The block diagram is a set of three different blocks. The concerned blocks are inputs, PLC module and outputs. Inputs to the PLC module are fed from limit switches that are pressed by the train flanges and a push switch to be pressed by the console operator. The PLC module then scans the entire rungs of the ladder diagram to initiate the output loads. The output will then actuate as per the supply fed by the concerned bus. Here the outputs are fence motor, crossing gate motor, train signal, crossing gate signal and alarm circuitry.

*Figure 1. Schematic block diagram of the entire automated system of the concerned Indian traction*

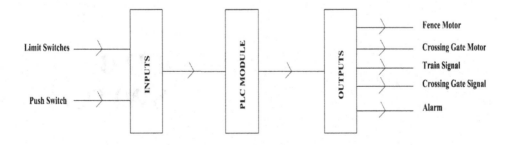

## INTERFACING WITH REAL WORLD

Here in this work we have selected limit switches as the input sources to the PLC module as it is SPDT (Single Pole Double Throw) in nature and as per constructional features it will assist the wheel to move over easily without any obstruction as well. In traction system trains are rolled forward over the rail by introducing ange attached to wheel that usually follows up the rail alignment. Vyas et.al. (Vyas and Gupta (2006)) have proposed the disadvantage of development of flats on wheel. That is why in this work flanges are taken as external contacts to the sequentially placed limit switches along the track. The

following mechanism is shown in Figure 2 and Figure 3. In Figure 2 the shaded portion is flanges which is extended to such limit compared to present engineered structure nowadays followed. The Limit switches are placed accordingly as shown in Figure 2 mounted along the track side capped with a typically designed contact point as presented under Figure 3. In Figure 3 the shaded portion is the switch head,

*Figure 2. Features of the relation between track, limit switch and wheel*

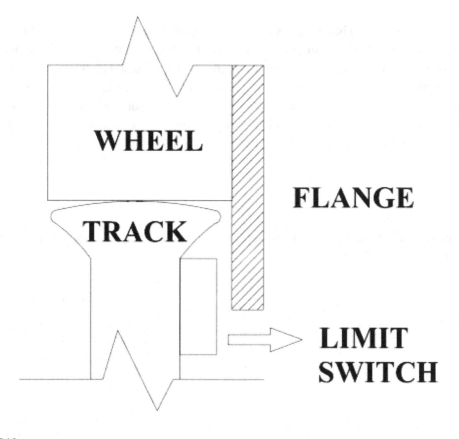

*Figure 3. Top view alignment of limit switch along the track with different forces and the direction of the flange*

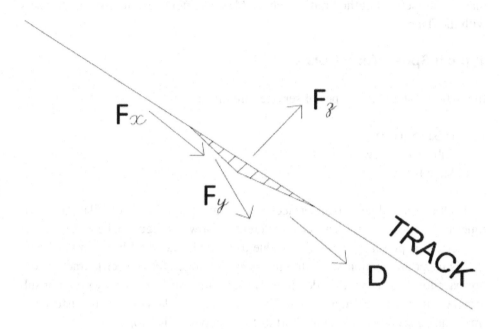

where $F\chi$ indicates the force exerted by the flange to the switch head tangentially due to its inclined structure. The force at the vertex point of the shaded triangle Fy hits the limit switch to send signal to the PLC module. The main actuating force is transferred from Fy to F$_3$ and connects the contact point of the limit switch as shown in Figure 3. The entire NO and NC are assembled together at the point just along the circumferential to the track as shown in Figure 2. This specific contact is operated by the force exerted to the cap of the switch by the flange and thus operates the entire ladder logic developed for the traction system. The non contact part of flanges usually make physical or mechanical contact with the limit switches placed accordingly as per Figure 3 to generate some electrical signals to operate entire automation scenario of traction system by introducing PLC module as the central controller. As per Figure 3 the right side portion of the wheel as well as the flange contact is the target frame to make contact with the accordingly placed limit switches. In Figure 3, D indicates the direction of the flange from the source towards the destination. A complete setup is presented under Figure 4 with an alternate hardware setup like the way it is discussed as per Figure 3. In Figure 4 the most important fact is the point contact. The purpose of selecting a point contact is due to less friction. Surface contact increases the friction and thus could change the retardation as well as the velocity of the train. The most negative impact due to wear and tear process as because of the coefficient of adhesion (Dover (1954)) is that the contact part of the limit switch could break after a few numbers of contacts with the flange.

## Typical Speed Time Curve

In traction system three types of services are there:

1.  Urban Service,
2.  Sub Urban Service,
3.  Main Line Service

Both urban and suburban services are designed to follow quadrilateral speed time curve. The main line service is different as shown in Figure 5, because the free run section is present in this case as due to long distance halt between the stops. In this paper automation algorithm has been developed for a specific track where no space for wagon carrier is deputed. Thus, for this work, especially urban or sub urban traction service, Figure 6 a and b respectively is taken due to no existence of free running section because of short distance between the stops.

Notations
m: metre
s: second
$\gamma$: acceleration (in m/s$^2$)
$\zeta_c$: coasting retardation (in m/s$^2$)

*Figure 4. Alternate alignment of limit switch along the track with a complete pictorial view*

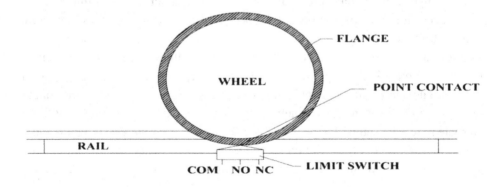

*Figure 5. Alternate alignment of limit switch along the track with a complete pictorial view*

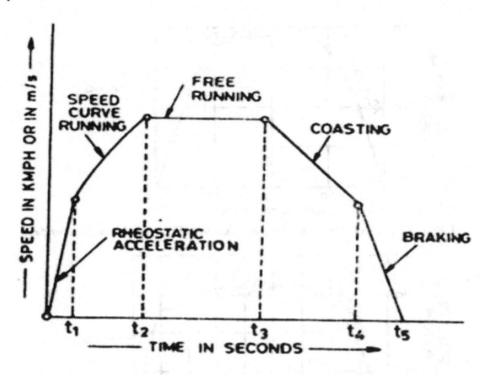

$\zeta$: braking retardation (in m/s$^2$)

X: distance covered by train (in m)

$T_1$: acceleration time (in s)

$T_2$: coasting time (in s)

$T_3$: braking time (in s)

## Real Equations

The typical speed time curve is the most important section covered (Dover (1954)) in any of the book associated with traction and drives. In case of quadrilateral curve $T_1$ and $T_3$ is less compared to $T_2$. The Equation - 4 is indicating distance traversed by the train during a single journey between each stop.

$$T1 = \frac{v1}{3} \tag{1}$$

*Figure 6. a) Coasting period with less slope due to short distance, (b) Coasting time is more due to distance*

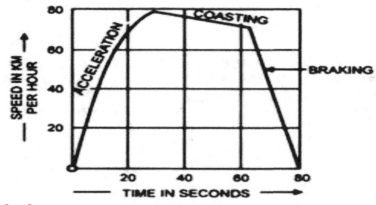

(a) *Typical Speed-Time Curve For Urban Service*

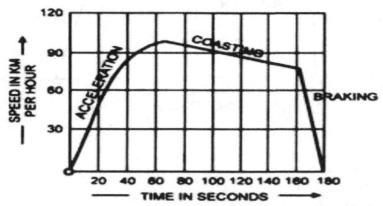

(b) *Typical Speed-Time Curve For Suburban Service*

$$T2 = \frac{v2 - v1}{\zeta c} \tag{2}$$

$$T3 = \frac{v2}{\zeta} \tag{3}$$

$$X = \frac{T(v1 + v2)}{2} - kv1v2 \tag{4}$$

*Figure 7. Quadrilateral speed time curve for sub urban service*

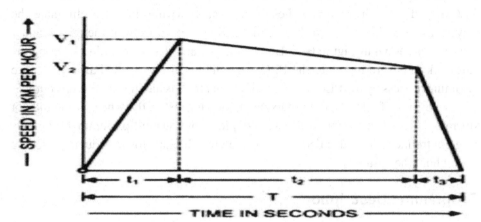

Where,

$$k = \frac{\gamma + \zeta}{2\gamma\zeta} \quad \text{Also,} \quad \zeta c = \frac{v2 - v1}{T2} \quad \text{and} \quad v2 = \frac{v1 - \zeta c\left(T - \frac{v1}{\gamma}\right)}{1 - \frac{\zeta c}{\zeta}}, \quad T = T1 + T2 + T3$$

In Equation 4, it is clear as per Figure 7, that the entire distance travelled by a train is dependent on velocity, acceleration and retardation. Therefore adhesion of coefficient (Dover (1954)) is also another major part which is also associated with the design features of the entire contact part of the coupled portion or capped part of the limit switch for traction system. Thus to avoid frictions between track and flanges a special kind of switch head has been developed and presented under Figure 3.

## RESEARCH METHODOLOGY

### Model Circuitry Layout

In Figure 8, the structure of hardware circuit developed excluding two controlling domains that is platform fence and road vehicles' traffic signalling. To ensure a better reliable system the above deficit controlling domain is hereby introduced in the PLC ladder diagram as it was getting very difficult to control the fence perimeter in case of through trains with the implementation of above proposed circuitry module. In the above circuit, Figure 8; source is taken as 12V, 7.5 Ah Rechargeable Battery. Figure

8 is basically comprised of physical relays and complicated wiring methodologies. PLC would assist in reducing these complicated wiring and also eliminate the physically available relays with its coil existing in each rung of the entire ladder diagram as shown in Figure 0-13 Limit switches are placed accordingly along the rail track to ensure inputs to the PLC. The outputs are controlled after the entire scanning process by the PLC. It is very often that train is having a numerous number of wheels, now if one hits the limit switch, then for rest of the wheels it should not operate, which means, latching is mandatory for avoiding multiple numbers of inputs to get introduced. It is decided to introduce virtual relays for introducing latching throughout the system.

## Programme Description

### Step 1:

1. When the limit switch1 as shown in Figure 8 is pressed it is basically actuating relay 1,
2. Fence motor,
3. Yellow signal to passengers and red signal to the vehicles at the crossing gate.
4. Normally Open (NO) contact of relay 1 usually fed supply to relay 7 which in turn makes NO change to Normally Closed (NC) and actuates crossing gate motor.

### Step 2:

*Figure 8. Conventional validated circuitry design of the concerned automated traction system*

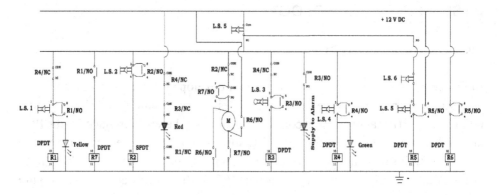

*Figure 9. Implementation Steps with a Proper Flow Chart*

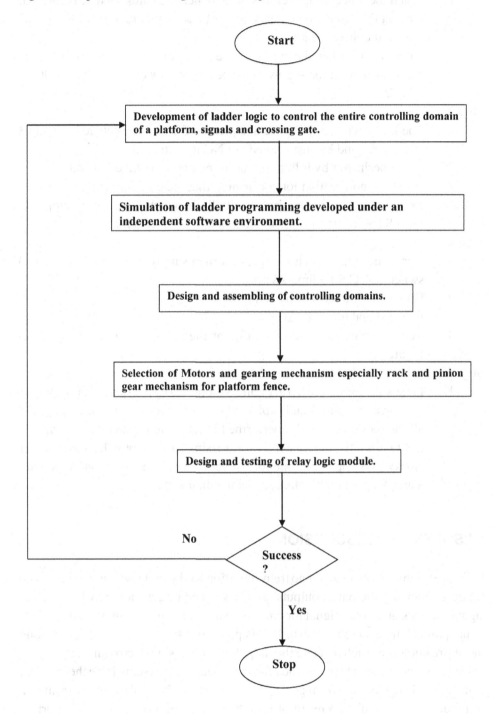

1. When the fence perimeter hits limit switch 7 as presented in Figure 8 it will cut the supply to the fence motor by actuating relay 6 to change NC to NO of concerned relay.

2. After closing when the crossing gate motor hits limit switch 2 in Figure 8, it will also cut the supply to the gate motor by changing NC to NO of relay 2.

**Step 3:**

1. The limit switch 3 in Figure 8 is pressed then supply gets fed to relay 3 of Figure 8 and by ensuring NO to NC it controls the

2. Fence perimeter by rolling motor in the opposite direction and

3. An alarm notification for confirming that the train has arrived.

4. Now when the fence perimeter hits limit switch 8 it ensures supply to relay 8 and cut the supply to fence motor via NC contact.

**Step 4:**

1. Again the limit switch 4 is pressed then supply goes to relay 4 as NO switch to NC for a limit switch,

2. Fence motor to cover up again,

3. Green signal to train and

4. Yellow signal to vehicles waiting at the crossing gate as designed in Figure 8.

**Step 5:**

1. Finally the limit switch 5 in Figure 8 is pressed by the flange of train wheel as shown in Figure 2 and explained under Section - 3 to make changes in all the sequences hereby performed in its default state by changing NC to NO instantly. In this step again crossing gate motor will rotate counter clockwise to open the gate for the vehicles waiting for a long time with a green signal notification to change their state.

## RESULTS AND DISCUSSION

In Figure 9, simulation result for no train condition has been shown. In the concerned figure two among the entire outputs are active. The outputs are classified as red signal for track and green signal for crossing gate. In Figure 10, simulation result of train approaching is hereby shown. In this particular simulation result five among the entire outputs are active. Here the outputs are track signal, crossing gate signal, fence motor, crossing gate motor and relay coil to latch the system. Here the crossing gate signal changed to red from green and track signal changed to yellow from red. In Figure 11 the simulation result of train halt has been intimated. In this portion the change is only the fence motor. As on while crossing the half of the platform length fence motor starts operating in the reverse direction to pull it down due to a supply fed from limit switch pressed by the flange. The results are shown in Figure 10, Figure 11 and Figure 12 are the belongings of the first phase. After this phase passengers rush usually takes around 1 minute. The end of intermediate phase will introduce the second phase to be executed after the push switch to be pressed for the notification of the platform to be cleared to the driver of the train. Figure 13 and Figure 14 presenting the actual operation during the time of simulation. Figure 13 is showing the simulation output of the train leaving the platform. In this particular possession a manual switch gets operated from the control room to notify the train to leave the platform by showing a green signal using track signal by changing it from yellow to green and a parallel supply is fed to the fence motor to set the temporary fence. In Figure 13 the last part of the entire automation system is hereby shown. In this simulation result the entire frame is similar to that of no train condition. While leaving the entire scenario the train usually presses the last limit switch to reset the entire automation system to its default state. The entire ladder operation is clearly explained under Table 2 by taking the status of each rung with respect to its concerned activities.

The entire setup is also stable enough as it has a dual power source associated with it. 12 V supply is directly fed to it by using a 12 V transformer and apart from this a selector switch is also available to feed supply to it using a dry cell of 12 V with 7.5 Ah rating source as well. This selector switch works on the basis of manual selection and even if necessary it can be converted into automatic transfer switch based power backup for emergency shutdown. In Table 1, it is clearly shown that

*Figure 10. Simulation validates the operation of the concerned algorithm developed for the entire traction system in case of when there is no train*

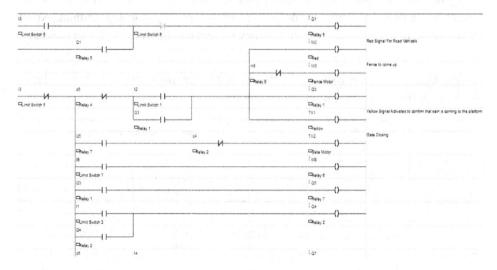

*Figure 11. Simulation validates the operation of the algorithm developed for the condition when train is arriving platform*

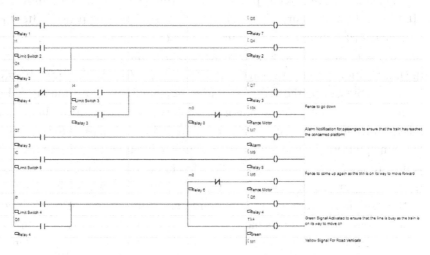

the PLC based system is more reliable as compared to the conventional system. The running cost of the conventional system is high enough as compared to the PLC based system. PLC can easily operate both the digital and analog system. Conventional system needs more auxiliary components to manipulate the same.

## CONCLUSION

Simulation result of automation in the Indian traction system by introducing PLC is hereby reported. Incorporation of the discussed control system in the Indian traction system might bring a change in the Indian automation engineering domain. Apart from this it will also provoke a tight security system during most of the unavoidable

*Table 1. Comparative analysis of the PLC based system along with the conventional system with respect to the concerned estimate*

| Particulars | PLC | Conventional System |
|---|---|---|
| Controller | Micro, 22000/- | Relays 10000/- |
| Wires | 2000/- Max | 8000/- |
| Limit Switch | 8 Nos, 1600/- | 12 Nos, 2400/- |
| Indication | No Investment | 16 Nos, 3200/- |
| Misllaneous | Operator and Lines Man | Comparatively huge due to complex wiring and major maintenance. |

*Figure 12. Simulation validates the operation of the concerned algorithm developed for the entire traction system in case of halt*

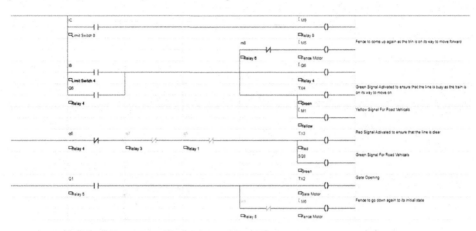

*Figure 13. Simulation validates the operation of the concerned algorithm developed for the entire traction system in case of train is on its way to depart*

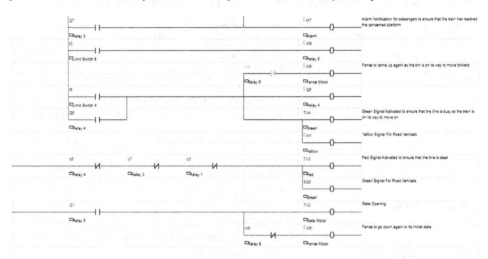

accidental cases and might help in reducing the death rate due to traction system. It is also very often that by introducing PLC in Indian traction system might set an asset to ensure a very reliable control system for the betterment of railway departmental delegates and the passengers as well. This paper has presented and validated that the replacement of an identically functional features based conventional circuit is easily possible by implementing process control based Programmable Logic Controller

*Figure 14. Simulation validates the operation of the concerned algorithm developed for the entire traction system in case of train left the scenario*

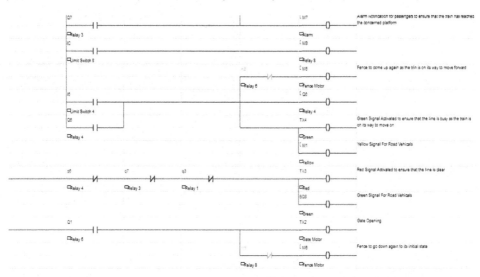

*Table 2. Analysis of the ladder result obtained while performing simulation*

| Stages | Status | Activities |
|--------|--------|------------|
| Stage 1 | No Train is there in the platform | • Green Signal to Vehicle,<br>• Red Signal to ensure no train |
| Stage 2 | Train is arriving towards the platform | • Red Signal to vehicles,<br>• Fence along the side of the platform to come up,<br>• Yellow signal activated to confirm that the train is arriving to the platform,<br>• Level crossing gate would close. |
| Stage 3 | Halt | • Fence to go down,<br>• Alarm notification to passengers |
| Stage 4 | Departing | • Fence to come up again,<br>• Green signal to train,<br>• Yellow signal for vehicles |
| Stage 5 | Train left the scenario | • Red signal activated to ensure line clearance,<br>• Green Signal to vehicles,<br>• Level crossing gate opened,<br>• Fence to go down to initial state |

with emergency power backup and low running cost as discussed under Section - 4.1, Section - 4.3 and Section - 5. It is evident that by uploading this ladder diagram in any 128 I/O module PLC hardware kit the chances of evolution in the Indian traction system is very natural. In future this entire concept will be implemented with an upgraded ladder logic for any junction based Railway station. The motivation of this work is to reduce accidental features and to improve the control system of the process as well.

## ACKNOWLEDGMENT

We, gratefully acknowledge the contributions of Railway Department of India. Inspired by the present scenario of the train route available from Katwa, Burdwan to Azimganj Junction, Murshidabad. This case was previously carried out by some students of a polytechnic institute of West Bengal by implementing SPDT relays in partial form. After that it has been decided to develop more controlling domain which was not very easy to set with the physically available change over relays.

## REFERENCES

Banuchandar, J., Kaliraj, V., Balasubramanian, P., Deepa, S., & Thamilarasi, N. (2012). Automated unmanned railway level crossing system. [IJMER]. *International Journal of Modern Engineering Research, 2*(1), 458–463.

Dewangan, A. K., Gupta, M., & Patel, P. (2012). Automation of railway gate control using frequency modulation techniques. *International Journal of Electrical, Electronics Communication Engineering, 2*(6), 288–298.

Dewangan, A. K., Gupta, M., & Patel, P. (2012). Automation of railway gate control using microcontroller. *International Journal of Engineering Research & Technology (IJERT), 1*(3).

Dhande, B. S., & Pacharaney, U. S. (2017). Unmanned level crossing controller and rail track broken detection system using ir sensors and internet of things technology. In *Proceedings International Conference on Inventive Communication and Computational Technologies (ICICCT)*, IEEE., pp. 206–210.

Dover, A. T. (1954). *Electric traction*. Pitman.

Hnin, N. Y. P., Tun, Z. M., & Tun, H. M. (2014). Automatic railway gate control system using microcontroller. *International Journal of Science* [IJSETR]. *Engineering and Technology Research, 3*(5), 1547–1551.

Mahdi, AS Al-Zuhairi. (2013). Automatic railway gate and crossing control based sensors & microcontroller. [IJCTT]. *International Journal of Computer Trends and Technology, 4*(7).

Priyanka, J. C., Saranya, A., Shanmathi, C., & Baranikumar, S. (2015). Automatic level crossing gate with database collection. In *Proceedings International Conference on Computation of Power, Energy, Information and Communication (ICCPEIC)*, IEEE, pp. 0388–0392. 10.1109/ICCPEIC.2015.7259483

Reddy, E. A., Kavati, I., Rao, K. S., & Kumar, G. K. (2017). A secure railway crossing system using iot. In *Proceedings International Conference of Electronics, Communication, and Aerospace Technology (ICECA)*, IEEE, 2, pp. 196–199. 10.1109/ICECA.2017.8212795

Sharad, S., Bagavathi Sivakumar, P., & Ananthanarayanan, V. (2016). An automated system to mitigate loss of life at unmanned level crossings. *Procedia Computer Science*, *92*, 404–409. doi:10.1016/j.procs.2016.07.397

Vyas, N. S., & Gupta, A. K. (2006). Modeling rail wheel-flat dynamics. In *Engineering Asset Management* (pp. 1222–1231). Springer. doi:10.1007/978-1-84628-814-2_135

Younis, M. B., & Frey, G. (2006). A formal method based re-implementation concept for plc programs and its application. *International Conference on Emerging Technologies and Factory Automation*, IEEE, pp. 1340–1347. 10.1109/ETFA.2006.355346

# Chapter 14
# An IoT–Based Remote Health Monitoring System for Smart Healthcare:
## Cardiac Health Monitoring-Based Approach

**Uday Maji**
*Haldia Institute of Technology, India*

**Rohan Mandal**
*Haldia Institute of Technology, India*

**Saurav Bhattacharya**
*Haldia Institute of Technology, India*

**Shalini Priya**
*Haldia Institute of Technology, India*

## ABSTRACT

*Many automated health monitoring devices detect health abnormalities based on gleaned data. One of the effective approaches of monitoring a senior cardiac patient is the analysis of an Electrocardiogram (ECG) signal, as proven by various studies and applications. However, diagnosis results must be communicated to an expert. An intelligent and effective technology gaining wide popularity known as 'internet of things' or 'IoT' allows remote monitoring of the patient.*

DOI: 10.4018/978-1-7998-2584-5.ch014

# INTRODUCTION

Twenty first century's most alarming issue is public health care as the greatest number of people suffering from different diseases due to uncertain changes in environment specially for pollution and also due to unhealthy food qualities. World health organization (WHO) is reported that many people dies annually from different diseases mainly from cardiovascular diseases (CVD). Moreover 80% of CVD death is observed in low and middle economic countries among men and women both in almost equal percentage. It is also reported that by 2030, almost 23.6 million people may die from cardiovascular diseases and stokes [WHO 2013]. Different organizations have been taken several initiatives to reduce this miserable trained of human health issues. But another way to reduce and save human from this trained is to employ continuous or regular health monitoring system. Effective health monitoring systems can diagnosis human health with proper care of experts. But the availability of experts especially in rural area in the country like India is very difficult. An automated health monitoring system can help to overcome this problem with its self-diagnosis capability. This type of expert system diagnoses health condition based on the given data from the patient with the help of wearable sensors. The system is also capable to communicate with the experts of patients' relatives in emergency condition. This literature mainly focuses on modern health monitoring system on cardiovascular diseases.

At present time IoT (internet of things) based system [Yang Z, 2016] is gaining popularity in all the fields from human daily appliance to big industries. Looking at its popularity, this system has also adapted in the diagnosis of human health condition and makes our life better. In the following sections, how this can be used to monitor the ECG signal for cardiac health diagnosis is described.

# CONVENTIONAL ECG MONITORING SYSTEMS

The electrocardiogram (ECG) is a main tool used by the doctors to diagnose and monitor heart patients. It is the graphical representation of the time variant voltage produced by the muscle tissue of heart (myocardium) during cardiac cycle. Fig1 shows basic waveform of the normal ECG signal. The P-wave generates due to atrium contraction, QRS complex generates due to atrium relaxation and ventricle contraction and T-wave is produced due to ventricle relaxation. This waveform represents the rhythmic electrical depolarization and repolarization of the myocardium. Basically ECG waveform is used to diagnosis different kind of heart diseases. For the diagnosis of the heart disease cardiologist first checks the heart rate and in normal health condition its value lies in between 60 to 100 beats per minute. Heart rate of any person can be slower or faster than the normal range, former is termed as bradycardia whereas latter situation is called tachycardia. The cardiologist checks the ECG waveform and detect the various disease on the basis of change in rhythmic oscillation like, if the cycles are not evenly spaced the person suffers from arrhythmia (abnormal heart rhythm) or if the P-R interval is greater than the normal range (0.12 to 0.20 sec), it can indicate the blockage of the autrio ventricular (AV) node etc.

The instrument is used to obtain and record the ECG waveform is known as electrocardiograph. The first ECG monitoring device was appeared in the hospitals around the year 1910. As the year passes lots of technical changes occurred in the electrocardiograph. But still the conventional method is preferred in the most of the health center. Few conventional ECG monitoring systems are briefly described below:

## Conventional Eletrocardigraph

In the conventional electrocardiograph ECG is recorded from a number of leads placed at different parts of the body, usually 12-lead Ag-AgCl electrodes are required which are placed to the specific of chest, arms, hands and legs. The 12 standard leads are used to ensure that no important detail of the ECG waveform is missed and to get the better ECG signal quality and it is divided into two parts – six limb leads which are placed in coronal plane (vertical) are used to record electrical potential transmitted into frontal plane and six chest leads (precoidial leads) are placed in horizontal plane. The conventional ECG measurement provides the better waveform but it requires a trained healthcare professionals and is also very complicated as upto twelve leads are placed in precise locations on the patient body. Before placing the electrodes, the patient is prepared by shaving the area and applying a gel and electrodes. Then these electrodes are attached by cables to the ECG machine. The principal parts or building blocks of electrocardiograph are shown in the fig2.

*Figure 1. The normal ECG waveform*

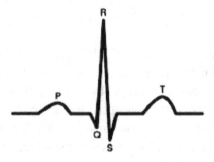

*Figure 2. Electrocardiograph building blocks*

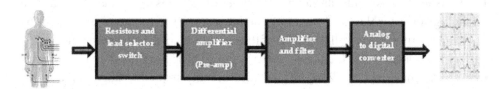

Physiological signal from human body acquired by ECG electrodes are connected to the selector switch and the resistor which are essential for unipolar leads. This ECG signal amplified by two stage amplifier – in first stage signal is amplified by high common mode rejection ratio differential amplifier (Pre-amp) followed by amplifier and filter circuits. It is also ac- coupled in order to block the small dc voltage generates from polarization of electrodes. The preamplifier has the switch to set the gain. After that the signal goes into dc amplifier which is followed by filter and analog to digital conveter. Then ECG waveform is displayed or recorded for diagnosis purpose . There are various types of ECG recorder like single-channel recorder, three channel recorder, vector electrocardiographs, electrocardiograph systems for stress testing, electrographs for computer processing, holter recording etc.

Thus the 12 leads conventional electrocardiograph is used to provide more comprehensive information about heart with greater accuracy, but the electrodes used here contain electrolytic paste which may cause skin infection [Elena B. Sgarbossa, 2004] . Also this method can be performed only in the guidance of specialist. For this reason the use of this conventional method in remote health monitoring is impractical. But nowadays mobile telemedicine systems has become very popular and mobile computing platforms are going to dominate the information communication technology (ICT) sector with the rapid technological developments. These innovative systems will help us to monitor the patients without conventional clinical setup may be within the home environment. Hence the system will reduce the health care delivery cost but enhance the access to care the patient.

## Biotelemetry

The term telemetry is an abbreviation of Tele Metering which means measurement of some physical parameter from a remote location. The primary block of any measurement system is sensor and it is obvious that the sensor must be installed at the measurand site whereas the concept of remote measurement makes sense by displaying and recording the sensed information at a remote place. For this purpose the sensed signal is modulated with proper carrier signal and transmitted via suitable antenna. In the receiver side this modulated signal is received by suitable receiver antenna then demodulated and the measured data is retrieved. The application of telemetry in biology, medicine and other healthcare is known as biotelemetry [D. C. Jeutter, 1983]. It is also referred as measurement of biological parameters over distance. The simple example of biotelemetry is stethoscope in which the heartbeat signal is amplified and transmitted through a hollow tube to be picked by the ear of the doctor for diagnosis. The first true biometric system was come in knowledge in year 1903 by Linthoven. He designed the electrocardiograph to monitor the electrical activity of the heart but it is very large in size and also immobile. If the person wanted to measure his ECG he had to remain attached to the device. Linthoven used the telephonic wire to transfer the bio data. The next major improvement in the biotelemetry came in the year 1957 when Soviet Union launched Sputnik in space. The aim of the mission was basically to determine the physiological effects of zero-gravity but machine which was used to measure the biological parameter was very bulky. As we see that earlier the wires are used to transmit the signals from one place to other but in 1961, NASA set the base of modern biotelemetry where the use of wire is eliminated for the transmission of bio-data also the machine used to measure the bio-data is not bulky so that it could easily be carried by human. They made the spacesuits which had sensor to measure the heart rate, body temperature, $CO_2$ and $O_2$ levels in blood. The invention of integrated circuits and microelectronic devices revolutionized the biotelemetry as the bio-data is transmitted wirelessly without the use of wires. The elimination of the wire is the major advantage as it makes the concept of remote health monitoring system which is based on modern biotelemetry where the biological parameters are wirelessly transfer between the patient and data collection equipment.

The components of modern biotelemetry system are shown in the figure 3. The first component is the sensor which is used to measure the biological parameter after that the analog signals (voltage, current etc.) from the sensor is converted into the form which is suitable for transmission. Normally for wireless transmission

*Figure 3. Components of biotelemetry*

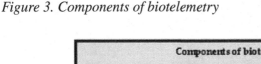
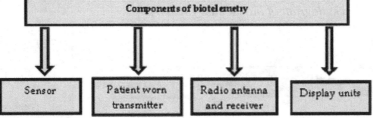

analog signal is modulated (FM/AM) using some radio frequency carrier signal and transmitted using FDM technique. At the receiver end these signals are decoded and converted into its original form. FDM is frequency division multiplexing using which signals from different sensors can be sent through a single channel. According to the Wireless Planning Commission of India the frequency ranges 402-405MHz and 2.4-2.4835GHz can be used for bio-telemetry applications in India. Here the bio-data is transmitted from one place to another. So when the direct diagnosis of patient is impossible, the biotelemetry is used in such medical cases and the most widespread use of biotelemetry is the transmission of the ECG because for the cardiac disease to be detected the patients must be observed for a period of time following intensive coronary care. For proper diagnosis of such patients are generally allowed a certain amount of mobility. To make such kind of monitoring possible, coronary care units equipped with patient monitoring systems with the use of biotelemetry. In this type of monitoring system the ECG electrodes are placed to the patient chest and it is connected to small transmitter which also contains signal conditioning equipment as shown in figure 4. Instrumentation at the transmitting end is simple as only electrodes and amplification are required to prepare the signal for transmission.

The receiver side consists of the tuner (select the transmitting frequency), demodulator (separate the signal from the carrier wave) and display unit (for recording of signal) shown in figure 5. In the ECG telemetry system, each receiver is connected to the one of the channel of the patient monitor.

With the new technology development the biotelemetry transmitting and receiving system has also evolved. Earlier the problem with ECG monitoring using biotelemetry

*Figure 4. Block diagram of a biotelemetry transmitter*

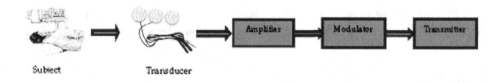

*Figure 5. Block diagram of biotelemetry receiver*

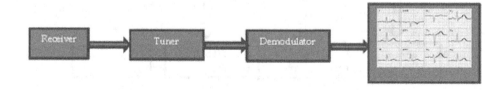

is that it can properly work only in limited area. If the patient goes beyond the range of system his ECG signals are no longer monitored and this limits the use of telemetry in health monitoring system. But nowadays there is lots of technology available which help in proper use of telemetry in remote patient monitoring like mobile cardiac outpatient telemetry (MCOT) where three leads sensor are used to record the ECG signal. The monitoring device which is capable of communicating with sensor continuously is carried by patient. By using the cellular telephone technology the bio-data is transmitted to the health centre. If there is problem with communicating with health centre the data is stored in the monitor upto 24 hours until the connection is established. The cardiac outpatient telemetry helps the cardiologist for better diagnosis as this system can record the electrical activity of heart continuously for 30 days. But the best use of modern biotelemetry is in the underwater ECG monitoring system which is basically used in scuba diving.

The scuba diving is basically underwater diving in which the diver uses the breathing apparatus scuba for continuous supply of oxygen. It is popular sport which is practiced by the professionals and military. But it is very dangerous and can lead to death. Decompression sickness which occurs due the excess amount of nitrogen inhaled by the diver which gets dissolved in the blood and it is very dangerous as it may block the blood vessels. BY using the ECG waveform we can able to detect this disease before severe effect it causes [B.Woodward, 1995]. So the system which can continuously monitor the diver current condition can save the life. The modern health monitoring system provides the underwater ECG monitoring facility shown in figure 6. Here the ECG electrodes are hydrophobic in nature and made up of a mixture of carbon black powder (CB) and polydimethylsiloxane (PDMS). In this scenario if it uses the conventional ECG electrode (Ag-AgCl), the signal quality is degraded so CB-PDMS electrode is preferred. Here, wearable sensors are used for

*Figure 6. Underwater ECG monitoring system*

Data acquisition using wearable sensor with hydrophobic ECG electrodes

Sensor data is transmitted to the mobile device using Bluetooth or Wi-Fi

Display unit for the diagnosis of ECG waveform

ECG waveform. Three hydrophobic electrodes are used in which two electrodes are placed at the diver's right and left clavicle and the third one is placed on the abdominal region above the right leg. The bio-data from the sensor is transferred to the mobile device using Bluetooth or Wi-Fi. The scuba diver kept the mobile device with itself in a waterproof diving bag and it is attached to his chest. The transmitter transmits the signal to the diagnosis room outside the water where the ECG waveform diagnosis and warn the diver when the heart rate goes above or below the normal heart rate which is calculated from the detected QRS complex of the ECG waveform through the alert system provided to the diver. So the risk of scuba diving can be reduced by using real time ECG monitoring system with alert function.

**Modern Electrocardiograph:** William Einthoven is known as the father of modern electrocardiograph. The first clinical use ECG was developed after he invented the string galvanometer in the year 1901. Earlier the ECG machines were very bulky and large and it could not be connected to the patient's bedside. The ECG signal was transmitted (telemetry) from the patient's room to another room where ECG machine were kept through wires. But the modern day ECG machines are portable for example cardiac event recorder and can transmit the ECG signal to the doctor's office through internet. The concept remains the same as the traditional ECG machine but the system become light, portable, user friendly, wirelessly transmit data etc. Now a day also the ECG electrodes are no directly connected to the recording machine. They also wirelessly transmit the ECG data to receiver attached to the ECG machine. Wireless ECG machine are very flexible and useful as patient can transmit the data from his home to doctor's office. There is no need of frequent visit to hospital. Many wireless ECG devices like Monebo Cardio Belt, AliveCor Kardia Mobile ECG, Qardio Core, Apple Watch etc. are available in the market.

- The Monebo Cardio Belt which is shown in figure 7, is an ECG recording device used for remote patient monitoring and it can be used in the home healthcare and biotelemetry. The advantage of this over the conventional ECG is that it can be easily used and worn across the chest by the patient and also there is no use of sticky electrodes and trained health professionals. Cardio Belt provides an effective useful platform to the doctors in association with Monebo's analyzing software with the Bluetooth as the communication medium.

- The AliveCor Kardia Mobile ECG is used for early detection of atrial fibrillation. It is a single channel ECG recorder. It consists of a device and app that helps to record ECG anywhere, anytime. The device is basically designed for cardiologists and heart patients. We can attach this device in the back of smart phones and by using the free Kardia app it can communicates and display the ECG signals. It can instantaneously detect if atrial fibrillation

*Figure 7. Monebo cardio belt*

is present in ECG. By using this patient has the facility to share their data to the health centre or specialists. Moreover, patients can also visualize these information through synced online account. This information is stored in the cloud, thus the patient can access their data confidentially, consult with physician, email it to caregivers and health professionals through secure login in to their account from anywhere anytime.

- QardioCore is another chest wearable ECG monitoring device that offers medical grade data while fitting our normal lifestyle. It's a very small dimensional (185 x 87 x 9 mm) device that is fixed on human chest with a belt for long hours without hampering any activity of the patient. It collects ECG signal through a single channel electrode, converts it into 16bit digital data with a sampling rate of 600 samples per second and sends it to iOS devices like iPhone, iPad, Apple Watch etc. through Bluetooth 4.0 medium. From these devices these data are shared with doctors or healthcare providers in a remote place ensuring a better health monitoring and preventive care. Apart from ECG, the device also provides other biometric data like skin temperature, heart rate, heart rate variability (HRV), activity tracking, and respiratory rate to the medical experts giving them a greater insight into patient's overall heart health and behavior.

Apart from these many ECG machine like Holter ECG machine which is portable and can be worn by patient for more than 24 hours. In this system a special magnetic tape recorder is used to obtain the ECG during his normal daily life activity. It has less lead than the clinical ECG and the patient can freely move and able to perform their daily routine. But these present ECG monitoring devices have some problems like in AliveCorKardia Mobile ECG, the patients have to rest two or more fingers on Kardia Mobile and also rest their arms on a flat surface and remain still with their fingers on the electrodes for 30 second. This device can display the ECG only when patient put their finger on it. So, it cannot be used for continuous monitoring as it is not possible to put their finger on it for long hours. In the same way Monebo CardioBelt supports wireless facility, e.g. Bluetooth which provide short range low rate wireless data transfer and also there is security issue.

## INTERNET OF THINGS (IOT)

In this century everybody is cognizant and associated with the term internet. At present a term called 'things', has coupled with internet to produce a very interesting subject called Internet of Things (IoT). But what this 'things' is referred to? The 'things' is referred to the various physical devices home appliances, automobiles, industrial equipment and even human beings. Thus IoT implies a concept of inter-linking of these elements with embedded system, software, sensors through some network connectivity that facilitate these objects to exchange information among themselves. It has been initiated by Global Standards Initiative (GSI) in 2013 and defined the IoT as the infrastructure of the information society" [Vermesan, 2013]. This system mainly allows certain object to be accessed remotely over the existing inter-networking setup. Hence physical devices are integrated more with the computer world which improves devices performances and economic benefits with less human effort. Moreover IoT is expected to offer more advanced facilities that goes beyond machine to machine connectivity and covers a wide variety of domains, protocols and application such as smart power grid, virtual power plant, intelligent transportation, smart home as a results smart cities i.e. the technology setup an example of more general class of cyber-physical systems.

Successful application of IoT concept in industries and home appliances is not limited any more but it also uses in wide variety of human health care systems like cardiac health monitoring, farm animal monitoring through biochip transponders, DNA analysis devices for environmental/food/pathogen monitoring, automobiles controlling and tracking as well as rescue operation. Based on these various field of application, Legal scholars advised to consider 'Thing' as an "inextricable mixture of hardware, software, data and service". Basically in all applications these devices acquire necessary information with the help of various sensors and by using network protocol communicate to other devices.

Devices and appliances communicate with each other are expected to generate large amount of data. Thus it requires strong data handle capable network and server. With the enhancement of the versatility of the internet connected devices, IoT will be applicable in all these areas with the necessity for quick accumulation of the data, and an increase in the need to index, process and store the information effectively. Moreover, making of Smart City, Smart Energy Management in present day is possible by the application IoT platform and can turn into Smart heath care system as well.

## IoT in Medical and Healthcare

Information in fingertip is the most essential entity of quality living at present time. So if human health status is also available, life status could be better. With the advancement of technology and wide applicability of IoT remote heath monitoring is also becoming possible. IoT in medical and healthcare help us to remotely monitor patient blood pressure, heart activity moreover specialised pacemaker implant, advanced hearing aids etc. Many super-speciality hospitals implant the concept of 'Smart bed' that can communicate to respective place detecting whether patient is present on the bed or not. Most interesting feature of this system is it can automatically regulate itself to ensure patient appropriate support and pressure without anybody's help.

Some medical and healthcare areas where IoT is applying:

**Real Time Location Tracking:** A new concept called aged person tracking during their outing has been implemented in IoT environment by using Bluetooth Low Energy (BLE) devices. This system helps to automatically track the person if someone leaves the hospital bed or goes for outing.

**Patient Information Collection:** Remote health monitoring system is mostly depending on patient physiological data collection and transmission which is known as bio-telemetry system. Collection and processing of this large amount of data is a very crucial task. Advancement of IoT technology and machine learning help to process the data efficiently and automatically diagnose the disease which in turn help the doctor to treatment the patient easily.

**Elder Care:** Caring of senior citizen is a big issue for IoT based medical devices. IoT based elder care system has been developed by installing specialized sensor and camera within living area to monitor regular activities of the person as well as detect the abnormal situation and ensure proper care is being done. This is at most important in present day's busy world as peoples are unable to always present at home to take care of elder/disabled person.

This type of many specialised healthcare IoT is slowly introducing. This system is basically trying to reduce the human interface with machine by automatic decision-making capability. Hence this will further reduce the human error. Despite of this advantage IoT is not gaining popularity in regular healthcare consumers. It still needs many improvements in early detection of serious disease and prescribes the probable primary treatment.

## System Architecture of IoT Based Cardiac Monitoring System

Availability of the cardiac specialist in rural area specially in third world country like India is very less. In this scenario bio-telemetry of ECG data plays an important role for the treatment of cardiac patients. Existing system of data collection and analysis has carried out by lot of human intervention and the process is time consuming as well. This method cannot provide the real time monitoring of the patient health condition. But with the advancement of IoT this purpose can be served remotely.

In an IoT based Electrocardiogram monitoring system Rapid Application Development (RAD) methodology is adapted where the hardware and software systems underwent a prototyping cycle for development [Ortiz Kristine Joyce P.,2018]. After that the systems are integrated to construct a complete IoT-based ECG monitoring system. This device uses a single lead electrode to collect ECG signal from patient's body and converts it into ASCII data through an Arduino PSoC. This data is send to a computer through USB device. A program gives login provision in two modes; either as a patient or as a doctor. In the patient mode after login through ID and password verification the COM port is enabled to receive ASCII data from Arduino and display it in the GUI. If the data is valid the program sends it to a MATLAB DLL program which plots and analyses the data to get different ECG parameters like RR interval, PP interval, PR interval, QRS duration, ST segment

*Figure 8. Schematic diagram of IoT based remote health monitoring system*

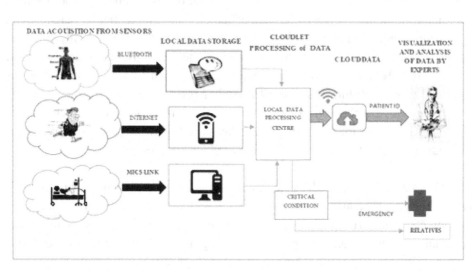

etc. Then it returns the collected data into the program which is displayed in the GUI and stored into a MySQL database. This database is linked with a webpage. The data acquisition from patient's body and uploading the vital information to the internet cloud continues until the user is logged off. The doctor mode login is also possible only after successful verification of ID and passkey. After successful login a list of patients attributed to the doctor is downloaded from the MySQL database and represented in GUI in tabulated form. Upon selection of a particular entry, the .mat file of that patient is downloaded from the web server. The user is then prompted for analysis of the data if necessary. If yes, the MATLAB program is executed and the ECG parameters along with some possible diagnosis (Tachycardia, Bradycardia and A systole) are displayed in the GUI. The user can choose to add a message or comment to the file, which will be uploaded into the MySQL database in the patient's record, and subsequently displayed in the webpage. The .mat file will be automatically deleted after its information is displayed in the C# GUI, for security purposes and prevention of file duplication. Once the user logs out, the program will return into the user preference selection form. Thus this device enables remote interaction between patient and doctor ensuring better preventive care for the patients.

Schematic diagram of IoT based health monitoring system is shown in figure 8. Overview of each stage is described below:

## DATA ACQUISITION

The initial step of a health monitoring system is the proper collection of data (DATA ACQUISITION) from the wearable sensors so as to monitor the patient remotely. Data is the form of various physiological parameters such as ECG, skin temperature, respiratory rate, EMG muscle activity and gait (posture). A number of parameters are to be kept in mind while designing these sensors which leads to the increased complexity. The sensors must be light, robust, small should not obstruct the free movement of the patient and should be energy efficient. Wearable Health Monitoring System is becoming a top notch for medical applications due to the increased accuracy in the recent times. An example of recent designed flexible sensors which can be mounted on the skin in different body parts (epidermal electronic systems is shown in figure 9.) are becoming attractive for medical applications as it measures the physiological parameters with greater accuracy.

An IOT based framework provides various stratagem like when energy is limited according to patient's condition, it will focus on a particular biomaker. This helps to prevent energy consumption as other sensors will be powered off. Moreover, instead of logging data continuously into the data centre, intelligent sensor node transmits only the critical data. This results in low traffic over network and also provides for

*Figure 9. Epidermal electronic system*

Wireless Flexible Band

power consumption. This flexibility and intelligent system cannot be achieved by conventional DAQ system which passively transmit the collected data. This feat has been achieved in modern real time ECG monitoring system [Deshpande Uttam U, 2017] with the help of low power Programmable System on Chip (PSoC).The PSoC has a built in microcontroller which allows programming of analog and digital components used in embedded systems. This microcontroller has pre-amplifier, transimpedance amplifier, programmable gain amplifier, filter, compression/ suppression etc. It can be used for signal conditioning of sensors allowing to built a complete system for monitoring and control avoiding the employment of separate analogous components and hence enhancing battery life. This data is then transmitted to the data centre in the data transmission step.

## DATA TRANSMISSION

Data transmission can be defined as the transfer of information from the wearable sensor to the local storage unit or from the local storage unit to the data centre of the health organization in a secure manner. This system has a three-tier architecture: mobile devices, cloudlets and cloud. This three-level infrastructure is named as MOCHA (Mobile Cloud Hybrid Architecture) which has been developed in the University of Rochester. Using MOCHA technology mobile devices are connected to the cloud data services such Amazon Web Services, Windows Azure etc. through the intermittent cloudlet step. The general client server model is divided into two parts a front end client program (presentation layer) and a back end server program (data access layer). This basic model has several cons like it may involve several network hops, high latency, low bandwidth and may also have the problem of signal loss or distortion due to disturbances. To reduce these errors the emerging scheme of the client server model is to bring the cloud offload infrastructure (cloudlet) closer to the mobile to decrease latency. The data acquisition layer is connected to the data transmission layer through short range communication technology involving low power consumption like Bluetooth, Zigbee etc. The local data centre is connected to the cloud server through WiFi or cellular connection. Chunk of local data has sent to the data centre for long term storage. This reduces traffic in the network which would be generated by the direct and continuous transmission of data from the wearable sensors to the data centre. Cloudlet is a small size cloud data centre which operates from the edge of the Internet. A desktop or a smartphone can be used as a cloudlet processing unit. The cloudlet basically determines how to divide the computing data among itself and multiple servers and it also provides temporary storage prior to transfer of data to the cloud. In this cloudlet the data undergoes basic processing. If the data of certain physiological parameters are beyond certain critical limits it uses the SMS system of the smartphone or the Internet facility of the computer to send EMERGENCY text to the ambulance and relatives. All data are passed on to the cloud. Cloud processing has three distinguishable steps: storage, analytics and visualization. For long term analysis of patient condition the data collected by the concentrator or aggregator (a device that connects a large number of links to one target and forward data transmission signal efficiently) requires to be stored in the cloud. In this IOT framework mobile is acting as the concentrator. The advent of cloud computing converted the Healthcare System from professional dominant system to distributed and mobile healthcare system. Data science and analytics are being employed to this large amount of data to develop pattern which has led to a breakthrough in disease diagnosis. In near future we would be able to develop and design intelligent system that would not only diagnose but also may provide with the treatment procedure. This would in no way be less than a revolution in the clinical and healthcare practices. All because of the tetra bytes of data collected by this network. As of now the visualization of the data helps the physicians to provide proper diagnosis. This cloud-based system would be economical for patients who require frequent health check-ups and also for those who lives in areas where proper medical facilities are not available.

In another approach Cyress WICED (Wireless Internet Connectivity for Embedded Devices) IOT platform is used for real time ECG monitoring. The WICED sensor module is designed using Broadcom BCM20737 SoC. It uses Bluetooth Low Energy (BLE) in order to transmit the sensed data with minimum energy consumption. The data assembled from the three wearable electrodes are transmitted to the programmable ROM of WICED sensor module via USB-UART. Smartphone has Bluetooth connectivity option. It pairs up with the WICED sensor. Through the smartphone we can configure and control the WICED module. The smart device receives encoded bytes of data from the WICED device. Now the smart device is connected to the Web Cloud Platform through port number and client ID. The sensor data is passed on and published in the IOT platform. The cloud is responsible for long term data storage, visualization of data, analysis of data and derivation of potential patterns. An IOT cloud based wearable ECG Monitoring System for Smart Healthcare [Yang Zhe, 2016] make use of WiFi to directly transmit the data from the sensor to the cloud without involving the middle tier of the three tier IOT architecture. WiFi provides fast data transfer, wide area coverage and is able to process large amount of data as compared to Bluetooth or Zigbee. Data rates are high 11-54Mbps as compared to 3-24Mbps and 10-250kbps for Bluetooth and Zigbee respectively. MQTT and HTTP server are deployed in the cloud to provide the user with easy and timely access to ECG data. To provide for a greater speed and flexibility data can be stored in non-relational database. A web-based GUI enables the doctor to access the data of the patient in his smartphone or desktop by providing with the patient ID. It helps in the timely check of critical patients. Another IoT based low-cost distant patient ECG monitoring system collects the Bio-signals from the Body of the patient using ECG electrodes and after the required processing using development boards, sent to distant cloud Bluemix, which is an web service (like AWS) owned by IBM, for further analysis by a physician or other authorized person. The Bluemix cloud uses MQTT (Message Queuing Telemetry Transport) protocol which is used to connect different types of internet enabled devices together across the globe.

Epidermal Quadruple Loop Antenna [Damis Haitham Abu, 2018] can be used for transmission of biomedical data from patient body to cloud server. These are body worn antennas (BWA) proposed for transmission of bio data collected from outpatient's body to remote healthcare persons. Three types of antennas have been designed to work on three popular frequency band GSM-900 (890 to 915 MHz uplink and 935 to 960 MHz downlink), GSM-1800 (1710 to 1785 MHz uplink and 1805 to 1880 downlink), and BLE (2400 to 2483.5 GHz including guard bands). Though BLE is used for short range communication the GSM compatible QL antennas are capable of communicating patient's vital signs to specific health centers without hampering the patient's mobility. LoRa (Long Range) is another IOT network which can be used for health care solution [N. Sornin, 2015]. LoRa network can be used for monitoring of any bio data including cardiovascular information of outpatients over a large area. LoRa is a physical layer technology for a LPWAN (low-power wide-area network). It operates in globally unlicensed Industrial Scientific and Medical (ISM) 868 MHz radio frequency bands [Catherwood Philip A., 2018]. Patient data security is ensured by three layers of encryption Its key benefits include easy installation, subscription-free service (no mobile SIM card), highly secure two-way communication, long battery life (5-10 years) and low cost.

The study of different IOT protocols cannot be completed without knowing their energy requirement as the transmitter is generally wearable device low power consumption is desirable. A comparative study of power consumption of the different Wireless Protocols along with their data rate and range is shown in the table 1.

*Table 1. Range and Power consumption comparison of different wireless protocols*

| Wireless Protocol | Max Range | Max Data Rate | Power Consumption |
|---|---|---|---|
| Bluetooth (before version 4.0) | 100 m | 1–3 Mbps | 2.5–100 mW |
| Bluetooth Low-Energy (BLE) | 100 m | 1 Mbps | 10 mW |
| Wi-Fi | 150–200 m | 54 Mbps | 1 W |
| ZigBee | 100 m | 250 kbps | 35 mW |
| LoRa | 50 km | 700 bps | (customizable) |

## IOT HEALTH CARE CHALLENGES

Cyber Security is the prime concern in the IOT Industry. There are increasing number of cases of data breaching. Data protection becomes even more important when patient's sensitive information is involved. Securing the information is critical in the IoT based health system, while transmitting data from sensor to cloudlet or from cloudlet to cloud it is very important to do it in a private and secure manner. But there is a lack of nominal security standards and framework to curb data stealing. The number of devices connected to the Internet is increasing at an exponential rate and so is the risk of data stealing. Providing proper cyber security is one of the biggest challenges in the IOT Industry. The diversity of devices involved in the networks is another hurdle because a lack of uniformity among the connected medical devices may reduce the opportunities of scaling the use of IOT in healthcare. HIPAA stands for Health Insurance Portability and Accountability Act (1996) is a United States Law that consists of a set of provisions that provides for data privacy and security developed by the Department of Health and Human Services. These norms provide the patients more control over how their personal health information is being used and disclosed to third party. But the IOT based health monitoring system has used cloud-based architecture where security of data is still a problem. Also there are various incidents occurred which question on the safety of the data in cloud based architecture like a famous incident of Department of Veterans Affairs where an employee had stolen the sensitive data of 26.5 million military veterans which contains their social security numbers and health data and in early 2010, Google reported that there is a malicious attacks to its Gmail accounts. Building a health system using IoT is a critical task because here not only the patient's privacy has been priority but since here wearable sensors are used to collect and store medical data of the patients, security is even more critical since cloud computing is an open platform there is more chances of outside hacker attacks.

## IOT INTEGRATION AND CYBER-SECURITY

Cyber security is a topic of utmost importance in every sector where data is being exchanged across the network. Health care Industry has been affected adversely by cybercrimes in the recent years. For example, according to Healthcare IT News, 1.4 million patient records were breached in Unity Point Health, US. This was the biggest breach in 2018 in healthcare services. Health facilities in California, Massachusetts, Kentucky, Singapore and Maryland have been hit by ransom ware recently. In Singapore hackers breached 1.5 million records including the Prime Minister's. In March 2016, a renowned health care group MedStar was attacked by a ransom ware. This occurred when the hackers found that MedStar uses IBoss an application server with a recognized flaw. The attack rendered their computer system and patient records unusable. These incidents are the Major potholes in the development of IOT based health services. Hospitals are becoming more hesitant in trying this new technology.

Cloud Computing is a great tool to store the data in the virtual cloud by reducing the hassle of maintaining resources on site. Here privacy and security becomes an important concern. Obviously the smart healthcare systems store and deal with very sensitive data, a proper security and privacy framework and mechanisms are very essential because the disclosure of health data may lead to severe damage to the interest and day to day life of the patient .It is important to maintain the privacy of the patient and undertake methods so that the information is only made available to the authorized user. There are basically three types of access control: User Based Access Control (UBAC), Role Based Access Control (RBAC) and Attribute Based Access Control (ABAC). All these use a cryptographic primitive known as Attribute Based Encryption (ABE). Using ABE, the health data is stored in the cloud and can be encrypted under some access policy. The users are provided with a set of attributes and corresponding keys. The user having a matching set of attributes can decrypt the information stored in the data centre. In this way, each patient has full control over his data. This is only a proposed framework to secure cloud data. To protect the data from all kinds of cyber theft is still a challenge.

## PROTOTYPE MODEL FOR IOT BASED HEALTH CARE SYSTEM

Online monitoring of human health through live physiological data from human body is always a challenging task as it requires high baud rate data transmission. A prototype model for remote monitoring of human health is proposed in this literature. The system is designed as per the block diagram shown in figure4.

*Figure 10. Electrode placement*

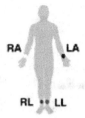

## Data Acquisition and Processing

In this work ECG signal is acquired by using disposable ECG electrode and processed by AD8232 amplifier module. Placement of the electrodes is shown in figure10. AD8232 is an integrated signal conditioning block for ECG and other bio potential measurement applications. It is designed to extract, amplify, and filter small bio potential signals in the presence of noisy conditions, such as those created by motion or remote electrode placement.

Amplified signal is connected to the next stage Arduino microcontroller board as shown in figure 11. Acquired signal is displayed in Arduino serial plotter (figure 12). This signal is further processed to eliminate the base line and other noises and transferred to next stage to communicate to the local server.

## Signal Communication

Most important part of remote health monitoring system is the uploading of signal to the web server, from where expert can visualise the health status. In this work Arduino Ethernet Shield is used to connect the local system with the web server. The Arduino Ethernet Shield allows the Arduino to easily connect to the internet. This shield enables the Arduino to send and receive data from anywhere in the world with an internet connection. Arduino Ethernet plugin is shown in figure 13.

Arduino Ethernet Shield further requires a local web server to upload the data. This work uses XAMPP local server for this purpose. XAMPP is a free and open source cross-platform web server solution stack package developed by Apache Friends, consisting mainly of the Apache HTTP Server, MariaDB database and interpreters for scripts written in the PHP and Perl programming languages. This platform is used here to upload the physiological data in web server. Thus it is possible to monitor the live data as well as experts are able to get the historic information of the patients.

*Figure 11. Connection of Arduino with AD8232*

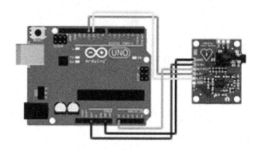

*Figure 12. ECG waveform in Arduino serial plotter*

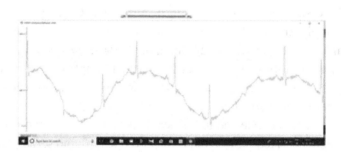

The uploaded data in the web server is displaying on the webpage as shown in the figure 14. The Id, value, time and date of the data taken is displayed so that the exact behavior of the patient health is monitored time to time from the graphical plot of the same. At the top of the page, there is also a link for downloading the data and the downloaded data is saved as an excel file and can be used for keeping a record.

This work can be extended by developing software modules to detect any ECG pattern and in case of any emergency health condition it should be able to send

*Figure 13. Arduino-Ethernet plugging*

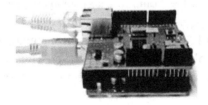

*Figure 14. Displaying data on the webpage*

E-mail or SMS notification or any web-based notification to the doctor which makes the system automated. The ability of healthcare organizations to turn the data collection by IoT into meaningful insights will influence the future of IoT. It must be taken into account that IoT is not here to replace healthcare providers, but to provide them with the data it gathers from the patients in order to facilitate diagnosis and treatment and to reduce time. Wearable sensors such as fitness trackers, blood glucose monitors and other connected medical devices have taken healthcare by storm. These devices have been embraced by the consumers and are being adopted by them for various purposes, with or without prescription. Such wearable sensors allow patients to manage and track illnesses on their own. All these devices can be connected to the internet to reach the information to experts such that adequate facilities can be provided in emergency situation from the distance.

## FUTURE PATH MEDICAL'S UROSENSE

A smart fluid management solution is developed by Future Path Medical which is beneficial to both the patient and caregivers. UroSense is the latest device developed by Future Path Medical which not only measures the urine output but also records the core body temperature for catheterized patients. UroSense measures the parameters and transmits it wirelessly to the monitoring or nursing station. By recording and monitoring the trend in the above-mentioned vital parameter the medical professionals can provide prior diagnosis for heart failure, kidney injury, infectious disease, prostate tumours, diabetes, sepsis, and burns. Measuring CBT can also indicate infection or hypothermia.

## CONCLUSION

It is seen that the conventional ECG monitoring system is basically used in the cardiology department of the hospital. It is very complex and requires trained professionals. The patient also feels uncomfortable during conventional method. But as the technology developed instead of using 12 leads we can use 3 leads to record ECG. This reduces the complexity but still conventional method is preferred in many hospitals so that no information is missed regarding ECG waveform for proper diagnosis. ECG waveform is basically used to detect the heart related diseases. For 24-hour ECG monitoring we don't prefer 12 leads ECG, here we can use Holter ECG monitoring. In this system a special magnetic tape recorder is used to obtain the ECG during his normal daily life activity. So we can say that for remote health monitoring system modern ECG monitoring system like (MCOT) is preferred over conventional one.

This article provided an insight into the current state and curved a path for future improvements in order to integrate remote health monitoring technologies into the clinical practice of medicine. The use of wearable sensors especially those with IOT Intelligence provide an opportunity of recording and analysing data in dynamic environments. Is saves the time invested in clinics and laboratory for regular health check-ups. We have a check on our health in real time. In remote areas where health services are not so well developed IOT based health care services can be of great use. Internet of Things has a large number of uses in healthcare, remote monitoring of health parameters and medical device integration and also the healthcare sectors are slowly adopting this effective and efficient technology as there is a continuous surveillance on the health status of the patient irrespective of the presence of the doctor. These systems collect the health information of patients and update the same to the doctor. So in the near future the healthcare system will be available which can monitor the patient 24 hours.

## REFERENCES

Abu, D. H., Nabil, K., Rashid, M., Hyun-Joong, C., & Pedram, M. (2018). Investigation of Epidermal Loop Antennas for Biotelemetry IoT Applications. *IEEE Access : Practical Innovations, Open Solutions*. doi:10.1109/ACCESS.2018.2814005

Catherwood, P. A., Steele, D., Little, M., Mccomb, S., & Mclaughlin, J. (2018, May). A Community-Based IoT Personalized Wireless Healthcare Solution Trial. *IEEE Journal of Translational Engineering in Health and Medicine.* doi:10.1109/JTEHM.2018.2822302

Deshpande Uttam, U., & Kulkarni Milan, A. (2017). IoT based Real Time ECG Monitoring System using Cypress WICED, International Journal of Advanced Research in Electrical [February.]. *Electronics and Instrumentation Engineering, 6*(2), 710–720.

Jeutter, D. C. (1983). Overview of biomedical telemetry techniques. *IEEE Engineering in Medicine and Biology Magazine, 2*(1), 17–24. doi:10.1109/EMB-M.1983.5005875

Ortiz, K. J. P., Davalos, J. P. O., Eusebio, E. S., & Tucay, D. M. (2018). IoT: Electrocardiogram (ECG) Monitoring System. *Indonesian Journal of Electrical Engineering and Computer Science, 10*(2), 480–489. doi:10.11591/ijeecs.v10.i2.pp480-489

Saurabh, P. (2017). *ECG Monitoring: Present Status and Future Trend.* Elsevier.

Sgarbossa, E. B., Barold, S. S., Pinski, S. L., Wagner, G. S., & Pahlm, O. (2004). Twelve-Lead Electrocardiogram: The Advantages of an Orderly Frontal Lead Display Including Lead-aVR. *Journal of Electrocardiology, 37*(3), 141–147. doi:10.1016/j.jelectrocard.2004.04.002 PubMed

Singh, P., & Jasuja, A. (2017, May). IoT based low-cost distant patient ECG monitoring system. In *Proceedings 2017 International Conference on Computing, Communication and Automation (ICCCA)* (pp. 1330-1334). IEEE.

Sornin, N., Luis, M., Eirich, T., Kramp, T., & Hersent, O. (2015, October). LoRaWAN specification version 1.0.1, LoRa Alliance, San Ramon, CA, Tech. Rep. V1.0.1 Draft 3.

Vermesan, O., & Friess, P. (2013). *Internet of Things: Converging Technologies for Smart Environments and Integrated Ecosystems.* Aalborg, Denmark: River Publishers.

Welch, A. (2014). MC11587 "Telemetry Monitoring on the Medical/Surgical Floor".

Woodward, B. (1995). The use of underwater acoustic biotelemetry for monitoring the ECG of a swimming patient, Engineering in Medicine and Biology Society, 1995 and Proceedings of the 14th Conference of the Biomedical Engineering Society of India. doi:10.1109/RCEMBS.1995.533058

World Health Organisation. A Global Brief on Hypertention- Silent killer, global public health crisis, Document number: WHO/DCO/WHD/2013.2.

Yang, Z., Zhou, Q., Lei, L., Zheng, K., & Xiang, W. (2016). An IoT-cloud Based Wearable ECG Monitoring System for Smart Healthcare. *Journal of Medical Systems*, *40*(12), 286. doi:10.1007/s10916-016-0644-9 PubMed

Zhe, Y., Zhou, Q., Lei, L., Kan, Z., & Xiang, W. (2016). An IoT-cloud Based Wearable ECG Monitoring System for Smart Healthcare. Journal of Medical Systems, 1–18.

# Compilation of References

Aarabi, A., Grebe, R., & Wallois, F. (2007). A multistage knowledge-based system for EEG seizure detection in newborn infants. *Clinical Neurophysiology, 118*(12), 2781–2797. doi:10.1016/j.clinph.2007.08.012 PMID:17905654

Abd-Alghafour, N. M., Ahmed, N. M., Hassan, Z., & Bououdina, M. (2016). High-performance p–n heterojunction photodetectors based on V2O5nanorods by spray pyrolysis. *Applied Physics. A, Materials Science & Processing, 122*(9), 1–9. doi:10.100700339-016-0346-7

Abdolkader, T. M., Shaker, A., & Alahmadi, A. N. M. (2018). Numerical simulation of tunneling through arbitrary potential barriers applied on MIM and MIIM rectenna diodes. *European Journal of Physics, 39*(4). doi:10.1088/1361-6404/aab5cf

Abu, D. H., Nabil, K., Rashid, M., Hyun-Joong, C., & Pedram, M. (2018). Investigation of Epidermal Loop Antennas for Biotelemetry IoT Applications. *IEEE Access: Practical Innovations, Open Solutions.* doi:10.1109/ACCESS.2018.2814005

Agilent Technologies, User's Guide AC. (2004). *Power Solutions Agilent Models 6811B, 6812B, and 6813B.*

Ahad, A., Tan, J., Kim, H., & Ishikawa, S. (2010). Motion history image: Its variants and applications. *Machine Vision and Applications.*

Aharon, M., Elad, M., & Bruckstein, A. (2006). K-SVD: An algorithm for designing over complete dictionaries for sparse representation. *IEEE Transactions on Signal Processing, 54*(11), 4311–4322. doi:10.1109/TSP.2006.881199

Aia, W., & Xu, Q. (2014). Overview of flexure-based compliant microgrippers. *Advances in Robotics Research, 1*(1). 001-019. DOI: . doi:10.12989/arr.2014.1.1.001

Aiello, M., Cataliotti, A., Cosentino, V., & Nuccio, S. (2005). A self-synchronizing instrument for harmonic source detection in power systems. *IEEE Transactions on Instrumentation and Measurement, 54*(1), 15–23. doi:10.1109/TIM.2004.834600

Akle, B., & Leo, D. J. (2004). Electromechanical transduction in multilayer ionic transducers. *Institute of Physics Publishing Smart Materials and Structures, 13*(5), 1081–1089. doi:10.1088/0964-1726/13/5/014

Alex, K. V., Jayakrishnan, A. R., Ajeesh Kumar, S., Ibrahim, A. S., Kamakshi, K., Silva, J. P. B., ... Gomes, M. J. M. (2019). Substrate temperature induced effect on microstructure, optical and photocatalytic activity of ultrasonic spray pyrolysis deposited MoO 3 thin films. *Materials Research Express, 6*(6). doi:10.1088/2053-1591/ab0f7a

Al-Faiz, M. Z., Ali, A. A., & Miry, A. H. (2010). A k-Nearest Neighbor Based Algorithm for Human Arm Movements Recognition Using EMG Signals, Iraq. *Journal of Electrical and Electronics Engineering (Oradea), 6*(2), 158–166.

Aliman, N., Ramli, R., & Haris, S. M. M. (2017). Design and development of lower limb exoskeletons: A survey. *Robotics and Autonomous Systems, 95*, 102–116. doi:10.1016/j.robot.2017.05.013

Allen, W. G., & Anand, K. V. (1971). Orientation dependence of the diffusion of boron in silicon. *Solid-State Electronics, 14*(5), 397–406. doi:10.1016/0038-1101(71)90190-0

Amargianitakis, E. A., Miziou, F., Androulidaki, M., Tsagaraki, K., Kostopoulos, A., Konstantinidis, G., Delamadeleine, E., Monroy, E., & Pelekanos, N. T. (2019). Improved GaN Quantum Well Microcavities for Robust Room Temperature Polaritonics. *Physica Status Solidi B: Advances in Physics of Semiconductors, 256*(6).

Amiribesheli, M., Benmansour, A., & Bouchachia, A. (2015). A review of smart homes in healthcare. *Journal of Ambient Intelligence and Humanized Computing, 6*(4), 495–517. doi:10.100712652-015-0270-2

Amrutha, N., & Arul, V. H. (2017). A Review On Noises in EMG Signal and its Removal. *International Journal of Scientific and Research Publications, 7*(5), 23–27.

Anderle, M., Barozzi, M., Bersani, M., Giubertoni, D., & Lazzeri, P. (2003). Ultra shallow depth profiling by secondary ion mass spectrometry techniques. In *Proceedings International Conference on Characterization and Metrology for ULSI Technology*. 10.1063/1.1622547

Andersen, L. L., Kjaer, M., Andersen, C. H., Hansen, P. B., Zebis, M. K., Hansen, K., & Sjøgaard, G. (2008). Muscle activation during selected strength exercises in women with chronic neck muscle pain. *Journal of the American Physical Therapy Association, 88*(6), 703–711. PMID:18339796

Andronic, L., Manolache, S., & Duta, A. (2007). TiO2 thin films prepared by spray pyrolysis deposition (SPD) and their photocatalytic activities. *Journal of Optoelectronics and Advanced Materials, 9*(5), 1403–1406.

Androulidakis, C., Zhang, K., Robertson, M., & Tawfick, S. (2018). Tailoring the mechanical properties of 2D materials and heterostructures, *2D Materials, 5*(3).

Ansari, A. N., Navada, A., Agarwal, S., Patil, S., & Sonkamble, B. A. (2011). Automation of Attendance System using RFID, Biometrics, GSM Modem with Net Framework. In *Proceedings International Conference on Multimedia Technology [ICMT 2011]*, pp. 2976-2979.

**Compilation of References**

Apetrei, V., Filote, C., & Graur, A. (2014, March). Harmonic analysis based on Discrete Wavelet Transform in electric power systems. In *Proceedings of the 2014 Ninth International Conference on Ecological Vehicles and Renewable Energies (EVER)* (pp. 1-8). IEEE.

Aranovich, J., Ortiz, A., & Bube, R. H. (1979). Optical and electrical properties of ZnO films prepared by spray pyrolysis for solar cell applications. *Journal of Vacuum Science and Technology, 16*(4), 994–1003. doi:10.1116/1.570167

Arshad, A. N., Wahid, M. H. M., Rusop, M., Majid, W. H. A., Subban, R. H. Y., & Rozan, M. D. (2019). Dielectric and Structural Properties of Poly(vinylidene fluoride) (PVDF) and Poly(vinylidene fluoride-trifluoroethylene) (PVDFTrFE) Filled with Magnesium Oxide Nanofillers. *Journal of Nanomaterials, 2019*, 1–12. doi:10.1155/2019/5961563

Arya, S. P. S. (1986). Study of Upward and Downward Sprayed Fluorine-Doped Tin Oxide Films. *Crystal Research and Technology, 21*(3), K38–K42. doi:10.1002/crat.2170210322

Ashworth, D. G., Bowyer, M. D. J., & Oven, R. (2007, October). Representation of Ion Implantation Distributions in Two and Three Dimensions. In *Proceedings of the 7th WSEAS International Conference on Wavelet Analysis & Multirate Systems,* France. Academic Press.

Ashworth, D. G., Oven, R., & Mundin, B. (1990). Representation of ion implantation profiles by Pearson frequency distribution curves. *Journal of Physics. D, Applied Physics, 23*(7), 870–876. doi:10.1088/0022-3727/23/7/018

Atieh, M., Mustapha, O., Tahini, H., Zibara, A., Al Awar, N. F., Marak, R. A., Eljammal, S., Diab, M. O., & Moubayed, N. (2014). Modeling and Utilization Of An IPMC Muscle, *International Journal of New Computer Architectures and their Applications (IJNCAA), 4*(3), 137-145.

Attri, R. K. (1998). Various noise sources & noise reduction techniques in instrumentation. In Instrumentation Design Series (Electronics), Paper No. 1, June 1998.

Ayouchi, R., Leinen, D., Martın, F., Gabas, M., Dalchiele, E., & Ramos-Barrado, J. R. (2003). Preparation and characterization of transparent ZnO thin films obtained by spray pyrolysis. *Thin Solid Films, 426*(1–2), 68–77. doi:10.1016/S0040-6090(02)01331-7

Baietto, M., & Wilson, A. D. (2015). Electronic-Nose Applications for Fruit Identification, Ripeness and Quality Grading. *Sensors (Basel), 15*(1), 899–931. doi:10.3390150100899 PMID:25569761

Banuchandar, J., Kaliraj, V., Balasubramanian, P., Deepa, S., & Thamilarasi, N. (2012). Automated unmanned railway level crossing system. [IJMER]. *International Journal of Modern Engineering Research, 2*(1), 458–463.

Barai, R. K., Dey, A., & Rudra, S. (2013). Sliding Mode Compensation for Model Uncertainty, Payload Variation and Actuator Dynamics for Inverse Dynamics Velocity Control of Direct Drive Robot Manipulator. *Journal of Control Engineering and Technology, 3*(4), 203–211.

Batabyal, T., Chattopadhyay, T., & Mukherjee, D. P. (2015). Action recognition using joint coordinates of 3d skeleton data, in *Proceedings IEEE International Conference on Image Processing (ICIP)*, 10.1109/ICIP.2015.7351578

Bauquier, S. H., Lai, A., Jiang, J. L., Sui, Y., & Cook, M. J. (2015). Evaluation of an automated spike-and-wave complex detection algorithm in the EEG from a rat model of absence epilepsy. *Neuroscience Bulletin, 31*(5), 601–610. doi:10.100712264-015-1553-5 PMID:26242485

Benech, P., Chamberod, E., & Monllor, C. (1996). Acceleration Measurement Using PVDF. IEEE Transactions On Ultrasonics, Ferroelectrics, and Frequency Control, 43(5). doi:10.1109/58.535484

Beneteau, A., Caterina, G. D., Petropoulakis, L., & Soraghan, J. J. (2014). Low-cost wireless surface EMG sensor using the MSP430 microcontroller, In *Proceedings of the 6th European Embedded Design in Education and Research,* 264-268.

Bennett, R. J., & Parish, C. (1975). Determination of diffusion, partition and sticking coefficients for boron, phosphorous and antimony in silicon. *Solid-State Electronics, 18*(10), 833–838. doi:10.1016/0038-1101(75)90003-9

Bevan, O. J., & Townsend, W. G. (1972). A method of measuring the diffusion of boron into silicon from a localized surface source. *Journal of Physics. E, Scientific Instruments, 5*(7), 704–706. doi:10.1088/0022-3735/5/7/029

Bhattacharya, S., Bepari, B., & Bhaumik, S. (2014). IPMC-Actuated Compliant Mechanism Based Multifunctional. *Multifinger Microgripper, 42*(3), 312–325.

Bhattacharyya, N., Bandyopadhyay, R., Bhuyan, M., Tudu, B., Ghosh, D., & Jana, A. (2008). Electronic nose for black tea classification and correlation of measurements with "Tea Taster" marks. *IEEE Transactions on Instrumentation and Measurement, 57*(7), 1313–1321. doi:10.1109/TIM.2008.917189

Bhattacharyya, S., Biswas, A., Mukherjee, J., Majumdar, A. K., Majumdar, B., Mukherjee, S., & Singh, A. K. (2013). Detection of artifacts from high energy bursts in neonatal EEG. *Computers in Biology and Medicine, 43*(11), 1804–1814. doi:10.1016/j.compbiomed.2013.07.031 PMID:24209926

Bilgera, G., Nebela, C. E., Bauera, G. H., & Mohring, H. D. (1985). Boron diffusion in amorphous silicon analyzed by SIMS and temperature dependent conductivity. *Journal of Non-Crystalline Solids, 77-78*(1-2), 503–506. doi:10.1016/0022-3093(85)90708-2

Bobick, A., & Davis, J. (2001). The recognition of human movement using temporal templates. *IEEE Trans. PAMI, 23*(3), 257–267. doi:10.1109/34.910878

Bonomo, C., Fortuna, L., Giannone, P., & Graziani, S. (2005). A method to characterize the deformation of an IPMC sensing membrane. *Sensors and Actuators. A, Physical, 123–124,* 146–154. doi:10.1016/j.sna.2005.03.012

Borden, P. (2001). Junction Depth Measurement using Carrier Illumination. *AIP Conference Proceedings, 550,* 175–180. doi:10.1063/1.1354393

Bozzi, M., Pierantoni, L., & Bellucci, S. (2015). Applications of graphene at microwave frequencies. *Wuxiandian Gongcheng, 24*(3), 661–669.

Brand, M., Oliver, N., & Pentland, A. (1997). Coupled hidden Markov models for complex action recognition. *CVPR, 97*, 994.

Brann, D. W., Dhandapani, K., Wakade, C., Mahesh, V. B., & Khan, M. M. (2007). Neurotrophic and neuroprotective actions of estrogen: Basic mechanisms and clinical implications. *Steroids, 72*(5), 381–405. doi:10.1016/j.steroids.2007.02.003 PMID:17379265

Brown, S. (2011). Measures of shape: Skewness and kurtosis. Retrieved on August, 20, 2012.

Bruhn, A., Weickert, J., & Schnorr, C. (2005). Lucas/Kanade meets Horn/Schunck: Combining local and global optic flow methods. *International Journal of Computer Vision, 61*(3), 211–231. doi:10.1023/B:VISI.0000045324.43199.43

Bryant, W. A. (1977). The fundamentals of chemical vapour deposition. *Journal of Materials Science, 12*(7), 1285–1306. doi:10.1007/BF00540843

Budrevich, A., & Hunter, J. (1998). Metrology Aspects of SIMS Depth Profiling for Advanced ULSI Processes. *AIP Conference Proceedings, 449*, 169–181.

Burke, P, V., & Bullen, L. (1988). *Bertha*. Poff L Kenneth, Frequency Distribution Histograms for the Rapid Analysis of Data; doi:10.1104/pp.87.4.797

Burnett, A., Green, J., Netto, K., & Rodrigues, J. (2007). Examination of emg normalization methods for the study of the posterior and posterolateral neck muscles in healthy controls. *Journal of Electromyography and Kinesiology, 17*(5), 635–641. doi:10.1016/j.jelekin.2006.06.003 PMID:16899375

Candès, E. J., Romberg, J., & Tao, T. (2006). Robust uncertainty principles: Exact signal reconstruction from highly incomplete frequency information. *IEEE Transactions on Information Theory, 52*(2), 489–509. doi:10.1109/TIT.2005.862083

Cao, S. (2009). GSM Modem-based Mobile Auxiliary Learning System. In *Proceedings International Conference on Computational Intelligence and Software Engineering [CISE 2009]*, pp. 1-4.

Cao, Z., Simon, T., Wei, S.-E., & Sheikh, Y. (2017). *Realtime multi-person 2d pose estimation using part affinity fields*. CVPR. doi:10.1109/CVPR.2017.143

Cardenas, A., Guzman, C., & Agbossou, K. (2010, July). Real-time evaluation of power quality using FPGA based measurement system. In *Proceedings 2010 IEEE International Symposium on Industrial Electronics* (pp. 2777-2782). IEEE. 10.1109/ISIE.2010.5636556

Cardenas, A., Guzman, C., & Agbossou, K. (2012). Development of a FPGA based real-time power analysis and control for distributed generation interface. *IEEE Transactions on Power Systems, 27*(3), 1343–1353. doi:10.1109/TPWRS.2012.2186468

Castrodad, A., & Sapiro, G. (2012). Sparse modeling of human actions from motion imagery. *IJCV, 100*(1), 1–15. doi:10.100711263-012-0534-7

Cataliotti, A., Cosentino, V., Di Cara, D., Lipari, A., & Nuccio, S. (2015). A DAQ-based sampling wattmeter for IEEE Std. 1459-2010 powers measurements. Uncertainty evaluation in nonsinusoidal conditions. *Measurement, 61*, 27–38. doi:10.1016/j.measurement.2014.10.033

Cataliotti, A., Cosentino, V., & Nuccio, S. (2004, May). A time domain approach for IEEE Std 1459-2000 powers measurement in distorted and unbalanced power systems. In *Proceedings of the 21st IEEE Instrumentation and Measurement Technology Conference (IEEE Cat. No. 04CH37510)* (Vol. 2, pp. 1388-1393). IEEE. 10.1109/IMTC.2004.1351325

Catherwood, P. A., Steele, D., Little, M., Mccomb, S., & Mclaughlin, J. (2018, May). A Community-Based IoT Personalized Wireless Healthcare Solution Trial. *IEEE Journal of Translational Engineering in Health and Medicine*. doi:10.1109/JTEHM.2018.2822302

Cemil, A., & Orhan, E. (2016) Comparison of Different Time and Frequency Domain Feature Extraction Methods on Elbow Gesture's EMG, ISSN 2411-4138 (Online)

Chai T., & Draxler, R. R. (n.d.). Root mean square error (RMSE) or mean absolute error (MAE)? – Arguments against avoiding RMSE in the literature, doi:10.5194/gmd-7-1247-2014

Chamberlin, R. R., & Skarman, J. S. (1966). Chemical spray deposition process for inorganic films. *Journal of the Electrochemical Society, 113*(1), 86–89. doi:10.1149/1.2423871

Chang, G. W., Chen, C. I., Huang, B. C., & Liang, Q. W. (2008, September). A comparative study of two weights updating approaches used in ADALINE for harmonics tracking. In *Proceedings 2008 13th International Conference on Harmonics and Quality of Power* (pp. 1-5). IEEE. 10.1109/ICHQP.2008.4668760

Chang, B. S., & Lowenstein, D. H. (2003). Epilepsy. *The New England Journal of Medicine, 349*(13), 1257–1266. doi:10.1056/NEJMra022308 PMID:14507951

Chattopadhyay, S., Roy, G., & Panda, M. (2011). Simple Design of a PID Controller and Tuning of Its Parameters Using LabVIEW Software. *Sensors & Transducers Journal, 129*(6), 69–85.

Chen, C. H., Buysman, A. A. J., Kelder, E. M., & Schoonman, J. (1995). Fabrication of LiCoO2 thin film cathodes for rechargeable lithium battery by electrostatic spray pyrolysis. *Solid State Ionics, 80*(1–2), 1–4. doi:10.1016/0167-2738(95)00140-2

Chen, S., Donoho, D. L., & Saunders, M. A. (1999). Atomic decomposition by basis pursuit. *SIAM Journal on Scientific Computing, 20*(1), 33–61. doi:10.1137/S1064827596304010

Chen, S., Kim, S. P., Chen, W., Yuan, J., Bashir, R., Lou, J., ... King, W. P. (2019). Monolayer MoS2 Nanoribbon Transistors Fabricated by Scanning Probe Lithography. *Nano Letters, 19*(3), 2092–2098. doi:10.1021/acs.nanolett.9b00271 PMID:30808165

Chinnathambi, S., & Shirahata, N. (2019). Recent advances on fluorescent biomarkers of near-infrared quantum dots for *in vitro* and *in vivo* imaging. *Science and Technology of Advanced Materials, 20*(1), 337–355. doi:10.1080/14686996.2019.1590731 PMID:31068983

Chitanu, E., & Ionita, G. (2010). Obtaining thin layers of ZnO with magnetron sputtering method. *International Journal of Computers, 4*(4), 243–250.

Choi, J., Yoo, K. S., & Kim, J. (2018). Spray pyrolysis synthesis of mesoporous TiO2 microspheres and their post modification for improved photocatalytic activity. *Korean Journal of Chemical Engineering, 35*(12), 2480–2486. doi:10.100711814-018-0176-8

Chung, C. K., Fung, P. K., Hong, Y. Z., Ju, M. S., Lin, C. C. K., & Wu, T. C. (2005). A novel fabrication of ionic polymer-metal composites (IPMC) actuator with silver nano-powders, 117(2006) 367-375.

Cippitelli, E., Gasparrini, S., Gambi, E., & Spinsante, S. (2016). A human activity recognition system using skeleton data from RGB-D sensors. *Computational Intelligence and Neuroscience*, 1–14. doi:10.1155/2016/4351435 PMID:27069469

Cyr, H. F. S., Noshkina, E., Stevie, F., Chow, L., Richardson, K., & Zhou, D. (2001). Secondary ion mass spectrometry characterization of the diffusion properties of 17 elements implanted into silicon. *Journal of Vacuum Science & Technology. B, Microelectronics and Nanometer Structures: Processing, Measurement, and Phenomena: An Official Journal of the American Vacuum Society, 19*(5), 1769–1774. doi:10.1116/1.1396638

da Silva, L. F., M'Peko, J. C., Catto, A. C., Bernardini, S., Mastelaro, V. R., Aguir, K., ... Longo, E. (2017). UV-enhanced ozone gas sensing response of ZnO-SnO2 heterojunctions at room temperature. *Sensors and Actuators. B, Chemical, 240*, 573–579. doi:10.1016/j.snb.2016.08.158

Das, K., Chakladar, D. D., Roy, P. P., Chatterjee, A., & Saha, S. P. (2020). Epileptic seizure prediction by the detection of seizure waveform from the pre-ictal phase of eeg signal. Biomedical Signal Processing and Control, DOI: . doi:10.1016/j.bspc.2019.101720

Das, K., Maitra, M., Sharma, P., & Banerjee, M. (2019). Early started hybrid denoising technique for medical images. In Recent Trends in Signal and Image Processing. Advances in Intelligent Systems and Computing, vol: 727 (pp. 131–140). Springer Singapore; doi:10.1007/978-981-10-8863-6_14

Dash, P. K., Panda, S. K., Liew, A. C., Mishra, B., & Jena, R. K. (1998). A new approach to monitoring electric power quality. *Electric Power Systems Research, 46*(1), 11–20. doi:10.1016/S0378-7796(98)00015-7

Dash, P. K., Panda, S. K., Mishra, B., & Swain, D. P. (1997). Fast estimation of voltage and current phasors in power networks using an adaptive neural network. *IEEE Transactions on Power Systems, 12*(4), 1494–1499. doi:10.1109/59.627847

Dash, P. K., Swain, D. P., Liew, A. C., & Rahman, S. (1996). An adaptive linear combiner for on-line tracking of power system harmonics. *IEEE Transactions on Power Systems, 11*(4), 1730–1735. doi:10.1109/59.544635

Das, K., Maitra, M., Sharma, P., & Banerjee, M. (2020). Embedded Implementation of Early Started Hybrid Denoising Technique for Medical Images with Optimized Loop. In *Emerging Technology in Modelling and Graphics, Advances in Intelligent Systems and Computing, vol: 937* (pp. 295–308). Springer; doi:10.1007/978-981-13-7403-6_28

Davies, D. E. (1970). The implanted profiles of boron, phosphorous and arsenic in silicon from junction depth measurements. *Solid-State Electronics*, *13*(2), 229–232. doi:10.1016/0038-1101(70)90055-9

Deepa, K. G., Sajeesh, T. H., & Jampana, N. (2018). Opto-Electronic Properties of Cu2ZnSnS4 Thin Films Grown by Ultrasonic Spray Pyrolysis. *Journal of Electronic Materials*, *47*(1), 530–535. doi:10.100711664-017-5803-3

Deepmind. (n.d.). Kinetics dataset. Retrieved from https://deepmind.com/research/open-source/kinetics

Degenhardt, A., Engelhardt, U. H., Lakenbrink, C., & Winterhalter, P. (2000). Preparative separation of polyphenols from tea by high-speed counter current chromatography. *Journal of Agricultural and Food Chemistry*, *48*(8), 3425–3430. doi:10.1021/jf0000833 PMID:10956128

Degenhardt, A., Engelhardt, U. H., Wendt, A. S., & Winterhalter, P. (2000). Isolation of black tea pigments using high-speed counter current chromatography and studies on properties of black tea polymers. *Journal of Agricultural and Food Chemistry*, *48*(11), 5200–5205. doi:10.1021/jf000757+ PMID:11087459

Deokate, R. J., Kalubarme, R. S., Park, C. J., & Lokhande, C. D. (2017). Simple Synthesis of NiCo2O4 thin films using Spray Pyrolysis for electrochemical supercapacitor application: A Novel approach. *Electrochimica Acta*, *224*, 378–385. doi:10.1016/j.electacta.2016.12.034

Deshpande Uttam, U., & Kulkarni Milan, A. (2017). IoT based Real Time ECG Monitoring System using Cypress WICED, International Journal of Advanced Research in Electrical [February.]. *Electronics and Instrumentation Engineering*, *6*(2), 710–720.

Devanne, M., Wannous, H., Berretti, S., Pala, P., Daoudi, M., & Bimbo, A. D. (2015). 3-D human action recognition by shape analysis of motion trajectories on riemannian manifold. *IEEE Transactions on Cybernetics*, *45*(7), 1340–1352. doi:10.1109/TCYB.2014.2350774 PMID:25216492

Dewangan, A. K., Gupta, M., & Patel, P. (2012). Automation of railway gate control using microcontroller. *International Journal of Engineering Research & Technology (IJERT)*, *1*(3).

Dewangan, A. K., Gupta, M., & Patel, P. (2012). Automation of railway gate control using frequency modulation techniques. *International Journal of Electrical, Electronics Communication Engineering*, *2*(6), 288–298.

Deyasi, A. (2007, January). Junction Depth Estimation of Si p+nn+ diode Designed at Ka-Band for IMPATT. In *Proceedings International Conference in Emerging Trends in Electrical Engineering*, pp. 52-53.

Deyasi, A., & Banerjee, J. P. (2010, February). Investigation of Junction Depth for Boron Implantation in Silicon Designed for IMPATT Structure at Ka-Band. In *Proceedings National Conference on Electrical, Power Engineering, Electronics & Computer*, pp. 122-125. Academic Press.

Deyasi, A. (2010). Numerical Analysis of Moment Parameters for Ion Implantation of Boron in n-Si Designed for SDR IMPATT Structure in Ka-Band. *International Journal BITM Transaction on EECC*, 2, 23–29.

Deyasi, A., & Bhattacharyya, S. (2014). Investigating Penetration Depth of Boron into P-Doped Silicon by Diffusion Process For p+nn+ SDR IMPATT Structure at Ka-Band. *Journal of the Association of Engineers*, *83*(3-4), 18–24. doi:10.22485/jaei/2013/v83/i3-4/119923

Deyasi, A., & Sarkar, A. (2018). Analytical computation of electrical parameters in GAAQWT and CNTFET using NEGF Method. *International Journal of Electronics*, *105*(issue: 12), 2144–2159. doi:10.1080/00207217.2018.1494339

Dhande, B. S., & Pacharaney, U. S. (2017). Unmanned level crossing controller and rail track broken detection system using ir sensors and internet of things technology. In *Proceedings International Conference on Inventive Communication and Computational Technologies (ICICCT)*, IEEE., pp. 206–210.

Donoho, D. L. (2006). Compressed sensing. *IEEE Transactions on Information Theory*, *52*(4), 1289–1306. doi:10.1109/TIT.2006.871582

Dover, A. T. (1954). *Electric traction*. Pitman.

Dreifuss, F. E. (1981). Proposal for revised clinical and electroencephalographic classification of epileptic seizures. *Epilepsia*, *22*(4), 489–501. doi:10.1111/j.1528-1157.1981.tb06159.x PMID:6790275

Drouin, D., Droulers, G., Labalette, M., Sang, B. L., Harvey-Collard, P., Souifi, A., ... Ecoffey, S. (2017). A Fabrication Process for Emerging Nanoelectronic Devices Based on Oxide Tunnel Junctions. *Journal of Nanomaterials*. doi:10.1155/2017/8613571

Dundar, I., Krichevskaya, M., Katerski, A., & Acik, I. O. (2019). TiO2 thin films by ultrasonic spray pyrolysis as photocatalytic material for air purification. *Royal Society Open Science*, *6*(2). doi:10.1098/rsos.181578 PMID:30891278

Dunkle, S. S., Helmich, R. J., & Suslick, K. S. (2009). BiVO 4as a visible-light photocatalyst prepared by ultrasonic spray pyrolysis. *The Journal of Physical Chemistry C*, *113*(28), 11980–11983. doi:10.1021/jp903757x

Dutta, J., Perrin, J., Emeraud, T., Laurent, J.-M., & Smith, A. (1995). Pyrosol deposition of fluorine-doped tin dioxide thin films. *Journal of Materials Science*, *30*(1), 53–62. doi:10.1007/BF00352131

Dutta, R., Kashwan, K. R., Bhuyan, M., Hines, E. L., & Gardner, J. W. (2003). Electronic nose-based tea quality standardization. *Neural Networks*, *16*(5-6), 847–853. doi:10.1016/S0893-6080(03)00092-3 PMID:12850043

Elad, M., & Aharon, M. (2006). Image denoising via learned dictionaries and sparse representation. In *Proceedings of CVPR '06 Proceedings of the 2006 IEEE Computer Society Conference on Computer Vision and Pattern Recognition* (vol. 1, pp. 895-900). Washington, DC: IEEE Computer Society. 10.1109/CVPR.2006.142

Elavsky, T. (n.d.). A Condensed Guide to Automation Control System Specification, Design, & Installation: White Paper, Automation Direct.

El-Ghaish, H., Shoukry, A., & Hussein, M. (2018). CovP3DJ: Skeleton-parts-based-covariance Descriptor for Human Action Recognition, in *Proceedings of the 13th International Joint Conference on Computer Vision, Imaging and Computer Graphics Theory and Applications (VISIGRAPP 2018)*, pp. 343-350. 10.5220/0006625703430350

Engan, K., Skretting, K., & Husøy, J. H. (2007). Family of iterative LS-based dictionary learning algorithms, ILS-DLA, for sparse signal representation. *Digital Signal Processing*, *17*(1), 32–49. doi:10.1016/j.dsp.2006.02.002

Esterly, D. M. (2002). *Manufacturing of Poly (vinylidene fluoride) and Evaluation of its Mechanical Properties*. Blacksburg, VA: Virginia Polytechnic Institute and State University.

Fair, R. B. (1975). Boron diffusion in silicon: Concentration and orientation dependence, background effects and profile estimation. *Journal of the Electrochemical Society*, *122*(6), 800–805. doi:10.1149/1.2134326

Fanti, C. (2008) Towards automatic discovery of human movemes. PhD Thesis, California Institute of Technology. Retrieved from http://www.vision.caltech.edu/publications/ phdthesis_fanti.pdf

Farina, D., Madeleine, P., Graven-Nielsen, T., Merletti, R., & Arendt-Nielsen, L. (2002). Standardising surface electromyogram recordings for assessment of activity and fatigue in the human upper trapezius muscle. *European Journal of Applied Physiology*, *86*(6), 469–478. doi:10.100700421-001-0574-0 PMID:11944093

Farooq, H., & Sharma, S. (2015). A Review paper on EMG Signal and its Classification Techniques. *International Journal of Emerging Research Management & Technology*, *4*(4).

Figueiredo, R. C., Riberio, A. M. O., Arthur, R., & Conforti, E. (2011). *Remote SMS Instrumentation Supervision and Control Using LabVIEW, Practical Application and Solutions Using Labview Software* (pp. 317–342). PA: Intechopen.

Filote, C., Apetrei, V., & Graur, A. (2014, September). Topologies of three-phase rectifier with near sinusoidal input currents—A comparative analysis of power quality indices using FFT and DWT. In *Proceedings 2014 16th International Power Electronics and Motion Control Conference and Exposition* (pp. 731-736). IEEE.

Firat, Y. E., Yildirim, H., Erturk, K., & Peksoz, A. (2017). Sulphide Thin Films for Solar Cell Applications, *2017.*

Fischler, M. A., & Bolles, R. C. (1981). Random sample consensus: A paradigm for model fitting with applications to image analysis and automated cartography. *Communications of the ACM, 24*(6), 381–395. doi:10.1145/358669.358692

Francis, A., Mohan, N., & Roy, R. (2017). Multi-Tasking EMG Controlled Robotic Arm. *International Journal of Advanced Research in Computer and Communication Engineering, 6*(4), 108–111.

Franckié, M., Bosco, L., Beck, M., Mavrona, E., & Faist, J. (2019). Optimization and fabrication of two-quantum well THz QCLs operating above 200 K. In *Proceedings 2019 Conference on Lasers and Electro-Optics (CLEO)* (pp. 1-2). IEEE.

Franco, A., Magnani, A., & Maio, D. (2017). Joint Orientations from Skeleton Data for Human Activity Recognition, ICIAP 2017, Part I, LNCS 10484, pp. 152–162. doi:10.1007/978-3-319-68560-1_14

Fung, C. K. M., Elhaj, I., Lil, W. J., & Xi, N. (2002). A 2-D PVDF Force Manipulation Sensing System for Micro and Micro-assembly. In *Proceedings of the 2002 IEEE.* 10.1109/ROBOT.2002.1014754

Gaglio, S., Re, G. L., & Morana, M. (2015). Human activity recognition process using 3-D posture data. *IEEE Transactions on Human-Machine Systems, 45*(5), 586–597. doi:10.1109/THMS.2014.2377111

Galal, A., & Hesselbach, X. (2018). Nano-networks communication architecture: Modeling and functions. *Nano Communication Networks, 17*, 45–62. doi:10.1016/j.nancom.2018.07.001

Ghorai, S., Mukherjee, A., & Dutta, P. K. (2010). Discriminant analysis for fast multiclass data classification through regularized kernel function approximation. *IEEE Transactions on Neural Networks, 21*(6), 1020–1029. doi:10.1109/TNN.2010.2046646 PMID:20421179

Ghorai, S., Mukherjee, A., & Dutta, P. K. (2012). *Advances in Proximal Kernel Classifiers.* Germany: LAP LAMBERT Academic Publishing.

Ghosh, A., Tudu, B., Tamuly, P., Bhattacharyya, N., & Bandyopadhyay, R. (2012). Prediction of theaflavin and thearubigin content in black tea using a voltammetric electronic tongue. *Chemometrics and Intelligent Laboratory Systems, 116*(7), 57–66. doi:10.1016/j.chemolab.2012.04.010

Giraud, P., Hou, B., Pak, S., Sohn, J. I., Morris, S., Cha, S. N., & Kim, J. M. (2018). Field effect transistors and phototransistors based upon p-type solution-processed PbS nanowires. *Nanotechnology, 29*(7). doi:10.1088/1361-6528/aaa2e6 PMID:29324436

Goswami, S. (2013). A Comparative Study of the ADALINE Method with S-ADALINE Approach for Harmonics Tracking. In Proceedings of Recent Development in Electrical, Electronics & Engineering Physics (RDE3P-2013), 94–97.

Goswami, S., Sarkar, A., & Sengupta, S. (2016). Electrical Power and Energy Measurement Under Non-sinusoidal Condition, in S. L. Sergey, & Y. Yurish (Ed.), *Sensors and Applications in Measuring and Automation Control Systems, 19, pp. 369–382,* International Frequency Sensor Association (IFSA) Publishing, Retrieved from http://www.sensorsportal.com/HTML/BOOKSTORE/Advance_in_Sensors_Vol_4.htm

Goswami, S., & Sarkar, A., & Sengupta (2019, August), S. Digital Metering of Electrical Power Components Using Adaptive Non-Uniform Discrete Short Time Fourier Transform. *International Journal of Emerging Electric Power Systems, 20*(4).

Goswami, S., Sarkar, A., & Sengupta, S. (2017). Power Components Measurement Using S-ADALINE. *International Journal of Engineering Innovation & Research, 6*(3), 120–126.

Gottlieb, B., Koropecki, R., Arce, R., Crisalle, R., & Ferron, J. (1991). Characterization of fluorine-doped tin oxide produced by the pyrosol method. *Thin Solid Films, 199*(1), 13–21. doi:10.1016/0040-6090(91)90047-2

Greene, B. R., Faul, S., Lightbody, G., Korotchikova, I., Marnane, W. P., & Boylan, G. B. (2008). A comparison of quantitative EEG features for neonatal seizure detection. *Clinical Neurophysiology, 119*(6), 1248–1261. doi:10.1016/j.clinph.2008.02.001 PMID:18381249

Gudarzi, M., Smolinski, P., & Wang, Q. M. (2017). Compression and Shear Mode Ionic Polymer-metal Composite (IPMC) Pressure Sensors: Sensors and Actuators A, Elsevier, 99–111.

Gudarzi, M., Smolinski, P., & Wang, Q.-M. (2017). Compression and shear mode ionic polymer-metal composite (IPMC) pressure sensors, *Sensors and Actuators A 260,* Elsevier, 99–111.

Guitouni, S., Khammar, M., Messaoudi, M., Attaf, N., & Aida, M. S. (2016). Electrical properties of Cu4ZnSnS2/ZnS heterojunction prepared by ultrasonic spray pyrolysis. *Journal of Semiconductors, 37*(12), 0–4. doi:10.1088/1674-4926/37/12/122001

Gurland, J., & Tripathi, R. C. (1971). A Simple Approximation for Unbiased Estimation of the Standard Deviation. *The American Statistician, 25*(4), 30–32.

Gu, Y., Zhang, Q., & Yu, L. (2018). Some Inequalities Combining Rough and Random Information. *Entropy (Basel, Switzerland), 20*(3), 211. doi:10.3390/e20030211

Gwet, K. L. (2008). Computing inter-rater reliability and its variance in the presence of high agreement. *British Journal of Mathematical & Statistical Psychology, 61*(1), 29–48. doi:10.1348/000711006X126600 PMID:18482474

Haifeng, C. (2010). SQL-based Educational Management System Design. In *Proceedings 2nd International Conference on Computer Engineering and Technology [ICCET 2010],* pp. v3 (441-445).

Hall, M. N., Robertso, A., & Scotter, C. N. G. (1988). Near-infrared reflectance prediction of quality, theaflavin content and moisture content of black tea. *Food Chemistry, 27*(1), 61–75. doi:10.1016/0308-8146(88)90036-2

Hanscomb, A., & Hughes, L. (1995). *Epilepsy*. Family Health Guides. Ward Lock.

Hansen, M. S., & Dørup, J. (2001). Wireless access to a pharmaceutical database: A demonstrator for data driven Wireless Application Protocol applications in medical information processing. *Journal of Medical Internet Research, 3*(1), e4. doi:10.2196/jmir.3.1.e4 PMID:11720946

Haykin, S. (2001). *Neural Networks – A Comprehensive Foundation* (2nd ed.). London, UK: Pearson Education.

Hazarika, M., Goswami, M. R., Tamuly, P., Sabhapondit, S., Baruah, S., & Gogoi, M. N. (2002). Quality measurement in tea- biochemist's view. *Two and a bud, 49*, 3-8.

He, Q., Vokoun, D., & Shen, Q. (2018). Biomimetic Actuation and Artificial Muscle Applied Bionics and Biomechanics Volume. *Article ID, 4617460*, 1–2.

Hirai, H., Matsui, K., Iimura, T., Mitsumori, K., & Miyazaki, F. (2010). Modular control of limb kinematics during human walking. In *Proceedings 2010 3rd IEEE RAS and EMBS International Conference on Biomedical Robotics and Biomechatronics, BioRob 2010*, 716–721. 10.1109/BIOROB.2010.5628042

Hnin, N. Y. P., Tun, Z. M., & Tun, H. M. (2014). Automatic railway gate control system using microcontroller. *International Journal of Science* [IJSETR]. *Engineering and Technology Research, 3*(5), 1547–1551.

Hobler, G., Langer, E., & Selberherr, S. (1987). Two-dimensional modeling of ion implantation with spatial moments. *Solid-State Electronics, 30*(4), 445–455. doi:10.1016/0038-1101(87)90175-4

Hofker, W. K., Oostheok, D. P., Koeman, N. J., & De Grefte, H. A. M. (1975). Concentration profiles of boron implantations in amorphous and polycrystalline silicon. *Radiation Effects, 24*(4), 223–231. doi:10.1080/00337577508240811

Hofker, W. K., Werner, H. W., Oostheok, D. P., & Koeman, N. J. (1974). Boron implantation in silicon: A comparison of charge carrier and boron concentration profiles. *Applied Physics (Berlin), 4*(2), 125–133. doi:10.1007/BF00884267

Howitt, D., & Cramer, D. (2008). *Introduction to Statistics in Psychology* (4th ed.). Prentice Hall.

Hu, Q., Lee, D. L., & Lee, W. C. (1999). Performance Evaluation of a Wireless Hierarchical Data Dissemination System. In Proceedings IEEE International Conference on Mobile Computing and Networking, pp. 163-173. doi:10.1145/313451.313528

Huang, C. S., Tao, C. S., & Lee, C. H. (1997). Nebulized Spray Deposition of Pb (Zr, Ti) O 3 Thin Films. *Journal of the Electrochemical Society, 144*(10), 3556–3561. doi:10.1149/1.1838047

Hummel, A., Laubli, T., Pozzo, M., Schenk, P., Spillmann, S., & Klipstein, A. (2005). Relationship between perceived exertion and mean power frequency of the EMG signal from the upper trapezius muscle during isometric shoulder elevation. *European Journal of Applied Physiology, 95*(4), 321–326. doi:10.100700421-005-0014-7 PMID:16096843

Huynh-The, T., Le, B.-V., & Lee, S. (2016). Describing body-pose feature - poselet - activity relationship using Pachinko allocation model, in *Proceedings 2016 IEEE International Conference on Systems, Man, and Cybernetics (SMC)*, pp. 40–45. 10.1109/SMC.2016.7844218

Ibraheam, A. S., Rzaij, J. M., Fakhri, M. A., & Abdulwahhab, A. W. (2019). Structural, optical and electrical investigations of Al:ZnO nanostructures as UV photodetector synthesized by spray pyrolysis technique. *Materials Research Express*, *6*(5). doi:10.1088/2053-1591/ab06d4

Iltgen, K., MacDonald, B., Brox, O., Bennlnghoven, A., Weiss, C., Hossain, T., & Zschech, E. (1998). Ultra-shallow junction depth profile analysis using TOF-SIMS and TXRF. *AIP Conference Proceedings*, *449*, 777–781.

Inamdar, S. I., Ganbavle, V. V., & Rajpure, K. Y. (2014). ZnO based visible-blind UV photodetector by spray pyrolysis. *Superlattices and Microstructures*, *76*, 253–263. doi:10.1016/j.spmi.2014.09.041

Inamdar, S., Ganbavle, V., Shaikh, S., & Rajpure, K. (2015). Effect of the buffer layer on the metal-semiconductor-metal UV photodetector based on Al-doped and undoped ZnO thin films with different device structures. *Physica Status Solidi (A)*. *Applications and Materials Science*, *212*(8), 1704–1712. doi:10.1002/pssa.201431850

Inderherbergh, J. (2017). Polyvinylidene Fluoride (PVDF) Appearance, General Properties and Processing. *Journal Ferroelectrics.*, *115*. doi:10.1080/00150193.1991.11876614

Ioannou, D. E., & Davidson, S. M. (1979). Diffusion length evaluation of boron-implanted silicon using the SEM-EBIC/ Schottky diode technique. *Journal of Physics. D, Applied Physics*, *12*(8), 1339–1344. doi:10.1088/0022-3727/12/8/014

Islam, M., Mohammadpour, H. A., Ghaderi, A., Brice, C. W., & Shin, Y. J. (2014). Time-frequency-based instantaneous power components for transient disturbances according to IEEE standard 1459. *IEEE Transactions on Power Delivery*, *30*(3), 1288–1297. doi:10.1109/TPWRD.2014.2361203

Ismail, R. A., Habubi, N. F., & Abbod, M. M. (2016). Preparation of high-sensitivity In2S3/Si heterojunction photodetector by chemical spray pyrolysis. *Optical and Quantum Electronics*, *48*(10), 1–14. doi:10.100711082-016-0725-5

Ivarsson, P., Holmin, S., Höjer, N. E., Krantz-Rülcker, C., & Winquist, F. (2001). Discrimination of tea by means of a voltametric electronic tongue and different applied waveforms. *Sensors and Actuators. B, Chemical*, *76*(1-3), 449–454. doi:10.1016/S0925-4005(01)00583-4

Jahanshah, F., Sopian, K., Abdullah, H., Ahmad, I., Othman, M. Y., & Zaidi, S. H. (2007, October). Investigation on ion implantation models impact on i-v curve and thin film solar cell efficiency. In *Proceedings of the 7th WSEAS International Conference on Wavelet Analysis & Multirate Systems,* France. Academic Press.

Jain, R. K., Datta, S., Majumder, S., Mukherjee, S., Sadhu, D., Samanta, S., & Banerjee, K. (2010). Bio-mimetic Behaviour of IPMC Artificial Muscle Using EMG Signal, In *Proceedings International Conference on Advances in Recent Technologies in Communication and Computing*, 186-190. 10.1109/ARTCom.2010.49

James, D. (1985). Automatic recognition and characterization of epileptiform discharges in the human EEG. *Journal of Clinical Neurophysiology*, 2(3), 231–249. doi:10.1097/00004691-198507000-00003 PMID:3916845

Jamil, T. (2008). Design and Implementation of a Wireless Automatic Meter Reading System. In *Proceedings of the World Congress on Engineering [WCE 2008]*, vol. I, UK.

Jaseja, H., & Jaseja, B. (2012). EEG spike versus EEG sharp wave: Differential clinical significance in epilepsy Jaseja. *Epilepsy & Behavior*, 25(1), 137. doi:10.1016/j.yebeh.2012.05.023 PMID:22809496

Jeutter, D. C. (1983). Overview of biomedical telemetry techniques. *IEEE Engineering in Medicine and Biology Magazine*, 2(1), 17–24. doi:10.1109/EMB-M.1983.5005875

Jia, C., Kong, Y., Ding, Z., & Fu, Y. (2014). *Latent tensor transfer learning for rgb-d action recognition*. ACM Multimedia. doi:10.1145/2647868.2654928

Jiao, Z., Wu, M., Qin, Z., Lu, M., & Gu, J. (2003). The NO2 sensing ITO thin films prepared by ultrasonic spray pyrolysis. *Sensors (Basel)*, 3(8), 285–289. doi:10.339030800285

Jin, C.-B., Li, S., & Kim, H. (2017). Real-Time Action Detection in Video Surveillance using Sub-Action Descriptor with Multi-CNN. *arXiv*.

Kamamichi, N., Yamakita, M., Asaka, K., & Luo, Z.-W. (2006). A Snake-like Swimming Robot Using IPMC Actuator/Sensor, In *Proceedings of the IEEE International Conference on Robotics and Automation*, pp. 1812-1817, Orlando, FL.

Kamble, V. B., & Umarji, A. M. (2012). Chromium oxide thin films by ultrasonic nebulized spray pyrolysis of aqueous combustion mixture for gas sensing application. *Proceedings - ISPTS-1, 1st International Symposium on Physics and Technology of Sensors*, 181–184. 10.1109/ISPTS.2012.6260915

Kane, J., Schweizer, H. P., & Kern, W. (1976). Chemical Vapor Deposition of Antimony-Doped Tin Oxide Films Formed from Dibutyl Tin Diacetate. *Journal of the Electrochemical Society*, 123(2), 270–277. doi:10.1149/1.2132802

Kanetkar, R. V. (n.d.). AR/01-Grounding and Earthing of Distributed Control Systems and Power Electronic Systems. *Asia Power Quality Initiative*.

Karmakar, S. (2019). Design of Multi-state DRAM Using Quantum Dot Gate Non-volatile Memory (QDNVM). *Silicon*, 11(2), 869–877. doi:10.100712633-018-9879-z

Karpathy, A., Toderici, G., Shetty, S., Leung, T., Sukthankar, R., & Fei-Fei, L. (2014). Large-scale video classification with convolutional neural networks. In Proceedings of the IEEE conference on Computer Vision and Pattern Recognition (pp. 1725-1732).

Kerner, J. (2018). On pairs of interacting electrons in a quantum wire. *Journal of Mathematical Physics, §§§,* 59.

Khakon, D., Khorat, D., & Sharma, S. K. (2020). An Embedded System for Gray Matter Segmentation of PET-Image, in *Proceedings of the Global AI Congress 2019 in Advances in Intelligent Systems and Computing book series,* Springer Singapore.

Khan, Y. U., Farooq, O., & Sharma, P. (2012). Automatic detection of seizure onset in pediatric EEG. *International Journal of Embedded Systems and Applications, 2*(3), 81–89. doi:10.5121/ijesa.2012.2309

Kim, J., Mastnik, S., & André, E. (2008). EMG-based Hand Gesture Recognition for Realtime Biosignal Interfacing, In *IUI '08 Proceedings of the 13th International Conference on Intelligent User Interfaces,* 30-39.

Kim, H., Fortunato, M. E., Xu, H., Bang, J. H., & Suslick, K. S. (2011). Carbon Microspheres as Supercapacitors. *The Journal of Physical Chemistry C, 115*(42), 20481–20486. doi:10.1021/jp207135g

Kitagawa, N., Ito, S., Nguyen, D.-C., & Nishino, H. (2013). Copper Zinc Sulfur Compound Solar Cells Fabricated by Spray Pyrolysis Deposition for Solar Cells. *Natural Resources, 4*(01), 142–145. doi:10.4236/nr.2013.41A018

Klipec, E. B. (1967). Reducing Electrical Noise in Instrument Circuits. In Vol. IGA -3, No. 2 MAR/APR 1967. doi:10.1109/TIGA.1967.4180749

Kocer, B., & Weiland, L. M. (2013). Experimental investigation of the streaming potential hypothesis for ionic polymer transducers in sensing. *Smart Materials and Structures, 22*(3). doi:10.1088/0964-1726/22/3/035020

Kong, Y., & Fu, Y. (2015). Bilinear heterogeneous information machine for RGB-D action recognition, in *Proceedings 2015 IEEE Conference on Computer Vision and Pattern Recognition (CVPR),* Boston, MA, 10.1109/CVPR.2015.7298708

Korzo, V. F., & Chernyaev, V. N. (1973). Electrophysical properties of indium oxide pyrolytic films with disordered structure. *Physica Status Solidi. A, Applied Research, 20*(2), 695–705. doi:10.1002/pssa.2210200232

Korzo, V. F., & Ryabova, L. A. (1967). *Conductivity of Thin Indium Oxide Films.* USSR: SOVIET PHYSICS SOLID STATE.

Krýsová, H., Krýsa, J., & Kavan, L. (2018). Semi-automatic spray pyrolysis deposition of thin, transparent, titania films as blocking layers for dye-sensitized and perovskite solar cells. *Beilstein Journal of Nanotechnology, 9*(1), 1135–1145. doi:10.3762/bjnano.9.105 PMID:29719764

Kulaszewicz, S. (1980). Electrical, optical and structural properties of SnO2: Sb films deposited by hydrolysis. *Thin Solid Films*, *74*(2), 211–218. doi:10.1016/0040-6090(80)90083-8

Kumar, N., Saha, T. K., & Dey, J. (2016). Sliding-Mode Control of PWM Dual Inverter-Based Grid-Connected PV System: Modeling and Performance Analysis. *IEEE Journal of Emerging and Selected Topics in Power Electronics*, *4*(2), 435–444. doi:10.1109/JESTPE.2015.2497900

Langella, R., & Testa, A. (2010). IEEE standard definitions for the measurement of electric power quantities under sinusoidal, non sinusoidal, balanced, or unbalanced conditions, IEEE Standard 1459-2010.

Laptev, I. (2005). On space-time interest points. *International Journal of Computer Vision*, *64*(2), 107–123. doi:10.100711263-005-1838-7

Larramona, G., Bourdais, S., Jacob, A., Choné, C., Muto, T., Cuccaro, Y., ... Dennler, G. (2014). 8.6% Efficient CZTSSe solar cells sprayed from water-ethanol CZTS colloidal solutions. *The Journal of Physical Chemistry Letters*, *5*(21), 3763–3767. doi:10.1021/jz501864a PMID:26278747

Lediaev, L. M. (2006). *Modeling Piezoelectric PVDF Sheets with Conductive Polymer Electrodes*. Bozeman, MT: Montana State University.

Lee, C., Chang, H., & Jang, H. D. (2019). Preparation of CoFe 2 O 4 -graphene composites using aerosol spray pyrolysis for supercapacitors application. *Aerosol and Air Quality Research*, *19*(3), 443–448. doi:10.4209/aaqr.2018.10.0372

Lee, J. C., Won, J., Chung, Y., Lee, H., Lee, E., Kang, D., ... Kim, J. (2008). Investigations of semiconductor devices using SIMS; diffusion, contamination, process control. *Applied Surface Science*, *255*(4), 1395–1399. doi:10.1016/j.apsusc.2008.06.129

Lee, S. (2011). Crystal Structure and Thermal Properties of Poly(vinylidene fluoridehexafluoropropylene) Films Prepared by Various Processing Conditions. *Fibers and Polymers*, *12*(8), 1030–1036. doi:10.100712221-011-1030-3

Lee, W. J., Choi, C. J., Park, G. C., & Yang, O. B. (2016). Characterization of boron diffusion phenomena according to the specific resistivity of n-type Si wafer. *Journal of Nanoscience and Nanotechnology*, *16*(2), 1665–1668. doi:10.1166/jnn.2016.11945 PMID:27433642

Lehnertz, K., Mormann, F., Kreuz, T., Andrzejak, R. G., Rieke, C., David, P., & Elger, C. E. (2003). Seizure prediction by nonlinear EEG analysis. *IEEE Engineering in Medicine and Biology Magazine*, *22*(1), 57–63. doi:10.1109/MEMB.2003.1191451 PMID:12683064

Liang, S. F., Chang, W. L., & Wang, H. C. (2010). Combination of EEG complexity and spectral analysis for epilepsy diagnosis and seizure detection. *EURASIP Journal on Advances in Signal Processing*, *2010*(1), 853434. doi:10.1155/2010/853434

Liao, Z., Gauquelin, N., Green, R. J., Macke, S., Gonnissen, J., Thomas, S., ... Rijnders, G. (2017). Thickness dependent properties in oxide heterostructures driven by structurally induced metal–oxygen hybridization variations. *Advanced Functional Materials*, *27*(17). doi:10.1002/adfm.201606717

Li, H. B., Huang, T. Z., Zhang, Y., Liu, X. P., & Gu, T. X. (2011). Chebyshev-type methods and preconditioning techniques. *Applied Mathematics and Computation, 218*(2), 260–270. doi:10.1016/j.amc.2011.05.036

Ling, J., Tian, L., & Li, C. (2016). 3D Human Activity Recognition Using Skeletal Data from RGBD Sensors, in *Proceedings International Symposium on Visual Computing (ISVC)*, 10.1007/978-3-319-50832-0_14

Lin, W., Sun, M.-T., Poovandran, R., & Zhang, Z. (2008). Human activity recognition for video surveillance, in *Proceedings 2008 IEEE International Symposium on Circuits and Systems*, 2737-2740. 10.1109/ISCAS.2008.4542023

Lin, Z., Wang, Z., Yuan, G., & Leburton, J. P. (2018). Numerov Schrödinger solver with complex potential boundaries for open multilayer heterojunction systems. *Journal of the Optical Society of America. B, Optical Physics, 35*(7), 1578–1584. doi:10.1364/JOSAB.35.001578

Liptak, B. G. (2018). Instrument Engineers Handbook Volume II: Process Control and Optimization, CRC Press.

Liu, H. Y., Lin, W. H., Sun, W. C., Wei, S. Y., & Yu, S. M. (2017). A study of ultrasonic spray pyrolysis deposited rutile-TiO2-based metal-semiconductor-metal ultraviolet photodetector. *Materials Science in Semiconductor Processing, 57*(August 2016), 90–94. doi:10.1016/j.mssp.2016.10.005

Liu, A. A., Su, Y. T., Jia, P. P., Gao, Z., Hao, T., & Yang, Z. X. (2015). Multiple/single-view human action recognition via part-induced multitask structural learning. *IEEE Transactions on Cybernetics, 45*(6), 1194–1208. doi:10.1109/TCYB.2014.2347057 PMID:25167566

Liu, F., Lu, G., Li, D., Zhang, Y., Liu, D., Yao, S., ... Wang, B. (2016). Hierarchical core/shell ZnO/NiO nanoheterojunctions synthesized by ultrasonic spray pyrolysis and their gas-sensing performance. *CrystEngComm, 18*(41), 8101–8107. doi:10.1039/C6CE01621A

Liu, H. Y., Hong, S. H., Sun, W. C., Wei, S. Y., & Yu, S. M. (2016). TiO2-based metal-semiconductor-metal ultraviolet photodetectors deposited by ultrasonic spray pyrolysis technique. *IEEE Transactions on Electron Devices, 63*(1), 79–85. doi:10.1109/TED.2015.2436701

Liu, Z., Zhang, C., & Tian, Y. (2016). 3D-based deep convolutional neural network for action recognition with depth sequences. *Image and Vision Computing, 55*, 93–100. doi:10.1016/j.imavis.2016.04.004

Li, X., Liao, D., & Zhang, Y. (2017). Mining key skeleton poses with latent SVM for action recognition. *Applied Computational Intelligence and Soft Computing*.

Li, X., Zhang, Y., & Zhang, J. (2018). *Improved Key Poses Model for Skeleton-Based Action Recognition*. Advances in Multimedia Information Processing. doi:10.1007/978-3-319-77383-4_35

Li, Y., Cichocki, A., & Amari, S. (2004). Analysis of sparse representation and blind source separation. *Neural Computation, 16*(6), 1193–1234. doi:10.1162/089976604773717586 PMID:15130247

Look, D. C., Reynolds, D. C., Litton, C. W., Jones, R. L., Eason, D. B., & Cantwell, G. (2002). Characterization of homoepitaxial p-type ZnO grown by molecular beam epitaxy. *Applied Physics Letters*, *81*(10), 1830–1832. doi:10.1063/1.1504875

Lughmani, W. A., Jho, J. Y., Lee, J. Y., & Rhee, K. (2009). Modeling of Bending Behavior of IPMC Beams Using Concentrated Ion Boundary Layer. *International Journal of Precision Engineering and Management*, *10*(5), 131–139. doi:10.100712541-009-0104-2

Lu, J., Wang, R., Ren, J., Kulkarni, M., & Jiang, J. H. (2019). Quantum-dot circuit-QED thermoelectric diodes and transistors. *Physical Review B: Condensed Matter and Materials Physics*, *99*(3). doi:10.1103/PhysRevB.99.035129

Magee, C. W., Hockett, R. S., Biiyiiklimanli, T. H., Abdelrehim, I., & Marino, J. W. (2007). SIMS analyses of ultra-low energy B ion implants in Si: Evaluation of profile shape and dose accuracy. *AIP Conference Proceedings*, *931*, 142–145. doi:10.1063/1.2799359

Magee, C. W., & Honig, R. E. (1982). Depth profiling by SIMS-depth resolution, dynamic range and sensitivity. *Surface and Interface Analysis*, *4*(2), 35–41. doi:10.1002ia.740040202

Mahanta, P. K. (1988). Colour and flavor characteristics of made tea. In H. F. Linskens, & J. F. Jackson (Eds.), *Modern method of plant analysis* (pp. 221–295). Berlin, Germany: Springer-Verlag.

Mahdi, AS Al-Zuhairi. (2013). Automatic railway gate and crossing control based sensors & microcontroller. [IJCTT]. *International Journal of Computer Trends and Technology*, *4*(7).

Mallat, S. G., & Zhang, Z. (1993). Matching pursuits with time frequency dictionaries. *IEEE Transactions on Signal Processing*, *41*(12), 3397–3415. doi:10.1109/78.258082

Manifacier, J. C., Fillard, J. P., & Bind, J. M. (1981). Deposition of In2O3 SnO2 layers on glass substrates using a spraying method. *Thin Solid Films*, *77*(1–3), 67–80. doi:10.1016/0040-6090(81)90361-8

Manifacier, J.-C., Szepessy, L., Bresse, J. F., Perotin, M., & Stuck, R. (1979). In2O3:(Sn) and SnO2:(F) films—Application to solar energy conversion; part 1—Preparation and characterization. *Materials Research Bulletin*, *14*(1), 109–119. doi:10.1016/0025-5408(79)90238-1

Marescaux, C., Vergnes, M., & Depaulis, A. (1992). Genetic absence epilepsy in rats from Strasbourg—a review. *Journal of Neural Transmission. Supplementum*, *35*, 37–69. PMID:1512594

Masaaki, K., Wilman, S., Toshiyuki, H., Yasuhiro, N., Takashi, H., & Shigeru, I. (2015). Fabrication of Cu(In,Ga)(S,Se) 2 thin film solar cells via spray pyrolysis of thiourea and 1-methylthiourea-based aqueous precursor solution. *Japanese Journal of Applied Physics*, *54*(9). doi:10.7567/JJAP.54.091203

Masetti, G., Solmi, S., & Soncini, G. (1976). Temperature dependence of boron diffusion in <111>, <110> and <100> silicon. *Solid-State Electronics*, *19*(6), 545–546. doi:10.1016/0038-1101(76)90020-4

Mata, V., Maldonado, A., & de la Luz Olvera, M. (2018). Deposition of ZnO thin films by ultrasonic spray pyrolysis technique. Effect of the milling speed and time and its application in photocatalysis. *Materials Science in Semiconductor Processing, 75*(November 2017), 288–295. doi:10.1016/j.mssp.2017.11.038

MathWorks. (2019). Simscape. Retrieved October 3, 2019, from https://in.mathworks.com/products/simscape.html

Maudes, J. S., & Rodriguez, T. (1980). Sprayed SnO2 films: Growth mechanism and film structure characterization. *Thin Solid Films, 69*(2), 183–189. doi:10.1016/0040-6090(80)90035-8

Mazumder, O., Lenka, P. K., Kundu, A. S., Gupta, K., Chattaraj, R., & Bhaumik, S. (2015). Development of series elastic actuator based myoelectric knee exoskeleton for trajectory generation and load augmentation. *ACM International Conference Proceeding Series*. 10.1145/2783449.2783472

McGrogan, N. (1999), Neural network detection of epileptic seizures in the electroencephalogram. (PhD thesis), Oxford University, UK.

Md Atiqur Rahman Ahad. (2011). *Computer vision and action recognition: a guide for image processing and computer vision community for action understanding.* Springer Science & Business Media.

Md Atiqur Rahman Ahad. (2012). *Motion history images for action recognition and understanding.* Springer Science & Business Media.

Md Atiqur Rahman Ahad. (2019). *Anindya Das Antar.* Masud Ahmed, IoT Sensor-based Activity Recognition, Springer Nature.

Meel, K., Mahala, P., & Singh, S. (2018). Design and fabrication of multi quantum well based GaN/InGaN blue LED. *IOP Conference Series. Materials Science and Engineering, 331*(1). doi:10.1088/1757-899X/331/1/012008

Mikaeili, F., Topcu, S., Jodhani, G., & Gouma, P.-I. (2018). Flame-Sprayed Pure and Ce-Doped TiO2 Photocatalysts. *Catalysts, 8*(9), 342. doi:10.3390/catal8090342

Miki-Yoshida, M., & Andrade, E. (1993). Growth and structure of tin dioxide thin films obtained by an improved spray pyrohydrolysis technique. *Thin Solid Films, 224*(1), 87–96. doi:10.1016/0040-6090(93)90463-Y

Mirabella, S., De Salvador, D., Napolitani, E., Bruno, E., & Priolo, F. (2013). Mechanisms of boron diffusion in silicon and germanium. *Journal of Applied Physics, 113*(3). doi:10.1063/1.4763353

Modur, P. N.Alvarado-Rojas, C. (2014). High frequency oscillations and infraslow activity in epilepsy. *Annals of Indian Academy of Neurology, 17*(5), 99–106. doi:10.4103/0972-2327.128674 PMID:24791097

Molla, M. Z., Zhigunov, D., Noda, S., & Samukawa, S. (2019). Structural optimization and quantum size effect of Si-nanocrystals in SiC interlayer fabricated with bio-template. *Materials Research Express, 6*(6). doi:10.1088/2053-1591/ab102a

Muñoz-Fernandez, L., Alkan, G., Milošević, O., Rabanal, M. E., & Friedrich, B. (2019). Synthesis and characterisation of spherical core-shell Ag/ZnO nanocomposites using single and two – steps ultrasonic spray pyrolysis (USP). *Catalysis Today, 321–322*(November 2017), 26–33. doi:10.1016/j.cattod.2017.11.029

Murphy, C., Campbell, N., Caulfield, B., & Ward, T. (2008). Micro electro-mechanical, systems-based sensor for mechanomyography, In 19th International Conference BIOSIGNAL, Brno, Czech Republic.

Myong, S. Y., Baik, S. J., Lee, C. H., Cho, W. Y., & Lim, K. S. (1997). Extremely transparent and conductive ZnO: Al thin films prepared by photo-assisted metalorganic chemical vapor deposition (photo-MOCVD) using AlCl3 (6H2O) as new doping material. *Japanese Journal of Applied Physics, 36*(Part 2, No. 8B8B), L1078–L1081. doi:10.1143/JJAP.36.L1078

Nakasone, A., Prendinger, H., & Ishizuka, M. (2005, September). Emotion recognition from electromyography and skin conductance. In *Proc. of the 5th International Workshop on Biosignal Interpretation* (pp. 219-222), Retrieved from http://www.miv.t.u-tokyo.ac.jp/papers/arturo-BSI-05.pdf,1-4

Nandy Chatterjee, T., Banerjee Roy, R., Tudu, B., Pramanik, P., Deka, H., Tamuly, P., & Bandyopadhyay, R. (2017). Detection of theaflavins in black tea using a molecular imprinted polyacrylamide-graphite nanocomposite electrode. *Sensors and Actuators. B, Chemical, 246*(7), 840–847.

Nasser, S., Zamani, S., & Tor, Y. (2006). Effect of solvents on the chemical and physical properties of ionic polymer-metal composites. *Journal of Applied Physics, 99,* pp. 104902-1 to 104902-17.

Ngurea, F. M., Wanyokob, J. K., Mahungua, S. M., & Mahungua, A. A. (2009, July). Catechins depletion patterns in relation to theaflavin and thearubigins formation. *Food Chemistry, 115*(1), 8–14. doi:10.1016/j.foodchem.2008.10.006

Nguyen, T. H., Septina, W., Fujikawa, S., Jiang, F., Harada, T., & Ikeda, S. (2015). Cu$_2$ZnSnS$_4$ thin film solar cells with 5.8% conversion efficiency obtained by a facile spray pyrolysis technique. *RSC Advances, 5*(95), 77565–77571. doi:10.1039/C5RA13000J

Nise, N. S. (2011). *Control System Engineering* (6th ed.). Hoboken, NJ: John Wiley & Sons.

Nister, D. (2003). Preemptive RANSAC for live structure and motion estimation. *International Conference on Computer Vision.* 10.1109/ICCV.2003.1238341

Nunes, P., Fernandes, B., Fortunato, E., Vilarinho, P., & Martins, R. (1999). Performances presented by zinc oxide thin films deposited by spray pyrolysis. *Thin Solid Films, 337*(1–2), 176–179. doi:10.1016/S0040-6090(98)01394-7

Obandaa, M., Owuora, P. O., Mang'okab, R., & Kavoi, M. M. (2004). Changes in thearubigin fractions and theaflavin levels due to variations in processing conditions and their influence on black tea liquor brightness and total colour. *Food Chemistry*, *85*(2), 163–173. doi:10.1016/S0308-8146(02)00183-8

Obradovic, B. J. (1997, October). Low energy model for ion implantation of As & B in <100> single-crystal silicon, In *Proceedings of SPIE 1997 Symposium on Microelectronic Manufacturing, Device technology*. Academic Press.

Oliver Faust, U. R. (2015). Wavelet-based EEG processing for computer-aided seizure detection and epilepsy diagnosis. *Seizure*, *26*, 56–64. doi:10.1016/j.seizure.2015.01.012 PMID:25799903

Olshausen, B., Sallee, P., & Lewicki, M. (2001). Learning sparse image codes using a wavelet pyramid architecture. In *NIPS'00 Proceedings of the 13th International Conference on Neural Information Processing Systems*, (pp. 887–893). Denver, CO: MIT Press. Cambridge, MA.

Ong, C. F., Hicks, J. L., & Delp, S. L. (2016). Simulation-Based Design for Wearable Robotic Systems: An Optimization Framework for Enhancing a Standing Long Jump. *IEEE Transactions on Biomedical Engineering*, *63*(5), 894–903. doi:10.1109/TBME.2015.2463077 PMID:26258930

Onofre, Y. J., Catto, A. C., Bernardini, S., Fiorido, T., Aguir, K., Longo, E., ... de Godoy, M. P. F. (2019). Highly selective ozone gas sensor based on nanocrystalline Zn 0.95 Co 0.05 O thin film obtained via spray pyrolysis technique. *Applied Surface Science*, *478*(January), 347–354. doi:10.1016/j.apsusc.2019.01.197

Ortiz, K. J. P., Davalos, J. P. O., Eusebio, E. S., & Tucay, D. M. (2018). IoT: Electrocardiogram (ECG) Monitoring System. *Indonesian Journal of Electrical Engineering and Computer Science*, *10*(2), 480–489. doi:10.11591/ijeecs.v10.i2.pp480-489

Otte, S., Schwanecke, U., & Zell, A. (2014). *ANTSAC: A Generic RANSAC Variant Using Principles of Ant Colony Algorithms*. ICPR.

Oweis, R. J., & Abdulhay, E. W. (2011). Seizure classification in EEG signals utilizing Hilbert-Huang transform. *Biomedical Engineering Online*, *10*(38), 38. doi:10.1186/1475-925X-10-38 PMID:21609459

Pahlavan, K., & Levesque, A. H. (1994). Wireless Data Communications. *Proceedings of the IEEE*, *82*(9), 1398–1430. doi:10.1109/5.317085

Pal, A., & Sarkar, A. (2014). Analytical study of Dual Material Surrounding Gate MOSFET to suppress short-channel effects (SCEs). *Engineering Science and Technology, an International Journal*, *17*(4), pp. 205-212.

Palit, M., Tudu, B., Dutta, P. K., Dutta, A., Jana, A., Roy, J. K., ... Chatterjee, A. (2010). Classification of black tea taste and correlation with tea taster's mark using voltammetric electronic tongue. *IEEE Transactions on Instrumentation and Measurement*, *59*(8), 2230–2239. doi:10.1109/TIM.2009.2032883

Panda, A. K., Dash, G. N., & Pati, S. P. (1994). Effect of the diffusion impurity profile on the microwave properties of silicon p+nn+ IMPATT diodes. *Semiconductor Science and Technology*, *9*(3), 241–248. doi:10.1088/0268-1242/9/3/002

Park, K., Lee, B., Kim, H. M., Choi, K. S., Hwang, G., Byun, G. S., & Lee, H. K. (2013). IPMC Based Biosensor for the Detection of Biceps Brachii Muscle Movements. *International Journal of Electrochemical Science*, (8), 4098–4109.

Park, J. A., Yang, B., Lee, J., Kim, I. G., Kim, J. H., Choi, J. W., ... Lee, S. H. (2018). Ultrasonic spray pyrolysis synthesis of reduced graphene oxide/anatase TiO 2 composite and its application in the photocatalytic degradation of methylene blue in water. *Chemosphere*, *191*, 738–746. doi:10.1016/j.chemosphere.2017.10.094 PMID:29078195

Patil, L. A., Suryawanshi, D. N., Pathan, I. G., & Patil, D. G. (2014). Nanocrystalline Pt-doped TiO 2 thin films prepared by spray pyrolysis, *37*(3), 425–432.

Patil, J. M. (2016). Low-operable and Low-ppm H2S Gas Sensing Performance of Nanocrystalline WO3 Thin Films. *Journal of Nanoscience and Technology*, *2*(24), 197–200. Retrieved from http://jacsdirectory.com/journal-of-nanoscience-and-technology/admin/issues/20161230144337_2-4-05 JNST16044 published.pdf

Patranabis, D. (1976). *Principles of industrial instrumentation* (3rd ed.). Tata McGraw Hill Education Pvt. Ltd.

Pavan, M., Rühle, S., Ginsburg, A., Keller, D. A., Barad, H. N., Sberna, P. M., ... Fortunato, E. (2015). TiO2/Cu2O all-oxide heterojunction solar cells produced by spray pyrolysis. *Solar Energy Materials and Solar Cells*, *132*, 549–556. doi:10.1016/j.solmat.2014.10.005

Pelzel, R. (2013). A Comparison of MOVPE and MBE growth technologies for III-V epitaxial structures. In *Proceedings CS MANTECH Conference*, pp. 105-108. New Orleans, LA. Academic Press.

Pfeiffer, C. J. (2001). *Principles of Electrical Grounding*. Pfeiffer Engineering Co.

Pham, H., Khoudour, L., Crouzil, A., Zegers, P., & Velastin, S. A. (2018). *Exploiting deep residual networks for human action recognition from skeletal data* (Vol. 170). Computer Vision and Image Understanding.

Phinyomark, A., Limsakul, C., & Phukpattaranont, P. (2009). A Novel Feature Extraction for Robust EMG Pattern Recognition. *Journal of Computers*, *1*(1), 71–80.

Pommier, R., Gril, C., & Marucchi, J. (1981). Sprayed films of indium tin oxide and fluorine-doped tin oxide of large surface area. *Thin Solid Films*, *77*(1–3), 91–98. doi:10.1016/0040-6090(81)90363-1

Prabhakar, T., & Nagaraju, J. (2010). Ultrasonic spray pyrolysis of CZTS solar cell absorber layers and characterization studies. In *Conference Record of the IEEE Photovoltaic Specialists Conference*, 1964–1969. doi:10.1109/PVSC.2010.5616709

Pratt, J. E., Krupp, B. T., Morse, C. J., & Collins, S. H. (2004). The RoboKnee: An exoskeleton for enhancing strength and endurance during walking. *Proceedings - IEEE International Conference on Robotics and Automation*, 2430–2435.

Priyanka, J. C., Saranya, A., Shanmathi, C., & Baranikumar, S. (2015). Automatic level crossing gate with database collection. In *Proceedings International Conference on Computation of Power, Energy, Information and Communication (ICCPEIC)*, IEEE, pp. 0388–0392. 10.1109/ICCPEIC.2015.7259483

Punning, A., Kruusmaa, M., & Aabloo, A. (2007). Surface resistance experiments with IPMC sensors and actuators. Sensors and Actuators. A, Physical, 133, 200–209.

Quhe, R., Li, Q., Zhang, Q., Wang, Y., Zhang, H., Li, J., ... Lu, J. (2018). Simulations of quantum transport in sub-5-nm monolayer phosphorene transistors. *Physical Review Applied*, *10*(2). doi:10.1103/PhysRevApplied.10.024022

Raham, S., Sunil, M. A., Singha, M. K., & Ghosh, K. (2019, August). Temperature dependent growth of $Cu_2SnS_3$ thin films using ultrasonic spray pyrolysis for solar cell absorber layer and photocatalytic application. *Materials Research Express*, *6*(10). doi:10.1088/2053-1591/ab3928

Raut, R., & Gurjar, A. A. (2015). Bio-Medical (EMG) Signal Analysis and Feature Extraction using Wavelet Transform, *Journal of Engineering Research and Application*, 17-19.

Reaz, M. B. I., Hussain, M. S., & Mohd-Yasin, F. (2006). Techniques of emg signal analysis: detection, processing, classification, and applications, *Biol. Procedures Online*, *8*(1), pp. 11-35, doi:10.1251/bpo115

Reddy, E. A., Kavati, I., Rao, K. S., & Kumar, G. K. (2017). A secure railway crossing system using iot. In *Proceedings International Conference of Electronics, Communication, and Aerospace Technology (ICECA)*, IEEE, 2, pp. 196–199. 10.1109/ICECA.2017.8212795

Rezage, G. A. L., & Tokhi, M. O. (2016). Fuzzy PID Control of Lower Limb Exoskeleton for Elderly Mobility. In *Proceedings 2016 IEEE International Conference on Automation, Quality and Testing, Robotics (AQTR)*, 1–6. 10.1109/AQTR.2016.7501310

Robertson, A. (1983). Effects of physical and chemical conditions on the in vitro oxidation of tea leaf catechins. *Phytochemistry*, *22*(4), 897–903. doi:10.1016/0031-9422(83)85018-3

Robertson, A. (1992). The chemistry and biochemistry of black tea production, the non-volatiles. In K. C. Wilson, & M. N. Clifford (Eds.), *Tea: Cultivation to consumption* (pp. 555–601). London, UK: Chapman and Hall. doi:10.1007/978-94-011-2326-6_17

Robertson, A., & Bendall, D. S. (1983). Production and HPLC analysis of black tea theaflavins and thearubigins during in vitro oxidation. *Phytochemistry*, *22*(4), 883–887. doi:10.1016/0031-9422(83)85016-X

Roy, G., Jacob, T., Bhatia, D., & Bhaumik, S. (2020). Optical Marker- and Vision-Based Human Gait Biomechanical Analysis. In S. Bhattacharyya, D. Konar, P. J. C. Kar, & K. Sharma (Eds.), Hybrid Machine Intelligence for Medical Image Analysis. Studies in Computational Intelligence, vol. 841. Springer, Singapore (pp. 275–291). doi:10.1007/978-981-13-8930-6_11

Ruan, L., Yao, X., Chang, Y., Zhou, L., Qin, G., & Zhang, X. (2018). Properties and Applications of the β Phase Poly (vinylidene fluoride). *Polymers*, *10*(3), 228. doi:10.3390/polym10030228 PMID:30966263

Rubinstein, R., Peleg, T., & Elad, M. (2013). Analysis K-SVD: A dictionary learning algorithm for the analysis sparse model. *IEEE Transactions on Signal Processing*, *61*(3), 661–667. doi:10.1109/TSP.2012.2226445

Ruiz-Rojas, E. D., Vazquez-Gonzalez, J. L., Alejos-Palomares, R., Escudero-Uribe, A. Z., & Mendoza-Vázquez, J. R. (2008). Mathematical model of a linear electric actuator with prosthesis applications. In *Proceedings - 18th International Conference on Electronics, Communications, and Computers, CONIELECOMP 2008*, 182–186. 10.1109/CONIELECOMP.2008.29

Sadeghzadeh, S., & Rezapour, N. (2016). The mechanical design of graphene nanodiodes and nanotransistors: Geometry, temperature and strain effects. *RSC Advances*, *6*(89), 86324–86333. doi:10.1039/C6RA18191K

Sadigh, B., Lenosky, T. J., Theiss, S. K., Caturla, M. J., de la Rubia, T. D., & Foad, M. A. (1999). Mechanism of boron diffusion in silicon: An *ab initio* and kinetic Monte Carlo study. *Physical Review Letters*, *83*(21), 4341–4344. doi:10.1103/PhysRevLett.83.4341

Saha, P., Ghorai, S., Tudu, B., Bandyopadhyay, R., & Bhattacharyya, N. (2014). A novel method of black tea quality prediction using electronic tongue Signals. *IEEE Transactions on Instrumentation and Measurement*, *63*(10), 2472–2479. doi:10.1109/TIM.2014.2310615

Saha, P., Ghorai, S., Tudu, B., Bandyopadhyay, R., & Bhattacharyya, N. (2016). Tea Quality Prediction by Autoregressive Modelling of Electronic Tongue Signals. *IEEE Sensors Journal*, *16*(11), 4470–4477. doi:10.1109/JSEN.2016.2544979

Saha, P., Ghorai, S., Tudu, B., Bandyopadhyay, R., & Bhattacharyya, N. (2017). Feature fusion for prediction of theaflavin and thearubigin in tea using electronic tongue. *IEEE Transactions on Instrumentation and Measurement*, *66*(7), 1703–1710. doi:10.1109/TIM.2017.2672458

Salvador, D. D., Napolitani, E., Mirabella, S., Bisognin, G., Impellizzeri, G., Carnera, A., & Priolo, F. (2006). Atomistic mechanism of boron diffusion in silicon. *Physical Review Letters*, *97*(25). doi:10.1103/PhysRevLett.97.255902 PMID:17280368

Sarkar, A., Choudhury, S. R., & Sengupta, S. (2011). A self-synchronized ADALINE network for on-line tracking of power system harmonics. *Measurement*, *44*(4), 784–790. doi:10.1016/j.measurement.2011.01.009

Sarkar, A., & Sengupta, S. (2009). On-line tracking of single-phase reactive power in non-sinusoidal conditions using S-ADALINE networks. *Measurement, 42*(4), 559–569. doi:10.1016/j.measurement.2008.10.001

Saurabh, P. (2017). *ECG Monitoring: Present Status and Future Trend.* Elsevier.

Sayed, M. H., Robert, E. V. C., Dale, P. J., & Gütay, L. (2019). Cu2SnS3 based thin film solar cells from chemical spray pyrolysis. *Thin Solid Films, 669*(October 2018), 436–439. doi:10.1016/j.tsf.2018.11.002

Scherg, M., & Ebert, A. (2012). Fast evaluation of interictal spikes in long-term EEG by hyper-clustering. *Epilepsia, 53*(7), 1196–1204. doi:10.1111/j.1528-1167.2012.03503.x PMID:22578143

Schroer, G., & Trenkler, D. (n.d.). Kolmogorov-Smirnov tests two or three samples, doi:10.1016/0167-9473(94)00040-P

Schuldt, C., Laptev, I., & Caputo, B. (2004) Recognizing human actions: A local SVM approach. *International Conference on Pattern Recognition.* 10.1109/ICPR.2004.1334462

Seidenari, L., Varano, V., Berretti, S., Bimbo, A. D., & Pala, P. (2013). Recognizing Actions from Depth Cameras as Weakly Aligned Multi-part Bag-of-Poses, in *Proceedings IEEE Conference on Computer Vision and Pattern Recognition (CVPR) Workshop.* 10.1109/CVPRW.2013.77

Sell, J., & O'Connor, P. (2014). The xbox one system on a chip and kinect sensor. *IEEE Micro, 34*(2), 44–53. doi:10.1109/MM.2014.9

Sgarbossa, E. B., Barold, S. S., Pinski, S. L., Wagner, G. S., & Pahlm, O. (2004). Twelve-Lead Electrocardiogram: The Advantages of an Orderly Frontal Lead Display Including Lead-aVR. *Journal of Electrocardiology, 37*(3), 141–147. doi:10.1016/j.jelectrocard.2004.04.002 PubMed

Shah, J. S. (2001). Field Wiring and Noise Considerations for Analog Signals 340224C-01, Application Note 025 National Instruments Corporation, July, 2001. BS:7430:2011, "Code of practice for protective earthing of electrical installations". IS:3043 -2001, "Code of practice for earthing". IEEE Std 1050 – 2004, "IEEE guide for Instrumentation and Control Equipment Grounding in Generating Stations". IEEE Std. 80 – 2000, "IEEE guide for safety in AC Substation Grounding".

Sharad, S., Bagavathi Sivakumar, P., & Ananthanarayanan, V. (2016). An automated system to mitigate loss of life at unmanned level crossings. *Procedia Computer Science, 92*, 404–409. doi:10.1016/j.procs.2016.07.397

Shasti, M., Mortezaali, A., & Dariani, R. S. (2015). Comparison of carrier transport mechanism under UV/Vis illumination in an AZO photodetector and an AZO/p-Si heterojunction photodiode produced by spray pyrolysis. *Journal of Applied Physics, 117*(2). doi:10.1063/1.4905416

Shinde, V. R., Mahadik, S. B., Gujar, T. P., & Lokhande, C. D. (2006). Supercapacitive cobalt oxide (Co 3 O 4) thin films by spray pyrolysis. *Applied Surface Science, 252*(20), 7487–7492. doi:10.1016/j.apsusc.2005.09.004

Shoeb, A. H. (2009). Application of machine learning to epileptic seizure onset detection and treatment. (PhD Thesis), Massachusetts Institute of Technology.

Siefert, W. (1984). Properties of thin In2O3 and SnO2 films prepared by corona spray pyrolysis, and a discussion of the spray pyrolysis process. *Thin Solid Films*, *120*(4), 275–282. doi:10.1016/0040-6090(84)90242-6

Singha, M. K., Patra, A., Rojwal, V., Deepa, K. G., & Kumar, D. (2019). Ultrasonic spray pyrolysis deposited ZnO thin film for photocatalytic activity, *030023*(March). doi:10.1063/1.5093841

Singha, B., & Solanki, C. S. (2016). Boric acid solution concentration influencing p-type emitter formation in n-type crystalline Si solar cells. In *Proceedings IOP Conf. Series: Materials Science and Engineering*, vol. 149. 10.1088/1757-899X/149/1/012174

Singh, P., & Jasuja, A. (2017, May). IoT based low-cost distant patient ECG monitoring system. In *Proceedings 2017 International Conference on Computing, Communication and Automation (ICCCA)* (pp. 1330-1334). IEEE.

Sinz, F. H., Candela, J. Q., Bakır, G. H., Rasmussen, C. E., & Franz, M. O. (2004). Learning depth from stereo. In *Pattern Recognition* (pp. 245–252). Springer. doi:10.1007/978-3-540-28649-3_30

Sirohi, J., & Chopra, I. (2000). *Fundamental Understanding of Piezoelectric Strain Sensors*. College Park, MD: University of Maryland.

Slobodian, O. M. (2019). Reduced graphene oxide obtained using the spray pyrolysis technique for gas sensing. *Semiconductor Physics. Quantum Electronics & Optoelectronics*, *22*(1), 98–103. doi:10.15407pqeo22.01.098

Smith, N. L., & Elad, M. (2013). Improving Dictionary Learning: Multiple dictionary Updates and Coefficient Reuse. *IEEE Signal Processing Letters*, *20*(1), 79–82. doi:10.1109/LSP.2012.2229976

Smola, A. J., & Schölkopf, B. (2004). A tutorial on support vector regression. *Statistics and Computing*, *14*(3), 199–222. doi:10.1023/B:STCO.0000035301.49549.88

Song, P. K., Shigesato, Y., Yasui, I., Ow-Yang, C. W., & Paine, D. C. (1998). Study on crystallinity of tin-doped indium oxide films deposited by dc magnetron sputtering. *Japanese Journal of Applied Physics*, *37*(Part 1, No. 4A4R), 1870–1876. doi:10.1143/JJAP.37.1870

Soomro, K., Zamir, A. R., & Shah, M. (2018). UCF101: A Dataset of 101 Human Actions. Classes from Videos in The Wild, CoRR.

Sornin, N., Luis, M., Eirich, T., Kramp, T., & Hersent, O. (2015, October). LoRaWAN specification version 1.0.1, LoRa Alliance, San Ramon, CA, Tech. Rep. V1.0.1 Draft 3.

Srividyadevi, P., Pusphalatha, D. V., & Sharma, P. M. (2013). Measurement of power and energy using arduino. *Research Journal of Engineering Sciences*, *2278*, 9472.

Starck, J., Elad, M., & Donoho, D. (2005). Image decomposition via the combination of sparse representation and a variational approach. *IEEE Transactions on Image Processing, 14*(10), 1570–1582. doi:10.1109/TIP.2005.852206 PMID:16238062

Stephens, M. A. (1974). EDF Statistics for Goodness of Fit and Some Comparisons. *Journal of the American Statistical Association, 69*(347), 730–737. doi:10.1080/01621459.1974.10480196

Stepnicki, P., Pietka, B., Morier-Genoud, F., Deveaud, B., & Matuszewski, M. (2015). Analytical method for determining quantum well exciton properties in a magnetic field. *Physical Review B: Condensed Matter and Materials Physics, 91*(19). doi:10.1103/PhysRevB.91.195302

Subbaramaiah, K., & Raja, V. S. (1994). Preparation and characterization of all spray-deposited p-CuIn (S0. 5Se0. 5) 2/n-CdZnS: In thin film solar cells. *Solar Energy Materials and Solar Cells, 32*(1), 1–6. doi:10.1016/0927-0248(94)90250-X

Su, Q., Zou, R., Su, Y., & Fan, S. (2018). Morphology control and growth mechanism study of quantum-sized ZnS nanocrystals from single-source precursors. *Journal of Nanoscience and Nanotechnology, 18*(10), 6850–6858. doi:10.1166/jnn.2018.15516 PMID:29954502

Su, T., Yang, M., Jin, T., & Flesch, R. C. C. (2018). Power harmonic and interharmonic detection method in renewable power based on Nuttall double-window all-phase FFT algorithm. *IET Renewable Power Generation, 12*(8), 953–961. doi:10.1049/iet-rpg.2017.0115

Tadeo, I. J., Mukhokosi, E. P., Krupanidhi, S. B., & Umarji, A. M. (2019). Low-cost VO2(M1) thin films synthesized by ultrasonic nebulized spray pyrolysis of an aqueous combustion mixture for IR photodetection. *RSC Advances, 9*(18), 9983–9992. doi:10.1039/C9RA00189A

Temko, A., Thomas, E., Marnane, W., Lightbody, G., & Boylan, G. (2009). An SVM-based system and its performance for detection of seizures in neonates. Annual International Conference of the IEEE Engineering in Medicine and Biology Society. Minneapolis, MN: Institute of Electrical and Electronics Engineers, pp. 2643–2646.

Terzija, V. V., Stanojevic, V., Popov, M., & Van der Sluis, L. (2007). Digital metering of power components according to IEEE standard 1459-2000 using the Newton-type algorithm. *IEEE Transactions on Instrumentation and Measurement, 56*(6), 2717–2724. doi:10.1109/TIM.2007.908235

Timotiom. (2019). TA1. Retrieved September 21, 2019 from https://www.timotion.com/_upload/files/datasheet_ta1-ac_en.pdf

Tischner, A., Maier, T., Stepper, C., & Köck, A. (2008). Ultrathin SnO2 gas sensors fabricated by spray pyrolysis for the detection of humidity and carbon monoxide. *Sensors and Actuators. B, Chemical, 134*(2), 796–802. doi:10.1016/j.snb.2008.06.032

Toda, T., Inoue, S., & Ueda, N. (2016). Mobile activity recognition through training labels with inaccurate activity segments. In *Proceedings of the 13th International Conference on Mobile and Ubiquitous Systems: Computing, Networking and Services*, pp. 57–64. ACM. 10.1145/2994374.2994378

Tombak, A., Kilicoglu, T., & Ocak, Y. S. (2020). Solar cells fabricated by spray pyrolysis deposited Cu2CdSnS4 thin films. *Renewable Energy, 146*, 1465–1470. doi:10.1016/j.renene.2019.07.057

Torr, P., & Davidson, C. (2000). IMPSAC: A synthesis of importance sampling and random sample consensus to effect multi-scale image matching for small and wide baselines. In *Proceedings European Conference on Computer Vision*, pp. 819–833.

Torr, P., & Zisserman, A. (2000). MLESAC: A new robust estimator with application to estimating image geometry. *Computer Vision and Image Understanding, 78*(1), 138–156. doi:10.1006/cviu.1999.0832

Tropp, A. J., & Gilbert, A. C. (2007). Signal recovery from random measurements via orthogonal matching pursuit. *IEEE Transactions on Information Theory, 53*(12), 4655–4666. doi:10.1109/TIT.2007.909108

Ullah, I., Hussain, M., Qazi, E.-H., & Aboalsamh, H. (2018). An automated system for epilepsy detection using eeg brain signals based on deep learning approach. *Expert Systems with Applications, 107*, 61–71. doi:10.1016/j.eswa.2018.04.021

Ullah, M. R., Gogoi, N., & Baruah, D. (1984). The effect of withering on fermentation of tea leaf and development of liquor characters of black tea. *Journal of the Science of Food and Agriculture, 35*(10), 1142–1147. doi:10.1002/jsfa.2740351014

Unaogu, A. L., & Okeke, C. E. (1990). Characterization of antimony-doped tin oxide films prepared by spray pyrolysis. *Solar Energy Materials, 20*(1–2), 29–36. doi:10.1016/0165-1633(90)90014-R

Uomi, K. (2018). "Ultra high-speed quantum-well semiconductor lasers", OSA Technical Digest: Optical Fiber Communication Conference, M2F.1, 2019. Academic Press.

Utkin, V. (1977). Variable Structure Systems with Sliding Modes. *IEEE Transactions on Automatic Control, 22*(2), 212–222. doi:10.1109/TAC.1977.1101446

Van de Pol, F. C. M., Blom, F. R., & Popma, T. J. A. (1991). Rf planar magnetron sputtered ZnO films I: Structural properties. *Thin Solid Films, 204*(2), 349–364. doi:10.1016/0040-6090(91)90074-8

van Lierde, P., Tian, C., Rothman, B., & Hockett, R. A. (2002). Quantitative Secondary Ion Mass Spectrometry (SIMS) of III-V Materials. In *Material Res. Society Symposium Proceeding*, vol. 692, H9.40, pp. 543-548. 10.1117/12.467668

Van, N. P., & Ngan, P. H. (2013). Use of co-spray pyrolysis for synthesizing nitrogen-doped TiO2 films. *Bulletin of Materials Science, 36*(5), 827–831. doi:10.100712034-013-0534-4

Vapnik, V. N. (1998). *The Nature of Statistical Learning Theory*. New York: John Wiley & Sons.

Vemulapalli, R., Arrate, F., & Chellappa, R. (2014). Human Action Recognition by Representing 3D Skeletons as Points in a Lie Group, in *Proceedings 2014 IEEE Conference on Computer Vision and Pattern Recognition*, Columbus, OH, 10.1109/CVPR.2014.82

Verlinden, G., Gijbels, R., & Geuens, I. (1999). Quantitative secondary ion mass spectrometry depth profiling of surface layers of cubic silver halide microcrystals. *Journal of the American Society for Mass Spectrometry, 10*(10), 1016–1027. doi:10.1016/S1044-0305(99)00064-1

Vermesan, O., & Friess, P. (2013). *Internet of Things: Converging Technologies for Smart Environments and Integrated Ecosystems*. Aalborg, Denmark: River Publishers.

Viguie, J. C., & Spitz, J. (1975). Chemical vapor deposition at low temperatures. *Journal of the Electrochemical Society, 122*(4), 585–588. doi:10.1149/1.2134266

Vink, T. J., Walrave, W., Daams, J. L. C., Baarslag, P. C., & Van den Meerakker, J. (1995). On the homogeneity of sputter-deposited ITO films Part I. Stress and microstructure. *Thin Solid Films, 266*(2), 145–151. doi:10.1016/0040-6090(95)06818-X

Vinodh Kumar, E., & Jerome, J. (2013). Robust LQR controller design for stabilizing and trajectory tracking of inverted pendulum. *Procedia Engineering, 64*, 169–178. doi:10.1016/j.proeng.2013.09.088

Vispute, R. D., Talyansky, V., Choopun, S., Sharma, R. P., Venkatesan, T., He, M., ... Li, Y. X. (1998). Heteroepitaxy of ZnO on GaN and its implications for fabrication of hybrid optoelectronic devices. *Applied Physics Letters, 73*(3), 348–350. doi:10.1063/1.121830

Vyas, N. S., & Gupta, A. K. (2006). Modeling rail wheel-flat dynamics. In *Engineering Asset Management* (pp. 1222–1231). Springer. doi:10.1007/978-1-84628-814-2_135

Wang, N. (2010). Material Information Management System Design in Enterprise. In *Proceedings of 2nd International Conference on Computer and Automation Engineering [ICCAE 2010]*, pp. 521-525. 10.1109/ICCAE.2010.5451597

Wang, H., Xie, J., Yan, K., & Duan, M. (2011). Growth mechanism of different morphologies of ZnO crystals prepared by hydrothermal method. *Journal of Materials Science and Technology, 27*(2), 153–158. doi:10.1016/S1005-0302(11)60041-8

Wang, J., Li, X., Huang, T. H., Yu, S., Li, Y., Chen, T., ... Su, H. (2018). Comfort-Centered Design of a Lightweight and Backdrivable Knee Exoskeleton. *IEEE Robotics and Automation Letters, 3*(4), 4265–4272. doi:10.1109/LRA.2018.2864352

Wang, K., Liu, Z., Huang, J., Dong, X., Song, L., Pana, Y., & Liu, F. (2008). Preparative isolation and purification of theaflavins and catechins by high-speed counter current chromatography. *Journal of Chromatography. B, Analytical Technologies in the Biomedical and Life Sciences, 867*(2), 282–286. doi:10.1016/j.jchromb.2008.04.005 PMID:18436487

Wang, S., Van Dijk, W., & Van Der Kooij, H. (2011). Spring uses in exoskeleton actuation design. In *Proceedings IEEE International Conference on Rehabilitation Robotics*, 1–6. 10.1109/ICORR.2011.5975471

Watkins, G. D. (1975). Defects in irradiated silicon: EPR and electron-nuclear double resonance of interstitial boron. *Physical Review B: Condensed Matter and Materials Physics, 12*(12), 5824–5839. doi:10.1103/PhysRevB.12.5824

Webber, W. R. S., Wilson, K., Lessera, R. P., & Litt, B. (1994). Practical detection of epileptiform discharges (EDs) in the EEG using an artificial neural network: a comparison of raw and parameterized EEG data, Electroencephalography and Clinical Neurophysiology, 91(3), pp. 194-204, Doi:10.1016/0013-4694(94)90069-8

Welch, A. (2014). MC11587 "Telemetry Monitoring on the Medical/Surgical Floor".

Westover, M. B., Shafi, M. M., Ching, S. N., Chemali, J. J., Purdon, P. L., Cash, S. S., & Brown, E. N. (2013). Real-time segmentation of burst suppression patterns in critical care EEG monitoring. *Journal of Neuroscience Methods*, *219*(1), 131–141. doi:10.1016/j.jneumeth.2013.07.003 PMID:23891828

Whitby, J. A., Östlund, F., Horvath, P., Gabureac, M., Riesterer, J. L., Utke, I., ... Michler, J. (2012). High spatial resolution time-of-flight secondary ion mass spectrometry for the masses: A novel orthogonal ToF FIB-SIMS instrument with in situ AFM. *Advances in Materials Science and Engineering*, *2012*, 180437. doi:10.1155/2012/180437

Whitlock, B. (2016). Understanding, Finding, & Eliminating Ground Loops, CEDIA Class EST016.

Wilson, A. D. (2013). Diverse Applications of Electronic-Nose Technologies in Agriculture and Forestry. *Sensors (Basel)*, *13*(2), 2295–2348. doi:10.3390130202295 PMID:23396191

Wisz, G., Virt, I., Sagan, P., Potera, P., & Yavorskyi, R. (2017). Structural, Optical and Electrical Properties of Zinc Oxide Layers Produced by Pulsed Laser Deposition Method. *Nanoscale Research Letters*, *12*(1), 253. doi:10.118611671-017-2033-9 PMID:28381074

Woodward, B. (1995). The use of underwater acoustic biotelemetry for monitoring the ECG of a swimming patient, Engineering in Medicine and Biology Society, 1995 and Proceedings of the 14th Conference of the Biomedical Engineering Society of India. doi:10.1109/RCEMBS.1995.533058

World Health Organisation. A Global Brief on Hypertention- Silent killer, global public health crisis, Document number: WHO/DCO/WHD/2013.2.

Wright, L. P., Mphangwe, N. K., Nyirenda, H., & Apostolides, Z. (2002). Analysis of the theaflavin composition in black tea (Camellia sinesis) predicting the quality of black tea produced in Central and Southern Africa. *Journal of the Science of Food and Agriculture*, *82*(5), 517–525. doi:10.1002/jsfa.1074

Wulf, U., Kučera, J., Richter, H., Horstmann, M., Wiatr, M., & Höntschel, J. (2017). Channel Engineering for Nanotransistors in a Semiempirical Quantum Transport Model. *Mathematics*, *5*(4), 68. doi:10.3390/math5040068

Yadav, A. A. (2016). SnO2 thin film electrodes deposited by spray pyrolysis for electrochemical supercapacitor applications. *Journal of Materials Science Materials in Electronics*, *27*(2), 1866–1872. doi:10.100710854-015-3965-4

Yadav, A. A., Deshmukh, T. B., Deshmukh, R. V., Patil, D. D., & Chavan, U. J. (2016). Electrochemical supercapacitive performance of Hematite α-Fe2O3 thin films prepared by spray pyrolysis from non-aqueous medium. *Thin Solid Films*, *616*, 351–358. doi:10.1016/j.tsf.2016.08.062

Yakimenko, I. P., Yakimenko, I. I., & Berggren, K. F. (2019). Basic modeling of effects of geometry and magnetic field for quantum wires injecting electrons into a two-dimensional electron reservoir. *Journal of Physics Condensed Matter, 31*(34).

Yang, X., Gao, A., Wang, Y., & Li, T. (2018). Wafer-level and highly controllable fabricated silicon nanowire transistor arrays on (111) silicon-on-insulator (SOI) wafers for highly sensitive detection in liquid and gaseous environments. *Nano Research, 11*(3), 1520–1529. doi:10.100712274-017-1768-z

Yang, X., & Tian, Y. (2014). Super normal vector for activity recognition using depth sequences, in *Proceedings EEE Conference on Computer Vision and Pattern Recognition (CVPR)*, 10.1109/CVPR.2014.108

Yang, X., Zhang, C., & Tian, Y. (2012). *Recognizing actions using depth motion maps-based histograms of oriented gradients*. ACM Multimedia. doi:10.1145/2393347.2396382

Yang, Y., Deng, C., Tao, D., Zhang, S., Liu, W., & Gao, X. (2017). Latent max-margin multitask learning with skelets for 3-D action recognition. *IEEE Transactions on Cybernetics, 47*(2), 439–448. PMID:27046919

Yang, Z., Zhou, Q., Lei, L., Zheng, K., & Xiang, W. (2016). An IoT-cloud Based Wearable ECG Monitoring System for Smart Healthcare. *Journal of Medical Systems, 40*(12), 286. doi:10.1007/s10916-016-0644-9 PubMed

Yen-Lung, K. (n.d.). Considerations for Instrument Grounding, Application Note. *Agilent Technologies Taiwan.*

Yi, C. H., Shigesato, Y., Yasui, I., & Takaki, S. (1995). Microstructure of Low-Resistivity Tin-Doped Indium Oxide Films Deposited. *Japanese Journal of Applied Physics, 34*(Part 2, No. 2B2B Pt 2), L244–L247. doi:10.1143/JJAP.34.L244

Yin, Z., & Collins, R. (2006). Moving object localization in thermal imagery by forward-backward MHI. In *Proceedings IEEE Workshop on Object Tracking and Classification in and Beyond the Visible Spectrum*, 133-140.

Younis, M. B., & Frey, G. (2006). A formal method based re-implementation concept for plc programs and its application. *International Conference on Emerging Technologies and Factory Automation*, IEEE, pp. 1340–1347. 10.1109/ETFA.2006.355346

Youssef, C. (2016). Spatiotemporal representation of 3d skeleton joints-based action recognition using modified spherical harmonics, Pattern Recogn. Lett. 83.

Yuliarto, B., Gumilar, G., Zulhendri, D. W., Nugraha, & Septiani, N. L. W. (2017). Preparation of $SnO_2$ thin film nanostructure for CO gas sensor using ultrasonic spray pyrolysis and chemical bath deposition technique. *Acta Physica Polonica A, 131*(3), 534–538. doi:10.12693/APhysPolA.131.534

Zaarour, B., Zhu, L., & Jin, X. (2019). Controlling The Surface Structure, Mechanical Properties, Crystallinity, and Piezoelectric Properties of Electrospun PVDF Nanofibers by Maneuvering Molecular Weight. Journal. *Soft Materials*, *17*(2), 181–189. doi:10.1080/1539445X.2019.1582542

Zabadaj, M., Ufnalska, I., Chreptowicz, K., Mierzejewska, J., Wróblewski, W., & Ciosek-Skibińska, P. (2017). Performance of hybrid electronic tongue and HPLC coupled with chemometric analysis for the monitoring of yeast biotransformation. *Chemometrics and Intelligent Laboratory Systems*, *157*(8), 69–77. doi:10.1016/j.chemolab.2017.05.003

Zhang, Z., Xu, Y., Yang, J., Li, X., & Zhang, D. (2015). A survey of sparse representation: Algorithms and applications. *IEEE Access: Practical Innovations, Open Solutions*, *3*(5), 490–530. doi:10.1109/ACCESS.2015.2430359

Zhe, Y., Zhou, Q., Lei, L., Kan, Z., & Xiang, W. (2016). An IoT-cloud Based Wearable ECG Monitoring System for Smart Healthcare. Journal of Medical Systems, 1–18.

Zheng, B., Lee, W. C., & Lee, D. L. (2007). On Searching Continuous k Nearest Neighbours in Wireless Data Broadcast Systems. *IEEE Transactions on Mobile Computing*, *6*(7), 748–761. doi:10.1109/TMC.2007.1004

Zheng, H., Wang, C., Zhang, X., Kong, L., Li, Y., Liu, Y., & Liu, Y. (2016). Ultrasonic spray pyrolysis assembly of a TiO2-WO3-Pt multi-heterojunction microsphere photocatalyst using highly crystalline WO3 nanosheets: Less is better. *New Journal of Chemistry*, *40*(4), 3225–3232. doi:10.1039/C5NJ02981C

Zheng, W., Zheng, B., Yan, C., Liu, Y., Sun, X., Qi, Z., ... Pan, A. (2019). Direct vapor growth of 2D vertical heterostructures with tunable band alignments and interfacial charge transfer behaviors. *Advancement of Science*, *6*(7). PMID:30989032

Zhou, Y., Lei, J., Wang, J., & Cheng, Z. (2012). Analysis and Selection of Features for Gesture Recognition Based on a Micro Wearable Device, IJACSA, 3(1).

Zhou, W., Mao, Y., Tang, M., Long, L., Chen, H., Li, Y., & Jia, C. (2018). Facile Synthesis of Tremella-Like V 2 O 5 Microspheres and Their Application as Cathode Materials in Lithium Ion Batteries. *Journal of Nanoscience and Nanotechnology*, *19*(1), 194–198. doi:10.1166/jnn.2019.16457 PMID:30327022

Znaidi, L., Illia, G. S., Benyahia, S., Sanchez, C., & Kanaev, A. V. (2003). Oriented ZnO thin films synthesis by sol–gel process for laser application. *Thin Solid Films*, *428*(1–2), 257–262. doi:10.1016/S0040-6090(02)01219-1

Zoss, A., Chu, A., & Kazerooni, H. (2006). Biomechanical Design of the Berkeley Lower Extremity Exoskeleton (BLEEX). *IEEE/ASME Transactions on Mechatronics*, *11*(2), 128–138. doi:10.1109/TMECH.2006.871087

Zoss, A., & Kazerooni, H. (2006). Design of an electrically actuated lower extremity exoskeleton. *Advanced Robotics*, *20*(9), 967–988. doi:10.1163/156855306778394030

# About the Contributors

**Srijan Bhattacharya** is presently working as Assistant Professor in Department of Applied Electronics & Instrumentation Engineering in RCC Institute of Information Technology, Kolkata, India, with more than 14 years teaching and research experience. Dr. Bhattacharya received Bachelor of Engineering (BE) in Electronics & Instrumentation from Gandhi Institute of Engineering & Technology (Presently GIET University), Orissa, India (2003), Master of Engineering (M. Tech) in Electrical Engineering (Specialization Mechatronics) With Gold Medal from National Institute of Technical Teachers Training & Research, Kolkata, India (2008) and Doctor of Philosophy from Department of Aerospace Engineering & Applied Mechanics (Specialization Mechatronics) from Indian Institute of Engineering Science and Technology, Shibpur, India (Formerly Bengal Engineering & Science University, Shibpur) (2017), Dr. Bhattacharya's area of research includes Mechatronics, Sensors, Smart Materials and Instrumentation, he has published more than 30 research papers in – international, national journals, book chapters, national and international conferences. He carrying out sponsored project by - The Institution of Engineers (India). He has organized more than 15 workshop, seminar (National & International) including IEEE International Conference as Organizing Secretary. Dr. Bhattacharya visited and associated with research in several labs at India, he also visited labs in Bangladesh, Japan and UK. He is associated with professional membership with IEEE - Sensors Council, Biometrics Council, Robotics and Automation Society and Life Membership with The Robotics Society (Robotic Society of India), The Institution of Engineers (India), Association for Machines and Mechanisms, Instrument Society of India (ISOI)

**Md Atiqur Rahman Ahad,** Senior Member, IEEE, is a Professor at the University of Dhaka (DU); specially appointed Associate Professor at Osaka University. He works on computer vision, imaging, IoT, & healthcare. He did B.Sc.(Honors) [1st class 1st position] & Masters [1st class 2nd position] from DU; Masters from University of New South Wales; & PhD from Kyushu Institute of Technology [KIT]. He was awarded prestigious UGC Gold Medal 2016 (handed by Honorable

President of Bangladesh), JSPS Postdoctoral Fellowship, & 20+ awards/scholarships in different conferences/etc. He was a Visiting Researcher at KIT. He has 4 books (available in Springer), 120+ journals/edited-books/conference papers. Ahad was invited as keynote/invited speakers ~60 times in different conferences/universities in Japan, BD, USA, India, Malaysia, & Indonesia. He is an Editorial Board Member, Scientific Reports, Nature; Associate Editor, Frontiers in ICT; Editorial Board Member, Encyclopedia of Computer Graphics and Games, Springer; Editor, Int. J. of Affective Computing; Assoc. Technical Editor (former), IEEE ComSoc Magazine; Editor-in-Chief: Int. J. of Computer Vision & Signal Processing http://cennser.org/ IJCVSP, General Chair, 9th Int. Conf. on Informatics, Electronics & Vision http:// cennser.org/ICIEV; 4th Int. Conf. on Imaging, Vision & Pattern Recognition http:// cennser.org/IVPR; 2nd Int. Conf. on Activity & Behavior Computing (ABC) https:// abc-research.github.io. More: http://ahadVisionLab.com

**Arif Ahmed** is a Post Doctoral Research Fellow in the Department of Physics and Technology at the University of Tromsø (UiT), Norway. From 2009 to 2019, he was an Assistant Professor of Computer Application at Haldia Institute of Technology, India. He holds invited position as Research Consultant in Imaging Media Research Center at Korea Institute of Sciece and Technology (KIST), Korea and in School of Electrical Sciences IIT Bhubaneswar, India. Arif completed his Ph.D. at National Institute of Technology Durgapur, India and his undergraduate studies at Burdwan University. His research interests lie in the area of Computer Vision and Artificial Intelligence, ranging from theory to design to implementation. He has collaborated actively with researchers in several other disciplines of computer science, physics, biology particularly computer vision application on problems at the multi disciplinary environment. Arif has served on roughly 15 conference and workshop program committees and served as the Organizing Chair for ICITAM 2017, Publication Chair in ICITAM 2019. He has served on the ICMC 2013, 2015, and 2019 as Organizing Member. He is a member of IEEE and Digital Life Norway (DLN).

**Mandakinee Bandyopadhyay** was born in India in 1989. She received her B. Tech degree in Electrical Engineering from Moulana Abul Kalam Azad University of Technology formerly known as West Bengal University of Technology and also received M. Tech degree in Mechatronics Engineering from National Institute of Technical Teachers' Training and Research, Kolkata, Under Ministry of Human Resource Development, Government of India. She is pursuing Ph. D in the Department of Electronics Engineering, Indian Institute of Technology [ISM], under Ministry of Human Resource Development, Government of India, Dhanbad, India in the research area of Instrumentation and control. She has more than 6 years of teaching experience. She started her professional career as an Asst. Professor of Electrical

Engineering in Gandhi Institute for Education and Technology, Bhubaneswar, India under Biju Pattnaik University of Technology, India and presently working as an Asst. Professor in Asansol Engineering College under Moulana Abul Kalam Azad University of Technology, India.

**Rajib Bandyopadhyay** received the Ph.D. degree from Jadavpur University, Kolkata, India, in 2001. He is currently a Professor with the Department of Instrumentation and Electronics Engineering, Jadavpur University and a Research Professor with the Laboratory of Artificial Sensory Systems, ITMO University, Saint Petersburg, Russia. His current research interests include machine olfaction, electronic tongue, and spectroscopic instrumentation.

**Saurav Bhattacharya** is a student of Haldia Institute of Technology, Presently pursuing B.Tech in Applied Electronics and Instrumentation Engineering. He is very much enthusiast in the domain of machine learning and IOT and has worked on various hands on projects on the same domain.

**Nabarun Bhattacharyya** received the Ph.D. degree from Jadavpur University, Kolkata, India, in 2008. He is currently Director with the Centre for the Development of Advanced Computing, Kolkata and a Research Professor with the Laboratory of Artificial Sensory Systems, ITMO University, Saint Petersburg, Russia. His current research interests include agri-electronics, machine olfaction, soft computing, and pattern recognition.

**Subhasis Bhaumik** received B.E. (Mechanical) from NBU, M.Prod.E. (Production) and Ph.D (Robotics) from Jadavpur University Kolkata. He is currently serving as Professor, Aerospace Engineering & Applied Mechanics Department, IIEST Shibpur. His research interest includes multi-fingered dexterous robot hands, bio-mimetic robotic systems, mechatronics, assistive devices, mobile robotics, continuum robots, BCI/HMI and smart material.

**Subrata Chattopadhyay** was born in India in 1965. He received his Ph. D (Tech) in Instrumentation Engineering from the University of Calcutta, India in 2006, preceded by M. Tech [Instrumentation], B. Tech. [Electrical] and B. Sc (Hons) in Physics , in 1993, 1991 and 1987 respectively. He served as a Deputy Manager [Projects & Maintenance] in Electrical and Instrumentation Engineering of Chemical and Manufacturing Industries in India and then joined as an Assistant Professor in Electrical Engineering Department of National Institute of Technical Teachers' Training and Research, Kolkata, under Ministry of Human Resource Development, Government of India in 2003. At present he is working as a Professor in Electrical

Engineering and In-charge of NITTTR Kolkata Extension Centre, Bhubaneswar, India. He introduced, as head of Electrical Engineering Department, a new Post Graduate Programme [M. Tech. in Mechatronics Engineering], first of its kind in Eastern India at NITTTR Kolkata, with required development of the Department to accommodate the same. He is highly involved in Teaching and Research and his present investigation is on innovation of noble techniques of measurement and control based on Sensor and Transducer development, Process Automation, PLC and Distributed Control System, Mechatronics, Robotics etc. He has guided one research scholar who have been awarded with Ph. D. (Tech.) degree from the National Institute of Technology, Durgapur, India. Presently, five scholars are working under him for the Ph. D. degree. He has around 100 papers in international and national journals and conference proceedings.

**Khakon Das** is former JRF & SRF in BRNS, Govt. of. India, funded research project. It is about an embedded segmentation of medical images. He completed his bachelor's degrees B.C.A from IGNOU in 2010 & B.Sc. from Calcutta University in 2010 and double master degrees M.C.A in 2012 from IGNOU and M.Tech (CSE) in 2015 from WBUT. His research interests are in the areas of EEG signal processing, pattern recognition, image processing, embedded system design, and FPGA design. Mr. Das has several publications in journals and conferences.

**Subir Das** was born in west bengal, India in 1984. He received bachelor's degree in electronics & instrumentation engineering from West Bengal University of Technology, west bengal, India in 2006 and M.Tech degree in instrumentation & control engineering from University of Calcutta, west bengal, India in 2010. He is pursuing PhD in positional sensor from Maulana Abul Kalam Azad University of Technology, west bengal, India. He is currently a faculty member with the School of Mechatronics & Robotics, Indian Institute of Engineering Science & Technology, Shibpur, howrah, west bengal, India. He worked with Danieli Automation,west bengal,India,Core-Technologies, west bengal, India and Stesalit India Ltd. west bengal,India between 2006 and 2008. His research interests include the design of sensors and transducers, robotics automation, industrial automation and Agricultural Sensors. He has authored or co-authored more than 20 research papers in the areas of the sensors and transducers, and design of electronics measuring system.

**Pampa Debnath** is presently working as Assistant Professor in the Department of Electronics and Communication Engineering in RCC Institute of Information Technology, Kolkata, INDIA. She has more than 12 years of professional teaching experience in academics. She received B.Tech, M.Tech Degree from the University of Burdwan. Her research interest covers the area of Microwave devices, Microstrip

Patch antennas, SIW based circuit and Antenna. She has published several research papers in IEEE Xpore, Microsystem Technologies- Springer, CRC Press and in some National and International conferences, and a few edited volumes under the banner of CRC Press, IGI Global etc. Her major teaching subjects are Electromagnetics, RF & Microwave and Antenna. She has already served as Editor as well as Technical chair of One International Conference (ICCSE 2016) which is published by CRC Press, coordinated a few Faculty Development Programmes, Workshops, Laboratory and Industrial visits, seminars and technical events under the banner of The Institution of Engineers (INDIA) Kolkata section. She is also associated with a few National and International conference. She is a reviewer of few journals of repute and some national and International conferences. She is the editor of various conference proceedings and edited volumes. She has conducted hands on session on Photonics, Electromagnetics and Microwaves in various FDP's, workshops, seminars. She is a member of The Institution of Electronics and Telecommunication Engineers (IETE), Indian Society for Technical Education (ISTE), International Association for Engineers (IAENG).

**Arpan Deyasi** is presently working as Assistant Professor in the Department of Electronics and Communication Engineering in RCC Institute of Information Technology, Kolkata, INDIA. He has 13 years of professional experience in academics and industry. He received B.Sc (Hons), B.Tech, M.Tech Degree from University of Calcutta. He is working in the area of semiconductor nanostructure and semiconductor photonics. He has published more than 200 research papers, some of which are in ELSEVIER, IEEE Xplore, SPRINGER, CRC Press, ACEEE, SPIE, IoP, OSA, IET, ASP etc. His major teaching subjects are Solid State Device, Electromagnetics, Photonics. He has already organized International and National Conferences, Faculty Development Programmes, Workshops, Laboratory and Industrial Visits, Seminars and Technical Events for students under the banner of IE(I) Kolkata section. He is also associated with a few reputed conference as member of programme committee. He is reviewer of a few journals of repute and some prestigious conferences in INDIA and abroad. He has delivered a few talks and conducted hands-on session on Nanolelectronics, Photonics and Electromagnetics in various FDP's, workshops, seminars. He is the editor of various conference proceedings and edited volumes. He is a member of IEEE Electron Device Society, IE(I), Optical Society of India, IETE, ISTE etc. He is working as SPOC of RCCIIT Local Chapter (NPTEL course), Nodal Coordinator of e-outreach programme and Faculty Advisor of the student chapter of Institution of Engineers (INDIA) in ECE Department.

**Santanu Ghorai** received the B. Sc degree in physics (Hons.) and the B. Tech. degree in Instrumentation Engineering from Calcutta University, Kolkata, in 1995 and 1998, respectively. He received the ME degree in Electrical Engineering from Jadavpur University, Kolkata, in 2000. He has received the PhD degree in 2011 from the department of Electrical Engineering, Indian Institute of Technology, Kharagpur. He is currently with the faculty of Applied Electronics and Instrumentation Engineering Department at the Heritage Institute of Technology, Kolkata. He has published about thirty papers in international journals and conferences. His present research interest includes signal processing, image processing and machine learning.

**Arijit Ghosh** currently works as an Assistant Professor at the Applied Electronics & Instrumentation Engineering, RCC Institute of Information Technology, Kolkata, India. He completed his B.Tech from West Bengal University of Technology in Electronics and Instrumentation Engineering in the year 2010 and M.Tech from the Dept. of Applied Physics with specialization in Instrumentation and Control Engineering, University of Calcutta in 2013. Presently, his area of research includes Instrumentation Engineering, Internet of Things, Wireless Sensor Network, and Machine Learning.

**Shreem Ghosh** has completed his B.Tech in Electronics & Instrumentation Engineering from WBUT & M.Tech in Instrumentation and Control Engineering from University of Calcutta and is presently working with Johnson Controls Inc. as Project Lead (Field Engineering Group). His area of interest is Process instrumentation & control systems and Microcontroller based system design.

**Soumyajit Goswami** is presently working as Managing Consultant in IBM India Pvt. Ltd. with around 14 years of industrial and research experience. Dr. Goswami obtained his B.E. in Electronics & Communication Engineering from Vidyasagar University, West Bengal, India (2004), M.Tech in Computer Science & Engineering from West Bengal University of Technology (Presently Maulana Abul Kalam Azad University of Technology), West Bengal, India (2006) and Doctor of Philosophy (Ph.D.) in Electrical Engineering from Maulana Abul Kalam Azad University of Technology, West Bengal, India (2020). His employment experience includes different roles and responsibilities in software giants like Tata Consultancy Services (TCS), Tech Mahindra and IBM. Dr. Goswami's area of research includes Power Quality, Digital Signal Processing, Soft Computing, Internet of Things and Artificial Intelligence.

**Debnarayan Khatua** is an Assistant Professor in Mathematics in the Department of Basic Science and Humanities in Global Institute of Science & Technology, West

Bengal, India. He qualified 'GATE' in the year 2015. He has received best award in poster presentation in Mathematics in 4th International Conference organized by World Science Congress, India, 2014. His research interests are in Inventory and optimal control of production systems in fuzzy, uncertain environments, fuzzy differential equations and fuzzy dynamical system, machine learning.

**Uday Maji** has completed his graduation from Haldia Institute of Technology in Applied Electronics and Instrumentation Department in the year 2005, post graduation from Jadavpur University in Power Engineering department in the year 2007 and PhD from Calcutta University in 2018. Presently working at Haldia Institute of Technology as Associate Professor and doing research work in the field biomedical signal processing.

**Rohan Mandal** is graduated from Haldia Institute of Technology in the year 2009 and completed his master from Calcutta University in 2011. He is presently working at Haldia Institute of Technology as an Assistant Professor in the department of Applied Electronics and Instrumentation Engineering.

**Vineet Rojwal** is a Master scholar in the department of Instrumentation and Applied Physics at Indian Institute of Science, Bangalore-INDIA since July 2015. Currently, He works in the laboratory of Dr. T.K. Mondal, Principal Research Scientist in the same department. In his master program, he investigated amorphous silicon (a-Si: H) thin film material and demonstrated the connection between the plasma deposition conditions and microcrystalline silicon ($\mu$c-Si: H) material quality for the application of optoelectronic thin film devices. Moreover, he studied and developed carbon nanotubes synthesis technique in his lab, known as electric arc discharge. He is currently working on ZnO nanostructures in order to develop high performance photodetector and photocatalysis in the collaboration with department colleagues.

**Ganesh Roy** (Born: 03.04.1986, Dakshin Dinajpur, West Bengal, India) received the B.E. degree in Applied Electronics and Instrumentation Engineering from University Institute of Technology, The University of Burdwan, Burdwan, India (2008) and M. Tech in Electrical Engineering (Specialization Mechatronics) from National Institute of Technical Teachers Training & Research, Kolkata, India (2011). He joined as an Assistant Professor in the Department of Instrumentation Engineering, Central Institute of Technology, Kokrajhar, Aassam, India on August, 2011. Currently he is working as a QIP Ph.D. Scholar in the Department of Aerospace Engineering & Applied Mechanics, Indian Institute of Engineering Science and Technology, Shibpur, Howrah, India from July, 2017. His area of research includes Mechatronics, Control System and Brain Computer Interface.

**Pradip Saha** received the Ph.D. degree from Jadavpur University, Kolkata, India, in 2018. He is currently an Assistant Professor with the Faculty of Applied Electronics and Instrumentation Engineering Department, Heritage Institute of Technology, Kolkata. His current research interests include machine learning and signal processing.

**Shankar Prasad Saha** is a former Professor and HOD of Neuro-Medicine at NRS Medical, RG-Kar Medical College in Kolkata and Bankura Sammilani Medical College. He was also a faculty member at Bangur Institute of Neurology. Dr. Saha has completed more than 32 years in the field of Neurology. Dr. Saha has more than 40 publications in national and international journals. He has contributed chapters in many Neurology books. Prof. Saha has been designated as a thesis guide for many DM (Neurology) and MD (General Medicine) students. He is an Examiner for the DM (Neurology) and DNB (Neurology) courses at several universities.

**Neeta Sahay** received her B.Tech degree in Electronics and Instrumentation Engineering from University of Kalyani, also received M.Tech degree in Mechatronics Engineering from NITTTR, Kolkata [MHRD]. She has more than 10 years of teaching experience. She started her professional career as an Asst. Professor in HIT, Haldia(Under MAKAUT, WB) and then joined AOT, Adisaptagram as an Asst. Professor. Presently she is pursuing Ph.D from NITTTR, Kolkata in research area of Mechatronics.

**Hano Jacob Saji** had obtained B.Tech in Electrical and Electronics Engineering from Mahatma Gandhi University, Kerala in 2016, and M.Tech in Mechatronics Engineering from Indian Institute of Engineering Science and Technology, Shibpur in 2019.

**Eshan Samanta** has obtained a master degree in Mechatronics Engineering form West Bengal University of Technology. Currently spearheading as an Assistant Professor at Global institute of Science and Technology and Ph.D. scholar of Maulana Abul Kalam Azad University of Technology, West Bengal, India. His area of interest is in the domain of Mechatronics, Power System Analysis, Artificial Intelligence and Robotics. He has already published several papers in international journals and conferences. He is a member of Institute of Engineer, Royal Charter and a Chartered Engineer as well.

**Arghya Sarkar** obtained his B. Sc. (Physics Honours), B. Tech., M.Tech and Ph.D. in Electrical Engineering from University of Calcutta, Kolkata, India. He is presently working with MCKV Institute of Engineering, Liluha, Howrah, West Bengal, India. His special fields of interest include Power Quality, DSP and Control System.

**Samarjit Sengupta** (MIEEE) obtained B. Sc. (Physics Honours), B. Tech., M.Tech and Ph.D. in Electrical Engineering from University of Calcutta, Kolkata, India. His employment experience includes about nine years in different industries and about twenty-five years of teaching and research in the Department of Applied Physics, University of Calcutta, Kolkata, West Bengal, India. His special fields of interest include Power Quality and power system stability.

**Kundan Kumar Singh** has completed his Diploma in Information Technology from Saroj Mohan Institute of Technology under W.B.S.C.T.E in the year 2009. After that he has completed his Bachelor's from B. P. Poddar Institute of Management & Technology, Kolkata in the year 2012. Then he completed his Master in Technology in Information Technology from RCC Institute of Information Technology Affiliated to Maulana Abdul Kalam Azad University of Technology. He worked as Technical Assistance in the Dept. Of Information Technology, RCCIIT Kolkata.

**Monoj Kumar Singha,** researcher at Indian Institute of Science, is presently working on MEMS, nanotechnology, microfluidics. He is developing low cost microstructure deposition technique for MEMS based devices and sensors applications than the conventional deposition techniques like sputtering, thermal,e-beam evapoartion. He has expertise in MEMS, nanotechnology, chemical sensors.

**Bipan Tudu** received the Ph.D. degree from Jadavpur University, Kolkata, India, in 2011. He is currently a Professor with the Department of Instrumentation and Electronics Engineering, Jadavpur University. His current research interests include pattern recognition, artificial intelligence, machine olfaction, and electronic tongue.

# Index

 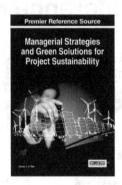  

Printed in the United States
By Bookmasters